# Doctrines of the Bible

## A Brief Discussion of the Teachings of God's Word

**DANIEL KAUFFMAN,** *Editor*

**ASSISTED BY A COMMITTEE OF TWENTY-ONE BRETHREN**

*"All scripture is given by inspiration of God, and is profitable"*

HERALD PRESS
Scottdale, Pennsylvania
Kitchener, Ontario

Published by order of Mennonite General
Conference

DOCTRINES OF THE BIBLE
Copyright © 1928 by Mennonite Publishing House, Scottdale, Pa. 15683
   Released simultaneously in Canada by Herald Press,
   Kitchener, Ont. N2G 4M5
International Standard Book Number: 0-8361-1358-6

Ninth Printing, 1977

### To Our Aged Pillars of the Faith

*Whose teaching, example, counsel, and presence among us is an inspiration to all*

### To Our Present-Day Leaders

*Parents, preachers, teachers, missionaries, Christian workers who are bearing the burden and heat of the day*

### To Our Active Young People

*Full of life and vigor, learners of today and leaders of tomorrow*

THIS VOLUME IS AFFECTIONATELY DEDICATED

# FOREWORD

Several valued books have been written on the subject, "How We Got Our Bible." A considerable portion of one of the chapters of this book is devoted to the same theme. Finding that subject interesting, we were encouraged in the thought that possibly some of our readers would be interested in a recital of how we got the book which you now hold in your hand.

At a number of meetings of the Mennonite General Conference the need of another book of Bible Doctrines was emphasized, and resolutions favoring the writing, compilation, and publication of such a treatise were adopted. At first the idea was simply to revise the book on "Bible Doctrine," formerly published by order of General Conference, but the plan of an entirely new book finally prevailed, and the present volume is the result.

At the meeting of the Mennonite General Conference held at Eureka, Ill., in August, 1925, the Executive Committee of the Mennonite Publication Board, working in co-operation with the Executive Committee of Mennonite General Conference, was authorized to proceed without further delay in the matter of securing writers and preparing the book on Bible Doctrines. The undersigned was selected to shoulder the principal share of the burden in preparing the work, and twenty-one other brethren, nearly all members of the above-named committees together with the Mennonite Publishing Committee and editors in the Mennonite Publishing House, assisted in a very material way in bringing this work to completion. The manuscripts were twice passed around to the different members of this combined committee—once in the formative stage and once after the work was practically complete. Following are the names of those who served in this capacity: D. H. Bender, J. K. Bixler, Oscar Burkholder, J. C. Frey, L. J.

Heatwole, Henry Hershey, John Horsch, J. L. Horst, D. J. Johns, D. G. Lapp, Aaron Loucks, N. E. Miller, S. H. Miller, John H. Mosemann, Levi Mumaw, J. A. Ressler, J. S. Shoemaker, John L. Stauffer, A. D. Wenger, C. F. Yake, and A. I. Yoder. Special acknowledgements are due to D. H. Bender, who furnished the introductory chapter as well as the chapters on The Ministry and The Congregation; to J. A. Ressler, Aaron Loucks, John L. Horst, and Ernest G. Gehman, whose careful reading and constructive criticisms of the completed manuscripts did much to enrich the thoughts found in the book and to give the volume its final form and finish; and to a number of other brethren whose names are not found in the above list but whose advice and counsel are much appreciated.

In the preparation of this volume we leaned heavily upon and copied copiously from our former work of a similar nature, "Bible Doctrine." Chief among other works consulted, besides concordances and cyclopedias, were Evans' "Great Doctrines of the Bible," and Torrey's "What the Bible Teaches." Other books of a similar nature were also consulted.

To God be the glory for His sustaining grace while this work was in the course of preparation. In all that we endeavored to say and teach we took it as a matter of course that a plain "thus saith the Lord" is the final word on any subject under consideration. We have tried to cover the entire range of Scripture, though limited space compelled us to be brief on many points that we would like to have considered at greater length, and the reader will no doubt find many other points that might have been very materially improved and strengthened. While the entire message is intended as an exposition of Christian doctrine, our aim was to reach the heart as well as the head, to appeal to the conscience as well as the understanding, to make the message practical as well as exegetical. How well we succeeded, or failed, we will let the reader judge.

Another thing that should be mentioned is that whatever the point under discussion our aim was to quote just enough Scripture to make the point clear and convincing, rather than to attempt to quote all scriptures bearing on said point. We endeavored to make the message brief, thus covering more ground without materially weakening the arguments put forth. This is not intended as an exhaustive treatise on any subject, as such an attempt on so many subjects would have made the volume entirely too large for practical use among the masses, for whom this message is intended.

The burden of this message is to hold up Jesus Christ, to magnify the Word of the Lord, and to endear the message of the Cross to the hearts of the readers. With a prayer that the blessing of the Lord may be added to the imperfect efforts put forth and that the entire body of readers may stand together in support of a full Gospel, a "pure religion," and a united effort to make this Gospel known to all the world, we submit this message for your consideration.

                                        Daniel Kauffman.

## THE CHURCH OF GOD

The Church of God, with solemn, virgin tread,
  With vesture luster-sheened, unwrinkled, white,
Demeanor calm, is to the world unwed.
  With zeal for garnering golden sheaves alight,
With sacrificial message all aglow,
  In consciousness of being Heaven's bride,
The Church awaits the mighty trumpet blow,
  When Christ, the Bridegroom, will not be denied.

Then, Eternity will see a glorious scene,
  The marriage of the Church with Jesus Christ!
Time's turmoil vanished by the smile serene
  Of Heaven, radiant with the Sacrificed!
The Church of God, with solemn, virgin tread,
  Walks humbly in unwrinkled, white array,
Glowing with love for Christ whom she will wed
  When God announces Heaven's bridal day.

—Ursula Miller.

# TABLE OF CONTENTS

# INTRODUCTORY

"Blessed is he that keepeth the sayings of the prophecy of this book." The sayings of the Bible are the doctrines of our Lord. To keep these doctrines is to be divinely blessed. The right keeping of the teachings of the Word of God necessarily depends on the right understanding of the truth. Christian doctrine involves the commandments, teachings, standards, and principles essential to saving faith and victorious life.

A book or treatise clearly setting forth these vital truths has always held, and must always hold, a unique place in the literature of the people of God. This book of Bible Doctrines is especially prepared to take this important place in the libraries of our Church institutions, our Sunday schools, our homes, and for study in Bible classes.

No sooner had God placed man upon the earth and surrounded him with the beauty and inspiration of the universe than He presented a series of teachings involving the principles that make for a successful life. The keeping of these teachings would have prolonged man's Edenic happiness through all eternity but his disobedience to his Creator in one thing, plunged the whole human family into disaster and death. In God's great plan for the redemption of man we have still more clearly presented doctrines and teachings fundamental to man's return to and enjoyment of conditions for which the redemption plan is made effective. All through the period of the Law, the period of the kings, the period of the prophets, down to the personal coming of the Saviour of men into the world was man's success or failure, his joy or sorrow, his victory or defeat, conditioned upon his accepting or rejecting the doctrines laid down by divine authority.

When Jesus, the Great Teacher, concluded His discourse in which He set forth the vital requirements for a life acceptable in His sight, He declared that the successful career depended upon hearing and doing His sayings. The Holy Spirit in instructing the leaders of the Christian Church constantly referred to the fact that in order to meet the approval of the Shepherd and Bishop of our souls it is essential to live, teach, and instill in the lives of His followers the doctrines of the Word of God. In II Tim. 16, 17 we are taught that all the teachings of the Word are essential in fully equipping the Christian for work. Again in I Tim. 4:16 we have this very direct teaching: "Take heed unto thyself, and unto the doctrine; continue in them: for in doing this thou shalt both save thyself, and them that hear thee."

The present volume of Doctrines of the Bible is the result of long years of searching, study, comparison, and practice, and comes to us in a straightforward manner, and in no uncertain tones sets forth as fully as is possible in a work of this size the teachings of God's Word on the subjects discussed. While it is not a revision of our former book on "Bible Doctrine," yet since the writers of the present volume were closely associated with the production of the former they had, besides other advantages, the experience involved in producing a work along the same lines before attempting this one. Also after the Church had studied and used the former book for a number of years, she was in a better position to suggest through her leaders and conferences the contents of a new book that would include all the vital elements of the old and in addition the improvements, additions, and subtractions that would make possible a superior work.

In this critical age of liberalistic and modernistic tendencies and positions, that characterize so many present day theologians and institutions of learning, it is very essential indeed that the Church have a work of vital doctrines that rings clear, and is free from the blasting influence of these false teachings. It is highly necessary that Christians know what are the teachings of the inspired Word, and that they make these doctrines a part of their faith and life. It makes a difference what we believe. It makes a difference as to what is our attitude toward the full inspiration of the Bible. It makes a difference as what we think of the Sonship of Christ, His virgin birth, His vicarious suffering, His atonement for sin, His bodily resurrection, His victorious ascension, His place at the right hand of the Father, His glorious coming again, the judgments He will measure out to the disobedient, and the eternal rewards He will give to the faithful. This book carefully studied and its teachings faithfully practiced must not only bring into the life of the individual a true attitude toward God, His being, His creative work, and the Church, but will qualify him to perform the highest and best service for his fellow men and be useful in the hands of his Master in helping lost and deluded souls into the glorious light of the Gospel and the salvation brought through Jesus Christ.

All Bible doctrines may be divided into three great classes: (1) the doctrines affecting the Deity; (2) the doctrines affecting man; (3) the doctrines affecting future conditions. The first division deals with the existence and work of the Trinity—Father, Son, and Holy Spirit. No one can understand the universe and physical life properly without the true conception of the Holy Trinity in the relations just mentioned. Scientists who do not recognize the proper place of God in the universe are entirely at sea in their vain attempt to account for the existence of matter, and regardless of the degree of education or worldly learning to which they may have attained, grope in absolute darkness, and present the most illogical and impossible theories in attempting to explain the laws of nature and the existence of life. Theologians who do not accept the Bible as the inspired Word of God and as being the literal truth in presenting the miracles as they pertain to the life of Jesus Christ and His work of atonement, are no less vague and illogical in their attempt to account for the marvelous existence of our Saviour and the deep spiritual truths regarding the fall, the redemption, and the future existence of man. In dealing with the third division of Bible doctrines, those affecting the future conditions of man, these spiritually ignorant teachers have no explanation whatever, and many of them ignore the existence of Satan, of angels, of heaven and of hell, and either allow each individual to build up his own idea of future existence or attempt to argue away the realities of a future world of woe or bliss. Worst of all, the poor dupes who swallow their sugar-coated but deadly poison arrive at the brink of the great divide, and plunge into the fearful abyss of uncertainty and darkness; as is testified by the deathbed utterances of many of these pitiable characters.

In view of these terrible facts and in the light of the knowledge we have of the eternal Word, and with a consciousness of the tremendous responsibility resting upon those whose mission it is to lead men into the glorious light and liberty of the Gospel of Jesus Christ, this volume has been prepared. The Church of Jesus Christ needs the sound, Biblical teachings presented in this work, and it is our prayer that through the divine blessings of our Heavenly Father these truths may be used in a better understanding of Himself and His great plan of salvation, and result in leading men into the glorious liberty of His grace, the building up of His Church, and the glory of His great name.

Hesston, Kansas.                    D. H. Bender.

# PART I

# The Doctrine of God

# THE DOCTRINE OF GOD

## Outline by Chapters

I. GOD—His Being and Attributes

   1. OUR FIRST INTRODUCTION TO HIM

   2. NAMES
     Elohim, Jehovah, etc.

   3. PROOFS OF HIS EXISTENCE
     a. Cause and Effect
     b. Testimony of Nature
     c. Universal Belief
     d. Man's Idea of the Infinite
     e. Bible Evidences
     f. Personal Experiences

   4. HIS ATTRIBUTES

| | |
|---|---|
| a. Eternity | i. Simplicity |
| b. Immutability | j. Goodness |
| c. Omnipotence | k. Mercy |
| d. Omnipresence | l. Justice |
| e. Omniscience | m. Love |
| f. Righteousness | n. Hatred |
| g. Faithfulness | o. Holiness |
| h. Incomprehensibility | p. Summary of Attributes |

II. GOD—His Works

  A. THE CREATION

    1. SIX DAYS OF CREATION

    2. THOUGHTS ON THE CREATION

    3. THE DEVELOPMENT THEORY

    4. GOD OUR ONLY RELIABLE WITNESS

  B. DIVINE RULERSHIP

    1. SUPREME RULER OF THE UNIVERSE

    2. THE DISPOSER OF EVENTS
     a. Sends Forth His Angels
     b. Overrules Shortcomings of Man
     c. Rules the Nations
     d. Sends us Rain
     e. Is the Preserver of His Creatures
     f. Holds Destiny of His Creatures in His Hands

    3. GOD'S LAWS

## III. THE TRINITY
### 1. THE TRIUNE GOD
a. One God
b. Three Persons
c. The Father Recognized as God
d. The Son Recognized as God
e. The Holy Ghost Recognized as God
### 2. INCOMPREHENSIBILITY OF THE TRINITY

## IV. GOD THE FATHER
### 1. CHARACTER AND OFFICE
### 2. HIS WORK
a. Architect of the Universe
b. Sent Son into the World
c. Approved Course of His Son
d. Sent Holy Spirit into the World
e. He is Our Saviour
f. Sanctifies Believers
g. Answers Prayer
### 3. THE ATTRIBUTES

## V. GOD THE SON
### 1. THE GOD-MAN
a. His Humanity
b. His Deity
### 2. THE SON OF GOD
### 3. HIS SEVENFOLD MISSION IN THE WORLD
a. The Son
b. Our Saviour and Redeemer
c. Our Example
d. Our New Testament Prophet
e. Our Lord
f. Our Intercessor
g. Our King
### 4. HIS ATTRIBUTES AND WORKS

## VI. GOD THE HOLY GHOST
### 1. HIS PERSONALITY
### 2. HIS WORK
a. Regenerates Believers
b. Indwells Believers
c. Sheds the Love of God Abroad in the Heart
d. Reproves the World of Sin
e. Directs the Affairs of His People
f. Our Guide and Teacher
g. Gives Spiritual Discernment of the Word
h. Confirms the Believer in Faith
i. Sanctifies the Believer
j. Empowers for Service
k. Inbreathes Scripture
### 3. EMBLEMS OR SYMBOLS OF THE HOLY SPIRIT
### 4. TO WHOM AND HOW GIVEN
### 5. FRUIT OF THE SPIRIT

# THE DOCTRINE OF GOD

The Infinite Being whom we call God can be described only in the language of infinity. His dominions are immeasurable, His wisdom unfathomable, His greatness beyond comparison, His riches "unsearchable," His ways "past finding out." We have reached the limit of our knowledge when we exclaim with the psalmist, "Even from everlasting to everlasting, thou art God."

And yet it is through Him only that the light of revelation is thrown upon the canvas of time and the realms of the past, present, and future are brought within the grasp of finite man. The heathen who knows not God is shrouded in ignorance, mysticism, and superstition. The agnostic who refuses to know God, though he often prides himself on his intelligence and knowlege, knows absolutely nothing beyond the reach of the finite mind. It is alone the child of God, through whose faith access is found to the hidden mysteries which mortal man unaided could never fathom, that can speak intelligently of the living God and His wonderful works.

On every hand there are evidences of a Supreme Being, conditions which can be accounted for only on the ground that there is a living, all-wise, all-powerful, supernatural, superhuman, Infinite Being who is without beginning or ending, a loving and living Creator who is without the limitations of all or any of His creatures. The very existence of matter is a miracle which necessitates the existence of a miracle-worker. The origin of matter, of life, of intelligence, and the relation between mind and matter are but the beginning of things that the human mind can never hope to fathom except through revelations from Him who created all things and in whom all power is vested. This Being we call **GOD**. In reverence we bow before Him, and bless His holy name.

# CHAPTER I

## GOD—His Being and Attributes

O magnify the Lord with me, and let us exalt his name together.—Psalm 34:3.

Reverence fills the soul of the worshiper as he finds himself in the presence of the Infinite Being whom we call God. High and holy, mighty and glorious, matchless and marvelous in all His wondrous works, perfect in wisdom and love, infinite in power, and great beyond the comprehension of all His creatures, far beyond the grasp of any human being and yet so simple and near that the humblest human being may have Him as a daily companion and intimate friend, His being fills us with a feeling of adoration and praise, and we acknowledge that it is but proper and right for Him to say: "Be still, and know that I am God." We have

### OUR FIRST INTRODUCTION TO HIM

in that significant expression found in the genesis of divine relevations: "In the beginning God. . . ." That was at the dawn of time, the time when God called the material universe into existence—but it was not the beginning of Him who is without beginning or ending.

As we thus get our first glimpse of Him we are impressed with the fact that He is a real BEING, just as man is a real being: for we are taught that man was created in His image; a Being having a personality, just as man has a personality. To the child of God He is revealed in four ways: (1) In the Book of Revelation (the Bible); (2) in the Book of Nature; (3) in the operation of the Divine in the hearts of His people; (4) in the divine Person of Jesus Christ—the Word made flesh. Aside from the Christian's handbook (the Bible) there is enough in God's handiwork in Nature, of God's impress in the intuition of man, of traditions received from generation to generation, that all the world is responsible before God. See Rom. 1:20-32.

## NAMES

by which He is known in the Holy Scriptures. The two names by which He is most commonly known in the Hebrew scriptures are *Elohim,* commonly translated GOD in our versions, and *Jehovah,* usually translated LORD. As Elohim He is held forth in His Creator relationship, conveying to us the idea of strength, supremacy, dominion, etc. As *Jehovah* (LORD) we have Him presented in His covenant relationship, impressing us as the great and mighty One, beyond our comprehension, the object of our most reverential worship. See Psa. 62:11, 12. Jehovah, we are told, is the name of God which was given to the Jews, who were so impressed with its sacredness and so seldom pronounced it that its pronunciation passed out of knowledge. And today, they who have a reverential regard for the name of the great Jehovah are never heard to pronounce this sacred name except in tones of reverence and worship. Profanity is entirely foreign to the language of the true child of God.

Our English versions bring to us a number of names of God combining the ideas suggested in these two names, each of these numerous names conveying a distinct idea of some trait or characteristic of God. Let us name a few: "LORD God" (Gen. 9:26); "God Almighty" (Ex. 6:3); "LORD of hosts" (Jer. 9:15); "God of hosts" (Psa. 80:7); "God of heaven" (Ezra 5:11); "Holy One" (Job 6:10); "Holy One of Israel" (Isa. 1:4); "the living God" (Deut. 5:26); "I AM" (Ex. 3:14); "King of kings" (I Tim. 6:15); "Lord of lords" (Rev. 17:14); "the most High" (Num. 24:16); "Lord of Sabaoth" (Rom. 9:29); "Father of lights" (Jas. 1:17). A study of these names, and of the other names by which the Deity is known in Scripture, will alone give us an illuminating idea of the greatness and blessedness of God.

## Proofs of His Existence

To one whose mind is open to receive the truth, and who gives the matter serious thought, the proofs of the existence of a God are many. Here are a few of them:

**1. For every created being or thing in existence there must be a cause.**

We reason back from the leaf to the trunk, to the root, to the seed. What caused the seed? Another plant. And as we go back along the chain of causation we finally come to the first seed and face the cause of its existence. A similar line of thought confronts us as we behold the starry heavens, the earth and sea and all that in them is, and the inevitable question arises, Whence came they? How do we account for the origin of matter, the origin of life, the origin of species, the origin of man? There must be a *First Cause*. This First Cause we call GOD. To believe in a God who is without beginning or ending, who by the breath of His mouth and His infinite power called all things visible and invisible into existence, requires less credulity than to believe that all these things came into being by mere chance. For a clear statement of this view read Romans 1:20 (in German, if you can, for that gives the sense more clearly than the King James Version). Weymouth's translation also is clear: "For from the very creation of the world his invisible perfections—namely his eternal power and divine nature—have been rendered intelligible and clearly visible by his works, so that these men are without excuse." No one has ever tried to argue away God as the First Cause of all things in existence but that he has found himself confronted with a miracle that is even more inexplainable than that of an Infinite God bringing all things into existence without the use of pre-existing material.

2. Nature abounds in things that can be accounted
for only on the ground of there being an Almighty Creator, a Supreme Intelligence, a Designer possessing superhuman wisdom and foresight.

Among these we may mention such problems as the
origin of matter, the origin of life, the origin of species,
the origin of man, and other "first things" for which no
man has ever been able to account (except on the ground
of faith in God the Creator). All nature abounds in questions which no atheist has ever been able to answer. For
instance, there is a law that substances are expanded by
heat and contracted by cold. One among a very few
exceptions is found in the fact that when water approaches
the freezing point it begins to expand, so that ice forms
on top of the waters instead of sinking to the bottom,
thus saving rivers and lakes from forming solid masses
of ice which no single summer's sun could ever melt.
Who designed this wise exception—or is it simply a freak
in nature? How does any one account for the fact that
the earth abounds in supplies for the needs of man and
beast? Coming a little closer home, and examining the
mechanism of the eye, ear, nose, mouth, brain, and cir-
culatory system of man, who has ever been able to account
for their delicate structure, to say nothing of their peculiar
location in the body and relationships to each other, except
on the ground of there being an all-wise Designer who
fashioned them according to His infinite purpose? But
we have hardly begun to ask questions. You need not
go a mile away from home to come face to face with hundreds of questions which the wisest and most scholarly of
men are not able to answer, save on the hypothesis of there
being a GOD.

### 3. The belief in a Supreme Being is universal.

Wherever the missionary goes, even in the densest
of heathen lands, he finds people with some kind of conception of a Supreme Being. What are idols but a coun-
terfeit of the living God? The Mohammedans, the Hindus,

the Buddhists, and others who worship in various forms, all
are worshipers of some being that they conceive to be
superhuman. Even atheists themselves have been known
to call upon the name of God in times of distress and
danger. That man who introduced his argument by saying, "I thank God that I am an atheist," is but typical
of his class. Yea, verily, "The fool hath said in his heart,
There is no God."

**4. Man's idea of the Infinite suggests the existence
of such a Being.**

Where does man get his idea of the Infinite? Certainly not from finite and imperfect beings like ourselves.
But this universal intuition, this world-wide conviction,
must have a Cause. The natural thing for fallen man to
do is to forget God rather than to create one in the
imagination. Turning again to Rom. 1:20, etc., we have
the cause for this in the fact that God has impressed the
fact of His being upon the minds and consciences of all
human beings. There is something within our hearts that
God appeals to, and often reaches, and thus succeeds in
winning fallen creatures back to Christ and to salvation.

**5. The Bible, as we have it, is an irrefutable argu-
ment in favor of its superhuman authorship.**

In our chapter on the Bible, found elsewhere in this
volume, this subject is considered at some length, so instead
of dwelling on that point here we invite the reader to turn
to that chapter for further study.

**6. The personal experiences of many of God's peo-
ple constitute another proof that there is a God, and that
He lives in the lives of His people.**

These experiences include such things as cleansed
lives, changed natures, the joy of the Lord in the soul,
answered prayers. The child of God who is rich in these
experiences can point to things that happened in his or
her own life and positively say, *"Now I know of a surety."*
Many who are not well versed in technical points that
stand as an evidence of the existence of a God have such

unmistakable evidences of the genuine salvation wrought in their souls by the true and living God that no amount of opposition or delusive arguments on the part of skeptics could shake them in their Christian faith.

This wonderful Being, whose impress is to be seen in every part and in all phases of His handiwork, becomes more precious to us as we turn to His Word and make a study of

### His Attributes

1. **Eternity.**—This thought, aside from Gen. 1:1, where God is represented as an active, creative Being "in the beginning," is gathered from such expressions as "The eternal God" (Deut. 33:27), "The everlasting God" (Gen. 21:33), "From everlasting to everlasting" (Psa. 103:17), "For ever and ever" (Rev. 11:15), and such like. Unlike His creatures, God has no time limitations.

2. **Immutability.**—"I change not" (Mal. 3:6), is the declaration from His own mouth. While He changes methods to meet the changing conditions presented from time to time, and has entered into new covenants with man to fit the conditions existing in the several dispensations, He Himself has never changed, and His truth "endureth to all generations" (Psa. 100:5). See also Jas. 1:17. It is "Jesus Christ the same yesterday, and to day, and for ever" (Heb. 13:8). "For ever, O Lord, thy word is settled in heaven" (Psa. 119:89).

3. **Omnipotence.**—In other words, God is all-powerful. The same God who in the beginning spoke the words and heaven and earth came into existence, who at the present time stretches forth His mighty arm and the earth trembles in earthquakes, storms, and other manifestations of His power, will in the end speak the word and a new order will come into being. II Pet. 3:10-13. The majesty and greatness of His power are eloquently set forth in the language of the prophet. Isa. 40:12-17. See also Gen. 17:1; Rev. 19:6. The same God who fills heaven and earth holds their very existence in the hollow

of His hands, and the mightiest nations are as nothing in His power.

4. **Omniscience.**—As in power, so in wisdom and knowledge, there is no limit with God, for He knows all things. "The eye of God is in every place, beholding the evil and the good" (Prov. 15:3). "From the foundation of the world" (Matt. 25:34) God looked ahead, foresaw the fall of man, conceived the divine plan of salvation, and prepared a Kingdom for the everlasting glory of His people. The Bible is full of evidence that its Author knows all things—past, present, future. I Kings 8:39; Ezek. 11:5; Matt. 10:30.

5. **Omnipresence.**—"Whither shall I go from thy spirit? or whither shall I flee from thy presence? If I ascend up into heaven, thou art there: if I make my bed in hell, behold, thou art there. If I take the wings of the morning, and dwell in the uttermost parts of the sea; even there shall thy hand lead me. . . . If I say, Surely the darkness shall cover me; even the night shall be light about me" (Psa. 139:7-11). The fact that the eye of God is in every place, that nothing can be hidden from His sight, that He knows even the innermost thoughts and intents of every human heart (Heb. 4:12) should lead us to regard Him at all times with holy reverence and never to harbor evil in our hearts. See also II Chron. 6:18.

6. **Righteousness.**—"The judgments of the Lord are true and righteous altogether" (Psa. 19:9); for "Righteous art thou, O Lord, and upright are thy judgments" (Psa. 119:137). No one need fear of not getting justice at His hands, for He is perfect in righteousness, even in His mercies. His righteousness is abundantly taught in the Word, and manifest in all His works.

7. **Faithfulness.**—"God is faithful" (I Cor. 10:13) is but one among many Biblical assurances of the faithfulness of God. His promises may be numbered by the thousands, and He has never broken a single one of them. His dealings with sinful man present one unbroken record

of faithfulness. We thank God that we can at all times approach Him in the fullest confidence, and feel assured that *"Thy word is truth"* (Jno. 17:17).

8. **Incomprehensibility.**—The wisest, most scholarly, most intellectual, most widely experienced among men come to many places in life where they must say, "I don't know." Job asked a very pertinent question when he wanted to know, "Canst thou by searching find out God" (Job 11:7)? On every hand we are surrounded by mysteries which the human mind can not fathom. Men who have spent a lifetime searching the Word of God have confessed that they made but a bare beginning. God is not hard to get acquainted with; yet in all that He is, or says, or does, it is impossible for man to reach the limit of knowledge about Him or of Him or in Him. Paul, who went far beyond the ordinary man in finding out things about God, even after having been lifted into "the third heaven" and having beheld things that were unlawful for man to utter, left this testimony: "O the depth of the riches both of the wisdom and knowledge of God! how unsearchable are his judgments, and his ways past finding out" (Rom. 11:33)!

9. **Simplicity.**—Notwithstanding all that may be said about God being both unsearchable and incomprehensible, simplicity is one of His most outstanding characteristics —it is written upon every page of His handiwork. While no human being may know *all* about Him, every rational being may know *something*—enough to encourage him to continue the study of His Word and work and rejoice in receiving progressive revelations of His divine truth. His Book (the Bible) is a model in simplicity and grandeur of thought, and they who shine in His image are noted for their simplicity and humility.

10. **Goodness.**—The goodness of God is everywhere in evidence. It is "the goodness of God" (Rom. 2:4) that leads to repentance. It was His goodness that made it possible for fallen man to be restored to divine favor.

And in a multitude of ways is the longsuffering and loving kindness of God manifesting the truth of the words of the psalmist: "The Lord is good to all" (Psa. 145:9).

11. **Mercy.**—This is a companion virtue, goodness and mercy being inseparably connected. "The mercy of the Lord is from everlasting to everlasting" (Psa. 103:17)—showing that there is no limit to His loving kindness. And what is considered "slackness" on His part is simply a manifestation of His "longsuffering to us-ward; not willing that any should perish" (II Pet. 3:9). His mercy, like His other attributes, is complete; without limit, without a flaw.

12. **Justice.**—Perfect justice and perfect mercy are in beautiful harmony. Because Jesus loved the rich young ruler that came to Him to inquire about the way of life He told him his condemning fault. Justice and mercy were in evidence when God drove sin-polluted man away from the tree of life, thus making it impossible for him to live forever in his sinful state. Sinners who spurn the mercy of God in time will have to face His justice in eternity. God is the Author of just laws which apply with equal force to all people under similar circumstances, for "God is no respecter of persons" (Acts 10:34).

13. **Love.**—"He that loveth not knoweth not God; for God is love" (I Jno. 4:8). The love of God for fallen humanity was so great that He gave His only begotten Son as a ransom to bring about our deliverance. Jno. 3:16. Paul refers to this amazing love in these words. "God commendeth his love toward us, in that, while we were yet sinners, Christ died for us" (Rom. 5:8). Oh, the matchless, priceless love of God—the whole record of His dealings with fallen man may be summed up in three words: "God is love."

14. **Hatred.**—We are so accustomed to thinking of God as a God of love that we sometimes forget that He

hates the evil quite as strongly as He loves the good. He declares Himself to be "a jealous God, visiting the iniquity of the fathers upon the children unto the third and fourth generation of them that hate me" (Ex. 20:5). In Prov. 6:16, 17 we are especially reminded of seven things which the Lord hates. He hates every evil way, hates all forms of iniquity, and in many ways He gives us a practical demonstration of the fact that it takes an ardent hater of iniquity to make a good lover of all that is good and righteous and holy.

15. **Holiness.**—We have reserved this for last because it is in this light that He stands out in all His dealings with man, because it is a quality in Him that should be sought and attained by all His people. The seraphim that appeared to Isaiah cried, "Holy, holy, holy, is the Lord of hosts: the whole earth is full of his glory" (Isa. 6:3). And thirty times does this prophet speak of the God of heaven and earth as "The Holy One." As we consider His righteousness, love, purity, faithfulness, goodness and marvelous grace and glory we are prepared to appreciate His loving admonition to all His people: "Be ye holy; for I am holy" (I Pet. 1:16).

Here we pause—not because we have named all the attributes of God, but because we think we have named enough of them to remind us of His infinite greatness, goodness, and majestic power and glory. Blessed, forever blessed, be His holy name.

Speaking of the attributes of God, it may be well to bear in mind that there are some—such as His omnipotence, omnipresence, omniscience, etc.—which apply only to the Infinite, and which none of His creatures can possess. In these He stands in a class all by Himself. Then there are moral attributes—such as holiness, loving kindness, righteousness, purity, etc.—which He has also enjoined upon all His people, and in which we may shine in His image. And not the least among the comforting thoughts enjoyed by the saints of God on earth is the fact that in the bright hereafter they will be "like HIM."

Following is a summary of the attributes of God as presented in Strong's "Systematic Theology:"

I. Absolute or Immanent Attributes:

1. Spirituality, involving
   (a) Life,
   (b) Personality.

2. Infinity, involving
   (a) Self-existence,
   (b) Immutability,
   (c) Unity.

3. Perfection, involving
   (a) Truth,
   (b) Love,
   (c) Holiness,

II. Relative or Transitive Attributes:

1. Related to Time and Space
   (a) Eternity,
   (b) Immensity.

2. Related to Creation
   (a) Omnipresence,
   (b) Omniscience,
   (c) Omnipotence.

3. Related to Moral Beings
   (a) Veracity and Faithfulness, or Transitive Truth.

   (b) Mercy and Goodness, or Transitive Love.

   (c) Justice and Righteousness, or Transitive Holiness.

Spirit, Infinite and Perfect, the Source, Support, and End of all Things. God is

# CHAPTER II

## GOD—His Works

O Lord of hosts . . . thou art the God, even thou alone,
of all the kingdoms of the earth: thou hast made
heaven and earth.—Isaiah 37:16.

Look where you will, in heaven above and the earth
beneath, on every hand you are surrounded with and confronted by the marvelous handiwork of God. David, the
shepherd king and "sweet singer of Israel," having beheld
the glory of God in the works of His hands, burst forth
in the eloquence of fervent praise as he sang:

> The heavens declare the glory of God;
> And the firmament sheweth his handywork.
>
> Day unto day uttereth speech,
> And night unto night sheweth knowledge.
>
> There is no speech nor language,
> Where their voice is not heard.
>
> Their line is gone out through all the earth,
> And their words to the end of the world.—Ps. 19:1-4.

On the day of Pentecost, when the apostles were
together in the Spirit and, filled with the Spirit, were
speaking "with other tongues, as the Spirit gave them
utterance," they set forth the words of life with such
wondrous power that the multitudes were amazed and
exclaimed, among other things, "We do hear them speak
in our tongues *the wonderful works of God*" (Acts 2:11).
When they beheld the wonder-working power of God as
wrought in the life and testimony of the disciples who had
just experienced the enduement of heavenly power, they
were ready to praise His holy name.

In "the wonderful works of God" around us there is
a wealth of glory that speaks of the greater glory to come.

Heaven and earth proclaim the glory of Him whom we adore for His matchless power, for His wonderful grace, for His tender love and compassion toward us unworthy worms of the dust. From our humble station we look into the fathomless realms above, and in our imperfect way attempt a study of the works of God. For convenience we shall divide this study into two parts: (1) The Creation; (2) Divine Rulership.

## A. THE CREATION

**"In the beginning"**—here is where our story begins —back of this, God has revealed nothing to man except in incidental references such as Jno. 17:5; Eph. 1:4 and others. Let us pause to remark here that whatever may be your conception of other worlds besides this present one having had existence, this expressive phrase marks absolutely *the beginning* of all things material, and that on the other side of Gen. 1:1 everything is an absolute blank, so far as the knowledge of man is concerned. Here is where God opens up His first chapter on revelation and says, "God created"—and here is where the worldly-wise skeptic begins his hypothetical gospel of "we may reasonably suppose—" Here is where the light begins to make known to man the mysteries of the past, and the humblest child of God may know that it was then that "God created the heaven and the earth." What happened between Gen. 1:1 and Gen. 1:2 is not stated, but the condition of the earth at the beginning is given—it "was without form and void"—a waste. As light had not been created, and as the sun, moon, and stars were not yet formed, there was no reckoning of time such as we know it now. How long this waste period lasted is all a mere guess. Some scientists assert that the earth is more than 6000 years old. The Bible does not state the age of the earth, alhough it gives fairly approximate data as to how long it is since man was created. The work of God during the followed by the seventh, a day of rest, is described in the first chapter of Genesis as follows:

**First Day.**—The light; day and night.

> And God said, Let there be light: and there was light. And God saw the light, that it was good: and God divided the light from the darkness. And God called the light Day, and the darkness he called Night. And the evening and the morning were the first day.—Gen. 1:3-5.

**Second Day.**—The waters below and the vapors above —the firmament.

> And God said, Let there be a firmament in the midst of the waters, and let it divide the waters from the waters. And God made the firmament, and divided the waters which were under the firmament from the waters which were above the firmament: and it was so. And God called the firmament Heaven. And the evening and the morning were the second day.—Gen. 1:6-8.

**Third Day.**—Land and sea; plant life.

> And God said, Let the waters under the heaven be gathered together unto one place, and let the dry land appear: and it was so. And God called the dry land Earth; and the gathering together of the waters called he Seas: and God saw that it was good. And God said, Let the earth bring forth grass, the herb yielding seed, and the fruit tree yielding fruit after his kind, whose seed is in itself, upon the earth: and it was so. And the earth brought forth grass, and herb yielding seed after his kind, and the tree yielding fruit, whose seed was in itself, after his kind: and God saw that it was good. And the evening and the morning were the third day.—Gen. 1:9-13).

**Fourth Day.**—Sun, moon and stars.

> And God said, Let there be lights in the firmament of the heaven to divide the day from the night; and let them be for signs, and for seasons, and for days, and years: and let them be for lights in the firmament of the heaven to give light upon the earth: and it was so. And God made two great lights; the greater light to rule the day, and the lesser light to rule the night: he made the stars also. And God set them in the firmament of the heaven to give light upon the earth, and to rule over the day and over the night, and to divide the light from the darkness: and God saw that it was good. And the evening and the morning were the fourth day.—Gen. 1:14-19.

### Fifth Day.—Marine life and fowls.

And God said, Let the waters bring forth abundantly the moving creature that hath life, and fowl that may fly above the earth in the open firmament of heaven. And God created great whales, and every living creature that moveth, which the waters brought forth abundantly, after their kind, and every winged fowl after his kind: and God saw that it was good. And God blessed them, saying, Be fruitful, and multiply, and fill the waters in the seas, and let fowl multiply in the earth. And the evening and the morning were the fifth day.—Gen. 1:20-23.

### Sixth Day.—(1) Creation of land animals. (2) Creation of man. (3) Man blessed and made responsible. (4) God views with complete satisfaction His work of creation.

And God said, Let the earth bring forth the living creature after his kind, cattle, and creeping thing, and beast of the earth after his kind: and it was so. And God made the beast of the earth after his kind, and cattle after their kind, and everything that creepeth upon the earth after his kind: and God saw that it was good. And God said, Let us make man in our image, after our likeness: and let them have dominion over the fish of the sea, and over the fowl of the air, and over the cattle, and over all the earth, and over every creeping thing that creepeth upon the earth. So God created man in his own image, in the image of God created he him; male and female created he them. And God blessed them, and God said unto them, Be fruitful, and multiply, and replenish the earth, and subdue it: and have dominion over the fish of the sea, and over the fowl of the air, and over every living thing that moveth upon the earth. And God said, Behold, I have given you every herb bearing seed, which is upon the face of all the earth, and every tree, in the which is the fruit of a tree yielding seed; to you it shall be for meat. And to every beast of the earth, and to every fowl of the air, and to every thing that creepeth upon the earth, wherein there is life, I have given every green herb for meat: and it was so. And God saw every thing that he had made, and, behold, it was very good. And the evening and the morning were the sixth day.—Gen. 1:24-31.

### Seventh Day.—The Sabbath.

And on the seventh day God ended his work which he had made: and he rested on the seventh day from all his work which he had made. And God blessed the seventh day, and sanctified it: because that in it he had rested from all his work which God created and made.—Gen. 2:2.

### Thoughts on the Creation

**1. The ease with which God accomplishes mighty things.**

He had only to speak the word, and it was so. For example:

> "And God said, Let there be light: and there was light."
> "And God said, Let the dry land appear: and it was so."
> "And God said, Let us make man . . . so God created man."

With even greater ease than man, who by simply pressing a button, sets a whole industrial establishment in motion, did God, by simply speaking the word, call heaven and earth into existence and set all things in their proper order. This marvelous, matchless power needs to be kept in mind, not only as we study the creation but also as we study His work in governing the universe.

**2. The perfect order in which God performs all His work.**

So perfect was God's order in the creation that men have made an idol of this orderly system and have tried to prove a creation without a living God in it.

**3. Separate and distinct creations.**

There was indeed a gradual unfolding of God's plan in the creation as He proceeded with His separate creations from the simpler to the more complex forms of life, but in connection with each form there was a distinct "God made," "God formed," "God created," etc. Ten times in this chapter are we reminded that each of the different species were to bring forth offspring "after his kind." And no naturalist has ever been able to prove that since that time any form of life has developed from lower into higher species.

**4. Man created in the "image of God."**

There is no way of harmonizing this simple, matter-of-fact statement that God created man in His own image, and "out of the dust of the earth," with the unscriptural theory that man evolved from the lower animals through a gradual process of development covering, perhaps, millions of years. The Bible and Evolution can not both be true.

### 5. The exalted position of man as God created him.

Man, as God created him, was "a living soul," bore the image of his Maker, was so intelligent that he could give names to all the animals which God brought before him, and had dominion over all the earth. No man, since the fall of man, has ever enjoyed such great distinction.

### 6. The wisdom of God manifest in the creation.

He overlooked nothing. Every plant and every animal filled the place for which God designed them. The animal world was placed in the care of the one creature of God who bore His image. All was so arranged that every creature of God was supplied with all that it needed, and full provisions were made for the happiness and well-being of both man and beast. And lest any man might get perverted ideas of the creation (as fallen man persists in holding) the principal events connected with the creation as mentioned in the first chapter of Genesis were enlarged upon in the second. The second chapter is simply a repetition of some of the things mentioned in the first, greatly enlarged and clarified. Everything that He had made was "very good."

Here our story ought to end. But since there are those who hold to

## The Development Theory

of the creation and of the origin of species, including man, we feel constrained to consider that theory a little while in the light of Scripture.

The prominent factor in this theory is Evolution. There are various modifications of it, ranging all the way from downright atheism to the attempt to make it harmonize with the Bible. But no matter which form of modification is considered, it is open to serious objections, for the following reasons:

1. It is hard to reconcile the specific six days of creation with the theory that these six days were six long geological ages covering millions of years.* It is still harder to reconcile the idea of there having been a gradual development from the original mass of floating chaos through the various stages of vegetable and animal life reaching its climax in man, with the scriptural statement that God "formed man of the dust of the ground," "created man in His own image." Read Heb. 11:3. The simplest child of God understands how the worlds were made because he believes Gen. 1.

2. It is admitted by the advocates of Evolution that they have nothing upon which to base their theory but unproved hypotheses; that the "missing link" between man and the lower animals has not yet been found; that all efforts to prove a spontaneous generation (that is, the bringing forth of life where life had not yet existed) have signally failed; that the development of life from one species to that next above it is as yet unknown. Matched against this failure is the fact that the Bible has stood the tests of time, that many of the most scholarly

---

* On this point we quote several paragraphs from a series of articles by Giorgio Bartoli, one of the outstanding scientific men of Italy. These articles were published in "The Sunday School Times" and have since been published in book form. Speaking of his qualifications to write on the subject the Times says: "Dr. Bartoli, as readers know, has taught chemistry, geology, physics, and kindred branches of science in prominent universities of Europe and Asia . . . . So he can write with authority concerning scientific matters, while at the same time his prolonged study of the Bible has satisfied him that it is wholly God's Word, without error, as accurate in matters of science and history as in spiritual truth."

"Geology tries . . . empirically to say something about the formation of the earth's crust, but sound reasoning and certain data from experiments forbid us to lay down any theory as certain and definite. Geology is a science in the making, a science of the future, not certainly a science today. Its three principal theories as to the origin of rocks—plutonism, neptunism, and vulcanism,—have ended in skepticism. Theories follow one another in quick succession and satisfy no one. Not a day passes that does not see new hypotheses, new schemes, new plans, new tabulated results, as to the formation

men do not hesitate to take the side of the Bible against
"science, falsely socalled," that what is considered scientific truth in one generation is often proved to be unscientific nonsense in the next—and in the light of all this
the monumental folly of trying to supplant the Genesis
account of the creation with the evolutionary hypothesis
becomes very apparent. God created the different species,
or kinds of flesh (I Cor. 15:39), and the theory of an evolution from one species to another is both unscriptural and
unscientific.

3. We object to calling that "Evolution" which is
merely development. It is indeed true that in many cases
there have been marvelous developments. But in most
cases this has been through the genius of man, while as
a rule in Nature it is the reverse. The peach has been
developed from a worthless, bitter thing into the luscious,
appetizing fruit that we now know it to be; the "razor-
back" hog has been developed into portly swine, in some
cases weighing half a ton; the fine Shire placed side by

of the earth's crust; in fact, there is a Babel of tongues and
nothing more. If any reader doubts this assertion, let him
consult books on geology and he will undeceive himself.

"Must we wonder at all this? By no means. Geologists
have undertaken an impossible task! Looking upon an im-
mense globe of ruins and broken fragments, they want to tell
us how the first fabric of the earth rose and came into being.
A vain labor, a useless effort! They will never succeed in their
efforts. If, however, laying aside preconceived ideas of evolution, they accept the Bible's account of the reconstruction of
the earth, they will have light in the darkness by which they
are surrounded. The internal structure of the earth will not
appear, then, as mysterious as now."

We may not agree, in every particular, with this scientific critic of
his fellow scientists. But it is very apparent, from this as well
as multitudes of similar scholarly testimonies, that it is the height
of folly to turn away from the tested testimonies of the Bible and
put superior faith in the suppositions of unproved hypotheses.
We can rest assured that when facts are so clearly revealed that
all scientists of present and past generations agree, it will be
found also that they are in agreement with the inspired Word of
God.

side with the scrawny broncho is convincing evidence of development in the horse family—but a few generations after the touch of man is taken away from these developed creatures will see a decided "reversion to type."

4. In endeavoring to explain away one miracle, the opponents of revealed truth find themselves face to face with a still more inexplainabe one. The creation of matter is a miracle. If we deny that it was called into being by the creative act of God, we have nothing left but to suppose that it must have come by chance. The origin of life was a miracle. If we deny that it was brought about by the creative act of God, we have no other recourse but to conclude that things commenced living through their own inherent power. And if we deny that God breathed into the nostrils of man "and man became a living soul," then we are faced by the alternative of rank atheism or spontaneous creation of spiritual life— that somewhere in the upward trend from monkey to man there was a gradual development into "a living soul." By what logic do men set aside the doctrine that heaven and earth and all things therein were called into being by the creative power and act of an Infinite God, and cling to the theory of a gradual development from nothing into the present status of the universe, including man, when not a single anti-Biblical theory on this point has been substantiated by proved facts?

5. Finally, we object to Evolution, now taught in most high schools, colleges, and seminaries, because it is but a way-station on the road to atheism. It has well been said that when a man gets a wrong vision of Genesis I and II he gets a wrong vision of the entire Bible. There is an alarming prevalence of unbelief—ranging all the way from a slight modification of the Genesis story of the creation to an out-and-out atheistic stand—among evolutionists, and not an atheist or infidel can be found who is not friendly to Evolution as against the Bible. On this point

all men of faith who have an interest in the rising generation need to take warning.

### GOD OUR ONLY RELIABLE WITNESS

The question has often been raised, Why, if the opposition to revealed truth is all based upon unproved hypotheses, do sincere searchers after truth often find things
that confirm them in the conclusion that the Bible is not
absolutely reliable? We answer: They base their conclusions upon the evidence of partial truth, and in this light
appearances are often deceitful. Let us submit a few illustrations:

There was a time when Daniel's story of Belshazzar
was generally discredited, for there were no traces to be
found in the records of Babylonia that such a character
had ever existed. For this reason scholars generally believed that on this point at least the Bible was not reliable. Later archeological discoveries proved, however,
that there was such a man as Belshazzar, and that it was
the scholars that were wrong, not the Bible.

There was a time when there was little question among
scientists but that the earth is flat. They had an un-
answerable argument: "If the world turns over, why
don't men fall off." But as time went on, Newton discov-
ered the fact of gravitation, and men actually did sail all
around the earth, thus utterly disproving the once well
established theory. Before this later evidence was dis-
covered it was the most reasonable thing in the world to
believe that the earth is flat, and very *un*reasonable to
believe it round. Partial knowledge was responsible for
the error.

These illustrations might be extended indefinitely.
In the absence of complete evidence, scientists often come
to conclusions that appear entirely reasonable and plausible, but which conclusions must later be given up in the
light of later and fuller revelations of fact. This accounts
for the fact that science has been compelled to reverse

itself on practically all points where the conclusions of scientific men ran counter to the revealed Word of God. Although Darwin is still held in high esteem by evolutionists generally, his fondest theories, like "the survival of the fittest" and "natural selection," have already been discredited. Why then, should any one, though he be a giant compared with other people, close his eyes to the fact that at best he is but a finite creature of limited attainments and knowledge, set himself up against the Infinite God and endeavor to substitute human speculations and unproved hypotheses for the revealed and unfailing Word of God?

We praise the Lord that we can put our trust in the only competent witness of things that transpired long before there was any human being to question the truth of His Word. In the language of the psalmist we feel to praise His name and to say: "Even from everlasting to everlasting, thou art God" (Psa. 90:2). And the question which concerns us most is not, Is God's Word true? but, Are we true to His Word?

## B. DIVINE RULERSHIP

The end of creation is but the beginning of the work of God pertaining to the welfare of His creatures. The story of the creation is but a recital of and introduction to the power and wisdom and work of the Creator. The creatures come and go, but the Creator continues on forever.

When we think of God we think of the One who has not only called heaven and earth into existence but who also holds the universe in the hollow of His hands, ruling and overruling all things in accordance with His divine wisdom and pleasure—the One who presides over the destiny of men and of nations, and who moves heaven and earth in behalf of and for the welfare of His creatures. It is as

## SUPREME RULER OF THE UNIVERSE

that we now behold Him. His eye "is in every place, beholding the evil and the good" (Prov. 15:3). Not a sparrow falls to the ground without His notice, and even the very hairs of our head are all numbered. While God has granted freedom to men and angels and the devil roams about at will, "as a roaring lion, seeking whom he may devour," yet the power of all His creatures is circumscribed by limitations beyond which they can not go. There is a way in which we may look at man as "monarch of all he surveys," but his frailty and utter dependence upon God are so manifest that we need not stop to discuss them. There is a way in which we may look at the archenemy of souls as the "god of this world," lord of all his dominions, yet even he is subject to certain limitations, as is seen in the first chapter of Job. Above the creation is the Creator who called all things into existence, and all His creatures are subject to His holy will, He being Lord over all. Acts 10:36. As

## THE DISPOSER OF EVENTS

God leaves His imprint upon all that He has made, and the touch of His mighty hand is in evidence in every stage of the onward sweep of events through the centuries.

1. **He sends forth His angels** as "ministering spirits" (Heb. 1:14) "to minister for them who shall be heirs of salvation." Of the "little ones" (Matt. 18:10), whom Christ so lovingly describes, it is said that "in heaven their angels always behold the face of my Father which is in heaven." The psalmist likewise informs us that "the angel of the Lord encampeth round about them that fear him, and delivereth them" (Psa. 34:7). In the end God will send forth His angels as reapers to "gather out of His kingdom all things that offend" (Matt. 13:39, 41)—important messengers and ministers of God in the great judgment to come.

## 2. He overrules the shortcomings of man.

Never did His grace appear in more refreshing clearness than when He thwarted the efforts of Satan by providing a Redeemer for the rescue of fallen man. Paul prayed three times that the Lord might remove his "thorn in the flesh," but he lovingly got the answer, "My grace is sufficient for thee," assuring him that his prayer was answered more wisely than he knew. The assurance, "Whom the Lord loveth he chasteneth," is but a reminder of the corrective power of God exercised in a fatherly oversight of His children. It is in line with that other assurance that "God . . . . will not suffer you to be tempted above that ye are able" (I Cor. 10:13), and that His promise, "I will never leave thee, nor forsake thee" (Heb. 13:5) is sure and steadfast forever.

## 3. He rules the nations.

By this we do not mean that He compels nations to do His bidding in spite of themselves, any more than He deals with individuals in that way; but nations, like individuals, have their limitations and are subject to His power of veto whenever He sees it wise to intervene. Moreover, the laws of nations are founded upon the laws of God. The history of nations proves that whenever the cup of iniquity of any nation is full, God in His own time and way brings it to judgment. Examples: Canaan, Egypt, Babylon, Israel, etc. God's power over the nations was manifest in the deliverance of Israel from the bondage of Egypt and later in the delivery of Israel into the hands of the enemy; in the destruction of Sennacherib's army; in the overthrow of Belshazzar's kingdom: in the delivery of the Syrian army into the hands of Elisha; and His directing hand may be seen in the affairs of nations today. Nations, like individuals, are often disobedient to God, and to some it looks as if "the god of this world" had full sway over them; but in the fullness of time it becomes evident that it is simply an illustration of the longsuffering and not of the powerlessness of

God, the ruling power of God being evident in their chastisement or overthrow. And finally, when the cup of iniquity of all the nations of earth is full, "all nations" (Matt. 25:32) will be brought to judgment and the present dispensation will be brought to a close. In all these things the overruling power and governing hand of God are plainly visible. Gen. 6; 11:1-9; 18:17—19:29; Ex. 3:7-17; Josh. 2:24; Judges 2:11-23; I Sam. 15:1-23; II Kings 17-19; Dan. 5.

### 4. He sends us the early and the latter rains.

That God rules the elements that are responsible for the different kinds of weather is evident in the fact that He answers the prayers of His people along these lines. Elijah prayed, and the rain ceased. Again he prayed. and it fell in abundance (I Kings 18; Jas. 5:17, 18). At the prayer of Samuel it thundered in harvest time, and the people quailed before this manifestation of the power of God. In modern times, some notable instances are on record where governors heeding the request of citizens, appointed a special day of prayer for rain. In several instances of this kind rain fell immediately after these united petitions were sent to the Throne. But some people, while not questioning the power of God, insist that the weather is governed by fixed laws. Grant it. But who called these fixed laws into being? And can not the Governor of the Universe, as well as any other law-making and law-enforcing power, suspend, reverse, or even repeal any law within His power? We have reasons to thank the Lord for any kind of weather that we may have; for His laws are perfect, and He orders all things in wisdom, and for our good.

### 5. He is the preserver of His creatures.

We might add truthfully that God is not only the Preserver of His creatures but also of all creation; as is evident from this declaration found in Neh. 9:6: "Thou, even thou, art Lord alone; thou hast made heaven, the heaven of heavens, with all their host, the earth, and all things that are therein, the seas, and all that is therein, and thou preservest them all." God is held forth in Scripture as the preserver of the faithful (Psa. 31:23; 97:10; 145:20; Prov. 2:8), the preserver of man and beast (Psa. 36:6), but not the preserver of the life of the wicked (Job 36:6). In other words, they that put their trust in the Lord have nothing to fear. He holds all things by His infinite power and faithfulness to His own. This adorable power and faithfulness is also manifest in the Son, as expressed in Heb. 1:3: "Who being the brightness of his glory, and the express image of his person, and upholding all things by the word of his power, when he had by himself purged our sins, sat down on the right hand of the Majesty on high."

6. **In His hands are the existence and destiny of all His creatures.**

In the language of Isaiah, "It is he that sitteth upon the circle of the earth, and the inhabitants thereof are as grasshoppers; that stretcheth out the heavens as a curtain, and spreadeth them out as a tent to dwell in; that bringeth the princes to nothing; he maketh the judges of the earth as vanity. . . . he giveth power to the faint; and to them that have no might he increaseth strength. . . . they that wait upon the Lord shall renew their strength; they shall mount up with wings as eagles; they shall run, and not be weary; and they shall walk, and not faint" (Isa. 40:22-31).

It is God who sits upon His throne in glory, beholding the innermost thoughts and intents of every human heart; who speaks the word, and the strongest nations crumble into the dust; who stretches forth His hand, and the earth trembles at the touch of His power; and every human being must some day stand before the judgment bar of God and give an account of his stewardship while in the flesh. See texts at close of paragraph 3; also Heb. 4:12; II Cor. 5:10.

### GOD'S LAWS

God is not an autocrat who decides the destinies of men according to an arbitrary will. He governs in mercy and in righteousness through laws founded upon the principles of everlasting truth and justice, and all will be judged according to the law and the evidence. What we call "the laws of nature" are but the laws of God, conceived in infinite wisdom and love and put into operation by His mighty power. By the laws of God we are governed here, and will be judged hereafter. As Jesus puts it, "The word that I have spoken, the same shall judge him in the last day" (John 12:48). Exact and perfect justice and mercy are possible because God has fixed laws, impartially administered; for "God is no respecter of persons" (Acts 10:34). The joys and sorrows of life are experienced as God's laws are obeyed or violated, for "whatsoever a man soweth, that shall he also reap" (Gal. 6:7).

As previously stated we should take into consideration, in connection with the laws of God, that He has power, in common with all law-making and law-enforcing powers, to enforce, suspend, modify, or repeal His laws. When He suspends or modifies the working of such laws (as He often does in answer to prayer), we call it a miracle. Examples: The sun and the moon standing still in the days of Joshua; drought and rain in the days of Elijah; Lazarus rising from the grave after having been dead four days; Jesus rising from the grave the third day.

Should we marvel at such manifestations of His power? The same God who called all things into existence has power to make such disposition of them as He may choose.

It is a noteworthy fact that the laws of God as found in the Ten Commandments, as well as some other Bible statutes, have also been made the basis for the laws of nations. These national laws, as we well know, are not always true to the Model, and governments often fail to administer them in righteousness; but the connection suggests the idea of God's rightful claim to the rulership of nations, and His wisdom is evident in the fact that the nearer the nations approach the Divine Model in the righteousness of both laws and administration of them the more prosperous and exalted such nations are.

Our highest interests are inseparably connected with that of keeping on the right side of all God's laws. Other things being equal, the more faithful we are in compliance with the laws of health, natural and spiritual, the more robust and healthy we become. The same application could be made with reference to all other kinds of laws. Keep on the right side of God's laws in time, and you will be on the right side of the great Lawgiver and Dispenser of blessings in eternity. Matt. 7:21-27.

# CHAPTER III

## THE TRINITY

Go ye therefore, and teach all nations . . . in the name of
the Father, and of the Son, and of the Holy Ghost.—
Matthew 28:19.

The word "Trinity" is not mentioned in Scripture, but
the doctrine of a Triune God is one of the most prominent
doctrines in the Bible.

There are two things about God that we believe with
equal emphasis: (1) There is one God. (2) There is a
trinity of personalities, each personality being recognized
as God. These two facts combined justify the designation:

### The Triune God

1. **One God.**—"Hear, O Israel; The Lord our God is
one Lord" (Mark 12:29). Hear again the voice of this
same God: "Look unto me, and be ye saved, all the ends
of the earth: for I am God, and *there is none else*" (Isa.
45:22). If there is anything clear about these two declarations it is that there is but one God—not three Gods, not
many gods, but *one God*. The unity of the Godhead is a
truth that should never be doubted. The theory of a plu-
rality of gods belongs to the realms of idolatry. The doctrine of the Trinity loses its power when we let go of the
idea of the unity of God. There is only one God—besides
Him there is none else. "Thou shalt worship the Lord thy
God, and him only shalt thou serve" (Matt. 4:10).

2. **Three Persons.**—Yet this one God appeals to us
in as many manifestations, as three distinct persons. And
when we speak of the Three, we want to speak with the
same emphasis that we used in speaking of the One. Let
us illustrate:

At the baptism of Jesus in the River Jordan (Matt. 3) we are called to witness the Son, baptized in the river; the Holy Ghost, appearing in the bodily form of a dove; the Father, speaking from heaven saying, "This is my beloved Son, in whom I am well pleased."

The fact of the Trinity is set forth in the testimony of our Saviour when He says, "But the Comforter, which is the *Holy Ghost,* whom the *Father* will send *in my name,* he shall teach you all things" (Jno. 14:26).

Again, the Trinity is mentioned in the command to baptize "in the name of the Father, and of the Son, and of the Holy Ghost."

Another thought worthy of recognition is the fact that each of these three persons is distinctly and personally recognized as God. This is important in view of the fact that some have held to the idea that the Father is God, that Jesus of Nazareth is His Son (not the very God Himself), and that the Holy Ghost is but a mere influence that draws the minds of men towards God. The Bible teaches us that each of the three persons named—Father, Son, and Holy Ghost—is recognized as God; and that neither the Father alone, nor the Son alone, nor the Holy Ghost alone, has such recognition. Unitarianism and radical trinitarianism unite in their opposition to the idea of a Triune God, in that both reject the Son and the Holy Ghost as being God Himself.

### 1. The Father is recognized as God.

Jesus gives Him this recognition when He says, "For God so loved the world, that he gave His only begotten Son" (Jno. 3:16). Peter recognizes Him as such when he says, "Blessed be the God and Father of our Lord Jesus Christ, which according to his abundant mercy hath begotten us" (I Pet. 1:3). Paul likewise gives Him the same recognition, saying, "Blessed be God, even the Father of our Lord Jesus Christ, the Father of mercies, and the God of all comfort" (II Cor. 1:3). Here are three reliable witnesses, speaking by inspiration of God, each of them giving the Father the distinction of being very God. It is not necessary to hear from any more.

## 2. The Son is recognized as God.

Hear this testimony from the pen of Isaiah: "Unto us a child is born, unto us a Son is given: . . . and his name shall be called Wonderful, . . . The mighty *God*, The everlasting Father, The Prince of Peace" (Isa. 9:6). Paul, telling of the recognition which the Father gave His Son, says, "Unto the Son he saith, Thy throne, O *God*, is forever and ever" (Heb. 1:8). See also John 20:28; Rom. 9:5; Titus 2:13, in which Jesus Christ is called God, besides many other references in which divine attributes are ascribed to Him.

## 3. The Holy Ghost is recognized as God.

When Christ says, "God is a Spirit" (Jno. 4:24), He teaches us that this Spirit is God. When He commissioned the apostles to go out into the world and baptize "in the name of the Father, and of the Son, and of the Holy Ghost," He gave equal recognition to the Holy Ghost, with Himself and the Father, as belonging to the holy Trinity. Another illustration is found in the language of Peter to Ananias. His question, "Why hath Satan filled thine heart to lie to the Holy Ghost?" was followed almost immediately with the declaration, "Thou hast not lied to men, but unto God" (Acts 5:3, 4), signifying that God and the Holy Ghost are the same Being.

The facts concerning the being and office of each of the persons of the Holy Trinity will be set forth in the three chapters to follow. Concerning the

### INCOMPREHENSIBILITY OF THE TRINITY

we quote from the pen of J. S. Hartzler ("Bible Doctrine," pp. 45, 46) as follows:

"It is sometimes argued that to speak of 'Three in one and one in Three' is a contradiction—that such a thing can not be. From a human standpoint that may be true, but God is not governed by the same laws which He has given for the government of His creatures. This is shown by the numberless things which He does for His creatures which are absolutely impossible for man to do, either for himself or for another. After Christ's resurrection He did that which to the disciples was an impossibility, but for Him it was a matter of perfect ease (Luke 24:31, 36, 51); hence the fact that man does not understand is no evidence that it is not true. If His 'ways are past finding out' it is very clear that His being is likewise so. We may not be able to explain how He can be three in one, but can we explain how there can be three, each separate and independent from the other and all of them absolutely perfect, or how there can be but one, thus ignoring both the Son and the Holy Ghost? The last two would be inexplainable because they are untrue but the other because He is incomprehensible to such finite minds as ours.

"Thou Blessed God, Thou Holy Trinity! Thou who art the Creator and Preserver of all things; the King of kings, and Lord of lords, the Ruler of heaven and earth, the Three in One and One in Three; may all the world stand in awe before Thee, beholding the 'goodness and severity of God' even in this life, and offer the gratitude of their hearts as the sacrifice most acceptable to Thee, 'Holy (Father), Holy (Son), Holy (Ghost), Lord God Almighty.'"

# CHAPTER IV

## GOD THE FATHER

Behold, what manner of love the Father hath bestowed upon us, that we should be called the sons of God.— I John 3:1.

When we say "God" we usually refer to Him in a sense that includes the three persons of the Godhead. In referring to Him as the Divine Head, Ruler, Executive, etc., we usually mean "God the Father."

God the Father is brought out in fuller light and prominence in the New Testament than in the Old, because of the greater prominence of the Son and His repeated references to the Father.

In the coming of Jesus Christ, the Son of God, to earth the "compound unity" of the Godhead is first brought into great prominence, and this prominence is still further heightened since the Holy Spirit, the third person in the Trinity, is performing His office in the present dispensation. In both the Son and the Holy Ghost is the Father glorified, and our attention is drawn to Him in a way that it could not have been had not the other two persons of the Godhead been magnified in the Gospel of Christ. Perhaps in no other place are the

### CHARACTER AND OFFICE

of the Father so clearly portrayed as in the Lord's Prayer, recorded in Matt. 6:9-13. For this reason we shall notice the repeated references to His office at some length, not to study the prayer but to consider the significance of the Son's references to the Father. In teaching His disciples how to pray Jesus directed them to address their messages to

**"Our Father."**—We have only to think of what a natural father is to his offspring to be impressed with our heavenly Father's relations to us. The scene of the father of the prodigal son, tenderly waiting for and finally welcoming him back into his family; or that of David's lamentations over the death of his beloved but misguided son Absalom, gives us a faint idea of the boundless and inexpressibly tender love which our Father in heaven has for us.

Since Jesus Christ is "the only begotten of the Father," there is a sense in which He alone can call upon God as *"My* Father." The rest of us must address Him as *"Our* Father;" but we thank Him for the privilege. And only such as have been born again and adopted into the family of God can address Him as *"Our* Father." True, He is *my* Father, *your* Father, *everybody's* Father in a natural sense, all of us being His by creation. But fallen man has rejected Him, so that Jesus said, "Ye are of your father the devil" (Jno. 8:44), and we must be "born again" before we can again claim a share in the "Father of lights" as our Father. There is no more misleading expression than this: "The Fatherhood of God and the brotherhood of man;" for upon a false conception of it is based the false hope of universal salvation.

**"In Heaven."**—While we associate the name of the Son with Bible lands (notably Palestine) and think of the Holy Ghost as being everywhere present, we invariably think of the Father as being in heaven. It is His eternal dwelling place. It was from this place that He spoke on numerous occasions to the patriarchs and prophets and later to and concerning His Son. And as we address our petitions to Him our feeling of reverence is heightened because we associate the Father with His (and our) eternal home. "Our Father—in heaven" suggests two thoughts and emotions which are inseparably connected.

**"Thy Kingdom."**—Thus the Son gives recognition to the fact that the eternal Kingdom belongs to the Father.

True, the Son represents Himself as a nobleman (Luke 19:12-27 to receive for Himself a kingdom, but it was the Father who gave Him this kingdom. When we approach the Father we feel that we are in the presence of a great and mighty and everlastingly glorious King.

"Thy Will"—is supreme in heaven, and we ought to give it similar recognition on earth. When our Saviour was in the Garden wrestling with the Father in prayer He qualified His petitions with "Nevertheless not as I will, but as thou wilt" (Matt. 26:39). Likewise Saul of Tarsus, at his conversion, expressed the Christian attitude when he inquired, "Lord, what wilt thou have me to do" (Acts 9:6)? If we give the Father the proper recognition we will make His will supreme in our minds, in our lives, in our Christian service. The true child of God has no will save to do the will of the Father.

"Lead Us."—We recognize Jesus Christ, the Holy Ghost, and to a certain extent men, as our leaders; but in the last analysis it is the Father who is our real LEADER. So long as our sincere prayer to our Father is that He *lead* us, we are safe from every foe, secure against any danger. and even in the gravest of temptations and dangers He will

"Deliver Us."—He is not only willing and able to safely *lead* but also to *"deliver* us from evil."  Recognizing our position and relationship in this vain and unfriendly world, full of snares and pitfalls and tempting allurements, our hearts go out to Him in gratitude and praise as we think of Him as the great Deliverer of our souls.

"For Thine—(O our Father) *is the kingdom, and the power, and the glory, for ever."* Is it any wonder, therefore, that when we pray we almost invariably address our petitions to "Our Father which art in heaven?" We also recognize the Son and the Holy Ghost in their respective spheres, and as such we sometimes address them personally: but in reality we pray to the Father, in the name of the Son, and through the Holy Ghost.

### His Work

As to His work, everything connected with the work of God as an Executive, Ruler, etc., belongs to God the Father. As such, most of the things mentioned in the preceding chapters are things pertaining to the work of God the Father. In addition to these things we might add a number of others which are ascribed to Him in a special way:

**1. He is the great Architect of the Universe.**

True, the Son and Holy Ghost have recognition as having had part in great events in history—as in the creation, etc.—but the work of God in such great epochal events of human history as the Deluge, the confusion of tongues, and dispersion of the human family at the Tower of Babel, the call of Abram, the giving of the Law on Mount Sinai, etc., are generally attributed to the Father as the great Disposer of events.

**2. He sent His Son into the world.**

"God so loved the world, that he gave his only begotten Son, that whosoever believeth in him should not perish, but have everlasting life. For God sent not his Son into the world to condemn the world; but that the world through him might be saved" (Jno. 3:16, 17). This is one among a number of scriptures which tells us in so many words that God sent His Son into the world. See Jno. 10:36.

**3. He gave approval of the course pursued by the Son.**

Twice in the career of the Son—once at His baptism (Matt. 3:17) and again on the mount of transfiguration (Matt. 17:5)—did He say, "This is my beloved Son, in whom I am well pleased."

**4. He sent the Holy Spirit into the world.**

"Whom the Father will send in my name" (Jno. 14:26), is the way that the Son expressed it. The Holy Ghost came, according to promise, on the day of Pentecost. See Acts 2.

### 5. He is our Saviour.

This office is also ascribed to the Son. Matt. 1:21; II Pet. 3:18. In fact, there is no salvation in which Father, Son, and Holy Ghost have no part. But we sometimes look upon Christ as our Saviour in such emphatic form that we forget that the Father, fully as much as the Son, is the Saviour of the soul. Paul sets forth the office of each very clearly when he says that "the gift of God is eternal life through Jesus Christ our Lord" (Rom. 6:23). The same thought is found in Jno. 3:17; Rom. 8:30-32; Eph. 1:1-5; 2:5-10; I Thess. 5:9; I Tim. 2:3, 4. It is of God the Father especially (not ignoring the other persons of the Trinity) that Paul speaks when he says, "We trust in the living God, who is the Saviour of all men, specially of those that believe" (I Tim. 4:10). Giving full recognition to the saving power of a Triune God, we say with Peter, ". . . Kept by the power of God through faith unto salvation" (I Pet. 1:5).

### 6. He has a part in the sanctification of believers.

Jude addresses his general epistle to "them that are sanctified by God the Father, and preserved in Jesus Christ" (Jude 1). In this work God the Father, God the Son, and God the Holy Ghost have a distinctly recognized part. The prayer of Christ the Son in behalf of His disciples that the Father should "sanctify them through thy truth" (Jno. 17:17) deserves special notice from every believer.

### 7. He answers the prayers of His people.

". . . that whatsoever ye shall ask of the Father in my name, he may give it you" (Jno. 15:16). God's promises to hear and answer prayer are numerous, and answered prayer is part of the record of every faithful life.

THE ATTRIBUTES

of the Father are identical with the list mentioned in the first chapter, for all that is said in that connection is especially applicable to God the Father. His infinite power as

Supreme Ruler of the universe. His wisdom and goodness and mercy in His righteous dealings with sinful men, His marvelous love in sending His only begotten Son into a sin-cursed world as its Saviour and Redeemer, His executive foresight in sending the Holy Spirit into the world to convince the world of sin and to guide His people into all truth, His watchful care over His creatures in longsuffering patience in supplying their every need, His "goodness and severity" which prove Him perfect both in justice and in mercy, His readiness and willingness to hear and to answer every petition of faith, His truthfulness which endures unto all generations, His unchangeable Word, and His loving kindness—all these reveal Him to us as the One who merits our confidence and praise, claims our obedience, and thrills our hearts with a recognition of His abounding grace, His infinite greatness, and His never ending glory.

# CHAPTER V

## GOD THE SON

Unto the Son he saith, Thy throne, O God, is for ever and
ever: a sceptre of righteousness is the sceptre of thy
kingdom.—Hebrews 1:8.

The state and standing of the Son of God are set forth
in the introductory part of John's Gospel as follows: "In
the beginning was the Word, and the Word was with God,
and the Word was God. . . . All things were made by him;
and without him was not any thing made that was made.
In him was life; and the life was the light of men. . . . And
the Word was made flesh, and dwelt among us, (and we
beheld his glory, the glory as of the only begotten of the
Father,) full of grace and truth" (Jno. 1:1-14). This twofold character of the Son of God has won for Him recognition as

### THE GOD-MAN

being perfect as both God and man. He referred to Himself frequently as "the Son of man" and also as "the Son
of God."

1. **His Humanity**—is evident from the fact that He
was (1) a child of a human mother (Matt. 1:18; 2:11;
Acts 13:23); (2) He grew up as other children do (Luke 2:
40); (3) He had a human body, being recognized as a Jew
(Luke 24:39; Jno. 1:14; 4:9); (4) He was tempted just
as other human beings were and are (Heb. 4:15); (5) He
performed human acts—such as eating, drinking, sleeping,
etc.—and received human treatment. Jesus was a perfect
man in two senses: (1) He had all the attributes belonging to human beings, so recognized by His associates. (2)
**While He was tempted in all points as other human beings**

were and are, He was nevertheless "without sin," the only human being that ever stood this test to perfection.

2. **His Deity**—is evident from the fact that (1) He was the Son of the living God, being conceived by the Holy Ghost (Matt. 1:18), born of a virgin (Isa. 7:14); (2) He is distinctly recognized as God, the Bible applying to Him a number of names pertaining only to the Deity. His recognition as

### THE SON OF GOD

is so everwhelming that no one who accepts the Bible as authoritative and reliable doubts His divinity and His Deity. His Divine Sonship is recognized—

1. **By the Father**—"This is my beloved Son, in whom I am well pleased; hear ye him" (Matt. 17:5).

2. **By Nebuchadnezzar**— ". . . . and the fourth is like the Son of God" (Dan. 3:25).

3. **By John the Baptist**—"This is the Son of God" (Jno. 1:34).

4. **By Nathanael**—"Thou art the Son of God" (Jno. 1:49).

5. **By Peter**—"Thou art the Christ, the Son of the living God" (Matt. 16:16).

6. **By the disciples**—"Of a truth thou art the Son of God" (Matt. 14:33).

7. **By the centurion**—"Truly this was the Son of God" (Matt. 27:54).

8. **By demons**—"What have we to do with thee, Jesus, thou Son of God" (Matt. 8:29)?

9. **By the angel**—"That holy thing that shall be born of thee shall be called the Son of God" (Luke 1:35).

10. **By the Ethiopian eunuch**—"I believe that Jesus Christ is the Son of God" (Acts 8:37).

11. **By Paul**—"He preached Christ in the synagogues, that he is the Son of God" (Acts 9:20).

12. **By Christ Himself**—"I am the Son of God" (Matt. 27:43).

With God the Father, God the Son, saints and sinners, men and devils, all uniting in testimony of the fact that Jesus of Nazareth is the Son of God, the proof is complete. Armed with this overwhelming evidence of His Divine Sonship, let us consider

### HIS SEVENFOLD MISSION IN THE WORLD

1. **The Son.**—As the "Son of God" He was sent into the world "that the world through him might be saved" (Jno. 3:17); and even at the early age of twelve He was about His "Father's business" (Luke 2:49). As the "Son of man" His mission was "to seek and to save that which was lost" (Luke 19:10)—identical with His mission as the Son of God. Conceived by the Holy Ghost, born of a woman, He was both the Son of man and the Son of God. As such His human mother was but "woman" to Him (Jno. 2:4), and whoever did the will of His Father was His mother, His brother, His sister. Mark 3:33-35. Christ being without a human father, all the world has an interest in Him as "the Son of man." As the Son of God He does us the honor to share with all the blood-bought sons and daughters of God the eternal inheritance belonging to "the saints in light," and we rejoice in the privilege of being His fellow heirs. Rom. 8:17.

2. **Our Saviour and Redeemer.**—He "came to seek and to save that which was lost," "to save his people from their sins" (Matt. 1:21); "to redeem us from all iniquity" (Tit. 2:14); and we therefore recognize Him as "the Saviour of all men, specially of those that believe" (I Tim. 4:10). Having given "his life a ransom for many" (Matt. 20:28), we gladly give Him recognition as "our Lord and Saviour Jesus Christ" (II Pet. 3:18). Being redeemed with "the precious blood of Christ" (I Pet. 1:18, 19), it is our priceless privilege to sing redemption's blessed story in time and in eternity.

3. **Our Example.**—But Christ did more than to save us, to bring about our redemption. He showed us how to

live, He showed us how to die. "I have given you an example," said He to His disciples on one occasion, "that ye should do as I have done to you" (Jno. 13:15). Peter tells us that Christ left us an example that we should "follow his steps" (I Pet. 2:21). "Being tempted in all points like as we are," Christ was "yet without sin," giving us a practical example of how to overcome the tempter. Matt. 4:1-11. In purity of life, in a loving interest in the welfare of others, in His prayer life, in going about doing good, in self-denial and humility, in helpfulness while bearing afflictions, in living for the good of others, in daily fellowship with the Father, in perfect obedience to the Father's will, and in many other ways did He set us a perfect example. Even leaders who are supposed to be "ensamples to the flock" should not forget to say with Paul, "Be ye followers of me, even as **I also am of Christ**" (I Cor. 11:1).

4. **Our New Testament Prophet.**—Moses prophesied that "A prophet shall the Lord your God raise up unto you of your brethren, like unto me" (Acts 7:37). As the leader and deliverer of His people, as the divinely appointed lawgiver and mediator between God and man in his own dispensation, Moses held an office similar to that of Christ in the Gospel dispensation, in these respects being a type of Christ. "God, who at sundry times and in divers manners spake in time past unto the fathers by the prophets hath in these last days spoken unto us by his Son" (Heb. 1:1). When John, the forerunner of Christ, was confronted with the question, "Art thou that prophet?" (Jno. 1:21) he promptly replied, "NO." Christ is the sole authorized Spokesman of the present dispensation, the central BEING in all revealed religion. His coming, His life, His preaching, His death, His going back to glory were all but a fulfillment of prophecies concerning the Messiah. The law being "our schoolmaster to bring us to Christ" (Gal. 3:24), He was the fulfillment of this law. His human mother said, *"Whatsoever* he saith unto you, *do* it" (Jno. 2:5). The

Father in heaven said, "This is my beloved Son, in whom I am well pleased; *hear ye* HIM" (Matt. 17:5). The inspired writer said, *"See that ye refuse not* HIM *that speaketh"* (Heb. 12:25). The message of this wonderful New Testament Prophet is not merely a message of authority, but also a message that is "full of grace and truth."

5. **Our Lord.**—"Ye call me Master and Lord; and ye say well;" is the way that Christ acknowledged His lordship, adding emphatically, "for so I am" (Jno. 13:13). Lordship means authority—meaning to rule, to serve as master. After He had delivered His Sermon on the Mount the people "were astonished at his doctrine: for he taught them as one having authority" (Matt. 7:28, 29). His declaration, "All power is given unto me in heaven and in earth," is further evidence of the source of His authority. His Lordship is manifest in His being the Author of our eternal salvation, in His giving the Gospel, in His establishing the Church of which He is the Head, in His sealing the Covenant with His own blood, and in His majestic flight to glory.

6. **Our Intercessor.**—When Christ, who on earth was "God in the flesh," left the scenes of earth (having, after His resurrection, "shewed himself alive after his passion by many infallible proofs") He ascended to Glory where He is at the right hand of God. It was there that Stephen saw Him at the time of his martyrdom (Acts 7:56); it is there that "he ever liveth to make intercession" (Heb. 7:25). Today He is our representative and advocate at the throne of God, and we have the consolation that "if any man sin, we have an advocate with the Father, Jesus Christ the righteous" (I Jno. 2:1).

7. **Our King.**—His kingly office was so clearly set forth in prophecy that when He finally came to earth the wise men came from the East, saying, "Where is he that is born King of the Jews" (Matt. 2:2)? When Pilate asked Him, "Art thou the king of the Jews?" Christ replied, "Thou sayest" (Matt. 27:11)— as much as to say, "Yes, I

3

am." In this He but acknowledged the kingship foretold by the prophet, "The Lord shall be King over all the earth" (Zech. 14:9). "My kingdom," is a common expression of His.

This introduces us to another phase of the mission of Christ to earth. What we have thus far said of Christ's mission to earth referred either to the events connected with His first coming or His present office of intercessor at the right hand of the Father. But there is a time coming when Christ will come again as Judge and King, as "King of kings and Lord of lords," to judge the world in righteousness and to claim His people as His own. Read Matthew, chapters 24, 25. This will be considered at greater length in a later chapter. His citizens have the consolation of looking forward with the blessed hope that He will come again to claim His own and to judge the world. See II Thess. 1:7-9. Hail to the King eternal, our Saviour and Lord, our Ransom and Redeemer, our Elder Brother, through whose sacrifice and suffering and intercession we will have the priceless privilege of reigning with Him "for ever and ever" (Rev. 22:5).

### His Attributes and Works

As for His attributes, we find them practically the same as those ascribed to God as noted in Chapter I. His pre-existence is set forth in Jno. 1:1, and He Himself declared that "Before Abraham was, I am" (Jno. 8:58). He is omnipotent (Matt. 28:18; Heb. 2:8), knows all things (Jno. 16:30; Col. 2:3), is everywhere present (Matt. 18:20; Eph. 1:20-23), is unchangeable (Heb. 13:8); in fact, "In him dwelleth all the fulness of the Godhead bodily" (Col. 2:9). Recognizing these qualities in Him, we are prepared to consider His works.

### 1. He had a part in the creation.

"All things were made by him; and without him was not any thing made that was made" (Jno. 1:3).

2. **He has part with the Father and the Spirit as the source of life and light.**

"For as the Father raiseth up the dead, and quickeneth them; even so the Son quickeneth whom he will" (Jno. 5:21). "In Christ Jesus have I begotten you through the gospel" (I Cor. 4:15). Recognizing Himself as "the light of the world" (Jno. 9:5), He imparts this quality to His disciples, saying, "Ye are the light of the world" (Matt. 5:14). Read Jno. 1:1-9.

3. **He is the Author of our eternal salvation.**

"And being made perfect, he became the author of eternal salvation unto all them that obey him" (Heb. 5:9).

4. **He is the Builder of the Church.**

"Upon this rock I will build my church; and the gates of hell shall not prevail against it" (Matt. 16:18). As such He is the Head (Col. 1:18), the Door (Jno. 10:9), the chief Cornerstone (Eph. 2:20), the Foundation (Eph. 2:20 cf. I Cor. 3:11), the Good Shepherd (Jno. 10:11), and everything else that makes the Church secure, steadfast, and meritorious in the sight of God the Father.

5. **He is the Upholder of all things.**

"Who being the brightness of his glory, and the express image of his person, and upholding all things by the word of his power, when he had by himself purged our sins, sat down on the right hand of the Majesty on high" (Heb. 1:3). "The universe is neither self-sustaining nor is it forsaken by God (Deism). Christ's power causes all things to hold together. The pulses of universal life are regulated and controlled by the throbbings of the mighty heart of Christ."—Evans.

6. **He forgives sins.**

"He said unto her, Thy sins are forgiven" (Luke 7:48). In His great, forgiving heart there is not only power and a constant readiness to forgive sins, but also an appealing reminder that we "should follow his steps."

7. **He, in common with the Father and the Holy Ghost, sanctifies the believer.**

"If the blood of bulls and of goats, and the ashes of an heifer sprinkling the unclean, sanctifieth to the purifying of the flesh: how much more shall the blood of Christ, who through the eternal Spirit offered himself without spot to God, purge your conscience from dead works to serve the living God" (Heb. 9:13, 14)? "By the which will we are sanctified through the offering of the body of Jesus Christ once for all. . . . for by one offering he hath perfected for ever them that are sanctified" (Heb. 10:10, 14).

8. **He atoned for the sins of the world.**

"Who gave himself for us, that he might redeem us from all iniquity" (Tim. 2:14). "Who his own self bare our sins in his own body on the tree, that we, being dead to sins, should live unto righteousness: by whose stripes ye were healed" (I Pet. 2:24). "We also joy in God through our Lord Jesus Christ, by whom we have now received the atonement" (Rom. 5:11).

9. **He is our Advocate at the Throne.**

"If any man sin, we have an advocate with the Father, Jesus Christ the righteous" (I Jno. 2:1). Read Heb. 7:25.

10. **He will judge the world in righteousness.**

"He hath appointed a day, in the which he will judge the world in righteousness by that man whom he hath ordained; whereof he hath given assurance unto all men" (Acts 17:31). "We must all appear before the judgment seat of Christ" (II Cor. 5:10). "When the Lord Jesus shall be revealed from heaven with his mighty angels, in flaming fire taking vengeance upon them that know not God, and that obey not the gospel of our Lord Jesus Christ" (II Thess. 1:7, 8).

11. **He will gather together His people, at His second coming, and they will be with Him forever.**

"If we believe that Jesus died and rose again, even so them also which sleep in Jesus will God bring with him. . . . For the Lord himself shall descend from heaven with a shout, and with the voice of the archangel, and with the

trump of God: and the dead in Christ shall rise first: then
we which are alive and remain shall be caught up together
with them in the clouds, to meet the Lord in the air: and
so shall we ever be with the Lord" (I Thess. 4:14-17).

# CHAPTER VI

## GOD THE HOLY GHOST

But the Comforter, which is the Holy Ghost, whom the Father will send in my name, he shall teach you all things, and bring all things to your remembrance, whatsoever I have said unto you.—John 14:26.

The Holy Ghost, like the Son of God, had eternal existence before His advent into the world. Scarcely had the inspired writer begun his description of the creation when he informed us that "the Spirit of God moved upon the face of the waters" (Gen. 1:2). The Old Testament makes repeated references to Him, but it is only when we get into the New Testament that we have a definite vision of Him as the third person of the Trinity. We shall begin our consideration of Him by examining a few scriptural evidences of

### His Personality

Christ refers to Him as "another Comforter" (Jno. 14: 16). That this Comforter is not merely a comforting influence is evident from the fact that the significant pronoun "He" is used so frequently in describing Him. One verse (Jno. 16:13) uses this personal pronoun seven times with reference to Him. Just twice in the New Testament writings is the neuter pronoun "itself" (Rom. 8:16, 26) used when referring to the Holy Ghost. The Revised Version changes this to "Himself," in harmony with the rest of the scriptures referring to the personality of the Holy Ghost. This is also in keeping with the fact, as heretofore shown from Scripture, that the Holy Ghost is God Himself, being so recognized in the Word of God. Jno. 4:24; Acts 5:3, 4.

Some have made much of the idea that since the Holy

Ghost is but "the Spirit of God," He can not be God Himself but simply God's Spirit, similar to the relationship between man and the spirit of man. But is it not a fact that the spirit of man **is man himself?** One illustration will make this clear:

Turn to Eccl. 12:7—"Then shall the dust return to the earth as it was: and the spirit shall return unto God who gave it." Now the question is, Which is the real man, the "dust" that returns to the earth, or the "spirit" that returns to God? This reference to the destiny of man throws light upon the assertion that Lazarus (the man) was "carried by the angels into Abraham's bosom" (Luke 16:22). It was Lazarus, the real Lazarus, though but "the spirit" of Lazarus, that was taken to heaven, while "the house he lived in," his body, returned to dust. Since "the spirit" of man is man himself, we may hold that "the Spirit" of God is none other than God Himself. "God is a Spirit" (Jno. 4:24), and this Spirit is God.

The personality of the Holy Ghost is evident, also, from the nature of

## His Work

### 1. He regenerates the believer.

"Just as Jesus was begotten of the Holy Ghost, so must every child of God who is to be an heir of the kingdom."—Evans. "Born of . . . the Spirit" (Jno. 3:5), is the way that Jesus describes the relationship between the Spirit and the child of God. "It is the Spirit that quickeneth" (Jno. 6:63). He who had recognition together with the Father and the Son, in the work of creation (Gen. 1:1-3; Jno. 1:1, 2) is still at work bringing to life the dead, changing the vile sinner into "the new man, which after God is created in righteousness and true holiness" (Eph. 4:24).

### 2. He dwells in the believer.

If you are a child of God, "your body is the temple of the Holy Ghost" (I Cor. 6:19). On the day of Pentecost the disciples were "all filled with the Holy Ghost" (Acts 2:4), and similar experiences are quite frequently recorded in the book of Acts. To the Corinthians Paul wrote, "Know ye not that ye are the temple of God, and that the Spirit of God dwelleth in you" (I Cor. 3:16)?

### 3. He fills the believer's heart with the love of God.

"Hope maketh not ashamed; because the love of God is shed abroad in your hearts by the Holy Ghost" (Rom. 5:5). It is of this love that John writes, saying, "Perfect love casteth out fear."

### 4. He reproves the world of sin.

"And when he is come, he will reprove the world of sin, and of righteousness, and of judgment" (Jno. 16:8). The sinner under conviction is simply feeling the convicting power of the Spirit, bringing him to a realization of his condition. God has wisely provided a twofold power to bring sinners to repentance: (1) the Spirit without, bearing to man a reminder of his sinful state; (2) the conscience within, to respond to the message of the Spirit and to constrain the individual to yield to His promptings. When the Spirit of God no longer strives with rebellious man (Gen. 6:3) it is an evidence that the hardened sinner is left undisturbed because his conscience is "seared."

### 5. He directs the affairs of His people.

For example, Philip (Acts 8), who was directed by the Spirit to go southward, and there came in contact with the Ethiopian eunuch; the Church at Antioch (Acts 13), which was directed by the Holy Ghost to set apart Barnabas and Saul as missionaries among the Gentiles; Paul and his coworkers (Acts 16), who were forbidden to preach in Asia, preparatory to going into Europe. They who "walk after the Spirit" will at all times be led and directed by the Spirit.

### 6. He testifies of the Son, and guides the believer into all truth.

"The Spirit of truth, which proceedeth from the Father, he shall testify of me" (Jno. 15:26). "He shall teach you all things, and bring all things to your remembrance, whatsoever I have said unto you" (Jno. 14:26). "He will guide you into all truth: for he shall not speak of himself; but whatsoever he shall hear, that shall he speak: and he will shew you things to come" (Jno. 16:13). The unity of the Father, Son, and Holy Ghost, together with the Gospel of Jesus Christ, is here set forth in emphatic form. Sometimes people profess to have received some Spirit-revelation which teaches them something different from that which the Word of God teaches. The references just quoted refute such false claims. The Word of God and the Spirit of God agree in all things, for He can not be a true God and contradict Himself.

7. **He gives the believer a spiritual discernment of the Word of God.**

The same apostles who failed to grasp the teachings of the Son of God with reference to His death and resurrection, and who were bewildered even after Christ rose from the dead, some of them doubting even to the very time of His ascension (Matt. 28:17), saw plainly and expounded the Scriptures with great clearness after they had received the Holy Ghost at Pentecost. When the Spirit of God takes possession of the heart of man the Word of God becomes a new message to him—resulting from a spiritual illumination, both of the heart and of the Word.

8. **He confirms the children of God in their Christian experiences.**

"The Spirit himself beareth witness with our spirit, that we are the children of God" (Rom. 8:16, R.V.). "He that believeth on the Son of God hath this witness in himself" (I Jno. 5:10).

9. **He has a part in the sanctification of the believer.**

The children of God are "sanctified by the Holy Ghost" (Rom. 15:16), "by God the Father" (Jude 1), "through the truth" (Jno. 17:17), "by the word of God" (I Tim. 4:5), "in Christ Jesus" (I Cor. 1:2), "through the washing of water by the word" (Eph. 5:26).

10. **He empowers the believer for service.**

It was the instruction of Christ to His disciples that they should tarry in the city of Jerusalem until they would be endued "with power from on high" (Luke 24:49). This enduement of power came when on the day of Pentecost they were all filled with the Holy Ghost and three thousand souls were converted and baptized. As a further evidence of the power of the Spirit, witness the efficient service of those who are fully consecrated, serving in the power of the Spirit. You have witnessed the fact that men of mediocre minds often outstrip those who are far more talented naturally but are much less spiritual, simply because they were fully upon the altar, where the Lord could make full use of them. The power accruing from wealth, intellect, executive ability, personality, etc., has its place; but it can never be a substitute for the power of the Spirit in Christian service. It takes the power of the Holy Ghost to enable any one to live the victorious life and to win souls for the Almighty.

11. **He is the Power through whom the Scriptures were given.**

"Holy men of God spake as they were moved by the Holy Ghost" ((II Pet. 1:21). Since the whole Bible was given "by inspiration of God" (II Tim. 3:16), we are made to understand that only as God breathed His Spirit into souls of men who were set apart to write God's Word into The Book was the human family favored with this divine revelation.

### Emblems or Symbols of the Holy Spirit

We gain a further knowledge of the nature of the Holy Spirit and a higher appreciation of His work as we take note of the emblems or symbols of the Spirit, as set forth in the Word of God. Let us notice a few of these:

1. **Water** (Jno. 3:5; 7:38, 39).—Remembering the uses and properties of water, this figure impresses us with the fact that the Holy Spirit is refreshing, invigorating, cleans-

ing in His effect upon the human heart; that He is freely given, and may be had in abundance.

2. **Fire** (Isa. 4:4, 5; Matt. 3:11).—No sooner do we grasp this symbol than we get the thought of the Holy Spirit's being illuminating, purifying, warming, penetrating, searching "the deep things of God" (I Cor. 2:9, 10).

3. **Oil** (I Jno. 2:20, 27; Isa. 61:1, 3).—This suggests the idea of consecration, comfort, and healing power.

4. **Wind** (Acts 2:2-4).—And again we think of great power, this time the power being manifest in revival of life and service. See Ezek. 37:9-14.

5. **A Dove** (Matt. 3:16).—As we see the descending form of a dove lighting upon the head of our blessed Lord we are reminded of the illuminating, peaceable, gentle wooings of the Spirit, who comes not in mighty demonstrations of physical powers but rather as "a still small voice," as masterful and effective as He is gentle.

6. **A Voice** (Isa. 6:8; Acts 13:2).—Obey this voice, and the promise is that He "will guide you into all truth" (Jno. 16:13).

7. **A Seal** (Eph. 4:30)—by which God has anointed us and "given the earnest of the Spirit in our hearts" (II Cor. 1:22).

8. **Cloven Tongues** Acts 2:2-11)—reminding us that the Holy Spirit speaks in tongues which all people in every clime and age may understand, on condition of faith in God and in our Lord Jesus Christ.

Thus are the ministrations of the Holy Spirit made clearer to all who will listen to His Voice and receive Him as the Spirit of the living God, by the impressive symbols through which He is characterized in Scripture. These emblems also convey to our minds the characteristics of the people in whom the Holy Spirit dwells.

### To Whom and How Given

This practical question should not be overlooked. Much disputing along this line might be avoided if men everywhere sought the teaching of God's Word instead of impressing their own individual views upon others; were they as quick to read their Bibles as they are to argue with those of opposing minds. Turning to the Word of God to find out to whom and how the Spirit of God is given, we learn that He is given—

1. "To them that ask (for) him."—Matt. 7:11.
2. "To them that obey him."—Acts 5:32.
3. In answer to prayer.—Luke 11:13.
4. Through the intercession of Christ.—Jno. 14:16.
5. To penitent believers.—Acts 2:38.
6. To those who accept Christ.—Gal. 3:5, 13, 14.

While given freely and gladly, there are conditions upon which men receive Him and without which He can not be had. Simon the sorcerer was even willing to pay for this power, but Peter quickly told him the utter unreasonableness of his request, he being yet "in the gall of bitterness and bond of iniquity." There are things which men alone can and must do, before the Holy Ghost can enter their hearts. God is willing to set the house in order for the habitation of the Spirit, but men must surrender this house to God before He can cleanse it. Rom. 12:1, 2.

Briefly stated, if we meet the conditions of salvation we also meet the conditions of receiving the Holy Ghost. Acts 2:38.

### Fruit of the Spirit

Perhaps the most practical phase of the work of the indwelling Spirit is the effect of such indwelling upon the daily life of the individual. This is made very clear in the great contrast presented in Gal. 5:19-23. "The works of the flesh" are first enumerated, after which Paul concludes that "they which do such things shall not inherit the kingdom of God." He next enumerates the things belonging to "the fruit of the Spirit," concluding with, "against such there is no law." They in whom the Spirit of God dwells have the following as a part of their Christian experiences:

1. **Love**—"Beloved, if God so loved us, we ought also to love one another" (I Jno. 4:11).

2. **Joy**—"We . . . worship God . . . and rejoice" (Phil. 3:3).

3. **Peace**—"The peace of God, which passeth all understanding" (Phil. 4:7).

4. **Longsuffering**—"With longsuffering, forbearing one another in love" (Eph. 4:2).

5. **Gentleness**—"Be ye kind one to another, tenderhearted" (Eph. 4:32).

6. **Goodness**—"Ye also are full of goodness" (Rom. 15:14).

7. **Faith**—"And this is the victory that overcometh the world, even our faith" (I Jno. 5:4).

8. **Meekness**—"Blessed are the meek: for they shall inherit the earth" (Matt. 5:5).

9. **Temperance**—"Every one that striveth for the mastery is temperate in all things" (I Cor. 9:25).

Where this perfect fruit of the Spirit is manifest in daily life, there is the best of evidence of the abiding presence of the indwelling Spirit.

.

# PART II

# The Doctrine of Man

## CHAPTERS

# THE DOCTRINE OF MAN

## Outline by Chapters

I. MAN

1. WHAT IS MAN
   a. Image of God
   b. Noblest of God's Creatures
   c. Vilest of Creatures
   d. Object of Heaven's Love
   e. God's Servant

2. MAN'S DOMINION

II. MAN—Historical Sketch

1. MAN AS GOD CREATED HIM
2. FALL OF MAN
3. THE FAMILY OF ADAM
4. THE AGE OF MAN
5. THE DELUGE
6. DISPERSION OF MAN THROUGH CONFUSION OF TONGUES
7. GOD'S COVENANT WITH ABRAHAM
8. THE LAW
9. CHRISTIANITY

III. MAN IN HIS FALLEN STATE

1. STEPS IN THE FALL
   a. Entrance of Tempter
   b. Indifference
   c. Unbelief
   d. Ambition
   e. Disobedience
   f. Death

2. CONDITION OF FALLEN MAN
   a. Spiritually Dead
   b. "Child of the Devil"
   c. Rebellious Mind
   d. Evil Heart
   e. A Defiled Creature
   f. In Bondage to Satan
   g. "Children of Wrath"
   h. Under Condemnation
   i. Without Hope

3. RESPECTABILITY NO SUBSTITUTE FOR SALVATION

4. THE SPARK OF LIFE

## IV. MAN REDEEMED

1. A CHILD OF GOD
2. SUBJECT TO DISEASE, PAIN, AND DEATH
3. BESET WITH SHORTCOMINGS
4. ACCESS TO THE FATHER
5. BLESSED WITH A HEAVENLY ADVOCATE
6. BODY A TEMPLE OF HOLY GHOST
7. CREATURE OF HOPE
8. FELLOW HEIR WITH CHRIST
9. AWAITING COMPLETE AND ETERNAL RE-DEMPTION

## V. DEATH

1. WHAT IS DEATH
   a. A Separation
   b. Judgment upon Sin
   c. An Enemy Turned into a Blessing
   d. A Sleep

2. WHAT DEATH IS NOT
   a. Not Soul Sleeping
   b. Not Annihilation

3. THE STING OF DEATH

# THE DOCTRINE OF MAN

The most remarkable thing about man, outside of the fact that he was created in the image of God, is his capacity for development. This is true, both in paths of righteousness and in the ways of sin.

Man is of a dual nature, in this that he is both fleshly and spiritual. On the one hand, he is like God; while on the other, he is like the animal creation. As a being like unto God he is intelligent, enjoys spiritual fellowship, is the possessor of a soul that has eternal existence. As a being like unto the lower animals, he is subject to the limitations of the flesh—to sickness, pain, and death.

Comparing man with God, we find him inferior to God in every point on which the comparison is made. The difference may be expressed in two words: finite and IN-FINITE. Yet, as already pointed out, man has the capacity for development, his room for growth is unlimited, since he may continue to grow a whole life-time without reaching perfection, and the longer he serves God the more he becomes like the Divine Model. Man's largeness depends wholly upon how fully he yields himself to God and repudiates the dominion of the flesh.

Comparing man with the lower animals, he is far above them in intelligence, dominion, and power—his capacity far beyond them, either for good or for evil. While the lower animals are governed through instinct, man is blessed with reasoning powers which give him an immensely larger sphere. When an animal dies, all that is left is a carcass that returns to dust. When a man dies, his body returns to dust while the soul continues to exist forever. But when man, like the lower animals, submits to the dominion of the flesh, he sinks into depths of depravity unknown in the animal world.

The practical question continually confronting us is, Will we, like the lower animals, grovel in the dust? or will we, like God, dwell in the heavenlies?

# CHAPTER I

## MAN

So God created man in his own image, in the image of
God created he him; male and female created he them.
—Genesis 1:27.

The psalmist, evidently meditating upon the goodness
and mercy of God and considering the great contrast between the Infinite God and finite man for whom the Creator did so much, burst forth in wonder and praise, exclaim-
ing,

### "WHAT IS MAN

that thou art mindful of him?" Drawing our deductions
from the Word of God, as in the light of this Word we
make a study of ourselves and our fellow creatures, let us
attempt an answer:

### 1. Man is a finite image of the Infinite God.

After God had supplied the earth with vegetable and
animal life, there was still no creature that bore His own
image. So God said, "Let us make man in our image"
(Gen. 1:26). Man, like the Creator whose image he bears,
is a compound being. When God said. "Let *us* make," etc.,
He used language that indicated the Trinity of the Godhead (Father, Son, Holy Ghost), as the trinity of man is
indicated in that significant expression, "Spirit and soul
and body" (I Thess. 5:23). Man is a compound being, also,
in the fact that he resembles both God and the animal creation. In physical structure there is much in the way of
similarity between man and the lower animals, and, like
them, man is subject to sickness, pain, and death. On
the other hand he is endowed with a mind that enables
him to rule the world, and all the moral attributes of God,
named in a previous chapter and which God possesses to
perfection, are possessed by man to a limited degree. Man,
while bearing the image of God, can never hope to equal

Him; for in all things God is perfect and infinite while man is imperfect and finite.

## 2. Man is the noblest and greatest of all God's earthly creatures.

The intelligence of man gives him the mastery over the animal world. Man alone possesses a spirit that enables him to commune with his Maker, receiving revelations from God by which he governs his life. Moreover, he is the possessor of a soul which is not only in communion with his Maker here, but which will, at the point of dissolution between soul and body, take its flight to the great God who gave it. Well may we, with the psalmist, burst forth in reverent worship and say, "I will praise thee; for I am fearfully and wonderfully made: marvellous are thy works" (Psa. 139:14).

## 3. Fallen man is the vilest of creatures on earth.

The man described in the preceding paragraph is the man as God created him, or as restored through the atoning merits of the blood of Christ, and not the fallen, sin-polluted creature that now inhabits this sinful world. The beasts of the field, the birds of the air, and the fishes of the sea are all filling the places which God ordained them to fill. Some of them seem rather depraved, the whole animal creation having been affected by the fall of man; but they are all governed by instinct, accommodating themselves to their surroundings as best they know how, and filling their places as God designed that they should. Of man alone is it true that he has proved traitor to his Creator. He fell from his lofty station, and instead of shining in the image of God he has descended into the lowest depths of vice and degradation—in his sinful state an utterly depraved being. It is reserved for man alone to make the disastrous descent from the lofty state of being a child of God to that of being a child of the devil. Read Jer. 9:17; Rom. 1:18—2:2.

## 4. Man is the object of heaven's love.

When we think of the woefully depraved state of fallen

man, and then think of what God has done and is doing for him, we may well wonder with the psalmist, "What is man, that thou art mindful of him?" And here is where the amazing grace, the marvelous goodness, and the unerring wisdom of God become manifest. Man, notwithstanding his total depravity, is, after all, possessed of a soul that is worth saving, and God moved heaven and earth to bring this about. The love of the father of the prodigal son (Luke 15), in watching and longing for the return of his wayward son, is but a faint illustration of the love of the heavenly Father for His fallen creatures, in giving His only begotten Son as a sacrifice to bring about their redemption and restoration to Him. They who respond to this wonderful grace can truly say, "We love him, because he first loved us." Read Jno. 3:16, 17; Rom. 5:1-8; I Jno. 3.

### 5. Man is God's servant.

In the beginning God placed man into the garden of Eden and commanded him to dress it and keep it. Gen. 2:15. While many unfaithful men are the voluntary servants of sin rather than of God, there is a sense in which all men are the servants of God—the righteous willingly so, the unrighteous at times and under circumstances when it pleases God to use them in carrying out His plans. In the latter sense Nebuchadnezzar, whom God used in bringing chastisement upon rebellious Israel; Cyrus, whom God used as His servant in restoring Judah to the promised land; Pharaoh, whom God raised up to fill the place he did in connection with the children of Israel; and the men who had a part in crucifying Christ, "by the determinate counsel and foreknowledge of God," were all the servants of God. Willingly or unwillingly, constantly or at such times as God may have special need for their services in carrying out His will, all men are the servants of God. In unwilling service, however, wicked men receive no reward. See Acts 1:18-25 concerning the fate of Judas. Concerning the service of the obedient, read Rom. 6:16.

## MAN'S DOMINION

When God said, "Be fruitful, and multiply, and replenish the earth, and subdue it: and have dominion over the fish of the sea, and over the fowl of the air, and over every living thing that moveth upon the earth" (Gen. 1:28), He put man in undisputed possession of the whole earth. The command implies:

1. **Procreation.**—"Be fruitful, and multiply." Man did not need to fall into sin before this commandment could be fulfilled, but marriage was instituted immediately that children might be reared up under the shelter of the home and the benediction of a godly home life.

2. **Complete Dominion.**—There were no limitations to this command, but man was placed as a sovereign over all the beasts of the field, all the birds of the air, and all the fishes of the sea. And Adam even named them all. Dominion necessarily brings with it the responsibility of stewardship.

3. **Complete Subjugation of the Earth.**—As man was commanded to "subdue it," we infer that there was some work to be done, some unoccupied territory to inhabit. It will be remembered that at this time there was but one family in existence, only one garden really occupied. How thrilling the thought that had the whole human family remained true to God the whole earth would eventually have been made into a beautiful paradise of God, the perfect peace and subjection of the whole animal world being in keeping with the perfect bliss and holiness of man. Since Satan captured man, this complete subjugation has never been fully accomplished.

Thus did God, in the creation, make every provision for the happiness and well-being of man. "And God saw every thing that he had made, and, behold, it was very *good*"—until the day when the tempter appeared on the scene, caused man to sin, and the whole career of man was completely changed from what it would have been had he remained true to God's plan for his life.

# CHAPTER II

## MAN—Historical Sketch

God that made the world, and all things therein. . . . hath made of one blood all nations of men, for to dwell on all the face of the earth; and hath determined the times before appointed, and the bounds of their habitation.—Acts 17:24, 26.

The history of the human family reads like a romance. Men who pride themselves on their own knowledge and ignore the knowledge of God as revealed to man, have endeavored to picture the progress of life from the primordial cell through the aeons of time, tracing man through the various stages of savagery, barbarism, and semicivilization until finally reaching the human in his present magnificent and kingly state. But we thank God for more direct and more reliable information. To be exact, God the Creator revealed to one of His creatures (Moses, the lawgiver and mediator between God and man under the Old Covenant) that "in the beginning God created the heaven and the earth," and made plain to Moses what was the history of man from the time of the creation of Adam until the time when these revelations were made. Moses wrote these things in a book, now known to us as the book of Genesis, and to which we turn as the only authoritative and reliable record of the early history of man.

### MAN AS GOD CREATED HIM

The creation of man is thus described in the language of inspiration:

And God said, Let us make man in our image, after our likeness; and let him have dominion over the fish of the sea, and over the fowl of the air, and over the cattle, and over all the earth, and over every creeping thing that creepeth upon the earth. So God created man in his own image, in the image of God created he him; male and female created he them.—Gen. 1:26, 27.

And the Lord God formed man of the dust of the ground, and breathed into his nostrils the breath of life; and man became a living soul. . . . And the Lord God said, It is not good that the man should be alone, I will make him an help meet for him. . . .And the Lord God caused a deep sleep to fall upon Adam, and he slept: and he took one of his ribs, and closed up the flesh instead thereof; and the rib, which the Lord God had taken from man, made he a woman, and brought her unto the man. And Adam said, This is now bone of my bones, and flesh of my flesh: she shall be called Woman, because she was taken out of Man. Therefore shall a man leave his father and his mother, and shall cleave unto his wife: and they shall be one flesh.—Gen. 2:7, 18, 21-24.

Here is simple language, easily understood; language which no one has ever attempted to "improve" without spoiling the narrative. From this brief description we gather the following facts concerning the state of man as God created him:

1. **He bore the image of God**—as noted in the preceding chapter.

2. **He was intelligent**—as evident from his talking with God and being able to give names to all the animals.

3. **He was pure and holy**—made in the image of God, sinless, in communion with his Maker.

4. **He was trustworthy**—given the task of keeping the garden and placed in dominion over all the earth.

5. **He was "a living soul."** This implies two things: (1) He had the life of God within him, having been created in the image of God. (2) He was not subject to death; for the warning, "In the day thou eatest thereof thou shalt surely die," meant nothing to him if at that time death reigned in his body and soul. The death here spoken of we conceive to be both spiritual and natural. (Compare Gen. 3:22-24 with Rom. 5:12, 19.) Until then, man was "a living soul," in position to "live forever."

A most beautiful word picture of the ideal home life, is this inspired narrative of the exalted, blissful state of **primitive man in the beautiful earthly paradise of God.**

## Fall of Man

In an evil hour Satan entered man's blissful home, both Adam and Eve fell through disobedience, and man lost his first estate. The story of their shameful fall is here related:

> Now the serpent was more subtil than any beast of the field which the Lord God had made. And he said unto the woman, Yea, hath God said, Ye shall not eat of every tree of the garden? And the woman said unto the serpent, We may eat of the fruit of the trees of the garden: but of the fruit of the tree which is in the midst of the garden, God hath said, Ye shall not eat of it, neither shall ye touch it, lest ye die. And the serpent said unto the woman, Ye shall not surely die: for God doth know that in the day ye eat thereof, then your eyes shall be opened; and ye shall be as gods, knowing good and evil. And when the woman saw that the tree was good for food, and that it was pleasant to the eyes, and a tree desired to make one wise, she took of the fruit thereof, and did eat; and gave also unto her husband with her, and he did eat. And the eyes of both of them were opened, and they knew that they were naked; and they sewed fig leaves together, and made themselves aprons. And they heard the voice of the Lord God walking in the garden in the cool of the day: and Adam and his wife hid themselves from the presence of the Lord God.—Gen. 3:1-8.

The fall of man changed the entire career of the human family. But that God had foreseen this event and made provision for the redemption of man from his shameful fall is evident from the fact that the eternal Kingdom for the redeemed had been prepared "from the foundation of the world" (Matt. 25:34). And the wisdom and power and goodness of God are seen in that the eternal destiny of man redeemed is to be preferred to the state of man in the garden of Eden, glorious and blissful as was this Edenic home. Another important fact that should not be lost sight of as we think of the fall of man is that it can in no way be harmonized with the evolutionary theory of a gradual development of man from a savage state into his present state of super-intelligence and refinement. The theory that the fall of man was simply "a failure to rise" is contrary to both fact and revelation.

### THE FAMILY OF ADAM

After this event the history of Adam's family is the history of fallen man rather than the history of man in the paradise of God. Adam, like the rest of mankind, was a son of sorrow, subject to sickness and pain and death, living by the grace of God. Of his children, we have the names of three—Cain, Abel, and Seth—the rest being included in the general statement that Adam "begat sons and daughters" (Gen. 5:4). The burden of sin rested heavily upon the family, as the first-born became a murderer. Abel was slain, and God gave Adam another favored son in the person of Seth.

"Where did Cain get his wife?" asks the skeptic sneeringly. Where did Seth get his wife? Cain's wife was either his sister or his niece. The fact that Cain was a fugitive and a vagabond, and driven from the presence of the rest of the family does not prove that some other members of the family might not have become sinners and outcasts, and joined Cain in his sinful career.

### THE AGE OF MAN

is ascertained, approximately, by two genealogies found in the fifth and eleventh chapters in Genesis. The first gives the number of years from the creation of Adam to the birth of Noah, and the second tells how much older Adam was than Abraham. From that time there is enough contemporaneous history among other nations that we need not be far wrong as to the exact length of time since the creation of man. Archbishop Ussher computed the time from Adam to Christ at 4004 years. There is some variation in the estimates of different calculators on this point, but not enough to interfere with the conclusion that if Adam were living today he would be about 6000 years old.

### THE DELUGE

As centuries rolled on, the wickedness of the human family increased. The posterity of Cain seems to have become more prominent than that of Seth. It is among the descendants of Cain that we find the builder of the first city (Enoch), the pioneer stock raiser (Jabal), the inventor of musical instruments (Jubal), and the pioneer in commercialism (Tubal-cain). As time went on, conditions prevailed which brought forth the judgment of the Almighty. "It repented the Lord that he had made man on the earth" (Gen. 6:6). What was wrong? Among other things, there were mixed marriages and loose marriage laws. And while there were giants born to these unholy marriages, and "mighty men of renown" were the result, the wickedness became so great that God said, "I will destroy man, whom I have created, from the face of the earth" (Gen. 6:7). The time limit set was a hundred and twenty years. Gen. 6:3.

But Noah found grace in the eyes of the Lord, and through him God preserved the human seed. God directed Noah to build an ark of huge dimensions, so that both the righteous among men and a limited number of all the varieties of animals might find shelter while the earth was being destroyed in a mighty flood.

Noah did as the Lord commanded. But there were only eight souls—himself and his wife, and his three sons and their wives—that entered the ark at the command of God. On the appointed day these all entered the ark, after which God sealed the ark, and for forty days and forty nights the fountains of the deep and the windows of heaven were opened, the rain fell in torrents, until the face of the earth was covered with water and all outside the ark perished. After the flood the ark rested upon Mt. Ararat, and Noah and his family left it after having been in it a little over a year.

Was the Flood universal? That is, was the whole earth covered with water? On this point we would observe: (1) It was no less miraculous to cover that part of the earth supposed to have been inhabitated at that time than to cover the entire surface of the globe. (2) On this point the Bible is our highest authority, so we will turn to it for witness:

> In the six hundredth year of Noah's life, in the second month, the seventeenth day of the month, the same day were all the fountains of the deep broken up, and the windows of heaven were opened. And the rain was upon the earth forty days and forty nights. In the selfsame day entered Noah, and Shem, and Ham, and Japheth, the sons of Noah, and Noah's wife, and the three wives of the sons with them, into the ark .... And the flood was forty days upon the earth: and the waters increased, and bare up the ark, and it was lift up above the earth .... And all the high hills, that were under the whole heaven, were covered. Fifteen cubits upward did the waters prevail; and the mountains were covered. And all flesh died that moved upon the earth, both of fowl, and of cattle, and of beast, and of every creeping thing that creepeth upon the earth, and every man: all in whose nostrils was the breath of life, of all that was in the dry land, died. .... Noah only remained alive, and they that were with him in the ark.—Gen. 7:11-23.

Can any language be more clear and explicit than the language of God just quoted? It is when men try to read something into the Word of God that is not there, when they try to make it appear that it means something else than that which God's language says, that they get into trouble. That the Flood was universal, covered the whole earth, is evident, because:

1. The language of Scripture admits of no other interpretation.

2. The nations of the Orient have a traditional account of the Flood, as handed down from generation to generation, which finally got into their literature. Some of the primitive American races have a similar tradition.

3. There are many fossil remains of aquatic plants and animals which indicate that at one time places now far inland were under water.

4. There is nothing substantial that opponents of revealed truth have urged against the theory of the Flood being universal that can not be harmonized with the Genesis account of this great event, there being plenty of room

in the ark for all the varieties of animals which naturalists claim to have proved in existence at that time. And even if there were objects in the way of explaining all these things from a scientific viewpoint, let it not be forgotten that "with God all things are possible," and that other miracles as marvelous as this have been wrought at His hands. Many of the phenomena in Nature which cause men to stumble at the idea of a universal Flood can be explained by the theory of an upheaval of the ocean beds at this time. This theory can be harmonized very nicely with the description of the Flood as recorded in Genesis.

The first thing that Noah did after leaving the ark was to build an altar for worship and sacrifice.

### DISPERSION OF MAN THROUGH CONFUSION OF TONGUES

But it was not long after the Flood until evidences appeared that though Noah had found favor in the eyes of God he was after all but a son of Adam, and that the sin transmitted from generation to generation since the fall of man was not wiped away in the Flood. Gen. 9:20-27. As man increased, his wickedness became more and more apparent. Again let us turn to the language of Scripture for our narrative:

> And the whole earth was of one language, and of one speech. And it came to pass, as they journeyed from the east, that they found a plain in the land of Shinar; and they dwelt there. And they said one to another, Go to, let us make brick, and burn them thoroughly. And they had brick for stone, and slime had they for morter. And they said, Go to, let us build us a city and a tower, whose top may reach unto heaven; and let us make us a name, lest we be scattered abroad upon the face of the whole earth. . . . And the Lord said, Behold, the people is one, and they have all one language; and this they begin to do: and now nothing will be restrained from them which they have imagined to do. Go to, let us go down, and there confound their language, that they may not understand one another's speech. So the Lord scattered them abroad from thence upon the face of all the earth: and they left off to build the city.—Gen. 11:1-8.

Nobody knows of a certainty the exact place where this Tower of Babel was located. But the Jews, after they were carried captive to Babylon, were much impressed by the similarity between the massive structures in Babylon and their conception of the city and the tower as gathered from their literature.

From this time forth the history of man is written, not as one but as many nations. The history of the nations during the few hundred years immediately following the dispersion is very meager; but enough is known to justify the conclusion that the greater part of the descendants of Shem remained in Asia, that the descendants of Japhet became the leading tribes and nations in Europe, while the descendants of Ham became the dominating peoples of Africa.

### God's Covenant with Abraham

But while man was baffled in his designs and scattered to the four winds of earth, he was not turned from his sinful ways. Nations were built up, and the wickedness of man kept on increasing. It was then that the plan of God in dealing with sinful man was further revealed in the calling of Abraham, a citizen of Ur of the Chaldees, to become the head of a chosen nation. This is what God saw in Abraham:

> For I know him, that he will command his children and his household after him, and they shall keep the way of the Lord, to do justice and judgment.—Gen. 18:19.

On the east bank of the Mediterranean was a choice strip of land inhabited by the descendants of Canaan, the son of Ham. This land, then known as the land of Canaan and now known to us as Palestine, God promised to Abraham, saying:

> I will make of thee a great nation, and I will bless thee, and make thy name great; and thou shalt be a blessing.—Gen. 12:2.

This promise was confirmed a number of times, on different occasions, the most precious part of the covenant being the promise of Christ, to whom God referred when

He said, "In thy seed shall all the nations of the earth be blessed." Read Gen. 12; 15:12-18; 17:8; 24:7; 26:3, 4; 28:4, 13; Ex. 33:1; Deut. 34:4; Gal. 3:16. Abraham obeyed; but in his lifetime he did not see all the promises of God realized. He dwelt in tents, and while God prospered him materially, he had to take the promises of God by faith—which he did, and is known to us as "the father of the faithful."

At the time of the death of Abraham he had comparatively few descendants, but in his grandson, Jacob, there was the beginning of the great nation which God had promised. In the days of Jacob the family (then numbering seventy souls) migrated to Egypt, where, according to Bible chronology, they lived about 215 years, the whole time from God's covenant with Abraham to the giving of the Levitical Law upon Mt. Sinai being about 430 years. Gen. 15:16; Gal. 3:17. Here in Egypt, first in honor under the leadership of Joseph but afterwards in slavery under the oppression of a new dynasty of kings (Ex. 1—12), Israel grew to be a nation, and under the leadership of Moses the children of Israel were delivered from the bondage of Pharaoh and started on their journey to the land of promise.

## THE LAW

For forty years this journey continued, most commonly known to us as "wilderness wanderings." While Israel was on this journey God appeared to Moses on Mt. Sinai and delivered the Law. The Ten Commandments were written with the finger of God on two tables of stone (Ex. 31:18), and the Levitical Law gave the commandments of God in greater detail. This Law was in force as the law of God for His people during the remaining portion of the Old Testament dispensation, until it was supplanted by the Gospel of Christ, for He was the fulfillment of the Law.

As the nation increased in strength the wickedness of the people also increased. The zenith of power was reached in the days of Saul, David, and Solomon, after which the kingdom was divided and later on, first the northern and then the southern kingdom fell and the people were carried into captivity. But the Law was still in force, the priesthood continued to function, the national worship of the Jews was kept up, proselytes were gained from other peoples, until at the time of Christ the synagogue worship was established in many cities, both in Palestine and in other countries.

Meantime other nations flourished. Chaldea, Assyria, Egypt, Persia, Phoenicia, Greece, and Rome each rose to prominence in its day, and each fell before the rising power of rivals, its inherent weakness being its own sinfulness. At the time of Christ Palestine was in the hands of the Romans, and about forty years after His crucifixion Jerusalem was completely destroyed by the Roman emperor Titus, since which time the Jews have been strangers among the nations.

### CHRISTIANITY

When we write "A.D. 1928" we mean that 1928 years ago the long heralded Messiah made His appearance on the earth. The scepter of divine favor passed from Judah to Christ, from the Law to the Gospel, from Judaism to Christianity, and henceforth the record of God in the lives of His people is to be found in the record of the Christian Church. John the Baptist, as the forerunner of Christ, was God's servant in bringing about the transition from the Old to the New Covenant. Jesus Christ appeared as the Messiah of prophecy, called His disciples, established His Gospel, sealed the New Covenant with His blood, arose from the grave, ascended to glory, sent the Holy Comforter and empowered the Christian Church for service. Within a few centuries Christianity had become one of the most powerful influences in the world, a distinction held to this day.

But while the nations of today have become rich and powerful, they have followed the footsteps of their predecessors in wickedness, and today there is a prodigality which has brought most of the nations on the verge of bankruptcy, while "wars and rumours of wars" are heard on every hand. As in the days of Noah, mixed marriages and loose marriage laws are the rule, giants are being born, scenes and achievements of dazzling splendor are in evidence, and the "signs" portrayed in Matt. 24 and other scriptures are upon us.

In the midst of all these the Christian Church has a message—the message of salvation, the Gospel of Jesus Christ, which is to be preached among "all nations."

\*    \*    \*    \*

Here we pause. Another chapter concerning the career of man is yet to be written. That will be written when we come to that part of this book that is devoted to the future destiny of man and consider that part of the inspired Volume in which the divine light from heaven is thrown upon the canvas of the future and God reveals what will be the career of man beyond the grave.

# CHAPTER III

## MAN IN HIS FALLEN STATE

> There is none righteous, no, not one: there is none that
> understandeth, there is none that seeketh after God.
> They are all gone out of the way, they are together
> become unprofitable; there is none that doeth good,
> no, not one. . . . .All have sinned and come short of the
> glory of God.—Romans 3:10-12, 23.
>
> The heart is deceitful above all things, and desperately
> wicked.—Jeremiah 17:9.

Picture in your mind's eye, if you can, the brightness,
purity, and happiness of man in his primitive state in Eden
—then compare this with sinful, fallen, depraved, wretched
man in his fallen state, and you are in position to realize,
to some extent, what man lost in the fall!

Again, it is necessary to study the utter depravity and
wretchedness of fallen man to have some idea of the goodness, greatness, and compassionate love of God for making
it possible for us again to be brought into covenant relationship with Him.

The story of the fall of man, as recorded in Gen. 3:1-9,
was noted in the previous chapter. Let us take a further
look at this narrative, observing the five

### Steps in the Fall

1. **Entrance of the Tempter** (1-5).—Hear his deceptive plea: "Yea hath God said. . . . Ye shall not surely die.
. . . God doth know. . . . Ye shall be as gods"—it was the
charm of the serpent, captivating the eye and the soul of
the victim. When the tempter is around there is no place
of safety for us except at the foot of the cross.

2. **Indifference**—giving place to the devil (2). Eve
was so indifferent to the abundant evidence which she had

of the goodness and truthfulness of God, and of the wonderful blessings she had all along been enjoying, that she
gave a listening ear to the enemy of God. Here was her
first blunder.

3. **Unbelief**—doubting God's Word (6). She could
not give credence to the devil's, "Ye shall not," without
disbelieving God's, "Ye shall." Had there been no transfer
of faith and confidence from God to Satan, the words,
"When the woman saw," etc., would never have been written; for, had she believed God, in the light of truth the
forbidden fruit would not have appeared "good for food,"
nor "pleasant to the eyes," nor "desired to make one wise."

4. **Ambition**—wanting to be like God. Ambition follows in the wake of unbelief, as selfishness takes the place
of trust in God and desire to glorify Him. No sooner have
the eyes been closed to the goodness and love of God than
the sefishness of ambition begins to assert itself. Eve had
already experienced things that were far beyond anything
that the tempter had yet offered, but her eyes were now
closed to that fact and a rising ambition was leading her
to see imaginary stars.

5. **Disobedience** (6).—Ambition, coupled with blindness, prompted her to reach forth her hand after forbidden
things—through the disobedience of one, "sin entered into
the world" (Rom. 5:12).

6. **Death** (3).—God's warning, "In the day that thou
eatest thereof thou shalt surely die," was verified. "Sin,
when it is finished, bringeth forth death" (Jas. 1:15). Adam
and Eve were now dead spiritually, and the fact that God
made it impossible for man to eat of the tree of life "and
live for ever" (vv. 23, 24) in his sinful state is proof positive that physical death had also set in. Man had become
a mortal being.

In this first transgression we have a picture of what
happens every time a human being is tempted to forsake
God, yields to the temptation, and falls into sin. John refers

to the sum total of temptation as "the lust of the flesh, and the lust of the eyes, and the pride of life" (I Jno. 2:16). These three have their counterpart in what Eve saw (or imagined she saw): "Good for food. . . . pleasant to the eyes, . . . desired to make one wise." They were also in evidence when the devil attempted to destroy the Son of God in the temptation in the wilderness. Matt. 4:1-11. The difference beween Eve and Christ was that while Eve yielded Christ did not—Christ overcame; Eve was overcome. Let us now turn the Gospel light on the

### Condition of Fallen Man

1. **Spiritually Dead.**—"Dead in trespasses and sins" (Eph. 2:1) is the way Paul describes it. And again he writes to Timothy, and to us: "She (he) that liveth in pleasure is dead while she (he) liveth" (I Tim. 5:6). "The wages of sin is death" (Rom. 6:23), is the solemn warning that all men should heed.

2. **"Child of the Devil."**—"Thou child of the devil" (Acts 13:10) was the way that Paul addressed Elymas who was opposing the work of the Lord. Christ gave a similar and fitting rebuke to the Pharisees when He warned them that "Ye are of your father the devil" (Jno. 8:44). Since men have forsaken the Fatherhood of God they have no other recourse but to become the children of the devil.

3. **A Rebellious Mind.**—"The carnal mind is enmity against God; for it is not subject to the law of God, neither indeed can be. So then they that are in the flesh can not please God" (Rom. 8:7, 8). "The natural man receiveth not the things of the Spirit of God: for they are foolishness unto him" (I Cor. 2:14). By these testimonies we may readily see why the sinner invariably possesses a disobedient, rebellious mind.

4. **"An Evil Heart."**—"An evil heart of unbelief" (Heb. 3:12), is another way of saying that "the heart (of fallen man) is deceitful above all things, and desperately

wicked." Read also Mark 7:21, 22 and Rom. 7:18. The only way to get rid of this evil heart is to submit to God, to accept Jesus Christ as Saviour and Lord, to be converted, and to let Him replace the evil heart with "a new heart, and a right spirit."

5. **A Defiled Creature.**—"Unto them that are defiled and unbelieving is nothing pure; but even their mind and conscience is defiled" (Tit. 1:15). "An evil conscience" (Heb. 10:22), a defiled flesh (Rom. 7:18), and an enfeebled will (II Tim. 2:26) furnish the explanation of the utter depravity of the natural man. No wonder that Paul wrote that "in my flesh dwelleth no good thing." There is no such thing as a "good man" outside of Christ; for "all our righteousnesses are are filthy rags" (Isa. 64:6).

6. **In Bondage to the Devil.**—"That they may recover themselves out of the snare of the devil, who are taken captive by him at his will" (II Tim. 2:26). "Who through fear of death were all their lifetime subject to bondage" (Heb. 2:15). "The bondage of corruption" (Rom. 8:21) is another way of expressing the same truth. They who imagine themselves at liberty because they ignore God's proffered terms of salvation and reconciliation to Him, are in the very worst kind of slavery and the most galling bondage imaginable. Man knows no real freedom, outside of the freedom of the Cross.

7. **"Children of Wrath."**—"Among whom we also had our conversation in times past in the lusts of our flesh, fulfilling the desires of the flesh and of the mind; and were by nature the children of wrath" (Eph. 2:3). "Behold, I was shapen in iniquity, and in sin did my mother conceive me" (Psa. 51:5). Only spiritual blindness keeps people from seeing themselves while in this state, as God sees them.

8. **Under Condemnation.**—"And this is the condemnation . . . men loved darkness rather than light, because their deeds were evil" (Jno. 3:19). "He that believeth not is condemned already" (Jno. 3:18). "The Lord Jesus shall

be revealed from heaven with his mighty angels, in flaming fire taking vengeance upon them that know not God, and that obey not the gospel of our Lord Jesus Christ" (II Thess. 1:7, 8). "The wicked shall be turned into hell, and all the nations that forget God" (Psa. 9:17). Notice, the condemnation already exists in this life, and the consummation of it will come in fullness in eternity.

9. **Without Hope.**—"Strangers from the covenants of promise, having no hope, and without God in the world" (Eph. 2:12), is Paul's characterization of those outside of Christ. We often read or hear of men entombed in mines or other prisons of earth, living there for days and sometimes for weeks before being rescued, sometimes dying before the rescuer comes. This is but a feeble illustration, giving us a faint picture of the lost soul held captive in the prison house of sin. And, oh how sad it is when sin-blinded souls refuse the proffered help of Jesus Christ the great Rescuer of every willing soul, and sinful bondage in this life is transferred to the absolutely hopeless bondage in the lake of fire, where rescue will be impossible forever!

All of these Bible descriptions of fallen man are confirmed and verified in the lives of sinners. These lives, like the testimony of Scripture, prove them to be depraved, godless, spiritually dead, candidates for hell!

### RESPECTABILITY NO SUBSTITUTE FOR SALVATION

Unconverted men sometimes justify themselves on the ground of their respectability. They live comparatively clean lives, pride themselves in the thought that they have "no bad habits," often comparing themselves with church members, to their own credit. But Isaiah says that all such righteousness is as "filthy rags." Christ compared the poor sinner with the self-righteous Pharisee, and said that the first was "justified rather than the other." Hell is not only for the wicked, but also for all "that forget God" (Psa. 9:17). And as for the eternal wrath of God, that is pronounced against "them that know not God, and that obey not the gospel of our Lord Jesus Christ." The vile sinner and the self-righteous sinner stand on a common level before God—can be saved only by the grace of God, through the atoning merits of the blood of Jesus Christ.

### The Spark of Life

This is not the "spark of divinity" which some people seem to think may be found in every human soul. Dismiss that delusive thought, if you have ever entertained it. All unsaved souls are dead, absolutely "dead in trespasses and sins," depraved and defiled, without hope and "without God in the world." Yet there is something in all men that is capable of responding to the goodness and grace of God. As Adam, perfect and sinless, had something within to which the devil could appeal and get a response, so the soul that is "dead in trespasses and sins" has something within it to which God appeals and may get a response. Yea, the hour "now is, when the dead shall hear the voice of the Son of God: and they that hear shall live" (Jno. 5:25). In every human being there is a conscience capable of being reached—unless such person has sinned away the day of grace. It was this conscience that troubled Saul of Tarsus, and to which Jesus referred when He said, "It is hard for thee to kick against the pricks." It is this that the Holy Ghost reaches when sinners are convicted, convinced, and converted. With the hope that the most hardened sinner may be reached by the grace of God, we are encouraged to warn every one of them, in the language of inspiration, "To day if ye will hear his voice, harden not your hearts."

# CHAPTER IV

## MAN REDEEMED

Christ hath redeemed us from the curse of the law.—
Galatians 3:13.

The study of man includes a consideration of him in three phases: (1) as God made him; (2) as sin made him; (3) as God remade him. We have already discussed the first two; let us now briefly discuss the third.

When God conveyed to Adam the knowledge of the results of the fall, He graciously coupled with it the promise of the Redeemer. See Gen. 3:15. The subject of redemption, as such, will be considered in a subsequent chapter. In this chapter we shall confine ourselves to a look at man in his redeemed state.

Man redeemed, as man in his original state, enjoys fellowship with God and shines in His image; but, unlike Adam before the fall, he is still beset with the infirmities of the flesh, and will continue to be so until God touches him with the finger of death and bids his ransomed soul return to Him.

As compared with unsaved man, there is this which is common to both: They are beset with the infirmities of the flesh; but while both live in the flesh, the natural man allows the flesh to dominate, while the spiritually minded man keeps the body under; one walks "after the flesh," the other walks "after the Spirit" (Rom. 8:1). One is spiritually dead, the other is spiritually alive; one is being overcome of evil, the other is overcoming evil with good; one is on the broad road to destruction, the other is on the narrow way to life eternal.

Looking at redeemed man as God remade him, we recognize the following:

## 1. He is a child of God.

In his fallen state he had been the "child of the devil" (Acts 13:10; Jno. 8:44). But now, having been raised from death to life and brought from darkness to light, as one "born again" he is again recognized as belonging to the happy family of God.

## 2. He is subject to disease, pain, and death.

The results of sin are still manifest in the infirmities of the flesh, even though the soul is saved. There is therefore a warfare within "our vile body" (Phil. 3:21), as Paul describes it. "The flesh lusteth against the Spirit, and the Spirit against the flesh" (Gal. 5:17). Moreover, this warfare must be kept up constantly; as Paul expressed it when he said, "I keep under my body, and bring it into subjection; lest by any means, when I have preached to others, I myself should be a castaway" (I Cor. 9:27). It is this vile body that is responsible for all the corruption that is in the world, when not kept in subjection—and even when it is kept in subjection it must pay in part the penalty of sin in that it suffers pain and finally death. It is our inheritance from Adam, and can not be gotten rid of until the body returns to dust. Rom. 8:1-14; Eccl. 12: 1-7.

## 3. He is beset with shortcomings.

This is for two reasons: (1) Man is a finite creature. (2) Man inherits weaknesses from his ancestors. Judging from the standard of absolute perfection, we will never reach it so long as we are in this tenement of clay. But only such shortcomings as we are individually responsible for (willful sinning) will be held against us. We may pray that the "thorn in the flesh" be removed, but the removing of it rests with the Lord. II Cor. 12:7-10.

## 4. He has access to the Father.

This is not true of the unsaved sinner. There is indeed this gracious invitation, "Look unto me, and be ye saved, all the ends of the earth," but "he that turneth away his ears from hearing the law, even his prayer shall be abomination" (Prov. 28:9). The condition is, "Hear, and your soul shall live" (Isa. 55:3). To the children of God there is a continual, daily, hourly, momentary access to the Father, who in tender mercy and loving kindness hears our prayers and answers according to His unerring wisdom. The child of God can say of a truth, "Truly our fellowship is with the Father, and with his Son Jesus Christ" (I Jno. 1:4).

### 5. He is blessed with a heavenly Advocate.

"If any man sin, we have an advocate with the Father, Jesus Christ the righteous" (I Jno. 2:1). Weak and unworthy though we be, we thank our God the Father, and God the Son, for this very great favor to us. When we have Christ as our Advocate, we have nothing to fear.

### 6. He is the temple of the Holy Ghost.

"Know ye not that your body is the temple of the Holy Ghost which is in you" (I Cor. 6:19)? A number of times are the children of God, either individually or collectively, referred to as "the temple of God." At Pentecost, in the house of Cornelius, and on numerous other occasions are the people of God referred to as having been "filled with the Holy Ghost." It is the Christian's most exalted honor, while on earth, to be the dwelling place of the Most High God, and our most sacred duty is to keep these houses of ours in fit condition for the abiding presence of this heavenly Guest. Let us therefore keep ourselves cleansed from "all filthiness of the flesh and spirit, perfecting holiness in the fear of God" (II Cor. 7:1).

### 7. He is a creature of hope.

No sooner had the two men in white apparel said that this same Jesus would come again (Acts 1:11) than the disciples, remembering that their Lord had told them to tarry at Jerusalem until they should be endued with power from on high, returned to that city and continued steadfastly in prayer and worship until the promised enduement came. Their faith and hope were rewarded. So will every one be rewarded who looks steadfastly forward and keeps faithfully serving, expecting the promised return of the Lord, until the "earnest expectation of the creature" will have been realized. "Having no hope and without God in the world" is not written of the saved children of God. On the other hand, "the blessed hope" of the Lord's return and of the continuous bliss and glory thereafter stirs his soul and "Christ in you, the hope of glory" is the joy of his heart.

### 8. He is fellow heir with Christ.

The Bible speaks of the children of God as being "heirs of God" (Rom. 8:17), "heirs of salvation" (Heb. 1: 14), "heirs of promise" (Heb. 6:17), heirs "of the righteousness which is by faith" (Heb. 11:7), "heirs of the kingdom" (Jas. 2:5). Paul sums up the whole of our inheritance when he speaks of the children of God as being "joint-heirs with Christ" (Rom. 8:17). No wonder then that he should burst forth in joyous expectation when out of his prison cell he looked hopefully into the bright beyond and exclaimed, "Henceforth there is laid up for me a crown of righteousness, which the Lord, the righteous judge, shall give me at that day: and not to me only, but unto all them also that love his appearing" (II Tim. 4:8). "And every man that hath this hope in him purifieth himself, even as he is pure" (I Jno. 3:3).

### 9. He is awaiting the time of his eternal and complete redemption.

The child of God looks forward with joyous hope— and then as he thinks of the infirmities of the flesh he is reminded again and again that here on earth he is not only an heir of glory but also a child of sorrows. Paul expressed the feeling of many a Christian soldier when he said, "We that are in this tabernacle do groan, being burdened: not for that we would be unclothed, but clothed upon, that mortality might be swallowed up of life" (II Cor. 5:4). It is not that we are dissatisfied or unwilling to remain here in this earthly tenement of clay until our mission on earth is completed; yet the hope of fuller and richer glory, where human shortcomings and tears and pains are unknown, impels us to cry out with John, "Even so, come, Lord Jesus." Again let us turn to Paul to express our feelings: "Ourselves also, which have the firstfruits of the Spirit, even we ourselves groan within ourselves, waiting for the adoption, to wit, the redemption of our body" (Rom. 8:23). This redemption will be finally complete at the resurrection when Christ returns for His own, and when, with glorified bodies, we will meet Him in the air. I Thess. 4:16-18.

# CHAPTER V

## DEATH

*When this corruptible shall have put on incorruption, and this mortal shall have put on immortality, then shall be brought to pass the saying that is written, Death is swallowed up in victory. O death, where is thy sting? O grave, where is thy victory?—I Corinthians 15:54, 55.*

Briefly but impressively, the inspired writer introduces our subject by saying, "It is appointed unto men once to die, but after this the judgment" (Heb. 9:27). It is the last subject to be considered in connection with mortal man, as death stands at the gateway between time and eternity.

### WHAT IS DEATH

#### 1. Death is a separation.

When we speak of physical or natural death, we speak of a separation of soul and body. See Gen. 25:8; Eccl. 12:7. A separation of the soul from God constitutes what we usually speak of as spiritual death. Eph. 2:1, 12; I Tim. 5:6. Finally, when the doomed soul is eternally separated from God, to be with the devil and his angels forever, this is referred to as "the second death" (Rev. 2:11).

#### 2. Death is judgment upon sin.

God planted, in the midst of the garden, the tree of knowledge of good and evil, warning Adam that "in the day that thou eatest thereof, thou shalt surely die" (Gen. 2:17). After Adam had sinned he heard this judgment: "Dust thou art, and unto dust thou shalt return" (Gen. 3:19). It is the edict of God that "the soul that sinneth, it shall die" (Ezek. 18:4). Paul emphasized this fact when he said "Death passed upon all men, for that all have sinned" (Rom. 5:12).

### 3. Death is an enemy which, under the providence of God, has been turned into a blessing.

Here we speak of natural or physical death, only. One of the kindest things which God ever did for man was to make it impossible for him to live forever in his sinful state. That flaming sword which God placed just east of the garden (Gen. 3:24) to keep fallen man away from the tree of life may have seemed cruel to Adam and Eve (just as some people today look upon death as something cruel) but in reality it was a manifestation of God's kindness and goodness, as it kept Adam and Eve from the possibility of living forever in their sinful state and gave them an opportunity, along with the rest of humanity, to become partakers of a new Tree of Life (Jesus Christ). Even so today, while death in itself is an enemy, referred to by Paul as "The last enemy that shall be destroyed" (I Cor. 15:26), through the providence of God its sting is taken away for all the people of God, through the atoning merits of the blood of Jesus Christ, and the ministration of death has been made to the saved in Jesus a loving touch of a merciful Father, since by the separation of soul and body the way is opened for a more glorious life in the world beyond. The presence of death on every hand is a real blessing in that it is a constant reminder to us of the frailty of man and of the importance of being ready for the Great Change. Though we must often do so through our tears, we thank the Lord for this merciful providence and loving kindness to us unmerciful creatures of the dust.

### 4. Death is a sleep.

It is so characterized in Scripture. "Not dead, but sleepeth," was the way Christ referred to Jairus' daughter who had just died. Yes, she was dead! but after all it was but a "sleep." In this case she was sleeping only till the Lord touched her (but a few hours at most), but had she been permitted to sleep on until the resurrection morn the sleep would not have been different from what it was. When Christ received word that He should hasten to the bedside of His friend Lazarus He informed the disciples that "our friend Lazarus sleepeth" (Jno. 11:11); but He soon made it clear what He meant, saying, "Lazarus is dead." When death stills the body it sleeps until the time of the resurrection, when it will again come forth at the call of the Lord. This idea of death being but a sleep is prominent in Paul's message to the Thessalonians. Read I Thess. 4:13-15.

## What Death Is Not

### 1. It is not "soul sleeping."

The idea that both soul and body go down to the grave together to await the trumpet call of God at the resurrection has no support in Scripture. This is what God says happens at death: "Then shall the dust return to the earth as it was: and the spirit shall return to God who gave it" (Eccl. 12:7). When the beggar Lazarus died he "was carried by the angels into Abraham's bosom" (Luke 16:22), while the rich man, though his body was buried, opened his eyes "in hell." Paul gives comfort to the Thessalonians, saying, "If we believe that Jesus died and rose again, even so them also which sleep in Jesus will God bring with him" (I Thess. 4:14). How could He bring with Him those who are not with Him in His risen state?

### 2. It is not annihilation.

The theory of annihilation is held by three classes of people: (1) the atheist, who believes that when man dies he is like a dead animal—dead forever—and that death ends all existence; (2) the Russellite, who believes practically the same thing, adding an amendment which means virtually a second creation at the time of the resurrection: (3) the Seventh Day Adventist, who believes in "soul sleeping," the resurrection, and instant annihilation of the wicked after the judgment. The first class, avowedly rejecting all belief in Scripture, may be dismissed from further consideration; but the rest, professing faith in the Word of God which they deny, need to have their faith tested by this Word which they profess to reverence.

The theory of annihilation can have no foundation save on the ground that the soul has no separate existence from the body. There is no scripture which can be perverted into a support of that theory which will not, in such perverted construction, also support the theory of atheism. Some say, "Death means death, and that is all there is to it." Grant it. But when they try to say that there is but one kind of death, they run counter to Scripture. What did Paul mean when he wrote to the Ephesians, "You hath he *quickened,* who *were dead"* (Eph. 2:1)? or when he wrote to Timothy, "She that liveth in pleasure is DEAD *while she liveth"* (I Tim. 5:6)? Or where was the comfort in Christ's assurance to the thief on the cross when He said, "To day shalt thou be with me in paradise" (Luke 23:43), if after death the thief had no existence outside the grave? No; death is not annihilation. When it is ceasing to live naturally, we call it physical death; when it is ceasing to live spiritually, we call it spiritual death. Both the righteous and the wicked have eternal existence after physical death. Matt. 25:46.

### The Sting of Death

for the righteous is taken away in the fact that the grave does not end all. On the other hand, physical death liberates the spirit of man that now returns to God, while the body returns to dust awaiting the call of God to rise in the resurrection. We thank God that

> "Dust thou art, to dust returnest,
> Was not spoken of the soul."

Let it be understood, however, that physical death is a glorious deliverance for the saved in Christ only. It is simply an ushering in of the realization of what eternity has in store. For the unrighteous dead, "everlasting punishment" is ahead, while the righteous dead are cheered by the promise of "life eternal."

The child of God, looking beyond the river of death, is cheered by the thought, "We know that if our earthly house of this tabernacle were dissolved, we have a building of God, an house not made with hands, eternal in the heavens" (II Cor. 5:1). Our praises go up to God as we think of the cheering fact that for the child of God death means simply the release of the soul. "O death, where is thy sting? O grave, where is thy victory? . . . . Thanks be to God, which giveth us the victory through our Lord Jesus Christ" (I Cor. 15:55, 57). When loved ones who die in the Lord are laid away, our mourning hearts are comforted in the thought and hope that by and by we will meet again on the celestial shore where death will come no more.

# PART III

# God and Man

# GOD AND MAN

### or

# God's Provisions for the Welfare of Man

## Outline by Chapters

I. MAN'S FALL—GOD'S REDEMPTIVE GRACE
1. IN EDEN
2. THE FAMILY OF ADAM ⎱⎱ Man's Failure
3. THE FAMILY OF NOAH ⎰ ⎰
4. THE FAMILY OF ABRAHAM ⎱⎱ God's Grace
5. THE FAMILY OF GOD ⎰ ⎰

II. REVELATION
1. OUR ONLY AVENUE OF LIGHT
2. REVELATIONS, TRUE AND FALSE
   a. Revelations Defined
   b. Spurious Revelations
   c. The Whole Bible Authentic
3. HOW GOD REVEALS HIMSELF TO MAN
   a. Through the Written Word
   b. Through the Book of Nature
   c. Through the Holy Spirit
   d. Through the Ministry of Angels
   e. Through Visions and Dreams
   f. Through Faith
4. NO CONFLICT BETWEEN DIVINE REVELATIONS

III. THE BIBLE
1. WHY WE BELIEVE THE BIBLE
   a. Fulfillment of Prophecy
   b. Unity
   c. Test of the Ages
   d. Reliability
   e. Effect upon its Readers
   f. The Masterpiece in Literature

2. THE INSPIRATION OF SCRIPTURE
   a. Old Testament
   b. New Testament
   c. Imperfect Men and Perfect Message
   d. Distinction between Inspiration, Revelation, and Illumination

3. HOW WE GOT OUR BIBLE
   a. Old Testament
   b. New Testament

4. THE APOCRYPHAL WRITINGS

5. THE LAW AND THE GOSPEL
   a. The Law
   b. The Gospel
   c. Two Spokesmen
   d. Two Covenants
   e. Law and Grace

## IV. THE HOME

1. THE WHY OF THE HOME
   a. A Promoter of Unity
   b. A Promoter of Purity
   c. A Godsend for Children
   d. A Safe Retreat
   e. A Training School for Children

2. HOME DUTIES
   a. Husbands and Fathers
   b. Wives and Mothers
   c. Children
   d. Servants
   e. Masters

3. HOME ASSOCIATIONS
   a. Love
   b. Spirit of Worship
   c. Spirit of Loyalty
   d. Wholesome Literature
   e. Desirable Companions

4. THE BLESSINGS OF HOME LIFE

## V. THE CHURCH

1. THE WHY OF THE CHURCH
   a. A Shelter for People of God
   b. A Place of Spiritual Nourishment
   c. Means for Christian Fellowship
   d. Means for Keeping
   e. In Touch with Heavenly Influences
   f. Union of Forces

2. HISTORICAL

3. OUR OPPORTUNITIES

VI. **CIVIL GOVERNMENT**
  1. THE POWERS THAT BE
  2. THE PURPOSE OF GOVERNMENT
  3. OFFICIAL POSITION NO SIGN OF SPIRITU-
     AL STANDING
  4. DIRECTIVE AND PERMISSIVE WILL OF GOD
  5. CHRISTIAN'S RELATION TO GOVERNMENT
     a. Subjection
     b. Twofold Citizenship
     c. "Strangers and Pilgrims"
     d. An Uplifting Power
     e. An Intercessor

VII. **THE DAY OF REST AND WORSHIP**
  1. A FEW FACTS CONCERNING THE SABBATH
     a. Instituted by the Creator
     b. Has a Place in Every Dispensation
     c. Was Made for Man
     d. Christ the Lord of
  2. PROPER USES OF THE DAY
     a. A Day of Rest
     b. A Day of Worship
     c. To be Kept Holy
     d. Not a Holiday

A. **THE SEVENTH DAY**
  1. ITS INSTITUTION
  2. EVIDENCES OF ITS HAVING BEEN KEPT

B. **THE JEWISH SABBATH**
  1. THE FOURTH COMMANDMENT
  2. FACTS CONCERNING THE JEWISH SABBATH
     a. Observed the Seventh Day of the Week
     b. Kept in Memory of God's Sanctifying the Day
     c. Kept in Memory of the Deliverance from Egypt
     d. Stringent Laws
     e. System of Sabbaths
     f. An Opportunity for Godly Service

C. **THE LORD'S DAY**
  1. PREFIGURED IN OLD TESTAMENT
  2. SOME FUNDAMENTAL FACTS
     a. The Lord's Day
     b. Son of Man the Lord of
     c. Worship the Outstanding Object
     d. To be Kept the First Day of the Week
     e. First Day Observance by the Early Church
  3. WHY KEEP THE LORD'S DAY SACRED
  4. A COMPARISON

# VIII. ANGELS

1. WHO THEY ARE
2. THEIR ORIGIN
3. THEIR GREAT NUMBER
4. ORDERS OF ANGELS
5. ATTRIBUTES
   a. Spirituality
   b. Individuality
   c. Immortality
   d. Power
   e. Intelligence
   f. Goodness
   g. Benevolence
   h. Happiness
   i. Glory
6. OFFICE AND WORK
   a. Ministering Spirits
   b. God's Messengers
   c. Execute Purposes and Judgments of God
   d. Guides to the Believer
   e. Glorify God
7. SOME THINGS THE BIBLE DOES NOT TEACH

# GOD AND MAN

OR

## God's Provisions for the Welfare of Man

God's wonderful love for His creatures is manifest in His bountiful provisions for the safety, happiness, and well-being of the human soul.

After man's shameful fall in the garden of Eden, He graciously restored him to divine favor, making provisions for our redemption through the giving of His only begotten Son.

He has revealed to man such mysteries of the past, present, and future as man, unaided, could never have fathomed.

Man on earth is provided with a material home where children, during the habit-forming period of their lives, may be sheltered, trained for service, and taught to face the issues of life.

Man on earth is provided with a spiritual home—the Church—where the people of God may enjoy His and one another's fellowship, strengthen one another in faith and service, and unite their powers in winning the lost for God and salvation.

Civil government has been provided for man's material interests, while as "strangers and pilgrims" the children of God are traveling toward "a city whose builder and maker is God."

God has set apart a day—in our dispensation known as "The Lord's Day,"—in which we may rest from our earthly toils and cares, and devote the day to the praise of God and the strengthening of the inner man.

To all of these blessings He has added the ministry of angels, God's spiritual messengers to the "heirs of salvation," bearing a very important relationship with man in time and eternity.

"O that men would praise the Lord for his goodness. and for his wonderful works to the children of men!"

# CHAPTER I

## MAN'S FALL—GOD'S REDEMPTIVE GRACE

> But God commendeth his love toward us, in that, while
> we were yet sinners, Christ died for us. Much more
> then, being now justified by his blood, we shall be
> saved from wrath through him.—Romans 5:8, 9.

The record of man, apart from God, may be summed
up in one word—failure! But God's wonderful grace has
been so marvelously wrought in the soul of man that both
God and man will be glorified together in eternity. Briefly
let us review the career of man, together with God's gracious dealing with him.

### In Eden

"Lo, this only have I found, that God hath made man
upright; but they have sought out many inventions" (Eccl.
7:29).

**Man's Fall.**—Behold man in the beautiful paradise of
God, shining in the image of his Maker, free from the
dominion of sin and death, in undisputed possession of
the earth, cheered by a sinless world and in daily communion with God!

But in an evil hour man fell. Innocence was gone,
and in shame did he attempt to hide from the face of God.
Through disobedience man forfeited his place in the family of God and became a child of the devil.

**God's Grace.**—But God was merciful. In conveying
to man the full meaning of his shameful fall, He graciously
coupled this information with the promise of a Redeemer.
Eden was indeed ruined, so far as its furnishing a blissful
home for man was concerned; but a still more glorious
paradise, "the kingdom prepared for you from the foundation of the world" (Matt. 25:34), with Christ the ever-

green Tree of Life in the midst of it, loomed in the distance before man as his everlasting dwelling place. The abundance of God's grace is manifest, not only in restoring fallen man to favor and friendship with Him but also making it possible for man to gain a state that is to be preferred to man's state in Eden.

Thus man was given another start.

### The Family of Adam

**Man's Failure.**—A child was born to Adam and Eve. A mother's heart beat with exultant joy as she exclaimed, "I have gotten a man from the Lord" (Gen. 4:1). But this "man from the Lord" turned out to be a murderer. Filled with envy and rage because Abel's sacrifice was accepted while his own was rejected, Cain sought a quarrel with Abel and slew him. Though he was driven from the face of man, this object lesson was lost on his fellow men and in course of time the wickedness of men became so great that the judgment of God was visited upon the human family and man was wiped off the face of the earth (Noah and his family excepted).

**God's Grace.**—But God was merciful. Having found a righteous man in Noah, through him He preserved the human seed. He also preserved seed from the various species of animals, beasts, fowls of the air, and every creeping thing that was sheltered in the ark during the great Deluge at that time (Gen. 7). Through Noah—

Man was given another start.

### The Family of Noah

**Man's Failure.**—But again did man prove his unworthiness. In the course of a few hundred years the human family had again grown to be numerous and sinful. The judgment of God came upon them while they were building the Tower of Babel, and the people were scattered into various parts of the earth. This, however, while it frustrated the efforts of man, did not long stem the downward current of wickedness.

**God's Grace.**—But God was merciful. In Ur of the Chaldees He found a faithful man in the person of Abraham, and him He called out from among kindred and friends (Gen. 12) to become "the father of many nations," promising him that in his seed should "all the nations of the earth be blessed." Abraham obeyed. Through him—

Man was given another start.

### The Family of Abraham

**Man's Failure.**—But Abraham, though righteous and favored of God, proved himself human; and his posterity, like others gone before, trod the ordinary course of the peoples of the earth. Following their course through Palestine, Egypt, and the wilderness, and back again into Palestine, we see the family of Abraham growing into a mighty nation. The Law was given them at Sinai, the land of promise became their habitation, and a nation of God's people blessed the earth. But Israel forgot God. Sin preyed upon the vitals of the nation, until God finally delivered it into the hands of enemy nations. Today the term "Jew" is a reproach and a by-word among the nations of earth.

**God's Grace.**—But God was merciful. He had not forgotten His promise that in the Seed of Abraham should all the nations of the earth be blessed. In due time the promised Seed of Abraham, the living Redeemer who was first promised to Eve and afterwards minutely described by the prophets, came into this sin-cursed world to "seek and to save that which was lost" (Luke 19:10). "God so loved the world, that he gave his only begotten Son, that whosoever believeth in him should not perish, but have everlasting life" (Jno. 3:16). See also Rom. 5:15. Through Jesus Christ, "the Lamb of God, which taketh away the sin of the world" (Jno. 1:29)—

Man was given a new start.

### The Family of God

We have pointed out that the work of man, apart from God, invariably results in failure. And the reason for this failure is found in the fact of man's departure from the ways of God. The unfortunate condition of the human family ever since the fall of man may be explained in the fact that many do not believe in God, while among those who profess faith in Him too many are trying to reach heaven by way of the Tower of Babel (the work of men's hands) rather than by way of the Lord Jesus Christ (the plan of God for man's eternal redemption).

But while "All is vanity" is the verdict upon human effort, "All is glorious" is the only truthful way to describe the work of God in the hearts of the children of men. From the days of Adam the family of God has been growing, not a generation passing but that new members were added to His family. We have no reason to believe otherwise than that Adam and Eve accepted the terms of God's grace after their fall and lived faithful lives thereafter. Among the antediluvians the people of God called "upon the name of the Lord" (Gen. 4:26) and Enoch is mentioned in particular as having "walked with God, and . . . God took him" (Gen. 4:24). In the eleventh chapter of Hebrews Paul mentions a long list of faithful men who constitute a great "cloud of witnesses" to the truth and grace of God. Job, Melchizedek, Jethro, and the Magi in the time of Christ, present proof that there were others in Old Testament times besides the lineal descendants of Jacob who were believers and devout worshipers of the God of Abraham. Peter, referring to the people of God in the present dispensation, says, "Ye are a chosen generation. a royal priesthood, an holy nation, a peculiar people" (I Pet. 2:9). Go to any old cemetery where Christians are buried, and the markers over the graves reveal the names of Christians who have gone on before, even though the adjoining church may have closed its doors. Yes, the family of God is growing larger. At the close of the present dispensation, though it will be revealed that its close will be similar to preceding ones so far as man's unfaithfulness is concerned, it will also be found that an innumerable multitude will have been gathered home to God.

In this we need not depend upon human opinion for our conclusions, for the Bible gives us ample assurance along these lines. One single illustration must suffice:

John on Patmos beheld a number of soul-thrilling scenes which he was commanded to write down in a book. Among the things that he saw, this from Rev. 7:9-14 has brought great joy to many a weary soul: *"After this I beheld, and, lo, a great multitude, which no man could number, of all nations, and kindred, and people, and tongues, stood before the throne, and before the Lamb, clothed with white robes, and palms in their hands; and cried with a loud voice, saying, Salvation to our God which sitteth upon the throne, and unto the Lamb. And all the angels stood around about the throne and about the elders and the four beasts, and fell before the throne on their faces, and worshiped God, saying, Amen: Blessing, and glory, and wisdom, and thanksgiving, and honour, and power, and might, be unto our God for ever and ever. Amen. These are they which came out of great tribulation, and have washed their robes, and made them white in the blood of the Lamb."*

We will close by quoting from Tit. 2:11-14: "The grace of God that bringeth salvation hath appeared to all men, teaching us that, denying ungodliness and worldly lusts, we should live soberly, righteously, and godly, in this present world; looking for that blessed hope, and the glorious appearing of the great God and our Saviour Jesus Christ; who gave himself for us, that he might redeem us from all iniquity, and purify unto himself a peculiar people, zealous of good works."

# CHAPTER II

## REVELATION

God hath revealed them unto us by his Spirit: for the
Spirit searcheth all things, yea, the deep things of
God.—I Corinthians 2:10.

A world-renowned agnostic was standing at the side
of a grave, pronouncing a touching funeral oration over
the dead body of his brother. When he came to the question, "If a man die shall he live again?" he answered,
"Hope says, Yes; reason says, Perhaps." That was as far
as he could go, for the most brilliant mind has its limitations; and having rejected the thought of divine revelation
from God, he was limited by the finiteness of the human
mind. Yet the simple-minded child of God can say of a
surety, "I know that my Redeemer liveth, and that he shall
stand at the latter day upon the earth: and though after
my skin worms destroy this body, yet in my flesh shall I
see God. . . . for the trumpet shall sound, and the dead shall
be raised incorruptible. . . . and so shall we ever be with
the Lord" (Job 19:25, 26; I Cor. 15:52; I Thess. 4:17).

Why this difference? The answer is found in one
word—REVELATION. "The natural man receiveth not
the things of the Spirit of God" (I Cor. 2:14). Ingersoll,
rejecting the doctrine of direct revelation from God, was
confined to the limitations of the human mind and human
knowledge, and as such was unable to unravel the mysteries of the prehistoric past, or to penetrate the (humanly)
unfathomable realms beyond the grave. In this respect
the unbelieving American and the unenlightened heathen
in the jungles of Africa or India are alike. There are
mysteries which the human mind, unaided by revelation
from God, can never unravel. The origin of matter, the
origin of life, the origin of man, the eternal destiny of

man, and numerous other problems which have challenged and baffled the investigations of unbelieving man for thousands of years, must continue to remain mysteries and be made the subject for idle speculations—except as the light from heaven makes them clear. They are beyond us. The only way by which such things can be found out is by getting information from one who knows—and who, besides the Infinite God, can know them—except through revelation from Him?

So the child of God, grasping the opportunity for enlightenment which the unbeliever rejects, looks backward and learns that "in the beginning God created the heaven and the earth" (Gen. 1:1). Looking forward, he is assured that "we shall not all sleep, but we shall all be changed, in a moment, in the twinkling of an eye, at the last trump: for the trumpet shall sound, and the dead shall be raised" (I Cor. 15:51, 52). "As it is written, Eye hath not seen, nor ear heard, neither have entered into the heart of man, the things which God hath prepared for them that love him. But God hath revealed them unto us by his Spirit" (I Cor. 2:9, 10). The believer accepts these revelations and moves on to greater light. But the unbeliever rejects them, and continues to grope in darkness.

The impossibility of knowing the things beyond your range of vision except through revelation may be illustrated in this way: You know there was a George Washington. How do you know? Somebody told you, or you got it from history. Who wrote that history? Somebody who either wrote from first-hand information, or got the reliable information from some one who knew. Reduced to the last analysis, your information comes from some one who either saw Washington, heard him speak, or had other sources of information that enabled him to speak or to write from knowledge. Armed with this information, the historian or the reader may know of a surety that there was such a man as Washington.

### Our Only Avenue of Light

So with reference to things divine. "Canst thou by searching find out God" (Job 11:7)? What do you know about the origin of matter, of life, of things that had existence before the first man? What do you know about God. His personality, His dwelling place, His environments? What do you know about the realms beyond the grave? about plant or animal life on the other planets? about heaven or hell? Nothing—absolutely nothing—save through revelation from the One who knows, and who has seen fit to reveal some of these things to man. God had existence before the beginning of creation, hence He can speak from knowledge, and with authority. He knows all things, hence He can tell us what will be in the ages to come. But for this direct revelation from God, we might as well believe Socrates or Confucius or Mohammed as to believe Moses or Jesus of Nazareth; for if neither of these were enlightened by direct revelations from God, then the guesses, or prognostications, or deductions of one man's mind are as likely to be correct as those of another, and Christianity would stand on a common level with all other religions, so far as knowing the mind and will of God is concerned.

### Revelations, True and False

Revelations, to be authentic, need not necessarily come from God. Men may reveal thoughts or facts to us, or we may read in books, or discover with our own eyes, things which are a real revelation to us, and thus an addition to our store of knowledge is made. But whether the revelation comes from God, from our fellow man, from some book, from the book of nature, or from any other source, the revelator must have actual knowledge of the things revealed, or the so-called revelation is spurious. There can be no authentic revelation unless the revelator *knows* what he is revealing. There is no hypothesis in revelation.

Bearing this fact in mind, it is not hard to see that there can be no revelations from God except through channels that are God-inspired or Spirit-directed. What do you know about a home that you have never seen, nor heard described by some one having actual knowledge of that home? You may guess, but what does a guess amount to under such circumstances? What do you know about heaven, if you are ignorant of or disbelieve the story of the Bible? In what other way did God transmit to man a description of this wonderful Place and a knowledge of what it is like? Who, besides God, can have first-hand knowledge of all the things pertaining to eternity? And how could any man know unless God has in some way communicated this knowledge to him? If the doctrine that the Bible contains such record of revelations from God is unsatisfactory, where is there another story of God's revelations to man that is more authentic? One thing is sure: This touch between God and man must exist, or man is absolutely in the dark concerning the things of God. Deny the fact that there is such a thing as a direct revelation from God, and deny that the Bible is the authentic story of such direct revelation, and you place Christianity upon the same level with the rankest form of heathenism.

The Bible is very specific in its teaching on direct revelations from God. That God revealed Himself to Adam, to Noah, to Abraham, to Jacob, to the prophets, and through Jesus Christ and the Holy Spirit to the saints of the New Testament period, can not be denied without repudiating the authenticity of the Bible as God's Word. Moreover, the Bible is equally clear in that it tells of the *only* means of revelation from God to man. God does not reveal Himself through idols, for idolatry is absolutely forbidden and denounced in both Old and New Testaments. He does not reveal Himself through any other written or verbally delivered messages, for the Bible is very specific in its judgments upon those who bring any

5

"other gospel," or presume to make additions to or subtractions from the message as it is found in the completed
and sacred canon. Read Gal. 1:8, 9; II Jno. 10; Rev. 22:
18, 19. There is absolutely no scriptural ground for the
claims of Mormons, Christian Scientists, Adventists, and
other sects that their leaders receive special revelations
from time to time which must be given equal or greater
credence than revelations recorded in the Bible. The same
is true with so-called "revelations," claimed to have been
received in answer to prayer, on the part of some, that
they need not obey certain unpopular Bible commandments
that are not to their liking. Neither is the theory that God
has from the beginning given to man progressive revelations
which became clearer and clearer with successive ages,
and that today the will of God is revealed (through
advanced knowledge and enlightenment) even more clearly
than it was in apostolic times, in harmony with the teaching of God's Word. And for similar reasons the claims
of modernists that through enlightenment and self-cul-
ture they "know God through experience" are all spurious,
for the knowledge of man, aside from direct revelations
from God, can never ascend above the realms of mind and
matter. All such revelations are from man and not from
God.

The question is often raised, What part of the Bible
is reliable as a bearer of revelations from God? We answer, unhesitatingly, *All* of it. This point will be considered at greater length in the next chapter. At this time
we simply wish to recall the inspired message to the Hebrews (1:1, 2) that while in the Old Testament dispensation
God, "at sundry times and in divers manners spake in time
past unto the fathers by the prophets," in the present dispensation He "hath in these last days spoken unto us by
his Son." In other words, in both dispensations God had
His authorized spokesmen through whom His Word and
will were communicated to men. It was of the Old Testament Scriptures that Paul wrote that they were *all* "given

by inspiration of God." It was of Old Testament prophets
that Peter wrote when he said that they "spake as they were
moved by the Holy Ghost." Concerning New Testament
Scriptures some people have advanced the foolish and mischievous notion that part should be recognized as the
Gospel of Christ while the rest should be considered as
simply the writings of the apostles. But what do we know
of Christ and His Gospel except what has been revealed
through the preaching and writings of the apostles? The
New Testament is divided into three parts: (1) biographical,
or the four Gospels and the Acts of the Apostles; (2) epistolary, or the apostolic letters from Romans to Jude; (3)
apocalyptic, or the book of Revelation. Who wrote these
books? The apostles and their coworkers. If they are not
reliable as writers of epistles, by what manner of logic are
we to conclude that they were reliable in writing the other
books? Take John, for example. He wrote one of the Gospels, three of the epistles, and the book of Revelation. Concerning the latter book it was expressly stated that it is
"The Revelation of Jesus Christ." If he was inspired to
write the Gospel, why was he not also inspired to write the
epistles? Added to this we might say that the apostles were
especially commissioned to proclaim the everlasting Gospel
of Christ in its fullness to a perishing world (Matt. 28:18-
20; Mark 16:15; Luke 24:46, 47; Acts 1:8; 9:15), and it
was the Gospel of Christ that they proclaimed whether
by tongue or pen, wherever they went. Read Rom. 1:16;
2:16; I Cor. 14:37; II Cor. 4:5; Gal. 1:8, 9; II Thes. 2:15;
I Tim. 1:11; Rev. 14:6.

### How God Reveals Himself to Man

1. **Through the Written Word.**—Is it something that
we wish to know about the creation, about the destiny of
man or some other thing beyond the range of the human
mind? We find it "in the volume of the BOOK." Such
expressions as "Thus saith the Lord," "Saith God," "The

Lord said," "God said," etc., are quite numerous in the Bible, showing conclusively that this Book lays claim to being the Word of God. In it the reader may know about the past, the present, and the future, so far as God has seen fit to reveal Himself, His handiwork, and His plans to man. The Bible is the one source of information to which the reader may turn and gather light on many things that would of necessity have remained complete mysteries through the ages, but for the revelations in this Book of God.

2. **Through the Book of Nature.**—This book is of service only as it is illuminated by the Book already referred to. But with the aid of such illumination the psalmist, speaking by inspiration of God, could scan the starry heavens and say, "The heavens declare the glory of God, and the firmament sheweth his handywork." And as the Book of divine revelation sheds light upon the handiwork of God in Nature, so this book of Nature reflects its light upon the Bible. For instance, travelers in Bible lands are unanimous in the testimony that the words of Jesus have taken on an added meaning for them since they were permitted to see for themselves some of the scenes upon which our Saviour looked while He went about from place to place, preaching the everlasting Gospel. One generation of scientists, basing their conclusions upon the limited information at hand, decides that certain portions of the Bible are erroneous. Another generation of scientists, in the light of later and fuller revelations from the book of Nature, finds that it is not the Bible but the Bible critics that were in error. And so it will continue to be until man sees God "face to face," has perfect knowledge of all the words and works of God, and finds them to agree in every particular.

3. **Through the Spirit.**—Concerning those mysteries which the natural man can not grasp, Paul says, "God has revealed them unto us by his Spirit." When the Spirit of God enters the soul of man the Bible becomes a new mes-

sage to him. "The natural man receiveth not the things of the Spirit of God. . . . neither can he know them, because they are spiritually discerned" (I Cor. 2:14). The Spirit of God gives to the child of God an insight into the Word of God which the most talented unconverted man can never have. (Read, in Jno. 14—16, what Christ says of the work of the Holy Spirit.)

4. **Through the Ministry of Angels.**—It was through angels that Abraham learned of the coming of the child of promise (Gen. 18:1-15), and of the impending destruction of Sodom (Gen. 18:16-22); that Lot was warned of that city's doom (Gen. 19:1-3); that Balaam was reminded that he had been warned of his disobedience to God (Num. 22:26-35); that Zacharias was informed concerning the coming of John the Baptist (Luke 1:11-25); that Mary and Joseph were enlightened as to the manner of the birth of Jesus (Luke 1:26-38; Matt. 1:18-21); that the shepherds of Bethlehem were informed as to the birth of Jesus (Luke 2:10-14); that Joseph and Mary were directed to flee into Egypt (Matt. 2:13-15); that the disciples were reassured that Jesus Christ would come again (Acts 1:11); that Peter and Cornelius learned of each other, and the door of the Gospel swung open to the Gentiles (Acts 10); that Paul was reassured concerning the safety of himself and all his company in the shipwreck (Acts 27:23-26); that John received his wonderful revelations on the Isle of Patmos. Wonderful and numerous have been the revelations of God to man, through the ministry of angels, as the Bible abundantly teaches.

5. **Through Visions and Dreams.**—No less remarkable than God's revelations through the ministry of angels are His revelations to man through the medium of visions and dreams. It was in a vision that Abraham learned of the promised seed, also the four hundred years' sojourn in Egypt (Gen. 15:12-16). No less remarkable was Jacob's vision at Bethel (Gen. 28) where he saw the vision of a ladder reaching to heaven, the angels ascending and

descending upon it. Joseph's dreams, through which he earned the reputation of "this dreamer" (Gen. 37:19) were nothing short of visions and revelations from God while he slept. The dreams of Pharaoh and of the chief butler and chief baker showed that others besides the people of God may have similar visitations from God. A similar observation may be made with reference to the visions of Darius and of Nebuchadnezzar as recorded in the book of Daniel. The visions of the shepherds, of the wise men, of Peter, of Cornelius, of Paul, and of John are proof that this method of God's revelations to man extended into New Testament times. Even today there are instances where people have seen in dreams things that came to pass thereafter, while many are known to have had premonitions of impending death. We recognize that as a rule a hearty supper and undigested food have something to do with most dreams, but this fact does not do away with the other fact that oftimes there are actual revelations from God through such means.

6. **Through Faith.**—Paul testified of the Gospel that "therein is the righteousness of God revealed from faith to faith" (Rom. 1:17). While it is true that at times there is such a clear revelation of the power and glory of God that even unsaved people acknowledge it (as, for example, the Roman centurion who acknowledged that "truly, this was the Son of God"), it takes faith to receive these revelations. What was it that enabled "babes" to receive what "the wise and prudent" (Matt. 11:25) failed to grasp? Faith. What is it that enables the uneducated peasant to grasp more of the goodness and love and power of God than do some of the world's most gifted scholars? Faith. What is it that enables the child of God to delve into the mysteries of the past and of the future while men of the world who have spent a lifetime in grappling with such problems have learned but very little? Faith. It is through the faith of the individual that God unfolds the mysteries of the ages, and where faith does not exist such mysteries can not be revealed.

The child of God has many reasons to thank God for the many wonderful revelations through which a world of mysteries becomes a reality of light and knowledge. Looking backwards, we see the door to the past opening as we hear the words, "In the beginning God . . . ." Looking heavenwards, we see the floods of heavenly light poured out on the environments of the present time. Looking forwards, the door to the future begins to swing open to the eye of man as we hear the words, "Behold, I shew you a mystery . . . ." Thus heaven and earth are filled with the light of God, the universe of God is thrown open to the eye of man, as revelation after revelation crowns his investigations with success and transfers mystery after mystery into the realms of knowledge.

## No Conflict Between Divine Revelations

Do these revelations from God ever conflict with one another? Never—or some of the (supposed-to-be) revelations are not from God. Whether they come to us through the written Word, through the witness of the Spirit, or through some other channel, they come from the same God, are in accordance with the same principles of everlasting truth, and therefore can not but be in harmony with the God of revelations Himself. When therefore we hear of revelations purporting to come from God let us not fail to do as the Bereans did—search the scriptures diligently to see whether those things are so. There can be no revelation from God which is not in perfect agreement with the Word of God, the Bible.

# CHAPTER III

## THE BIBLE

All SCRIPTURE is given by inspiration of God, and is profitable for doctrine, for reproof, for correction, for instruction in righteousness: that the man of God may be perfect, throughly furnished unto all good works.—II Timothy 3:16, 17.

Speaking of revelations, we naturally think of the Bible; for it is the Book of God, the only book given by direct revelation from God to man. This Book is called "The Bible," the word being taken from the Greek word *biblos,* meaning "book." It is THE BOOK, because there is none other of like authority, of like authorship. Naturally, with such claims in mind, the first thing to present is reasons

WHY WE BELIEVE THE BIBLE

is what we claim for it. Here are a few of the principal reasons:

1. **The Fulfillment of Prophecy.**—If we can prove that the things prophesied in the Bible are such as no human beings, however scholarly or brilliant, could have foretold, then we have proved that the Bible is from a source that is superhuman. Space permits us to give only a very few illustrations:

First to deserve mention are the more than three hundred Old Testament prophecies referring to the Messiah, every one of which was fulfilled in Christ in minutest detail. The prophets foretold that He was to be of the tribe of Judah (Gen. 49:10), that He was to be born of a virgin (Isa. 7:14), that He was to be born in Bethlehem of Judea (Micah 5:2), that He was to be called out of Egypt (Hos. 11:1), that a messenger was to be sent before Him (Isa.

40:3; Mal. 3:1), that He should teach by parables (Psa. 78:2), that He should be patient under trial and persecution (Isa. 53), that He should be sold for thirty pieces of silver (Zech. 11:12, 13) with which a potter's field should be purchased, and many other things that could not possibly have been foretold by human wisdom or even guesses. Many of these prophecies seemed very improbable and unbelievable at the time they were uttered.

Again, Daniel's vision of the four beasts (Dan. 7) together with the interpretation of this vision, gives an accurate portrayal of the history of nations, details of history that are even to this day going into fulfillment.

The prophets not only foretold the destruction of cities and nations then flourishing, but details of destruction were given, which have literally come to pass, as recorded on the pages of profane history. For instance, Tyre, once the pride of merchant princes and envy of nations, was spoken against by Ezekiel (26:4-12), whose prophecies later came to pass in the days of Alexander, when even the dust was scraped from off the rocks. The city has become a total ruin. The desolation of Egypt, as described in Ezek. 29, 30 came to pass centuries after this description was given, the pages of history confirming in minutest detail the prophecies of Ezekiel. That "prophecy is history pre-written" is verified in the fact that the forecast of prophecy is confirmed in the history of the desolation of Babylon, Syria, Medo-Persia, Greece, Rome, Carthage, and other nations. "Daniel it is the fashion of Higher Critics just now to declare a forgery, perpetrated by some unknown writer in the second century before Christ. One of the first Higher Critics, an infidel named Porphyry, in the third century A.D., assailed the book as a forgery written in the time of the Maccabees, 164-170 B.C., as does Archdeacon Farrar. But what completely disproves the charge is that Daniel is mentioned as an accredited and well known book in the books of the Maccabees, as well as in various other books of the Apocrypha; and it was placed in the Septuagint as a part of Scripture before the time of the Maccabees. Even Tom Paine admits its authenticity."—Brookes. The utter desolation and destruction of Jerusalem, as foretold by Christ, and the dispersion of the Jews among the nations of the earth, as foretold by the prophets, is accurately given in the writings of Josephus and confirmed by the present status of the Jews.

This recital of the fulfillment of prophecy might be continued indefinitely. But the one fact that we wish at this time to impress upon the reader is that these prophecies could not possibly have been the result of mere human wisdom, and it is folly to suppose that they were mere human guesses. They prove conclusively that the Bible must have been written by men who were prompted and guided by the mind of the Infinite, who foresees and foreknows all things. But this is but one of the many evidences of the infallibility of the Bible as God's Word.

2. **Unity of the Bible.**—The Bible is composed of sixty-six books, written in about fifteen different centuries, by nearly forty writers who occupied different stations, from the king upon the throne to the captive in a heathen land, from the educated Moses and Paul to the "unlearned and ignorant" Peter and John; written before, during, and after Israel was a nation—and yet through it all there is a beautiful and impressive harmony that proves conclusively that there was a Master Mind which inspired all of it. In other words, "Holy men of God spake as they were moved by the Holy Ghost" (II Pet. 1:21).

3. **Test of the Ages.**—No book has ever been put to the severe tests that the Bible has. Though the Jews were carried into heathen lands, they carried the Bible with them and preserved it there. It has been imitated so ingeniously that many have been unable to distinguish between the canonical books and the apocryphal writings, between the inspired Word of God and that which has been set forth by false prophets as something just as good or better. Determined efforts were made during the early centuries

of the Christian era to stamp out this "sect everywhere spoken against," and for centuries determined efforts were made to suppress the Bible through fire and sword. In every generation there have been men who prided themselves on their superior intellects and knowledge and who lost no opportunity to lead people to believe that the Bible was believed in its entirety only by the ignorant and superstitious. But in the face of all these oppositions the old Book still stands, the same book that it has always been since the sacred canon was completed. Today it is in greater demand than any book that has ever been printed. Not a single dent has been made into it—save in the imagination of its critics.

4. **Its Reliability.**—The Bible is the only book that has never been compelled to reverse itself or to change its message because of the later revelations of science. While it is not intended as a book of science, as such, yet it is a fact that it is scientifically correct in everything that it says. This can not be said of any other book or treatise ever written. Naturalists, astronomers, geologists, historians, and men of renown in every department of knowledge have demonstrated their fallibility by teaching things that were afterwards proved to be erroneous. There is not a prominent theory held by scientific men today that is not different from (in many cases exactly the reverse of) theories held by scientific men generations ago. Their theories have been reversed, or at least radically changed, with reference to the creation, the principles of light, the nature and extent of the deluge, the shape of the earth, the glacial period, geology, the structure of the body, disease, laws of health, and every other field of thought known to science. The Bible alone, in the language of the learned Urquhart, "is the one and only Book that is entirely and eternally true." It is true that the Bible has been quoted, and that by men of faith, in support of many erroneous theories. It has been quoted in favor of the slave traffic, of polygamy, of the theory that the earth is flat, and of

other things equally unscriptural; but the Bible teaches none of these things, and never has. It is not strange, however, that such quotations have been and are still being made, for the devil himself is an adept in quoting Scripture in support of his own vicious propaganda. Gen. 3:1-6; Matt. 4:1-11. But as time rolls on, and later revelations of science shed light upon both the Bible and scientific theories it is found that the Bible is invariably sustained by the light of truth while its critics are found to be in error. Let us quote from the writings of I. M. Haldeman:

"In less than ten years a textbook is out of date, a cyclopedia is worthless, a library a cemetery of dead books and dead ideas; but this Book keeps living right on. . . . . .Science has laughed it out of court. One hundred fifty years ago Voltaire said, 'Fifty years from now the world will hear no more of the Bible.' Self-selected scholarship has pronounced it out of date and dead. Again and again its funeral services are held. . . . . . and lo! before the critical mourners have returned to their homes it has arisen from the dead, passed with surprising speed the funeral coaches, and is found—as of yore—in the busy centers of life, thundering against evil, revealing the secrets of the heart, offering consolation to the sorrowing, hope to the dying, and flashing forth from its quivering, vital pages the wonders of the coming age."—Christ, Christianity, and the Bible, Pp. 151, 152.

5. **Effect upon its Readers.**—This is another proof of its superhuman qualities. It is the center of light wherever it is found. It works a transformation in the human heart, and wherever it gets a foothold in a community or nation it brings about a transformation in purity, refinement, culture, civilization, in everything that contributes happiness and moral and spiritual uplift to the soul. The difference between the nations of Europe and America, and the nations in Africa and Asia may be summed up in one word— Bible. That is not saying that nations called "Christian" merit the name, but it does say that they own what enlightenment they have to the influence of the Bible. If the little foothold which the Bible has in the nations of Europe and America has produced such wonderful results, what might we expect of these nations if, in fact as well as

in theory, they would adopt the Bible in its fullness, as their rule in life, in the home, in the community, and in the nation!

6. **The Masterpiece in Literature.**—When we speak of literary nations we think of Phoenicia, Greece, Germany, England, America, and other nations which have left their impress upon the world because of their literary productions; but the Bible comes from none of these nations. On the other hand, it comes from a comparatively weak, obscure nation that was never conspicuous for its literature, outside the Holy Scriptures, and but few of the writers of the Bible are renowned for their scholarship. And yet it stands out today as the world's MASTERPIECE in literature, so recognized by both believers and unbelievers. It stands unrivaled in the loftiness of its standards of purity and righteousness and holiness, is a recognized authority in the laws of nations, has a transforming power that is recognized even among the heathen, and is studied as "literature" even in schools that refuse to give it recognition as the revealed Word of God.

Why this distinction? There can be but one answer: IT IS FROM GOD. Upon every page of this wonderful Book may be found the Divine impress. This fact suggests as the next appropriate theme for our consideration

### THE INSPIRATION OF SCRIPTURE

From the foregoing thoughts we gather the following conclusions concerning the Bible:

1. It is the Word of God.
2. It is absolutely reliable.
3. It is infallible.
4. It is the only message in book form given as a direct revelation from God to man.
5. It is given *by inspiration* of God.

On this last point we quote from a statement on the fundamentals of the Christian faith adopted by the Mennonite General Conference in 1921:

"We believe in the plenary and verbal inspiration of the Bible as the Word of God; that it is authentic in its matter, authoritative in its counsels, inerrant in the original writings, and the only infallible rule of faith and practice. Ex. 4:2; II Sam. 23:2; Psa. 12:6; 139:7-12; II Tim. 3:16; II Pet. 1:20, 21."

The doctrine stated, let us observe that:

## 1. The Old Testament Scriptures are inspired.

It is to these Scriptures that Paul refers when he says, "All scripture is given by inspiration of God" (II Tim. 3:16). Peter adds his testimony to the same sentiment, giving the additional thought that the writers as well as their writings were inspired, when he says that "no prophecy of the scripture is of any private interpretation. For the prophecy came not in old time by the will of man; but holy men of God spake as they were moved by the Holy Ghost" (II Pet. 1:20, 21). The Bible is not lacking in evidence that the Old Testament Scriptures were God-inbreathed, that God spoke through the means of His servants whom He authorized to write the books now included in the Old Testament canon. Throughout the Old Testament, we have such expressions as, "Thus saith the Lord," "The Lord said," "God said," etc., repeated over and over again. Thus we hear Jeremiah saying, "This word came unto Jeremiah from the Lord, saying Take thee a roll of a book, and write therein all the words that I have spoken unto thee against Israel" (Jer. 36:1, 2). In like manner the Lord came to Ezekiel, telling him to speak to the children of Israel, saying, "Speak with my words unto them" (Ezek. 2:7). Similar quotations could be repeated by the score.

That the New Testament writers understood the Old Testament writings to be the message from God speaking through His servants is also quite clear. At the time of the choosing of Matthias to the apostleship, Peter quoted Scripture, saying, "The Holy Ghost by the mouth of David spake" (Acts 1:16). The book of Hebrews opens with these words: "God, who at sundry times and in divers manners spake in time past unto the fathers by the prophets, hath in these last days spoken unto us by his Son" (Heb. 1:1, 2). "This Book we call the Bible comes to us with the enormous and uncompromising claim that it is not a man-made book, but a Book whose real and sole Author is the living and eternal God."—I. M. Haldeman. And, as we have already noted, facts outside as well as inside the Bible substantiate the claim.

### 2. The New Testament Scriptures are inspired.

The New Testament claims to inspiration are as strong and as emphatic as are those of the Old. Paul, writing to the Corinthians, says, "We speak, not in the words which man's wisdom teacheth, but which the Holy Ghost teacheth" (I Cor. 2:13). Later on, in the same epistle, he says, "If any man think himself to be a prophet, or spiritual, let him acknowledge that the things that I write unto you are the commandments of the Lord" (I Cor. 14:37). This claim corresponds with what the Lord told Ananias, as recorded in Acts 9:15. To the Thessalonians he writes: "When ye received the Word of God which ye heard of us, ye received it not as the word of man, but, as it is in truth, *the word of God*. . . . For this we say unto you by **the Word of the Lord**" (I Thess. 2:13; 4:15). In the light of such testimonies we understand why it is that the apostles gave such emphatic warnings against man-made substitutes for the Word of God as recorded in the four gospels, the Acts of the Apostles, the epistolary writings, and the Revelation. Read Gal. 1:8, 9; II Pet. 3:16-18; II Jno. 7-10; Jude 3; Rev. 22:18, 19.

### 3. God used imperfect men as vehicles of thought and words to bring a perfect message to men.

This fact, apparent to all Bible students, makes the miracle of inspiration all the more marvelous. Concerning the imperfections of the men whom God used to bring His message to the world, we have Bible evidences of some shortcomings on the part of Abraham, Moses, Elijah, Peter, Paul, John, and others. But none of these imperfections, though revealed in the inspired Word, in any way impair the value or perfection of the Divine Message. Yea, more. The Bible contains some words and sentences that were not only spoken by imperfect men but by wicked and idolatrous men, by demons, by the devil himself; yet none of these utterances in any way impair the Message from God, but on the other hand are valuable to us in putting us on our guard against the wiles of the devil and his followers. No matter who first uttered the words and sentences found in the Bible, every one of them is placed where it means most in making the Message as a whole the most serviceable to those who receive it.

Some have wondered why, if the Bible is not the writings of men but of God, the personality of the writers is so very evident. Let us illustrate: You pass a house freshly painted in many colors. You ask, "How many painters worked on that house?" "One," is the reply. "How did he get so many colors?" "Oh, that is not hard to explain; he used many pigments in mixing up his paints, and brought out many colors to suit his plans." Does this suggest anything to you about the Great Author of the Divine Book using many personalities in the compiling of His Book? It is all the more serviceable, all the more adapted to fit the needs of and to appeal to the greatest possible number of people because of these different personalities. Because part of the Bible is in the language of Moses, a part of it in the language of Paul, and other parts of it in the language of some other writers, it does not therefore follow that it is not all the language of God. All these "men of God spake as they were moved by the Holy Ghost."

We said that every word and every sentence in the Bible fills its peculiar place, as designed by its perfect Author. Let us extend this to the very letter. For illustration: Paul, in referring to the promise of God to Abraham (Gen. 13) calls attention to the fact that "He saith not, And to *seeds,* as of many; but, as of one, And to thy *seed,* which is Christ" (Gal. 3:16). The point made is this: Had God said, "seeds," He would have meant the chil-

dren of Abraham; but because He said, "seed," He meant
Jesus Christ. Upon one letter, in this instance, hangs a
very important Christian doctrine. We can understand,
therefore, why Christ should stress the importance of "one
jot or tittle" (Matt. 5:18) when speaking of the fulfillment
of the law.

One more point: God sometimes put it into the mouth
of the prophets to utter prophecies which they themselves
did not understand. For example, witness the perplexed
state of Daniel's mind as the Lord put the last prophecy
into his mouth (Dan. 12:4-8). Then turn to I Pet. 1:10, 11
for a testimony which shows that Daniel was not alone in
such perplexities. The only point we wish to make out
of this is that while God worked through imperfect men,
He brought, through them, a perfect message to the world.

**4. There is a difference between inspiration, revelation, and illumination.**

On this point we quote from the writings of J. B.
Smith:

> In considering the nature of inspiration, let us see how it
> differs from revelation and illumination. Failure to do this has
> frequently led to endless confusion and contention.
>
> **a. Inspiration Distinguished from Revelation.**—In revelation God makes known to man truth not known before, or not
> knowable to man in any other way. In other words, in revelation there is a discovery of new truth. "All scripture," we
> have noticed, "is given by inspiration." Not all, however, is
> given by revelation. Inspiration guides the writer in communicating truth given by revelation. It also guides him in
> selecting and faithfully recording truth previously known.
>
> **b. Inspiration Distinguished from Illumination**—Illumination may be defined as that operation of the Holy Spirit upon
> God's children whereby they are enabled to understand and
> appreciate divine truth. Illumination is common to all Christians while inspiration is confined to the writers of the scripture. Illumination is continuous; inspiration is intermittent.
> Illumination admits of degrees, some Christians being more
> enlightened than others, while inspiration does not admit of
> degrees. By way of illustration let us notice that there may be
>
> (1) Inspiration without revelation, as for example, the
> book of Chronicles, Esther, the greater parts of the Gospels
> and Acts and Philemon.
>
> (2) Inspiration with revelation: The Pentateuch. See Ex.
> 20:1; 24:4; Deut. 31:24. Paul's writings. See Gal. 1:11, 12.
> The book of Revelation. Rev. 1:1, 11.

(3) Inspiration without illumination. See Num. 24:15-24; Jno. 11:49-52; I Pet. 1:10, 11.

(4) Inspiration with illumination. See I Cor. 2:12, 13.

(5) Revelation without inspiration. See Jno. 21:25; II Cor. 12:4.

(6) Revelation without illumination. See Dan. 12:8, 9; I Pet. 1:12.

(7) Revelation with illumination. See Dan. 9:23-27; 10:1, 8, 21; Matt. 13:1-23.

(8) Illumination without inspiration. See Luke 24:32, 45; Jno. 14:26; I Jno. 2:27.

(9) Revelation and inspiration with illumination. See Dan. 10, 11; I Cor. 2:10-13.

(10) Revelation and inspiration without illumination. See I Pet. 1:10-12.—Bible Doctrine, Pp. 101, 102.

## How We Got Our Bible

The story of how we got our Bible is quite as interesting as the doctrine of its inspiration. We are so accustomed to the Book that we scarcely ever think of how man came to get it. Its compilation, and later, its preservation, is to us a very great reason for praising the Lord and prizing its message.

The Book is divided into sixty-six distinct and separate messages, thirty-nine in the Old Testament and twenty-seven in the New, bringing to us a united story that would be incomplete were any one of these books missing. The book of Job is by many thought to be the oldest of these messages. Next is the Pentateuch, written by Moses; afterwards the other historical, poetical, and prophetic books were written. The Old Testament was written by kings, judges, and prophets, the books being finally compiled in the days of Ezra and Nehemiah. So great was the demand for these Scriptures that they were translated into Greek more than three centuries before Christ. The most celebrated version was that of the Septuagint, begun about 285 B.C., prepared by Alexandrian scholars who translated the Scriptures out of the original Hebrew into Greek.

Centuries rolled on. The scepter passed from Greece to Rome, and at the time of the appearance of the Messiah of prophecy, Palestine was a Roman province. Jesus of Nazareth grew to maturity, was baptized, and began His active ministry. He delivered His Gospel of salvation, sealed it with His precious blood, returned to glory, sent "another Comforter" who endued the disciples of Christ with power from on high, and the work of world evangelization was begun. His disciples recorded His life and teachings in four books known to us as "the gospels," the activities of the disciples were compiled in a book known to us as "The Acts of the Apostles," and these, together with the epistolary writings and the book of Revelation, constitute the New Testament canon. They were compiled very early in the history of the Christian Church, and judging by the writings of Clement, Tertullian, and other ante-Nicene fathers, the entire New Testament must have been completed in their day.

What the Septuagint is to the Greek translations of the Old Testament, the Latin Vulgate is to the Latin translations of the Old and New Testaments. This was a translation of the Greek into Latin, by Jerome (385-405) and others, and passed through a number of revisions. The Latin Vulgate is said to have been the first book ever printed, issued in 1455, soon after the invention of the art of printing. Subsequent translations into many languages have made the Bible accessible to the people of many nationalities, the most widely used English translation being the King James Version, completed in 1610.

The question is sometimes raised as to how we may know that we have the same Bible as the one used when the sacred canon was completed. While the original manuscripts are no longer in existence, there is enough evidence in the writings of the ante-Nicene fathers to set at rest all doubts as to the authenticity of the "Old Latin" and "Syriac" versions of the second century. In this list of early Church writers are Clement and Polycarp, who lived early enough to know personally a few of the apostles. Handwritten manuscripts, several thousand of which are known to be in existence (the four oldest being the

Alexandrian, the Ephraem, the Vatican, and the Sinaitic), cover the time from the fourth to the fifteenth centuries. Since that time printed copies have been in existence. There is no doubt in the minds of men of faith that we have the same Gospel that was preached in apostolic days, the same message as that compiled when the New Testament canon was completed.

## THE APOCRYPHAL WRITINGS

Along with the sixty-six books that finally found their way into the sacred canon, there are a number of other works, most of them written during the interim between the Old and the New Testament writings, which many thought worthy of a place among canonical books. They form a historical link between the Old and New Testaments, contain much of historical interest and value, but lack the evidences of being inspired of God, as found in the books of the Bible. Bearing on the question as to why they were not included in the sacred canon, we quote the following from the pen of J. B. Smith:

> If the question be asked as to why the Apocrypha has not been included in the canon, the following facts are a sufficient answer:
> 1. The word "apocrypha" signifies that which is hidden away, whereas the Bible is a revelation.
> 2. The fourteen books comprising it were not included in the Hebrew Bible.
> 3. The Jews have never received them into their canon, though they were probably written by Jews.
> 4. Christ and His apostles never quoted them.
> 5. They do not claim divine inspiration while some, at least, disclaim it.
> 6. They contain statements contradictory with themselves, with history, and with Scripture.
> 7. They are not found in the catalogues of inspired books for the first four centuries of the Christian era. ("Bible Doctrine," P. 117.)

## THE LAW AND THE GOSPEL

We are introduced to the Levitical Law in the early history of the children of Israel. As Israel had now become a nation and was soon to be in possession of the land of promise, it was fitting that the nation of God's people should have a written law of God to govern them. This law was given at Sinai. Ex. 19. It was in force until the institution of the Gospel of Christ. Matt. 5:17-20; Jno. 1:17; Col. 2:6-17.

What the Levitical Law was under the Old Dispensation, the Gospel of Christ is under the New—the supreme law of God for the people of God under their respective dispensations. There is perfect harmony and unity between these two, yet they are essentially different in a number of respects.

Does God change? No. "I change not" (Mal. 3:6), is His answer to this question. Does His law change? Yes —no. The principles of everlasting truth are as firmly established under the Law as under the Gospel—the Word of God is the same in both. But God, like every wise administrator, changes the application of His laws to fit existing conditions from time to time. To illustrate: A son comes to the father one day and says, "Father, may I go to town?" "No," says the father. The next day the son comes again and says, "Father, may I go to town?" "Yes," says the father. Has the father changed? No; but conditions have changed, and this makes it proper for the son to go today though it would have been improper yesterday. In like manner has God inserted some things in the New Covenant which are "not according" to corresponding things in the Old, not because He has changed or that truth has changed; but because of changed conditions He applies eternal truth to existing conditions in the present dispensation. On this point George R. Brunk submits the following comparisons for consideration:

> To rightly divide the Word of truth it is necessary to keep in mind the following:
>
> 1. That God has given two distinct covenants, the Old and the New Testaments.—Heb. 8:6-10.
>
> 2. That in the light of changed conditions, God in His wisdom saw fit to forbid in the New some things that were commanded in the Old.—Matt. 5:38, 39; Ex. 21:23-25; Jer. 31: 31, 32; Heb. 7:12.

3. That the Old Testament was the rule of life to Israel up to the time of Christ's death on the cross.—Gal. 3:23-25; Col. 2:14; Eph. 2:14, 15.

4. That the New Testament is now the rule for Christian conduct until Christ comes.—II Cor. 3:6; II Thess. 1:7, 8.

5. That the Christian has the Old as a mine of rich instruction, essential to the proper understanding of the New. —I Cor. 10:6, 11; Gal. 3:24, 25.

6. That the Old was taken away that the New might be established as our only rule of life.—Heb. 10:9, 10; Gal. 1:8, 9.

7. That those who persist in substituting Old Testament doctrine for New Testament teaching subvert the souls of their hearers.—Acts 15:24; Tit. 1:9-11.

Had these facts always been observed, the Church would never have been cursed with war, slavery, divorce and polygamy, nor persisted in following the Old Testament in the oath and trampling under foot the plain commandments of Christ. ("Bible Doctrine," P. 553.)

1. **Two Spokesmen.**—Both Old and New dispensations are provided with a spokesman, a mediator, a prophet, a lawgiver, one authorized by Almighty God to speak for his own dispensation—Moses under the Old, Jesus Christ under the New. It was concerning Jesus of Nazareth that Moses spoke, saying, "A prophet shall the Lord your God raise up unto you of your brethren, like unto me; him shall ye hear" (Acts 7:37). An additional thought is given in Heb. 1:1, 2: "God, who at sundry times and in divers manners spake in time past unto the fathers by the prophets, hath in these last days spoken unto us by his Son." The Father speaking from heaven puts emphasis on the thought of Christ's being the authorized spokesman for this dispensation when He says (Matt. 17:5): "This is my beloved Son, in whom I am well pleased; hear ye him." Let us again quote from Hebrews (12:25): "See that ye refuse not him that speaketh. For if they escaped not who refused him that spake on earth, *much more shall not we escape if we turn away from him that speaketh from heaven.*"

The thought conveyed in the last scripture quoted makes it clear that while in the Old Dispensation they looked to the law of Moses for their rule of life, in our times we look to the Gospel as our supreme Law. This thought will be developed later.

2. **Two Covenants.**—Paul, in comparing these covenants, says: "But now hath he obtained a more excellent ministry, by how much also he is a mediator of *a better covenant,* which was established upon better promises. For if that first covenant had been faultless, then should no place have been sought for the second. For finding fault with them, he saith, Behold, the days come, saith the Lord, when I will make a new covenant with the house of Israel and with the house of Judah" (Heb. 8:6-8).

Two very remarkable expressions, among other things, are found in this scripture: "more excellent ministry," "better covenant." The first refers to Christ and His work, as compared with Moses and the work of the Levitical priesthood. The conclusion is natural, and accepted with little difficulty. But what are we to say with reference to the "better covenant?" Was the old one faulty?

By no means. "The law is holy, and the commandment holy, and just, and good" (Rom. 7:12). There is absolutely no flaw, no imperfection in the law of God. The law of Moses, like the Gospel of Christ, is the law of God, was conceived in the mind of God, and is therefore perfect, absolutely perfect. But it "was weak through the flesh" (Rom. 8:3); or, in other words, it required absolute perfection on the part of the individual before any individual could be justified by it, therefore by the law can no flesh be justified. Again, as the sacrifices under the law were but "a shadow of good things to come," the law could "never with those sacrifices which they offered year by year continually make the comers thereunto perfect" (Heb. 10:1). In other words, the law was perfect, and the sacrifices offered under it meritorious, only as they found their fulfillment in Christ. For this reason, therefore, the covenant of grace is the "better covenant" as compared with the covenant of law.

3. **Law and Grace.**—Paul writes to the Galatians. saying, "The law was our schoolmaster to bring us unto Christ" (Gal. 3:24). It was right in its place, in its time, for its purpose—pure, just, holy, righteous, perfect. It served its purpose, was fulfilled in Christ, nailed to the cross (Col. 2:14), so we today are not under the law but under the Gospel of Christ. We look to Him as our Saviour and Redeemer, our Lawgiver and Supreme Authority, and we no longer look to the ceremonial law to find what the will of the Lord is concerning us for our times, but rather to the Gospel of Christ.

John gives voice to a significant thought when he says, "The law was given by Moses, but grace and truth came by Jesus Christ" (Jno. 1:17). One symbolizes the justice and power of God, the other His mercy and grace. Under the first covenant the seal was by the blood of animals; under the second, the blood of Jesus Christ, "slain from the foundation of the world" (Rev. 13:8).

One of the marked distinctions between the Law and the Gospel is the manner of dealing with transgressors. That was a dispensation of justice; as evident from the number that perished during the wilderness journey from Egypt to Canaan, from the stoning of Achan, the smiting of Uzzah (II Sam. 6:6, 7) the judgment of God upon Israel and Judah for their unfaithfulness, etc. Ours is a dispensation of mercy; as evident from God's mercy in the midst of great wickedness on the part of people bearing His name, and the sacrifice of the Lamb of God that all the world may go free. But let not man get the idea that God will deal more leniently with His people of this dispensation than He did with the people in former times. In that day they looked forward by faith (Heb. 11), and though dying without realization of the promise in their day, God's dealings with His people in that day were intended as an ensample to us (I Cor. 10:6, 11), to the end that the grace of God may not have been bestowed upon us in vain. Emphatic warning is given us that they who spurn

God's grace in time must suffer His wrath in eternity. II Thess. 1:7-9; Heb. 12:25.

The Law and the Gospel are interdependent. All the sacrifices and the ceremonies under the Law were but typical of Christ (Heb. 6-12) and would have amounted to nothing but for their fulfillment in Christ who "by one offering perfected forever them that are sanctified" (Heb. 10:14). On the other hand, "the law was our schoolmaster to bring us to Christ," and today the Gospel means more to us because of the light shed upon it by the message of the Law and because of the types and shadows found in the Old Testament. Nevertheless, when it comes to the law now in force, we find it in the Gospel. That is now the discipline by which the Christian Church is governed, the Word of God by which our destiny is determined.

Centered in the Law are the thirty-nine messages or books of the Old Testament. Centered in the Gospel are the twenty-seven messages or books of the New Testament. The whole constitutes a perfect message from God to man, the sacred canon of the Holy Scriptures, the BOOK which we have learned to cherish and which we call

THE BIBLE.

# CHAPTER IV

## THE HOME

As for me and my house, we will serve the Lord.—Joshua 24:15.

The Home, like the Sabbath, had its origin in the creation. Our highest authority on this subject is Christ Himself, who, in response to some questions by the Pharisees. said:

"Have ye not read, that he which made them at the beginning, made them male and female, and said, For this cause shall a man leave father and mother, and shall cleave to his wife: and they twain shall be one flesh? Wherefore they are no more twain, but one flesh. What therefore God hath joined together, let not man put asunder.—Matt. 19:4-6.

From this we notice that family life existed from the time of the creation of man; also, that it was conceived in the mind of the Infinite, who ordered all things for our good. This leads us to consider

### THE WHY OF THE HOME

#### 1. It is a promoter of unity.

"For this cause shall a man leave father and mother, and shall cleave to his wife." Why? Because he has become "one flesh" with another; that is, a new family has come into existence. There is no better way to foster this unity than for the two to be in constant fellowship with each other, that they may labor together in a life in which their problems, aims, and struggles are one. The complete union of husband and wife is essential to a unification of the whole family, including children and "strangers within the gates."

#### 2. It is a promoter of purity.

There is no greater force in the promotion of purity among the human race than a satisfactory, happy home life. "Marriage is honourable in all . . . but whoremongers and adulterers God will judge" (Heb. 13:4). In every community the moral standard is determined by the way marriage and home life are regarded. Where God's marriage laws are faithfully observed there is not only purity in the life and character of the parents, but a powerful influence is exerted in securing and maintaining the purity of the children.

3. **It puts children into the care and training of their very best friends during the most impressionable period of their lives.**

In every normal home the child's best friends are its parents. It was no mere accident that children were put into the care of these best friends at a time when associations and training will make their deepest and most lasting impression on the children. If parents are wise and alive to their duty as well as opportunity, they will make the best use of their influence to give the children the right kind of start before the rest of the world gets into contact with them to any great extent.

4. **It provides a safe retreat from the storms of life.**

The comfortable fireside where children are happy and contented while the rain or snow or sleet or hail or wind or dust beat threateningly on the outside is typical of the protection which the home furnishes along other lines. While homeless or neglected children roam the streets at will and pick up all the moral filth known to a "wild life," the children in well-kept homes are comparatively free from and protected against such blighting influences. In the midst of a world where iniquity abounds and children are often polluted with sin before they know what sin means, that child is fortunate that is sheltered by a home where the name of Jesus is hallowed, where virtue is held at a premium, and the habit-forming period of life is spent in an atmosphere of purity, godliness, and holiness. Well may the poet write:

> " 'Mid pleasures and palaces though we may roam,
> Be it ever so humble, there is no place like home."

What place can equal the home in times of sickness, misfortune, or distress? Who besides loved ones around the family hearth can give such sympathetic help and comfort in times of perplexity and uncertainty, when the problems of life tax us to the last extremity. Thank God for the shelter and the comfort of a godly home.

5. **The Christian home is a training school where children are brought up for God and prepared to meet the issues of life.**

We said, "training school." It is here that children are trained to work, to sing, to pray, to study, to practice self-denial, to lend a helping hand to those in need, to develop body, mind, and soul. In training children, let us not fail to remember the serious problems of life and to teach the rising generation how to meet them. A home modeled after scriptural ideals is not only serviceable as a training school for children, but it is the most substantial support of Church and State. Describe conditions in the average home, and you are also describing community conditions where this average home exists.

### HOME DUTIES

Home is more than a mere sentiment, and the trials of home are more than something to be dreamed about. Parents, children, servants and visitors, are real human beings, with human shortcomings and possibilities. In every home there arise problems which mere planning and theorizing will not solve, things which the "Christian Science treatment" will not cure. There are real duties to perform, real problems to be met, real difficulties to be overcome, and these should be met and dealt with in a heaven-approved way. The Bible throws some light upon the duties of every member of the household which we shall endeavor to notice briefly:

**1. Duties of Husbands and Fathers.**—The two outstanding duties are thus set forth by Paul:

> Husbands, love your wives, even as Christ also loved the church, and gave himself for it.—Eph. 5:25.
> Fathers, provoke not your children to wrath: but bring them up in the nurture and admonition of the Lord.—Eph. 6:4.

Reduced to modern English, these two admonitions mean this: The man who has pledged hand and heart to any woman owes to her his very life—his affections, his brains, his hands, and his money-making powers being at her service. As for the children, it is upon him, rather than upon the mother, that the Lord lays the greater part of the responsibility in the matter of bringing them up. As the head of the home, it is his duty to lead out in the family devotions, in the discipline and training of the household, in everything pertaining to the welfare of the home—all this in the spirit of service rather than of lordship.

**2. Duties of Wives and Mothers.**—Again we turn to the Scriptures for light on this subject:

> . . . . . . .an help meet for him.—Gen. 2:18.
> For this child I prayed.—I Sam. 1:27.
> Wives submit yourselves unto your own husbands, as unto the Lord.—Eph. 5:22.
> Wives, be in subjection to your own husbands; that, if any obey not the word, they also may without the word be won by the conversation of the wives; while they behold your chaste conversation coupled with fear.—I Pet. 3:1, 2.

Each of these texts points out a very important duty of the wife and mother in the home. In the first place, she is to follow the leadership of the husband, taking a submissive attitude. Secondly, the responsibility of motherhood is something that requires prayerful willingness to assure best results. Where women are in line with these two cardinal duties, they can not be otherwise than real blessings to their own husbands and to their offspring.

The question frequently arises: If either the husband or the wife fails or refuses to fill his or her heaven-ordained place in the home, what should the other one do? In such cases the other one must make the most of circumstances and try to supply the lack. But it is sometimes the case that the faults of the one are aggravated or multiplied by the shortcomings of the other. If you should happen to live in that kind of home, be sure that you do your full share in meeting the conditions which God has ordained for your life. One of the laws of association is that we usually transmit our qualities to our associates—and the first to profit by your sterling Christian qualities ought to be your own bosom companion.

3. **Duties of Children.**—The Bible is not slack in its teaching concerning the duty of children toward their parents. We will quote but one of these instructions:

> Children obey your parents in the Lord: for this is right. Honour thy father and mother, which is the first commandment with promise, that it may be well with thee, and thou mayest live long on the earth.—Eph. 6:1-3.

Notice, Paul gives three reasons why children should be obedient to parents: (1) It is right. (2) It is to their own interest to do so. (3) It is conducive to long life. Each of these reasons is so self-evident that it needs no argument to sustain it. One of the worst things that can happen any child is to permit it to grow up as a disobedient and rebellious child in the home. Such a child is not only an enemy to self, but also a problem in the home, the community, the school, the Church, and the state.

4. **Duties of Servants.**—We are using this word in its broadest sense—that of employee, whether bond or free. All such may find their instructions in Eph. 6:5-8.

> 1. "Be obedient to them that are your masters according to the flesh.
> 2. "In singleness of your heart, as unto Christ;
> 3. "Not with eye-service as men-pleasers;
> 4. "Whatsoever good thing any man doeth, the same shall he receive of the Lord, whether he be bond or free."

In short, when we are under obligations to render service to others, whether through contract or by compulsion, it is our Christian duty to render faithful service—not merely to please men, but especially to please God.

Through such faithful service masters or employers have been brought to Christ.

5. **Duties of Masters.**—Employers of labor are asked to read their instructions in Eph. 6:9:

> "And, ye masters, do the same things unto them, forbearing threatening: knowing that your Master also is in heaven; neither is there respect of persons with him."

Whether serving in the capacity of employer or employee, our obligation is to act the part of the Christian man or woman. They who look upon the position of a servant with contempt would do well to remember that Jesus Christ was a servant in the fullest and highest sense of the word.

Where father, mother, sons, daughters, brothers, sisters, and those in the employ of the home are all constrained by love to God and men to take the place in the home enjoined upon them, there is to be found an ideal Christian home.

### HOME ASSOCIATIONS

Home is made sacred or otherwise, depending upon the kind of associations to be found in it. In some homes the members "come home to board and sleep" while they seek their enjoyment elsewhere. Such places are not really homes but rather second-class hotels. In other homes you find father, mother, children, and frequent visitors there because they regard it as a most satisfactory place to be. What makes the difference? Associations. When we speak of associations, we mean both associates and the things which contribute to the character of the associations. Let us therefore notice some of the things which make home associations pleasant and uplifting:

1. **Love.**—This is what Paul calls "the bond of perfectness" (Col. 3:14). It is the quality that makes members of the household companionable, self-sacrificing, and ready to contribute to one another's interests. It binds husband and wife together not only as "one flesh" but also as one heart and soul. It holds the children to "the first

commandment with promise." It is hard for the enemy of souls to gain a foothold in such a home, especially where the love is the kind that binds each member of the household to the Father of love.

2. **The Spirit of Worship.**—The Christian home, like a church, should be "a house of prayer." There is nothing that can take the place of the family devotions. We referred to the husband and father as "the head of the home." But if there is not also a recognition, on the part of all members of the household, of Jesus Christ as the Supreme Head, over and above any and every earthly head, this human headship is a failure. We have seen homes where the parents were not Christians that were fairly peaceable and happy; but the heavenly sanctity that makes the home ideal was lacking. With family worship a daily practice, Bible reading habitual, spiritual songs frequently heard, and religion a prominent factor in the daily conversation, there is an atmosphere that is very helpful in the training of children and which serves as a benediction upon all comers and goers.

3. **The Spirit of Loyalty.**—Loyalty to what? Loyalty to one another, loyalty to parents, loyalty to the best interests of children, loyalty to God and the Church, loyaly to the government, loyalty to every other cause that merits support. In such a home children learn to respect authority and become law-abiding citizens wherever they go.

4. **Wholesome Literature.**—Books and periodicals, as well as people, are our influential companions. Hence the importance of being surrounded with proper literature. Since "reading maketh a full man," it behooves us to keep our homes supplied with the kind of literature that keeps us full of the love of God, full of that which is noblest and best in man. That home is fortunate which is kept supplied with the kind of literature that both interests and edifies the young people and leads their minds heavenward rather than worldward.

5. **Desirable Companions.** — This includes, besides members of the immediate family, hired help, school asso-

ciates, companions in the social circle, etc., etc. Every home should be marked for two things: (1) a genuine Christian hospitality that makes visitors feel welcome; (2) a genuine spirit of godliness that makes that influence uppermost in the home. In other words, let us strive to make our homes a place where people love to come because of the warm, congenial, friendly atmosphere they find there; and let this congeniality be such as to discourage every form of frivolity and carnality. In many homes, perhaps with the best of intentions, the mistake is made of furnishing musical and other attractions of a questionable sort, which have the effect of attracting a class of companions and fostering a kind of associations which are not conducive to the best interests of either the children or their associates. It should be the desire of all parents to encourage for their children the kind of associations that will be conducive to strength of character, to moral and spiritual uplift, and that will in turn make of them worthy associates of the best of companions.

Keep these home ideals before you at all times, and you will find

### THE BLESSINGS OF HOME LIFE

a joy to your soul, an inspiration to your children, a benediction to the visitors that come and go, and a glory to God. Home then will be a hallowed spot where the ties of love and sympathy grow stronger as the years roll on, where children are molded over right patterns during the habit-forming periods of their lives, where the tenderest care is given to the sick and afflicted, where we may be mutually helpful to one another as we face the trials and problems of life, and where in our declining years we may find the care which only a Christian home can supply.

Meditate on these things, strive to reach these ideals, and you will have abundant reasons to praise the Lord for the privilege of living in such a home.

# CHAPTER V

## THE CHURCH

Upon this rock I will build my church; and the gates of hell shall not prevail against it.—Matthew 16:18.

This subject will be considered at greater length in subsequent chapters. Our purpose in listing it here is to give it recognition as one among many things which God has so generously provided for our well-being. One of the most wholesome provisions which God ever made for the welfare of His people was to call into being an organization to serve as the spiritual home for them while on earth. Let us therefore consider

### THE WHY OF THE CHURCH

#### 1. It affords a shelter for the people of God.

Christ refers to Himself as "the good shepherd" (Jno. 10:11), and commands His undershepherds to "feed the flock of God . . . taking the oversight thereof" (I Pet. 5:2). He also refers to Himself as "the door" (Jno. 10:9), and warns against the "thieves," "robbers," and "wolves" of this world that are liable to break in at any time to carry away or to destroy the members of the flock. What a fold, under the faithful care of a shepherd, is to a flock of sheep, so the Church of Christ on earth, under the care of "the Shepherd and Bishop of our souls," directing the undershepherds who have been set as spiritual overseers of the congregations, is to the members of the Church.

#### 2. It affords a place of spiritual nourishment for the people of God.

The psalmist, sometimes referred to as "the shepherd-king," recognized God's bountiful provision along this line when he said, "The Lord is my shepherd; I shall not want.

He maketh me to lie down in green pastures: he leadeth
me beside the still waters. He restoreth my soul: he leadeth me in the paths of righteousness for his name's sake."
As the children of Israel were fed with manna in the wilderness, so is this heavenly manna made to fall among the
people of God today through the ministry of the Word.
"Feed the flock of God," is a timely admonition, not only
in Peter's time but in all ages. The spiritual food that you
get in hearing the preaching of the Word, in religious meetings of any kind, in Bible reading and study, in Christian fellowship with God and saints, in the family devotions, etc., is not only nourishing to the soul, but is absolutely essential to spiritual life and growth. We die, spiritually, without it, just as people die physically when de-
prived of natural food for a considerable length of time.
The Church is God's wise provision for the systematic and
continual spiritual nourishment of God's people on earth.
We need not only the nourishment, but we need it as prepared by Jesus Christ the greatest Dietitian that ever lived.

3. **It provides an adequate means of Christian fellowship.**

"If we walk in the light as he is in the light, we have
fellowship one with another" (I Jno. 1:7). And this fellowship is all the more precious when "our fellowship is
with the Father, and with his Son Jesus Christ" (v. 4).
When God said, "It is not good that the man should be
alone," He referred not only to the matter of marriage but
uttered a fundamental truth connected with human life
in all its phases; namely, that man as a social being needs
the fellowship of his fellow creatures. For this reason we
have domestic fellowship in the home, business fellowship
in the material affairs of this world, friendship fellowship
in the social circle, spiritual fellowship in the Church, and
in the ages to come we will have everlasting fellowship at
the right hand of God. Do we wonder that God warns us
not to forsake "the assembling of ourselves together, as
the manner of some is" (Heb. 10:25)? that people who

neglect this means of grace invariably experience a leanness of soul? that people who are out of active fellowship with those "of like precious faith" sooner or later lose their fellowship with God? The Church is God's plan for providing the needed spiritual fellowship of His people while living in the flesh.

**4. It provides a means for keeping the commandments of the Lord.**

The Church affords an orderly way in which the commandments of the Lord, especially the ordinances of the Lord's house, may be kept. The argument that we might keep all the commandments of the Lord without a church organization may be met with the convincing fact that nobody has ever been known to do it. True, some who are not members of any church have been known to keep some of the commandments of the Bible: but we repeat that nobody has ever been known to keep all of them while outside the realms of the Church. Such things as water baptism, the communion, and all other Christian ordinances are church functions, and naturally we look to the Church to see that they are properly observed. Besides, the influence and work of the Church are needed in the way of encouraging people to obey God. Even with this wise provision of God for the proper observance of His commandments, many are slack in the matter of obedience to Him.

**5. It keeps us in touch with heavenly influences.**

The ring of heaven is heard in every Gospel sermon. The music of heaven is forcasted in the "psalms, hymns, and spiritual songs" heard in the assembly of God's people. The need of faithful Christian service is apparent as we think of the millions of souls now living who are without the Gospel, and of our own obligations toward them. The glory of heaven is seen just ahead as we "sit together in heavenly places in Christ Jesus" (Eph. 2:6), and worship God "in spirit and in truth." This need is the more keenly felt as we think of those who were lost to God because they drifted away from and beyond the influence of the Church. It can truthfully be said of the Church, as it was of the Sabbath, that "the Church was made for man, and not man for the Church." We certainly need the ministry and fellowship and shelter of the Church to keep us in touch with heavenly influence and power.

6. **It affords an opportunity for the people of God to unite their forces and their resources in the work of winning the lost.**

It is not only true that "united we stand; divided we fall," but in uniting in a common cause we also help others to arise, and stand. Christ's prayer for His disciples was "that they all may be one; as thou, Father, art in me, and I in thee, that they also may be one in us" (Jno. 17:21). It is a blessed unity toward which all people of God should strive—a consummation which will be realized as soon as every one professing the name of Christ will rise to the standard set forth in the Gospel of Christ, not before. It is in the Church of Jesus Christ where the members of the fold may be mutually helpful to one another in the home, in the Church, in business and social life; and where the members may unite in sending the Gospel into the dark corners of earth and maintaining the work of the Church in weak places.

### Historical

We shall leave, for a later chapter, a technical discussion of what constitutes the real Church of God. Suffice it to say here that God, from the time that there were both righteous and unrighteous people in the world, followed the rule of having His people separated from the children of darkness commonly called "the world." As for the word "Church" itself, it is said to have been handed down from the Greeks to the Goths, the first among the Teutonic tribes to embrace the Christian faith. The Greek word for Church, "ekklesia," signifies an assembly of called out ones by authority. By authority of God His people have been called out of darkness and given a place in the Kingdom of His dear Son. Peter calls them "a chosen generation, a royal priesthood, an holy nation, a peculiar people" (I Pet. 2:9). But the important thing that we want to remember is that the Church of God, in the sense of God's having a people for His own possession, had existence long before any name known to modern languages was invented.

When Cain fell he was driven from the face of man. In Noah's day the "called out" ones were found in the ark. When, after the Flood, man again fell into the depths of wickedness, God's rule of calling out the faithful ones was again in evidence when He called out Abraham from among his home and kindred to become the father of the faithful. On the return to the land of promise on the part of the descendants of Abraham, the assembly of worshipers in the tabernacle of God is referred to by Stephen as "the church in the wilderness" (Acts 7:38). When Christ finally came and collected and organized His followers He assured Peter that "upon this rock I will build my church, and the gates of hell shall not prevail against it" (Matt. 16:18). The Church of Christ was endued with power from on high on the day of Pentecost, since which time the faithful followers of Jesus have been busily engaged in sending the Gospel to the ends of the earth, and looking forward to that glorious time when the great "ekklesia" will be gathered together in the fullness of power and glory, a mighty congregation in the heavens, reigning with the great Head of the Church "for ever and ever."

### Our Opportunities

This age presents to us an era of opportunities—and the greatest of opportunities confronting us is that of using this world as a stepping stone for the higher world above. Among our God-given opportunities are the following:

1. **To make our "calling and election sure"** (II Pet. 1:10).

Through an acceptance of God's plan for our salvation this happy privilege is ours. Thank God for the "whosoever believeth" (Jno 3:16), "whosoever will" (Rev. 22:17) provision in the plan of salvation, for by this plan no one is barred out save those who refuse to accept God's plan for their lives. Christ's story of the rich man and Lazarus shows that the day of opportunity ends at death.

2. **To let our lights shine.**

This opportunity is held forth in Scripture as both a command (Matt. 5:16) and as a matter of fact (Phil. 2:15) in the lives of God's people. Recognizing that Christian people are "this world's Bible," it behooves us to put forth faithful efforts to the end that these "bibles" may be an exact and safe interpretation of the real *Bible* given to us by inspiration of God. The child of God, standing forth in the light and liberty of the Gospel, has well been called "a means of revealing the grace and glory of Christ."— S. F. Coffman.

3. **To maintain an attitude of loyalty to God and the Church.**

Since all our blessings come from God, it would be the grossest and basest of ingratitude not to show our appreciation of these blessings by rendering Him faithful service. Since Jesus Christ laid down His life for our sakes, we owe our lives to Him. And since the Church has been especially called into existence and ordained of God as our spiritual home on earth, we can not afford to withhold our whole-hearted support. It is both a privilege and a duty to show by a faithful, loyal, Spirit-filled, obedient life that we appreciate what God did for us when He instituted the Christian Church. Genuine loyalty to Christ guarantees loyalty to the Church that fully follows Christ.

4. **To attend to every means of grace designed for godly edification, spiritual growth, and useful service.**

Among these we may mention such things as prayer, Bible study, proper Lord's Day observance, faithful attendance at religious services, cheerful giving as the Lord has prospered us, Christian fellowship, and other things pertaining to life and godliness. By availing yourself of all these opportunities you will not only have many reasons for praising God for instituting the Christian Church, but you will also be a substantial help in making this Church a real blessing to yourself and to others.

# CHAPTER VI

## CIVIL GOVERNMENT

I exhort therefore, that, first of all, supplications, prayers,
intercessions, and giving of thanks, be made for all
men; for kings, and for all that are in authority; that
we may lead a quiet and peaceable life in all godliness
and honesty.—I Timothy 2:1, 2.

The goodness of God toward man is apparent in the
twofold provision made for man's government, care, and
protection: (1) Spiritual, through the Church; (2) material, through the State. That the power of civil government, as well as the power of the Church is ordained of
God is evident from the writings of inspired men. Paul's
teaching on this subject is especially clear. Writing to
the Romans he says: "There is no power but of God:

### THE POWERS THAT BE

are ordained of God. Whosoever therefore resisteth the
power, resisteth the ordinance of God" (Rom. 13:1, 2). It
has well been said that "order is heaven's first law." Or,
to use the exact language of Scripture, "God is not the
author of confusion, but of peace" (I Cor. 14:33). Even
among the lower animals there is in evidence a gift from
God that enables them to conduct their affairs in an orderly,
well-regulated manner; as, for instance, the ant and the
bee. What is more natural, therefore, than that God should
bring about a system whereby the righteous may be shielded
against the dishonesty and violence of the unrighteous;
that nations should be called into being to govern their
subjects through established laws based upon principles
of righteousness and equity; that the lawless should be
restrained through penalties against unrighteousness; that
when the cup of iniquity of any nation gets full, God will
deal with that nation as He does with an individual of

that character, destroy it off the face of the earth? When it comes to authority, we look upon a nation in its sphere precisely as we do upon a church in its sphere—vested with authority to carry out its decrees, responsible to God for faithfulness or unfaithfulness.

### The Purpose of Government

has already been stated. It is to restrain the lawless (I Tim. 1:9), to protect the law-abiding against the violence of the wicked (Acts 25:11), to secure to each individual a freedom of "conscience void of offence" toward God and man. And the wisdom of God in making such provision is very evident when we remember that "the whole world lieth in wickedness" (I Jno. 5:19)—something very evident, even without turning to the Bible to see what God thinks of "this present evil world"—and that without some restraining power the righteous would be in the world as sheep at the mercy of the wolves, as seen in countries where anarchy and lawlessness run riot.

### Official Position no Sign of Spiritual Standing

Here we pause to meet the chorus of objections which we imagine we hear coming from many quarters to some of the things thus far held forth. Is it not a fact that some of the most heinous sins are committed by those in positions of highest civil authority? and that nations often foster rather than suppress iniquity? What about the fanatical Turk who for many centuries has caused the crimson flood to gush forth from the veins of helpless Christians? of Soviet Russia, where the present government is committed to atheism and oppression? of the many instances in history where the State directed the martyrdom of Christians rather than giving them protection? Is God the Author of all these atrocities, some of them committed in His very name!

No, **no, No, NO!** not any more than He is the Author of everything which unfaithful church members and churches do. God is longsuffering, and sometimes in His unfathomable wisdom He waits long before He brings sinners in high or low positions in Church or State to justice. But God does hold nations as well as individuals to account for their betrayal of a sacred trust, and, in due time, according to His infinite wisdom which we may or may not be able to understand, He will bring judgment upon every kind of iniquity and every kind of evil-doer. He has done that in the past, and He will continue to do so in the future.

But this one thing must not be lost sight of: The position of man in affairs of civil government is no indication whatever of his spiritual standing before God. Whether that person be called President, King, Queen, Emperor, Mikado, Shah, or Sultan; whether he be recognized as Christian or pagan, adjudged faithful or unfaithful, he is after all "the servant of God." It was of the wicked Nero that Paul wrote: "He is the minister of God to thee for good" (Rom. 13:4). Whether rulers prove faithful or unfaithful to their trust; whether they acknowledge themselves Christians, idolaters, agnostics, or what not; none of these things have anything to do with the fact that they in their respective positions are the servants of God, vested with the responsibility of governing their subjects in a way that will mete out justice to every citizen. Whether a man is or is not a Christian must be determined by his individual life and heart experience, not by any position he may hold in Church or State. The only question in connection with any official position which affects a man's spiritual standing is: Can a Christian consistently do the things which the office requires? for every human being is personally responsible to God for his individual acts, whether he serves in an individual or official capacity.

### DIRECTIVE AND PERMISSIVE WILL OF GOD

This question enters largely into the matter of the government of nations. There are some things which God commands or directs, while other things are done by His permission. Let us give a few examples:

1. When Balaam came to the Lord to inquire whether he should curse Israel, God told him not to do it. That was God's directive will. Then Balaam, restive under this direction and prohibition, came to inquire again. God told him to go. That was God's permissive will.

2. In the days of Samuel the people in Israel wanted a king. Samuel told them what God's directive will was in the matter. But because the people were rebellious and refused to submit to this will, God told Samuel to grant their request; that they were not rejecting Samuel but God. That was God's permissive will, though it meant leanness of soul for the children of Israel.

In this connection it is well to note that *God's permissive will does not always mean that He enters willingly* into the plans of rebellious people; but because He created man a free moral agent, *He does not compel man* to go contrary to his will.

Again, God permits certain things, not because it is a pleasure to His creatures to have it so, but because good will come out of it, or because it is made to serve His ultimate purpose. Examples: Pharaoh's oppression of the children of Israel (Ex. 1-10), the crucifixion of Jesus Christ (Acts 2:23), the dispersion of disciples after the death of Stephen (Acts 8:1-3), etc. In the affairs of all nations, God permits many things because through oppression and other forms of unrighteousness "the wrath of men" (Psa. 76:10) has been the means of bringing praises to God in that "the blood of the martyr is (often) the seed of the Church." History abounds in such illustrations.

### THE CHRISTIAN'S RELATION TO THE GOVERNMENT

Recognizing the providence of God in the affairs of government, let us turn to the Scriptures for light on what should be the Christian's relation to the government under which he lives. Foremost among these are the following:

1. **Subjection.**—Our first duty toward government is that of subjection. Even in the case of distasteful laws we should not neglect to respect and obey them. And this submission should be that of willing loyalty rather than that of unwilling slavery. "We must needs be subject, not only for wrath, but also for conscience' sake" (Rom. 13:5). Therefore, "Let every soul be subject unto the higher powers." "Put them in mind to be subject to principalities, to obey magistrates, to be ready to every good work" (Tit. 3:1).

2. **A Twofold Citizenship.**—The child of God has a twofold obligation. On the one hand he is a citizen of the country in which he lives, while at the same time he is also a citizen of the heavenly country. Paul, a native of Tarsus, on several occasions acknowledged himself a Roman citizen. He was also a citizen of that kingdom which Christ said is "not of this world" (Jno. 18:36), an allegiance which he acknowledged in his letter to the Philippians, saying, "Our citizenship is in heaven" (Phil. 3:20, R.V.). This dual citizenship is apparent as we read the preceding paragraph, in connection with the one that follows.

3. **Strangers and Pilgrims."**—Through citizens here, we should not forget that we are but "strangers and pilgrims on the earth" (Heb. 11:13), looking for a city "whose builder and maker is God" (Heb. 11:10). Looking at the Christian's position in this light, we can readily see how that the apostles who so emphatically taught and practiced subjection to the powers that be, also took the position that Christians owe their highest allegiance to God and that no law on earth should in any way move them to disobey any of the higher laws of God. See Acts 5:25-29. Yet at no time did the apostles offer any physical resistance to their government, choosing (in times of persecution) to suffer as *strangers* rather than to exercise their *rights* as citizens.

The idea that it is the duty of the Church to take hold of Government and run things for God is neither taught in Scripture nor supported by the facts of history. The place for Christian people to take hold and work is in the Church, and the place of most effective power is at the Throne. Lot is referred to in Scripture as a "righteous man" (II Pet. 2:8). Yet this righteous man, taking an active part in the affairs of Sodom, not only failed in saving the city from destruction but actually exerted less influence there than did his uncle Abraham who had no relationship whatever with Sodom save that by way of the Throne. When Christianity was adopted as the religion of State in Rome, the result was that Rome corrupted the Church instead of the Church purifying Rome. It is ever thus. To-day the average church member in politics is not one whit cleaner morally or better spiritually than is the average non-church member in politics. Christianity and world politics do not mix. Their spheres are essentially different. Both Government and Church are better off if each remains in its sphere. The idea that the Christian can render substantial aid in the cause of righteousness by "mixing in politics" has often been proved a delusion.

4. **An Uplifting Power.**—It does not follow, however, that the Christian has no obligation toward his government, or that the government gets no benefit from its Christian citizens. Since Christian people are law-abiding, the government needs no police force, criminal courts, jails, and penitentiaries to keep them orderly. On the other hand, real Christians are honest, upright, industrious, thrifty, as a rule substantial taxpayers, on the right side on all questions pertaining to morality and virtue, causing a country to "blossom as a rose" wherever they settle and have a real chance to make good. The Christian citizen invariably exerts an uplifting influence in any country giving him shelter, and, except where blind passion prevails over the highest interests of the country, is usually welcomed by the nations. It is suicidal for any country to suppress its Christian subjects.

**5. An Intercessor.**—Finally, it is the Christian's privilege and duty to pray for his government and all that are in authority. "I exhort therefore, that, first of all, supplications, prayers, intercessions, and giving of thanks be made for all men; for kings, and for all that are in authority." The benefit is twofold: (1) to the government; (2) to the intercessor. Herein is the Christian's power, the Christian's greatest opportunity. That nation is fortunate that has within its borders an army of intercessors at the Throne, for this is the most formidable army that any nation can have. It has well been said that "prayer is the power that moves the Hand that rules the world." Let Christian citizens never fail to use this power.

# CHAPTER VII

## THE DAY OF REST AND WORSHIP

> Thus the heavens and the earth were finished, and all the host of them. And on the seventh day God ended his work which he had made; and he rested on the seventh day from all his work which he had made. And God blessed the seventh day, and sanctified it: because that in it he had rested from all his work which God created and made.—Genesis 2:1-3.

From the beginning God provided for man a day of rest. A study of the divine narrative, as above quoted, makes two things very clear: (1) God rested on this day; (2) God sanctified the day, or, in other words, "hallowed it" (Ex. 20:11).

In our times there has been much disputing as to what we should call this day. There are three very emphatic opinions expressed by various commentators, each class of advocates having good reasons for their contentions. But, as we view the merits and demerits of these contentions, we are more impressed with the importance of keeping the day in harmony with God's plans in setting it apart for a beneficent purpose than with what the day should be called. In fact, the name depends altogether upon what you have in mind when you use it.

1. If you have in mind the day of the week set apart for its observance in this dispensation, call it *Sunday.*

2. If you have in mind the day of rest as distinguished from the six work days in the week, call it *The Sabbath.*

3. If you have in mind the Christian Sabbath as distinguished from the Jewish Sabbath, call it *The Lord's Day.*

### A FEW FACTS

which the Scriptures make plain, in connection with this day, will help us to determine what the day should be called, how it should be kept, and why we should reverence it.

### 1. It is a day instituted by the Creator.

As stated in Gen. 2:1-3, on this day God "rested," and He "sanctified it"—"hallowed it," set it apart for a holy purpose.

### 2. It has a place in every dispensation.

It is mentioned in the creation (Gen. 2:2, 3), was in use before the Mosaic Law was given (Ex. 16:23), had a place in the Law (Deut. 5:14), and under the Gospel (Acts 20:7). Let it be remembered therefore that this is a day intended for all time, not for one dispensation only.

### 3. It was made for man.

"The sabbath was made for man, and not man for the sabbath" (Mark 2:27). That this refers to the day as an institution, not as a part of the ceremonial Law merely, is evident from circumstances under which these words were spoken.

### 4. Christ is Lord of the Sabbath day.

To use His exact language: "The Son of man is Lord also of the sabbath" (Luke 6:5). As one of the Trinity who called all things into existence (Jno. 1:2), it is within His province to change or to regulate it at will. His Word is law, and what He says or does with reference to this day is accepted by all His faithful followers without controversy.

#### PROPER USES OF THE DAY

### 1. It is a day of rest.

On this day God rested. As one of the Ten Commandments, it sets forth this obligation: "Six days shalt thou labour, and do all thy work: but the seventh day is the sabbath of the Lord thy God: in it thou shalt not do any work" (Ex. 20:9, 10). In all of Christ's work and teachings bearing on the proper use of the day, He never called this use of the day in question but observed it literally and in the proper spirit. As Lord of the Sabbath, His example is worth noticing. He corrected the Pharisees as to the proper use of the day, showing that even by their law it was in keeping with the idea of rest and worship to do deeds of mercy and works of necessity on this day. Matt. 12:12; Luke 13:14, 15.

This is not a mere arbitrary command, a religious dogma, a scriptural "blue law" to restrain man of his liberties; but it is, like all other laws of God, a wise provision of the Infinite God, who does that which is best for man and beast. It has been demonstrated over and over again that man is not at his best physically and mentally, when he ignores this provision for his well-being. Even cold, lifeless machinery does more satisfactory work when it gets its regular seasons of rest. Let us give this beneficent provision of an all-wise God our respect and obedience by laying all secular labor aside on the Lord's Day.

### 2. It is a day of worship.

Resting means change rather than cessation from activity. There are few things less restful than laziness. To act lazy on the Lord's Day, or to spend the day in sightseeing, pleasure, or idle vanity does not refresh the soul like that of spending the day in Christian service and worship. Having spent all week in secular toil, let us lay our work aside on the seventh day that the soul may be fed with the heavenly manna, the individual refreshed and strengthened in the Christian fellowship and holy meditation which alone can lift the soul into the presence of God.

### 3. It is a day to be kept holy.

We sometimes sing, "This is the day the Lord hath made." We manifest our sincerity in singing it when we keep the day sacred, dedicated to Him who directed us to keep it holy. "Ye can not serve God and mammon"—ye can not, after spending the week among things that draw the mind earthward rather than heavenward, spend all or part of the Lord's Day with Sunday newspapers, or foolish games, or amicable associations with ungodly people, or planning for the business of the coming week, without serious injury to your highest interests, the spiritual uplift and strengthening of the inner man. Keep the day holy. Let the time be spent in refreshing the soul as well as resting the body. The morning family devotions, attendance at worship in the house of God, edifying conversation, soul-stirring singing, visiting the sick, personal work among saved and unsaved—these are some of the things that may be done in the way of keeping the day holy. It puts you into the realms of the heavenlies, and prepares you to meet the temptations and trials of the week that follows.

To keep this as a *holy day* means health for the spiritual man, and strength to overcome in the battle with sin. To keep it as a *holiday* means frivolity, leanness of soul, dissipation, being overcome of evil. God knew beforehand that man needed this day to keep even and ahead in the battle royal between righteousness and sin, therefore "the Sabbath was made for man." No other day affords so many opportunities for direct service in winning souls for Christ and building them up in Christ.

We have already referred to the fact that this day has received recognition in all ages of man's history. We have purposely submitted the foregoing thoughts before taking up consideration of the day in its dispensational setting, for the things thus far set forth are not dispensational but are the embodiment of truth which is applicable at all times. Our further consideration of the day will be under three distinct divisions; namely, *The Seventh Day, The Jewish Sabbath,* and *The Lord's Day.*

## A. THE SEVENTH DAY

Again let us quote Genesis 2:1-3:

"Thus the heavens and the earth were finished, and all the host of them. And on the seventh day God ended his work which he had made; and he rested on the seventh day from all his work which he had made. And God blessed the seventh day, and sanctified it."

Here God set the example. If we are in doubt as to how the day should be spent, we can find no better example than that of God Himself.

It has been said that after this reference to the Sabbath we have no further light on it until we find it incorporated in the Levitical Law. But facts stand in the way of such a conclusion. Turn to Ex. 16:16-26 and read. This was before the giving of the Law at Sinai. Abstinence from work on the seventh day is set forth as distinctly there as it is in the Fourth Commandment. Moreover, the seven-day system was written into the very creation itself. There were seven days of creation—six of labor and one of rest. The time required for hatching eggs of the feathered tribes is in multiples of seven days. France, during its bloody revolution more than a century ago tried to substitute a ten-day period of rest instead of a seven-day period, but was compelled to abandon it on account of unsatisfactory results. It is the provision of Infinite Wisdom, not the dictum of the autocrat, that brought this seven-day system into existence.

The absence of direct reference (between Gen. 2 and Ex. 16) to the keeping of the seventh day as a day of rest is not any more remarkable than the absence of references to many other privileges and duties belonging to the people of God and which they doubtless performed. Remembering that there was no written law during this time, we are not surprised at the scarcity of written references to fundamental laws which have always had and always will have existence. For example: there was no written law against murder; but when Cain murdered Abel he was promptly punished for its violation. Again, why was God displeased with the antediluvians (Gen. 6) if there were no laws to violate? and why was judgment visited upon them if they had violated none of His laws?

The Scriptures are not wanting in indirect evidences that there was Sabbath observance prior to the reference to the Sabbath in Ex. 16. Turn to Gen. 8: 7-12. The "seven days" mentioned several times imply a weekly service.

Again, in Gen. 29:27, 28 the words, "fulfil her week," prove the measurement of time by weeks (seven-day periods). A study of such references reveals them to be matter-of-fact references to an established order—something that would have had a place in written law, had the laws then in existence been reduced to written form. This day having a well-organized place in the established order of worship and service among God's people, what should be more natural than for God to say, when the written law was finally given, *"Remember* the sabbath day?" How could they "remember" if there had been nothing for them to remember?

## B. THE JEWISH SABBATH

When the Law of God was finally reduced to written form, God simply incorporated (in a form adapted to the peculiar needs of the people in that dispensation) the living principles of everlasting truth which had existence from the beginning and which will continue to exist as long as time shall last. So far as fundamental truths are concerned, there was nothing new brought into existence when the Law of God was reduced to written form at Sinai, nor taken away when this Law was fulfilled in Christ and the "better covenant" took its place. But the day of rest, as well as the other things enumerated in the Ten Commandments, was vested with new meanings and applications peculiar to the needs and conditions of this dispensation. Read Ex. 31:12-18; Ezek. 20:12-14; Neh. 9: 13, 14. Two things to be remembered in connection with the Jewish Sabbath are: (1) Before the giving of the Law the Sabbath was not the sign between God and Israel (Deut. 5:16). (2) The Jewish Sabbath was not only a day of rest but also the Sabbaths were "holy convocations" (Lev. 23). The changes which took place with the dispensations were ceremonial rather than fundamental. A change in dispensations does not change fundamental truth.

But in connection with these never-changing fundamental laws there are regulations which are applicable only to the times or dispensations in which such regulations are in vogue. The ceremonial Law given through Moses directed how the Sabbath should be kept in that dispensation. For this reason, when we are talking about the Jewish Sabbath we are not talking about the day of rest and worship as it exists under the Gospel of Christ and which we now know as "The Lord's Day." The principle, one day in seven, is the same in all ages. The manner and the time of observing the day are determined by the dispensational laws in force. Those desiring to keep the Jewish Sabbath should go to the Levitical Law for their instructions. Those desiring to keep the Lord's Day holy find their instructions in the Gospel of our Lord.

### Facts Concerning the Jewish Sabbath

#### 1. It was observed the seventh day of the week.

"Six days shalt thou labour, and do all thy work: but the seventh day is the sabbath of the Lord thy God" (Ex. 20:9, 10).

#### 2. It was kept in memory of God's sanctifying the day.

"For in six days the Lord made heaven and earth, the sea, and all that in them is, and rested the seventh day: wherefore the Lord blessed the sabbath day, and hallowed it" (Ex. 20:11).

#### 3. It was kept in memory of the deliverance of Israel from Egypt.

"The seventh day is the sabbath of the Lord thy God. . . . And remember that thou wast a servant in the land of Egypt, and that the Lord thy God brought thee out thence through a mighty hand and by a stretched out arm: therefore the Lord thy God commanded thee to keep the sabbath day" (Deut. 5:14, 15).

4. **Its observance was circumscribed by very strict laws.**

The man who picked up sticks on the Sabbath day and was stoned to death as a penalty (Num. 15:32-36) simply paid the penalty for violating Ex. 35:2, 3. Such incidents throw some light on the very critical Sabbath day observance ideas of the Pharisees in the days of Christ.

5. **There was a system of Sabbaths, having both a literal and a symbolical use and significance.**

Among these were—

a.  The seventh day, as already noticed.

b. The seventh month, which marked the observance of three national feasts—the feast of trumpets, the feast of tabernacles, and the day of atonement. Lev. 23; Num. 29.

c. The sabbatical year—every seventh year being set apart to give the land a rest (Ex. 23:11) as well as to insure more bountiful crops for man and beast (Lev. 25:6, 7).

d. The year of Jubilee—every fiftieth year—a summary of Sabbaths, so to speak, in which time there was opportunity for the poor to redeem their lands, for the redemption of servants, a year of grace for all the oppressed and distressed.

All of these Sabbaths had their spiritual significance, being typical of "good things to come," among other things pointing forward to the Christian Sabbath, the divinely appointed day of rest and worship in the present dispensation.

6. **It afforded an opportunity for godly service and worship.**

The weekly Sabbath eventually gave rise to synagogue worship, said to have been fully established in the days of Ezra and Nehemiah and often spoken of in the days of Christ and the apostles. The seventh month, in which the national feasts were kept, afforded a yearly opportunity for cleansing and restoration, and an annual reunion of Jewish worshipers. The sabbatical year was the occasion for rest and restoration, while the year of jubilee was the climax of the entire system of Jewish Sabbaths.

The synagogue worship in the days of Christ and the apostles afforded an excellent opportunity for introducing to the Jews the Messiah to which the prophetic writings pointed, and this form of worship was largely patterned after by the early Christian congregations.

## C. THE LORD'S DAY

We call this "The Lord's Day" because in our dispensation it is the day of rest and worship set apart and hallowed in memory of our risen Lord. It is a significant fact that the day of the week observed by the Christian churches is not the day when Christ was dead in the tomb, but the day in which He rose triumphant over every foe, thus signifying a victorious rather than a purely formal life and service. The name of our day is found in Rev. 1:10 ("I was in the Spirit on the Lord's day") but the idea is found in the fact that immediately after our Lord's resurrection the disciples began the practice of assembling for worship on this day.

Concerning the foreshadowing of the Lord's Day in the Old Testament we quote from the pen of Henry Hershey:

> "The Lord's day is prefigured in the Old Testament as the first day, or the morrow after the Sabbath. Lev. 23:10, 11. What did the 'first-fruits' typify? Let us turn to I Cor. 15:20 —'But now is Christ risen from the dead and become the firstfruits of them that slept.' When did Christ rise from the dead? On the Sabbath day? No; on the day after the Sabbath. Jno. 20:1."

### Some Fundamental Facts

### 1. It is the Lord's Day.

While the name is probably taken from John's expression in Rev. 1:10, the day was held sacred and conscientiously observed by the disciples long before the book of Revelation was written. Since the day is kept in memory of our risen Lord, the name is quite appropriate.

2. "The Son of man is Lord even of the Sabbath day."

Not only do we call this "The Lord's Day," but recognizing Christ as Lord of the Sabbath we feel it both a privilege and a duty to heed all His teachings and follow His example with reference to the observance of the day.

3. While among the Jews rest was the principal thing in mind in connection with Sabbath day observance, among us we hold the idea of worship and Christian service as most prominent.

Does this fact suggest the propriety of calling the Jewish day the "Sabbath" (day of rest) while among us the appropriate name is "Lord's day" (day dedicated to and kept in memory of our risen Lord)? Read the Old Testament references to the Jewish Sabbath, hear what the Pharisees have to say about our Saviour's way of keeping it—nearly all of it hinges on the idea of cessation from secular toil. Among us it is different. We think of worship, Christian service, edifying the body of Christ, winning souls for Christ, doing good—all connected with the idea of glorifying God and remembering Christ as Lord of the Sabbath.

4. The proper time to keep the Lord's Day is the first day of the week.

Following are among the principal reasons for this conclusion:

a. As the Jews kept their Sabbath on the same day of the week that their deliverance from Egypt occurred, which event they were to remember in their Sabbath day observance, so we also should keep our Sabbath on the same day of the week that Christ rose from the dead, in whose memory we keep the day.

b. Christ set the example, by rising on this day.

c. The disciples commenced keeping the day to His memory immediately after His resurrection from the grave, and Christ met with them a number of times, thus sanctifying their act by His presence.

d. Through the crucifixion of Christ all Jewish ordinances were nailed to the cross (Col. 2:14, 16), the Jewish Sabbath included.

e. The apostolic Church assembled for worship on this day. Acts 20:7; I Cor. 16:2.

f. The Christian Church during the first few centuries of the Christian era continued the practice.

g. There is no law in force, either the law of the land or the law of God for New Testament times, commanding us to keep the seventh day as the Christian's Sabbath.

These facts being irrefutable, what right has any one to ignore the example of Christ and the apostles, to set aside the practice of the Christian Church from the beginning, to ignore the laws of the land, and to insist on re-establishing a law that was repealed by divine authority?

5. **The early Church kept Sunday as the day of worship.**

On this point there is an illuminating discussion in the book, "Bible Doctrine," pp. 136-138, from the pen of Geo. R. Brunk, from which we quote the following:

"From the time of Christ's resurrection the first day of the week has been the authorized rest day of the Christian Church. Of this, there can be no reasonable doubt. In I Cor. 16:1, 2 we learn that the first day of the week was the day for assembling the offerings of the Church and suggests it therefore as the meeting day of the Church. The object of these instructions was that 'there be no gatherings (collections) when I come.' Verse 2 seems to show conclusively that they were not to lay it by at home but have it together in a common treasury. What better time than on this day? In this (excepting the day) they followed the custom of the Jews who on the Sabbath put aside money for the poor. (See Adam Clarke on I Cor. 16:1, 2.) Justin Martyr (A. D. 140) says of Sunday: 'And on the day called Sunday all who live in cities or in the country gather together in one place, and the memories of the apostles or the writings of the prophets are read . . . . . .bread and wine and water are brought, and the president in like manner also offers prayers and thanksgiving, according to his ability, and the people assent, saying, "Amen;" and there is a distribution to each, and a participation of that over which thanks have been given, and to those who are absent a portion is sent by the deacons. And they who are well-to-do, and willing, give what each thinks fit; and what is collected is deposited with the president, who succors the orphans and widows.' (Apology, Ch. 67.)

"Here is testimony perhaps not over fifty years after the death of John, the apostle, showing what we have found in Scripture, that Sunday was the day for religious service, like Pentecost; for communion, as in Acts 20:6, 7; for the giving of charities, as in I Cor. 16:1, 2, and that the example was first set by the Lord Himself. The apostolic fathers very commonly spoke of the resurrection day as 'the first day of the week,' 'the eighth day,' 'Sunday,' 'the Lord's day,' after the usage of John, the revelator, in Rev. 1:10. (See Encyclopedia Britannica on 'Sunday;' Sozomen, A. D. 440; Augustine, A. D. 354; Eusebius, A. D. 324; Peter of Alexandria, A. D. 306; Anatolius, A. D. 270; Apostolic Constitutions, A. D. 250; Cyprian, A. D. 250; Origen, A. D. 231; Tertullian, born A. D. 160; Clement of Alexandria, A. D. 194; Dionysius, A. D. 170; Justin Martyr, A. D. 140, born about the time the apostle John died; Epistle of Barnabas, A. D. 119-126; Pliny, A. D. 104; 'Didache,' A. D. 90-100; John, the revelator, A. D. 96.) This long list of writers has left testimony that has come down to our times that the early Church held the first day of the week in religious observance, that it was called 'the Lord's day,' and entirely distinct from the Jewish Sabbath. We would gladly have given full quotations from each, but space forbids. They may be found collected in Vankirks 'Thirteen Chapters on First Day Observance.'

"By these testimonies we can see clearly what was the practice of the apostolic Church and stop the mouths (Tit. 1:10, 11) of vain talkers who scatter through the world the false statements that the pope changed the Sabbath to the first day of the week. By these testimonies it is shown conclusively that Sunday was the regular day of worship in the apostolic Church, even as we have shown by Scripture that it was so held, named, spoken and written about as a common thing centuries before there was a pope or a Roman Catholic Church."

## WHY KEEP THE LORD'S DAY SACRED

1. It is God's will that we should.

2. It is a day dedicated to a sacred cause.

3. The laws of our land command us to do so.

4. It is needed as a day of rest and worship.

5. It is of divine origin, sanctified by the Lord of heaven and earth.

6. It is one of our greatest opportunities to keep in touch with God and His Word.

7. Neglect of the Lord's Day means a speedy lapse into heathenism, as manifest in every community where that has been done.

8. Faithful Lord's Day observance means recuperation for the body, rest for the mind, refreshment for the soul, strength to meet the issues of life.

9. It keeps alive the institutions of God among men, affords an opportunity for Christian fellowship and associations, and helps to bring saint and sinner under the influence and power of the Gospel.

10. The fondest memories of Christian people are associated with the thought of past experiences in Christian fellowship with God and man. Faithful Lord's Day observance means a Gospel message in every church.

11. History proves that more people are saved through the influence of Lord's Day activities than through all other Christian agencies combined. There is not an enterprise in the Church that is not strengthened through Sunday Gospel sermons and other Christian services.

12. It fosters development of that which is noblest and best in man, enjoyment of that which contributes most to the soul, and furnishes the most effective antidotes to a sinful, careless, God-dishonoring life. Get people interested in a faithful observance of the Lord's Day—in fact as well as in theory, Sunday morning, afternoon, and evening—and most of your perplexing problems in Church affairs will be solved.

### A COMPARISON

In a pointed message on The Lord's Day, comparing it with the Jewish Sabbath, Oscar Burkholder has this to say:

"Paul after his conversion and many years of experience, shows in Rom. 14:5 and Col. 2:16 that, because the law was now fulfilled in the resurrection and ascension of Christ the believer is no longer bound to keep the law as did they who believed before the coming of the Messiah. Jesus Himself said, in stating the purpose of His appearance on the earth, 'I came not to destroy the law, but to fulfill it.' Paul argues that since the law is fulfilled it is kept in Christ, and as followers of Christ we must no longer depend on the law, which is dead, but on Christ, who is alive forevermore. For this reason, and others, we are led to believe that the day of rest for this dispensation is the Lord's Day as now observed, and not the Jewish Sabbath. Thus in the history of the Christian Church we find her observing the Lord's day for the following reasons:

"1. A day of rest.

"2. A day of worship.

"3. A day of memorial. (Resurrection of our Lord.)

"4. A day of re-creation. (Not worldly pleasure nor sport.)

"5. A day for giving. I Cor. 16:1, 2.

"6. A day for special meditation. (John, the revelator, on the Isle of Patmos.)

"7. A day typical of eternal rest in the glory for the saints.

"Seeing then the great significance of the Lord's Day, it behooves the believer to be as faithful in the keeping of this day as in any other part of his Christian experience. Yet how many there are among us, who would like to be recognized as firm and staunch believers in many of the fundamentals of the Bible, who seem not even to hestitate to break this day of rest! It was God's purpose that this day should be beneficial to man, not for the satisfying of his fleshly lusts, but to keep him fit for service according to the plans and intentions of God for his sojourn upon the earth."

# CHAPTER VIII

## ANGELS

The angel of the Lord encampeth round about them that
fear him, and delivereth them.—Psalm 34:7.

It may not be correct to say that God created the angels for man's special benefit, but it is a fact that there is a very close connection between these two classes of created beings. Paul says of angels that they are "ministering spirits, sent forth to minister for them who shall be heirs of salvation" (Heb. 1:14). Of God's "little ones" (Matt. 18:10) Christ says, "In heaven their angels do always behold the face of my Father which is in heaven." Man has special reasons to be thankful to God for these heavenly beings whose ministry is so little understood and still less appreciated by the average man.

The word angel signifies a messenger, a bearer of tidings, and as such the name is sometimes applied to Christ (Zech. 1:12; Rev. 10:1) the great Messenger from heaven, the Mediator between God and man; to prophets and preachers (Rev. 2:1, 8, 12, etc.), who as God's messengers have done so much to carry His message to a lost world; and to the intelligent and immaterial heavenly beings whom God uses as His ministers to execute the orders of His providences (Heb. 1:14; Rev. 22:8, 9), to whom the name is most frequently applied, and who are the subjects under consideration in this chapter.

Angels are vastly inferior to God but superior to man in intelligence and power. They are a class of invisible, incorporeal, spiritual beings concerning whom many questions have been asked that man can not answer. Their origin is not definitely stated, yet the Bible refers to them so frequently and in such a matter-of-fact way that the faithful reader of the Word may learn much concerning them and their work.

Because of this lack of definite information, on the one hand, and the numerous Bible references to them, on the other, many fanciful theories and wild speculations concerning them have found their way into print. These we shall endeavor to avoid. As we write we breathe a prayer that God may direct our thoughts and pen aright so as to say only such things as will lead the reader into a fuller knowledge and higher appreciation of this wonderful provision of God for the safety and well-being of man.

## THEIR ORIGIN

Angels are created beings. "All things were made by him" (Jno. 1:3 cf. Neh. 9:6). "For by him were all things created, that are in heaven, and that are in earth, visible and invisible" (Col. 1:16). "Angels are not spirits of the departed, nor are they glorified human beings (Heb. 12:22, 23)."—Evans.

Then another question arises: When God created the angels, did He also include the fallen angels? There seems no reason to think that God created more than one kind of angels. "Very Good" (Gen. 1:31) was His verdict upon all that He created or called into being, so that the fallen angels must have become so since their creation. When Jude refers to "the angels which kept not their first estate" (v. 6) he infers that in the beginning they were not the miserable creatures which they have since then become. As to Lucifer, the prince of devils, Isa. 14:12 tells us of his fall from heaven. When Christ says that he *abode not* in the truth" (Jno. 8:44), this indicates that he was once *in* the truth. We conclude, therefore, that in the beginning all angels were created "very good;" but that at some subsequent time they fell away from their "first estate" and became followers of the devil.

### Their Great Number

Jacob referred to a company of angels revealed to him as "God's host" (Gen. 32:2). Elisha and his servant were permitted to have a glimpse of what God had provided for man in the form of these "ministering spirits" when they beheld the mountains around them filled with horses and chariots which far outnumbered the mighty hosts of Syria. II Kings 6:13-17. Christ had only to say the word, and "more than twelve legions of angels" (Matt. 26:53) were at His command. Paul refers to an "innumerable company of angels" (Heb. 12:22), and John on Patmos saw "ten thousand times ten thousand, and thousands of thousands" (Rev. 5:11) of these heavenly creatures. As for the fallen angels, there are so many of them that God provided a special place for "the devil and his angels" (Matt. 25:41). See also Rev. 12:3, 4.

It has been said that if our eyes were opened to such scenes we might, as did Elisha's servant, behold myriads of angelic or celestial beings all around us, above us, everywhere. But God in His wisdom has seen fit to withhold such scenes from the eyes of mortal man, except in cases of special revelations. By and by, when the veil of mortality will have been removed, our undimmed eyes will behold a scene which mortal tongue can not describe and mortal eyes can not behold.

### Orders of Angels

The Bible speaks of various ranks or orders of angels, such as archangels, seraphim, cherubim, etc. On this point we quote the following from Evans' "Great Doctrines of the Bible," p. 217:

"We read of Michael, the archangel (Jude 9; I Thess. 4:16): angels, authorities, and powers—which are supposedly orders or ranks of angels (I Pet. 3:22; Col. 1:16). In the Apocryphal books we find a hierarchy with seven archangels, including Michael, Gabriel, Raphael, Uriel. The fact that but one archangel is mentioned in the Scriptures proves that the doctrine of angels was not derived, as some suppose, from the doctrine and Persian sources, for there we find seven archangels instead of one."

## Attributes

1. **Spirituality.**—Angels are spiritual, immaterial beings. "Of the angels he saith, Who maketh his angels spirits, and his ministers a flame of fire" (Heb. 1:7). True, they have appeared to man in visible form, just as God sometimes reveals Himself to man; but all such appearances were miraculous, God and angels appearing in tangible form that man might be able to comprehend. When the Holy Ghost appeared at the baptism of Jesus in the bodily form of a dove, this appearance gave nobody the idea that this was His real form or substance—it was simply a symbolical appearance that gives man a clearer idea of His character and work. Angels, like God, are *spiritual* beings.

2. **Individuality.**—We recognize the personality of individual angels as well as the personality of man; as, for instance, when Gabriel appeared to Zacharias and later to Mary (Luke 1:19, 26-35), and Michael contended for the body of Moses (Jude 9), we get the idea that angels have their individual traits and offices which distinguish them from other individuals of their class.

3. **Immortality.**—Angels are not subject to death. Concerning the future state of the righteous Christ says. "Neither can they die any more; for they are equal unto the angels" (Luke 20:36). Men and angels differ in this: While the soul of man is for a time housed in a mortal body, angels are not thus limited, for they have no material bodies. After the dissolution of man's "earthly house" men and angels are alike immortal—the righteous to dwell with God in glory, the unrighteous to spend eternity in the place "prepared for the devil and his angels" (Matt. 25:41).

4. **Power.**—Of angels it is said that they "excel in strength" (Psa. 103:20); that they are "greater in power and might" (II Pet. 2:11) than man. Angelic power was demonstrated in the destruction of Sodom and Gomorrah,

in the destruction of Sennacherib's army (Isa. 37:36), at the resurrection of our Lord (Matt. 28:2-5) and will be further demonstrated in the judgment to come (Matt. 13:39; II Thess. 1:7-9; Rev. 20:1, 2, 10). In strength, mighty deeds, motion, speed, etc., the power of angels can not be measured by any standard that marks the limitations of man.

5. **Intelligence.**—That angels have their limitations in intelligence is evident from the fact that to man were revealed things that angels desired to know (I Pet. 1:12) and that even now there are things unknown to them (Matt. 24:36). When Christ says, "Not even the angels of heaven" (R.V.), He infers that they are of superior intelligence yet not infinite in knowledge. That the Jews had a very exalted opinion of the intelligence of angels is evident from such testimonies as that given by the woman of Tekoah, "My lord is wise, according to the wisdom of an angel of God, to know all things that are in the earth" (II Sam. 14:20). Free from the impediments which limit the knowledge of men in the flesh and inquiring enough to "desire to look into" the mysteries of God, angels are a class which far outstrip man in intelligence, yet fall far below the sphere of the Infinite, which belongs to God alone.

6. **Goodness.**—This quality belongs, of course, to those angels only who have "kept their first estate." Fallen angels, like fallen men, have lost their goodness. The goodness of the angels of God is evident from their faithfulness in carrying out His commands, from the fact that they worship Him (Neh. 9:6; Phil. 2:9-11), and are subject to Him in all things. Subject to God in heaven, ministering spirits to His people on earth, never having fallen, and therefore still "very good," it is needless to produce arguments proving their goodness.

7. **Benevolence.**—Again we name a quality which belongs to the angels of God only. The devil's angels are as fully committed to the destruction of men as the angels

of God are to promote man's highest interests. Think of the work of angels among men and women like Abraham, Lot, Jacob, Joseph, Moses, Zacharias, Paul, Peter, John, Hannah, Elizabeth, Mary, etc.; of how they wafted home to God the ransomed spirit of the beggar Lazarus, and of their joy over sinners coming home to God; and we have sufficient regard for these benevolent creatures to appreciate their message to the pious shepherds on the Judean hills when they sang, "Glory to God in the highest, and on earth peace, good will toward men."

8. **Happiness.**—Who can think of the myriads of the heavenly hosts without being convinced of their unending joy as well as goodness? It is they who perform the pleasant task of ministering to God's elect; who rejoice over the conversion of sinners brought back into the fold of our Redeemer; who are the fellow workers and fellow worshipers of the saints of God in time, and will share with them the glory of God in eternity; who, in the presence of the Father, Son, and Holy Ghost, will join with the saints of God in singing the anthems of praise and glory to God in eternity.

9. **Glory.**—Angels abound in goodness, intelligence, wisdom, purity, happiness, benevolence. Glorifying God (Isa. 6:3; Luke 2:14; Rev. 4:8; 7:9-12) and serving as His messengers in every good work, they can not rightfully be classified as anything but glorious and glorified beings.

## OFFICE AND WORK

### 1. They are ministering spirits.

Which angels? The holy angels. "Are they not *all* ministering spirits?" See the angels of God ministering to Abraham, to Jacob, to Moses, to Daniel, to the Virgin Mary, to the shepherds announcing the birth of Jesus, to Jesus Himself, to Peter and Paul and other disciples in prison, to John on Patmos, to many others of God's people. Of the people that fear God it is said, "The angel of the Lord . . . delivereth them" (Psa. 34:7). "For this cause ought the woman to have power on her head because of the angels" (I Cor. 11:10). After Christ had triumphed over Satan, "angels came and ministered unto him" (Matt. 4:11).

## 2. They are God's messengers.

It was these messengers from God that brought to Abraham the knowledge of God's purpose to destroy Sodom; to Jacob at Padan-aram, comforting him when he felt utterly forsaken; to Isaiah, telling him of his life work; to Zacharias, telling him that he should be the father of John the Baptist; to Mary, announcing the coming birth of her Son Jesus; to the shepherds, announcing the birth of the infant King; to John on Patmos, revealing the coming trials and triumphs of the Christian Church. Oh, the riches brought to the faithful in Christ through the ministry of these heaven-sent messengers!

## 3. They execute the purposes and judgments of God.

God uses angels in carrying out His will concerning man. The angel of the Lord entered the camp of the Assyrians, and 185,000 men were corpses; stood in the way of Balaam, and convinced him that he was more stupid than the beast upon which he rode; overawed the guard at the tomb of Jesus, when the blessed Lord arose in triumph. Angels directed the work of separating Lot from his wicked companions, proclaimed the glad tidings of our Saviour's birth, bore the ransomed soul of Lazarus into Abraham's bosom, will be the servants of God in gathering together the golden sheaves in the Master's final great harvest (Matt. 13:41, 42), and will accompany the Lord Jesus Christ when He comes to judge the world. Matt. 25:31; II Thess. 1:7-9. As God uses angels in this dispensation to carry out His purposes, so will He use them in the work of bringing this dispensation to a close.

## 4. They serve as guides to the believer.

It was the angel that directed Philip southward and brought him and the Ethiopian eunuch together (Acts 8), that brought Peter and Cornelius together in the latter's house when the door of the Gospel was opened to the Gentiles (Acts 10), that led Peter out of prison while his fellow disciples were praying for him (Acts 12), that directed Paul in the eventful voyage to Rome (Acts 27:23). In this connection it has well been said that while "the angel directs, the Holy Spirit guides;" angels being the servants of God the Spirit.

### 5. They glorify God.

None are more fully devoted to the praise and glory of God than these celestial beings. "When God laid the foundation of the earth, these morning stars rejoiced and shouted together for joy."—Wakefield. Hear the message of the seraphim who, in the presence of Isaiah praised the Lord, saying, "Holy, holy, holy, is the Lord of hosts: the whole earth is full of his glory" (Isa. 6:3). Listen to the heavenly refrain heard on the hills of Bethlehem: "Glory to God in the highest, and on earth peace, good will toward men" (Luke 2:14). There never was an appearance of the angels of God among men in which God was not thereby glorified. No message from these heavenly beings was ever heard that did not have in it the elements of praise to God. By and by the voices of saints and angels will be heard in proclaiming the praises of God in glory, saying, "Blessing, and glory, and wisdom, and thanksgiving, and honour, and power, and might, be unto our God for ever and ever. Amen!"

## Some Things the Bible Does not Teach

As said before, some people let their imaginations take the place of Bible teaching, and assert with positiveness some things on which the Bible is not only silent but, in some cases, gives testimony against.

### 1. That angels are disembodied spirits of people who lived in former worlds.

The Bible is so absolutely silent on this point that we have nothing but pure speculation upon which to base the theory.

## 2. That angels are females.

Almost invariably they so appear in pictures. All the names of angels found in the Bible are masculine names. From such scriptures as Mark 12:25; Luke 20:35, etc., we infer that sex life in no way enters into the life of angels.

## 3. That angels inhabit the planets.

Perhaps they do. If God has need for them there, they are certainly there, just as they are in heaven and on earth. But as to them needing a place to live, let it be remembered that angels, being spirits, need no planet upon which to rest their feet.

## 4. That angels fell some time during the interim said to exist between the times referred to in the first and second verses in Genesis.

"This view can neither be proved nor refuted."—Evans.

## 5. That the righteous here will become angels in the glory world.

This theory has found its way into hymn books. Many of us have been stirred with the song:

> "I want to be an angel,
> And with the angels stand."

But the merit of that song ends with its poetic ring. The Bible nowhere teaches that saints here will become angels in heaven. Angels had existence before man was created. Christ's reference to resurrected saints as being "equal unto the angels" (Luke 20:36) or "as the angels which are in heaven" (Mark 12:25), proves that He had in mind two classes of beings being very much like each other, or He would simply have said that in the resurrection the people of God become angels. While saints are "as the angels in heaven" in a number of ways, it is quite clear that they are not now, nor will they ever become, angels. Saints and angels both have recognition in heaven (Rev. 7:9-12) as well as on earth.

Some find support of this theory in Rev. 22:8, 9, where the angel represented himself as being a fellow servant of

John and of the prophets. But a careful study of that reference warrants no such conclusion. Both men and angels serve as ministers and messengers of God, both classes in their respective spheres, and are therefore fellow servants of God; but John's fellow saints were recognized by the angel as *"thy* brethren," not *my* brethren or our brethren—showing that while he considered himself a fellow servant of John and his brethren, he after all recognized a distinction between himself and them which put them into two separate classes. This text is in harmony with all other scripture texts bearing on this subject, showing that while they are very closely associated in their work, saints and angels are after all two separate and distinct orders of beings, subject to God and in His service. This close relationship on earth promises to be continued in heaven.

# PART IV

## The Realms of Darkness

### CHAPTERS

# THE REALMS OF DARKNESS

## Outline of Chapters

# THE REALMS OF DARKNESS

"And darkness was upon the face of the deep," is the language of Scripture concerning conditions as they were just before God created the light. But this is not the darkness of which we speak in these chapters—but we refer rather to the spiritual darkness portrayed by the works of Satan and his hosts.

Throughout the Bible, truth and righteousness are held forth as "light," while sin and its results are referred to as "darkness." The darkness seen of men in the absence of light is but typical of the indescribable darkness where the face of God does not shine.

First, there is THE PRINCE OF DARKNESS, the author of sin, the "father of lies," the "god of this world," the enemy of righteousness. Next to him are the FALLEN ANGELS who, together with their chief, are responsible for the realms of darkness herein described and who, together with their chief and his human victims, are doomed to spend eternity in the "outer darkness" (Matt. 25:30) which God prepared for them. Then there are LOST SOULS, the victims of sin, who are described as "having no hope and without God in the world," and who are on the broad road to endless destruction. These complete the vision of the dark picture before us. With "an evil heart of unbelief" they have joined forces with "the devil and his angels" in a mighty effort to bring about the desolation of human souls.

This, however, is but the beginning of sorrows. For every sin on earth there will be a resulting condition in eternity. Sin on earth, dark and dismal as it is, is but a foretaste of the wretchedness and despair, the indescribable torture and woe in the realms of "outer darkness" where the devil and his victims will spend eternity.

It is a dark and horrifying scene; but we thank God that He has provided a means of escape. May we be impressed with the horrors of sin, that the blessedness of God's redeeming grace may be more fully appreciated.

# CHAPTER I

## SATAN, or THE DEVIL

Your adversary the devil, as a roaring lion, walketh about,
seeking whom he may devour.—I Peter 5:8.

And no marvel; for Satan himself is transformed into an
angel of light.—II Corinthians 11:14.

Let us begin the study of this awful, dreadful, villainous destroyer of human souls with a prayer that we may consider him in his true light, and that, by the grace of God, we may at all times be delivered from his power. He is known in Scripture by many names, the most common ones standing at the head of this chapter. As Satan he is the great archenemy, the *adversary* of human souls. As the devil, he is the *slanderer* or accuser, both of God and of man. In all the names by which he is known in Scripture, his qualities may be classified under one or the other of these two heads. But first, let us notice

### His Personality

In the first place, it is important that we recognize this adversary as having a real personality, not as a mere evil influence or evil propensity working in man. He is a real being, having a distinct personality, just as God and man have personalities. In the days of Job he came along with the sons of God as they assembled for worship. Job 1:6-12. He contended with Michael the archangel over the body of Moses. Jude 9. He tempted Christ in the wilderness. Matt. 4:1-11. We are assured that if we resist him he will flee from us. Jas. 4:7. In the end he will be cast into the lake of fire. Rev. 20:10. The saying that "every man is his own devil" has no scriptural foundation. The sooner that men recognize that there is an actual, personal devil in the world whose business it is to deceive men, to lead them astray, to attempt to thwart the plan of God for the restoration of fallen men, and, finally, to bring about their eternal destruction from the presence of God in glory, the better it is for their present and eternal welfare.

## His Abode

It has aptly been said that Satan's chief place of abode is within six feet from the surface of the earth. In other words, if he is not abiding in the hearts of men, he is not far away, and constantly seeking an entrance. He is described as "going to and fro in the earth, and walking up and down in it" (Job 1:7), as "a roaring lion, . . . . seeking whom he may devour" (I Pet. 5:8), as "the prince of the power of the air" (Eph. 2:2), as "the god of this world" (II Cor. 4:4), as "the prince of this world" (Jno. 14:30), etc. His purpose is, of course, to enter the hearts of men with the view of corrupting and destroying their souls. The Bible quite frequently speaks of Satan as dwelling in the hearts of sinful men. While it is natural to think of him as having his dwelling place in hell, just as the dwelling place of God is in heaven, the Bible is silent on this point, deferring reference to this until it discusses his eternal abode in connection with his destiny (Matt. 25:41; Rev. 20:10), but it speaks quite frequently about this earth as being the scene of his activities.

## His Origin

It has pleased God not to reveal, in so many words, where Satan came from, how he was created, and how he came to be a devil. Yet we are not without scriptural authority which throws at least an indirect light on this subject. That this person is among the "all things" which God created there can be no doubt. Gen. 1:2; Jno. 1:3. But we can not conceive that God would create a being of great power and resourcefulness, such as the Scriptures ascribe to Satan, whose mission it is to bring His work to nought.

We must conclude, therefore, that when God created the devil He created him as an angel of light; that, having exalted himself through pride, and with him a multitude of "angels which kept not their first estate" (Jude 6) he was cast out of heaven; and, that ever since that time he has been carrying on his nefarious work on earth. For confirmation of this conclusion, read Isa. 14:12-14; Ezek. 28:12-15; I Tim. 3:6.

Why did God permit such work? and how could it be possible for the holy angels in heaven to fall? how could evil originate in the pure environment of heaven? In such questions we are entering the realms of mystery and of speculation. In due time all things will be revealed; and when they are, we will see the wisdom and goodness and justice of God in it all. Suffice it to say that there is a difference between angels and human beings, and not all rules that apply to one will apply with equal force to the other; also that if God would have created man without the possibility of falling he could not have been a free agent and would have been a child of God from compulsion rather than from choice. But summing it all up we know that God created all things, that all that He created was "very good;" that the devil and his angels are depraved and vicious creatures for whom the eternal lake of fire was prepared (Matt. 25: 41), and therefore must have become so since their creation; that God has made every provision for the salvation of every human soul that comes to Jesus Christ by faith (Jno. 3:16), and we are willing to leave it to Him as to when the how and why and wherefore of these things will be more fully revealed.

## His Attributes

The character of his personality and work becomes apparent as we consider the names by which he is known in Scripture, together with the significance of these names. He is declared to be—

1. Satan—adversary of God and man. I Pet. 5:8.

2. The devil—the accuser and slanderer of God and man. Rev. 12:9, 10. As such he slanders God to man (Gen. 3:1-6) and man to God (Job 1:9; 2-4).

3. Beelzebub—"the prince of devils" (Matt. 12:24), "the prince of the power of the air" (Eph. 2:2).

4. Belial—worthless, reckless, lawless. II Cor. 6:15.

5. Apollyon—"the angel of the bottomless pit" (Rev. 9:11).

6. The dragon—the monster that seeks admission into the human heart at every opportunity. Rev. 20:2.

7. God of this world—the prince of demons, before whom every fallen creature bows his knees. II Cor. 4:4.

Besides these he is likened unto a fowler (Psa. 91:3), a sower of tares (Matt. 13:25, 28), a serpent (Rev. 12:9), a wolf (Jno. 10:12), a roaring lion (I Pet. 5:8), an angel of light (II Cor. 11:14).

He is presumptuous (Job 1:6), proud (I Tim. 3:6), wicked (I Jno. 2:13), malignant (Job 1:9), subtle (Gen. 3:1), deceitful (II Cor. 11:14), fierce (Luke 8:29; 9:39, 42), a murderer, and a liar (Jno. 8:44).

Ransack the whole catalogue of vices and destructive and diabolical traits of character known to sinful men, and you have in the characterization of these vices a faint description of this prince of evil angels, commonly known as the devil.

One must wonder how such a being can make such headway among intelligent beings. This will be considered at some length in the next chapter. Yet a description of this prince of darkness would be incomplete if we did not notice, to some extent,

### His Manner of Work

We spoke of his personality. Contrary to the common conception of this adversary of souls, and in spite of what we have just said of him, he has a personality that is most attractive. We frequently see him pictured as a hideous monster having a long tail, a forked tongue, a hellish grin, a pitchfork in his hand. And while the qualities thus indicated are all included in his personality, it is not thus that he makes his appeals to men. On the other hand, he comes with an attractive personality, transforming himself into

1. **An Angel of Light.**—It was in this guise that he appeared to Mother Eve in the Garden, convincing her that he had something to impart to her that was far to be preferred to anything she then enjoyed. He is still working this same kind of confidence game, and many of his followers are skilled in his art of charming deceptiveness. The infidel, the libertine, the pleasuremonger, and every other leader among the hosts of Satan's followers—all try to make it appear that the true religion of Jesus Christ is something that robs people of their "liberty," holds them to a "narrow," slavish, unsatisfactory course in life, and that the way *they* have to recommend is a deliverance from the bondage of oppression, a path of "higher light," the only worth while way to live. In this art of deception Satan stands as the prince and leader, the great pastmaster in this hellish achievement. Gen. 3:1-6; Eph. 5:1-6. Thus people are at first dazzled and deceived, charmed and blinded, after which the archenemy of souls plies his real trade as

2. **A Roaring Lion.**—It is when the lion has his victim within his power that he begins to roar. Under the leadership of Satan the sportsman becomes a gambler, the pleasure-seeker becomes a libertine, the tippler becomes a drunkard, the skeptic becomes an atheist, and so throughout the whole catalogue of sins. It is as an angel of light that he gets them started, as a roaring lion that he accomplishes their finish. The present rising tide of crime is but the roar of the mighty LION—bootlegging, immorality, murder, "wars and rumours of wars," labor troubles, etc.—but through it all there is a soothing strain, a deceptive siren song, a blinding of the eyes of the people, as

sin-cursed humanity listens to such charming refrains as, "The world is getting better," and "We are awakening to an era of higher light."

### The End

of all this is the spoliation of the world, the ruin of human souls, all of which will find its consummation in the great cataclysm at the end of time, when Satan and all his hosts will be cast into the lake of fire, where "the smoke of their torment ascendeth up for ever and ever." As the prince of devils, the chief of sinners, the archenemy of all that is pure and good and holy and righteous and blessed, Satan will be the chief sufferer in this place prepared for him and his angels.

# CHAPTER II

## SATAN—His Dominions

The god of this world hath blinded the minds of them
which believe not, lest the light of the glorious gospel
of Christ, who is the image of God, should shine unto
them.—II Corinthians 4:4.

Satan, being of commanding personality, is of necessity the leader of all the forces of iniquity. He is referred
to in Scripture as "the god of this world," "the prince of
this world" (Jno. 12:31), a ruler of darkness (Eph. 6:12),
and from such passages of Scripture as Dan. 10:5-13;
Luke 11:14-18; Eph. 6:11, 12, and others, it is evident
that he is "king over the realm of demons" (Torrey); and
that "the world of evil spirits is organized, and Satan is
at its head" (Evans). As the "god of this world" and the
"prince of devils," he is obeyed by these two classes of
beings more abjectly and much more faithfully than most
church members obey the God of heaven. It is but right,
therefore, that we refer to the hosts of fallen angels, as
well as fallen men, as belonging to his dominion. But
first let us notice

### HIS LIMITATIONS

Let us not forget that Satan is a creature and not the
Creator, and that therefore, like all other creatures, he has
his limitations. In other words, while he has absolute
sway so far as his dominion extends, there are limits beyond which he is not permitted to go. Let us cite a few
illustrations:

1. When God discussed with the devil the merits of
Job, the devil remarked: "Doth Job fear God for nought?
Hast thou not made an hedge about him, and about his
house, and about all that he hath on every side?" Then

God gave the devil permission to do the very things that he complained no one was permitted to do. The devil tried his hand on Job, and grievous afflictions befell this man of God, but Satan failed. Then another conversation took place between God and Satan. This time the devil accused Job of serving God through fear. God extended the devil's liberties with reference to Job, but again Satan failed. In the end Job came out victorious, was blessed with greater prosperity than ever before, and the world has an object lesson which too few people appreciate. But the point we wish to make is that the devil was not permitted to go any further than God permitted him to go. He had his limitations.

2. After Christ fasted forty days He was sorely tempted by the devil. Three times he tried desperately to overcome the Son of God, and three times he failed. Why? Because the Son of God remained true to the Word of God. And Satan could not touch Him. But let us not get the idea that Satan failed because Christ was the Son of God. The same power of resisting the devil is given to us, so long as we remain true to the Word of God. The assurance is given us that if we "put on the whole armour of God," we will be able to "quench all the fiery darts of the wicked" (Eph. 6:10-18); that if we resist the devil he will flee from us. Jas. 4:7. The Bible holds out abundant assurances that so long as we are faithful to God the devil has no power over us, for he has his limitations.

But because men fail to exercise their privilege of arming themselves with the full armor of God, the devil, as a roaring lion, "devours" them. In

### His Dominions

there are innumerable hosts of fallen creatures, which include—

1. **Evil Angels.**—Jude refers to "the angels which kept not their first estate, but left their own habitation," and says that God has reserved them "in everlasting chains

under darkness unto judgment of the great day." We get several thoughts from this reference: (1) It is one of the scriptures which support the idea that the devil and fallen angels were first created holy but afterwards fell, left their first estate, and went to other quarters. (2) Fallen angels are not, like fallen men, subject to redemption, but are "reserved in everlasting chains under darkness unto the judgment of the great day."

The frequent references in Scripture telling of Christ and His disciples casting out devils or demons show us that "the prince of devils" is well supported by his host of subservient followers in the great and frightful work of destroying human souls. As the angels who remained true to their Creator, the God of heaven, are ministering spirits to heirs of salvation, so the devil's angels are ministering spirits in the work of bringing about the corruption and destruction of human souls.

2. **Lost Souls.**—The Bible tells us that "the whole world lieth in wickedness" (I Jno. 5:19). That means the world of lost souls. They have rejected God, and "the god of this world" has taken possession of them. He is "the spirit that now worketh in the children of disobedience" (Eph. 2:2), and is therefore "the prince of the power of the air." Read our Saviour's estimate (Matt. 7:13, 14) as to which way the body of humanity is traveling. It is a fearful thought that "all the nations that forget God" (Psa. 9:17) belong to Satan's dominion, and will therefore "be cast into hell!"

### THE GREAT CONTROVERSY

for human souls is going on. God is offering freedom for every captive soul, having sacrificed His only begotten Son to this end. By authority of Jesus Christ there are messengers in every land, preaching "the good tidings of salvation." In the freedom from sin in time and the glory of heaven in eternity there is sufficient urge for every soul to accept Jesus Christ as Saviour and Lord and to press hopefully on towards the heavenly goal.

On the other hand, Satan is resting neither day nor night in prompting the cause of damnation and destruction. All that misrepresentation, deception, and lying slander can do is being done to subvert the hearers of the truth and to turn them aside unto fables. On the side of the Lord are the Spirit-directed churches and all allied institutions and enterprises. On the side of Satan are the evil angels and fallen men, evil inventions of men (Eccl. 7:29), and all the vain allurements of an evil world. The practical question that comes to every reader is, Who has the victory in *my* soul, God or the devil?

### Why Souls Are Taken Captive

The question naturally arises, Since salvation from sin means nobility of soul, freedom from condemnation, and the blessed hope of an everlasting crown in glory; and since a sinful life means a degraded life in time and banishment from God in eternity, why do so few decide for Christ and so many fall victims of the devil? Here are a few reasons:

1. **"The god of this world hath blinded their eyes."**
Like Eve they see only things that are "good for food," "beautiful to look upon," "desired to make one wise," and close their eyes to the real blessings from God which may be had only in a sinless life.

2. **Satan is transformed into an angel of light.**
Many have forsaken the true faith because some unbeliever has made them believe that they were stepping out into "higher light." Many a miserable wretch has died a horrible death and gone on to a dreadful eternity because somebody lured him on in the paths of sinful pleasure. Many a man has become a slave to the bottle or pipe because as a boy he thought he was exercising his "liberty" to drink and smoke. The "way that seemeth right" is traveled by multitudes of people because they

have been deceived by the blandishments of Satan and his dupes.

### 3. People are led astray through temptation.

Because of the blandishments and deceptions already referred to, people lust after evil things. "Then when lust hath conceived, it bringeth forth sin: and sin, when it is finished, bringeth forth death" (Jas. 1:15). Satan's appeal to the flesh is pleasing to the carnal man, and under this spell the only means of escape is in fleeing to the cross for cleansing in the blood, guidance by the Spirit, and protection in the love and power of God. For a contrast between defeat and victory in the hour of temptation compare Gen. 3:1-6 with Matt. 4:1-11.

### 4. Indifference on the part of God's professed people.

Satan's dominions are enlarged because there are too many professing Christians asleep. Contrast, for a moment, the ever watchful attitude and continual day and night activity of Satan and his hosts with the lethargic, listless, indifferent attitude of professing Christians. Is it any wonder that Satan makes such frightful headway in enlarging the borders of his kingdom, in extending his nefarious work of destruction? It was while men slept that the enemy sowed his tares. Read Eph. 5:11-14.

# CHAPTER III

## SIN

By one man sin entered into the world, and death by sin; and so death passed upon all men, for that all have sinned.—Romans 5:12.

As we compare this present dark and sinful world with what it was before man became polluted with sin, or with what it might be if every human being were sinless like Adam before the fall, we have some idea of the nature of the subject now under consideration.

Sin has been defined as "any thought, word, action, omission, or desire contrary to the law of God."—Cruden. The word is used in different senses. It may apply to the sum total of all iniquity, to the innate depravity of the human soul, or to individual acts, either of omission or commission. It is the opposite of all righteousness, the essence of corruption and godliness, the disease which corrupts the heart and kills the soul. An idea of what constitutes sin or sinning may be had by consulting a few

### Bible Definitions

1. The thought of foolishness is sin.—Prov. 24:9.

2. Whatsoever is not of faith is sin.—Rom. 14:23.

3. Therefore to him that knoweth to do good, and doeth it not, to him it is sin.—Jas. 4:17.

4. Sin is the transgression of the law.—I Jno. 3:4.

5. All unrighteousness is sin.—I Jno. 5:17.

Can you think of any sin that any one may commit—in thought, word, or deed—that may not be classified under one or the other of these definitions? Take the five together, and you have a perfect definition, at least one sufficient for all practical purposes. The

### Origin of Sin

in the world is described in Gen. 3:1-8. Before the advent of sin into the world we find man pure and holy, bearing the image of his Maker, happy and contented, knowing no such thing as guilt or death, free from all condemnation, in fellowship with God. But when once Satan "beguiled" Eve, as a result of the first transgression of man we find a condition that is thus described in the language of inspiration: "By one man sin entered into the world, and death by sin; and so death passed upon all men, for that all have sinned." The entire nature of man was changed, as noted in a previous chapter. Instead of being "very good," as man (together with the rest of the creation) was described before the fall, God was now compelled to say, "All have sinned, and come short of the glory of God."

### Sin, and Sins

1. **The Adamic Sin.**—One sin was enough to destroy the purity, the perfection, the holiness, the life of man. This sin did not consist merely in the stretching forth of the hand after the forbidden fruit, for that was merely a result of the act of turning away from God to Satan. The sin, therefore, was the condition of the soul, not the action of the hand. Man had lost the divine relationship, and was therefore sinful. The three things connected with this sinful state are corruption, mortality, separation from God. This condition has been transmitted from generation to generation. Even if it were possible to live an absolutely perfect life from infancy to death (something unknown, outside of Christ) this would not atone for the sinful quality transmitted from Adam to his posterity. The blood of Jesus Christ alone can take away this stain. Read Psa. 51:5; Acts 17:26; Rom. 3:10-23; 5:12-19; II Cor. 5:14; Eph. 2:3.

2. **Committed Sins.**—Where sin exists in the heart it will in some way manifest itself in the outer life. Because

"the heart is deceitful above all things, and desperately wicked" (Jer. 17:9), therefore "out of the heart proceed evil thoughts, murders, adulteries, fornications, thefts, false witness, blasphemies" (Matt. 15:19), which "are the things which defile a man."

The question is sometimes heard, "Am I responsible for the sin of Adam?" No; not if the Adamic sin, together with my own committed sins, has been brought to Christ and washed away in His blood. But the Adamic sin, or rather the proneness to sin because of hereditary weaknesses, will give rise to enough committed sins of my own that will condemn me before God.

Another question: Will I be responsible before God for committed sins if I do as well as I know? Yes; for "the soul that sinneth, it shall die" (Ezek. 18:4). Even for "every idle word that men shall speak, they shall give account thereof in the day of judgment" Matt. 12:38). Of course, there is a way of securing "remission of sins" (Luke 24:47; I Jno. 1:7), but the point we wish to emphasize here is that ignorance of sin in no way nullifies its effects. When you get into a yellow fever nest the fact that you are not aware that you are in a germ-laden community in no way makes you immune from the effects of the disease. But of the effects of sin we shall speak later.

This fact also sheds light on the question, "Is the heathen lost without the Gospel?" Rom. 1:20-32; 2:12 makes it very clear that the heathen, like the man who is next door neighbor to a church, has salvation only through Christ. In other words, his sins are remitted only through faith in Jesus Christ and the atoning merits of His blood. This fact reminds us that there are also

3. **Sins of Omission.**—These are but sins committed negatively; that is, we sin by not doing the things we know ought to be done. As God through James informs us, "To him that knoweth to do good, and doeth it not, to him it is sin."

One thing to bear in mind as we consider this subject is that to be a sinner does not depend upon the kind or the enormity of the deeds which one may commit. For illustration: One man steals an apple, another one a million dollars. Before God they are both guilty—not necessarily of stealing anything great or small, but of STEALING. When God says one thing and we do another, the thing which estranges us from God is that we were disobedient to Him, not necessarily the vileness of the sin committed. Let us not, therefore, console ourselves with the thought that our sins do not seem as black as those of some other people; but when we find ourselves to be guilty of sin, even though it may seem but *a very little thing*, it is nevertheless big enough to estrange us from our God, and the only way we can possibly get rid of the stigma of sin and its results is through repentance and by the grace of God through the atoning merits of the blood of Jesus Christ. Adam and Eve, by eating of the forbidden fruit, committed a transgression that seems unimportant as compared with some of the heinous sins and crimes committed today, yet their sin was enough to separate them from God and to bring the condemnation of death upon them and their posterity. The thing that separates us from God is SIN, not *sins*. But when the blood of Jesus Christ "cleanseth us from all sin," our sins likewise will disappear.

## THE UNPARDONABLE SIN

This theme is discussed a number of times by Christ and the apostles, and the seriousness of the subject demands that we give it more than a mere passing notice. Among the more direct scriptural references to the question are the following:

> All manner of sin and blasphemy shall be forgiven unto men: but the blasphemy against the Holy Ghost shall not be forgiven unto men. And whosoever speaketh a word against the Son of man, it shall be forgiven him; but whosoever speaketh against the Holy Ghost, it shall not be forgiven him, neither in this world, neither in the world to come.—Matt. 12:31, 32.
>
> There is a sin unto death.—I Jno. 5:16.

> It is impossible for those who were once enlightened, and have tasted of the heavenly gift, and were made partakers of the Holy Ghost, and have tasted the good word of God, and the powers of the world to come, if they shall fall away, to renew them again unto repentance; seeing they crucify to themselves the Son of God afresh, and put him to an open shame.—Heb. 6:4-6.

It will be seen that while these scriptures are discussing problems that are somewhat different from each other, they all bear upon the same phase of the sin question; namely, that of the unforgivableness of sin under certain circumstances. The thing which brought this solemn warning from the lips of our Saviour was the accusation by the Pharisees that Christ was casting out devils "by Beelzebub the prince of the devils," thus attributing to Satan the power which God alone possesses. Concerning the blasphemy against the Holy Ghost it has well been said that "the reason why this sin is never forgiven, is not because of any want of the sufficiency in the blood of Christ, nor in the pardoning mercy of God, but because such as commit it despise and reject the only remedy, i.e., the power of the Holy Spirit, applying the redemption of the Gospel to the souls of men." Similar comments could be made with reference to the other scriptures quoted. Some have professed fear that they might have committed the unpardonable sin. The fear is rather that they are not sincere in their expressions of fear; for true repentance or, in other words, a real sorrow for sins committed, is the best kind of evidence that the unpardonable sin has not been committed, since the Word says positively that "it is impossible" to renew such to repentance.

The two practical lessons which Christian people may glean from the Bible teaching on the unpardonable sin may be briefly stated as follows: (1) "Take heed lest ye fall." (2) The fact that sinning against the Holy Ghost can not be forgiven serves to emphasize the grace and goodness of God in this that it is the *only* sin which puts a man beyond repentance.

## CAUSES FOR COMMITTED SINS

1. **Inherent Depravity.**—As Paul says, we are "by nature the children of wrath;" that is, we have inherited the Adamic sin through our ancestors. God says that "the iniquity of the fathers" is visited upon "the children unto the third and fourth generation of them that hate me" (Ex. 20:5). Children have an inherited tendency to sin because their parents before them were sinners. Parents have a fearful responsibility resting upon them.

2. **Temptation.**—Satan takes advantage of the weaknesses of men by luring them on. For example, many people having a strong appetite and a craving for strong drink would after all leave it alone were they not tempted through the smell of it or through the influence of other men. "Every man is tempted, when he is drawn away of his own lust, and enticed" (Jas. 1:14). It is a reason why we should keep out of temptation's way whenever possible to do so. For meditation, read Matt. 4:1-11; 6:13; I Cor. 10:13; Jas. 1:2-6, 12-17.

3. **Ignorance.**—Many an unsuspecting person, for want of better knowledge, has fallen into grievous sins that blighted his whole life. Not the knowledge *of* sin, but the knowledge *about* sin, with instructions as to how to keep out of sin's deadly grasp, is what people need, especially young people. Read Lev. 4:2; Psa. 79:6; Jer. 9:3; Luke 12:48; Acts 17:29, 30; Eph. 4:18; I Thess. 1:9.

4. **Lack of Proper Employment.**—The old proverb, "Satan has some mischief still, for idle hands to do," is lost sight of by too many young people; for, "An idle brain is the devil's workshop." Keep busy doing something useful, something which may be done to the glory of God, and you will escape many a snare into which idlers have fallen. One of the greatest curses of modern times is the policy of having young people grow up without knowing how to work. Rid a town of its loafers and clean out its loafing places, and much of its wickedness

disappears. Prov. 10:4; 12:24; 13:4; 24:30-34; 26:15; II Thess. 3:10-12; I Tim. 5:13.

5. **Indifference.**—The "don't care" spirit has led many a person into the sinning life. Who can fathom this monster cause of evil!

6. **Influence of Evil Associations.**—Our worst enemy, outside of self, is our supposed-to-be friend that influences us to do things that we know to be wrong. "My son, if sinners entice thee, consent thou not" (Prov. 1:10). Did you ever know of an apple to remain uninfected very long after it was surrounded by rotten apples?

7. **A False Idea of Self-interest.**—People in business, for the sake of gain, have stooped to things that they knew to be wrong—not realizing that in sacrificing their integrity they lost something far more valuable than dollars. For the sake of high standing in society, some have sacrificed a tender conscience, not realizing that thereby they became losers rather than gainers. Men, for the sake of winning some coveted official position, have given way to corrupt means, thereby exchanging Christian manhood for the sake of earthly gain or fame. Such illustrations might be extended indefinitely. When godliness and purity are sacrificed for the coveted (supposed-to-be) treasures of earth, it may or may not secure these treasures; but it does mean sinful pollution, which loss can not be compensated for by anything this world has to offer. For illustration, read the story of the rich man and Lazarus (Luke 16:19-31) and of the rich fool. Luke 12:15-21.

8. **Flattery.**—This is something that is harder to withstand than open and direct opposition. It is true today, as it was in the days of Solomon, that "a flattering mouth worketh ruin" (Prov. 26:28).

Back of all these causes is the influence and work of the "father of lies," the archdeceiver of human souls, who knows the weaknesses and shortcomings of men and misses no opportunity to lead them into forbidden and ruinous paths. Summing it all up, every victim of sin can truthfully say, "The serpent beguiled me, and I did eat."

### RESULTS OF SIN

Sin is one of the many things that may be considered under the general head of cause and effect. Having noticed the cause, let us now turn the Gospel light on the effect.

1. **Death.**—The penalty for sin is summed up in God's warning to Adam, "In the day that thou eatest thereof, thou shalt surely die" (Gen. 2:17). Such expressions as "The soul that sinneth, it shall die," "The wages of sin is death," "Death passed upon all men, for that all have sinned," "Sin . . . bringeth forth death," "Dead in trespasses and sins," "She that liveth in pleasure is dead while she liveth," are further testimonies to the fact of death— physical and spiritual—being the penalty for sin.

2. **Depravity.**—Sin is not a mere academic question which men may study as an exercise for the mind, but it is a terrible reality that ought to make all men shudder. It is a putrefying process which makes the vile person loathsome in the eyes of God and shameful in the light of righteousness and true holiness. It is something that can not be gotten rid of through civilization or refinement or culture—for witness the fact that the most rotten mess of iniquity, the most shameful cesspools of vice, are often found in the heart of countries laying claim to the highest state of civilization. Where can you go, in this wide world, where human depravity is not evident in dishonesty, pride, murder, selfishness, lying, profanity, intemperance, licentiousness, strife, theft, incest, and uncleanness of many varieties! Sin is a mortal disease that first defiles and ultimately destroys both body and soul. Rom. 1:20-32.

3. **Wretchedness.**—People are often deceived into the idea that while religion is a good thing to die by the sinning life is preferable to live by, supposing that you get so much more satisfaction and pleasure out of it. But "be not deceived." What is the cause of all this wretched-

ness and poverty and distress that you see on every hand —poverty, pain, sickness, plagues, etc.? **S I N.** Why the jails, penitentiaries, lunatic asylums, reform schools? why the fights and brawls and lynchings and persecutions and wars and other sorrows of life? why the miserable hovels in the "red light" districts of our cities, the remorse of conscience and anguish of soul because of blasted lives and hopes and other disappointments and sorrows of life? **S I N.** "Who hath woe? who hath sorrow? who hath contentions? who hath babbling? who hath wounds without cause? who hath redness of eyes? They that tarry long at the wine" (Prov. 23:29). Nor is drunkenness the only sin that brings forth its catalogue of miseries and distresses. Similar results come from every form of persistent sinful indulgence. Language fails us as we attempt to depict the woes and heartaches and desolations brought on by sin!

It is true that sin often brings what men call pleasure. It gratifies, for the time being, the sinful desires of the depraved heart. Like an opiate, it creates a pleasurable sensation for the time being, and those under the influence of this receptive "soothing syrup" often look with pity or contempt upon others who walk in paths "of righteousness and true holiness." But such pleasures are only temporary. The tippler sooner or later becomes the miserable toper who staggers in the streets, a miserable, drunken wretch. The boy that smokes his cigarettes eventually becomes the nicotinized, enslaved, diseased man who emits an odor that reminds you of a tobacco warehouse. The seeker after pleasure becomes the gambler, the libertine, the prostitute, the wrecker of other people's homes. The end of it all is summed up in the language of the psalmist: "The wicked shall be turned into hell!" These mental opiates may be soothing for a time, but they simply lull the victim to sleep and make more sure the day of wrath and terrible retribution.

4. **Eternal Damnation.**—Speaking of the results of sin, the climax is reached, not in this life but in the next.

Whatever is experienced in this world is but a faint fore-taste of what is coming in the world to come. The edict has gone forth, "Whatsoever a man soweth, that shall he also reap" (Gal. 6:7). Here we sow, yonder we will reap. If, in this life, we "sow to the flesh," we will, in the world to come, "reap corruption." If here we sow "to the Spirit," over yonder we will "of the Spirit reap life everlasting." If the results of sin here, in plain sight of man, are beyond the power of the human tongue or pen to describe, what must be the anguish and woe when the doomed souls of earth will mingle their wails and gnashings and groans with those of the devil and his angels in the midst of "the everlasting burnings" where the smoke of their torment "ascendeth up for ever and ever!"

## DELIVERANCE FROM SIN

Is there no means of escape? no way in which the lost of earth who are held captive in the chains of sin may have release from their bondage and be spared "the ven-geance of eternal fire"? Thank God, yes. Save in the matter of blaspheming against the Holy Ghost (Matt. 12: 31, 32), and of "sin unto death" (I Jno. 4:16) there is for-giveness for every sin, provided we meet God's conditions for such forgiveness. Luke 24:47. "God hath not ap-pointed us to wrath, but to obtain salvation by our Lord Jesus Christ" (I Thess. 5:9). The grace of God extends to every soul, and to every one bound by the shackles of sin there comes the gracious heavenly invitation, "Look unto me, and be ye saved, all the ends of the earth: for I am God" (Isa. 45:22). But this promise is based on this condition: "Let the wicked forsake his way, and the un-righteous man his thoughts: and let him return unto the Lord, and he will have mercy upon him; and to our God, for he will abundantly pardon" (Isa. 55:7). "Except ye repent," the only alternative is "ye shall all likewise perish."

8

### VICTORY OVER SIN

Deliverance from sin is possible only as the individual places himself under the power of God and the guidance of His Spirit. Apart from Christ, life is an absolute, dismal failure. On the other hand, there is no power in earth or hell that can keep any one from perfect victory in our Lord Jesus Christ, provided the conditions of God's Word are fully met. While it is true of the strongest and most resourceful man that "without me"—that is. without Christ—"ye can do nothing" (Jno. 15:5) it is also true of the weakest saint that "I can do all things through Christ which strengtheneth me" (Phil 4:13). This naturally raises the question, How may we overcome? Turning to the Word of God, we have the following answers:

1. By the blood—"They overcame . . . . by the blood of the Lamb" (Rev. 12:11).

2. By faith—"This is the victory that overcometh the world, even our faith" (I Jno. 5:4).

3. By wearing the full armor of God—"Be strong in the Lord, and in the power of his might. Put on the whole armour of God, . . . . that ye may be able to withstand in the evil day . . . able to quench all the fiery darts of the wicked" (Eph. 6:10-16).

4. By the Word—"Thy word have I hid in mine heart, that I might not sin against thee" (Psa. 119:11).

Our conflict with sin means a continual warfare against the powers of the evil one. But remembering that "the weapons of our warfare are not carnal, but mighty through God" (II Cor. 10:4), and relying upon Him whose power is infinite, whose love is unfailing, and whose promise is never to leave nor forsake His own, it is our blessed privilege to have a continual, daily experience, which is so admirably described by Paul: "In all these things we are more than conquerors through him that loved us" (Rom. 8:37).

# CHAPTER IV

## UNBELIEF

Take heed, brethren, lest there be in any of you an evil
heart of unbelief, in departing from the living God.—
Hebrews 3:12.

Unbelief is the besetting sin which stands at the very
gateway to the realms of darkness. What faith is to salvation, unbelief is to damnation. As no treatise on God's
plan of salvation is complete without a discussion of faith.
so no write-up on the devil's work of damnation can be
complete without consideration of unbelief. If this sin
could be eradicated from the hearts of men the rest of the
conquest of souls for God would be comparatively easy.

Unbelief is to faith as darkness is to light. As the
light fades away, darkness settles in to take its place; and
by the time the light is all gone darkness has taken full
possession. Unbelief is a negative entity that is found only
where faith does not exist. Where faith is perfect and complete there can be no unbelief.

It was "by one man's disobedience" that sin entered
into the world, but this act of disobedience would never
have been perpetrated had there not been a transfer of
faith from God to Satan. Unbelief is at the foundation of
every other sin. Tit. 1:15. All humanity is included in unbelief. Rom. 11:32. Through the deception of "the father
of lies" and other causes the world has become the home of
all forms of unbelief, and many

### CLASSES OF UNBELIEVERS

have appeared to assist him in robbing men of their faith
and bringing the work of God to nought in the hearts of the
children of men. Let us name a few of them:

1. **The atheist** does not believe in the existence of a God. Like "the fool" referred to by the psalmist, he says, "There is no God."

2. **The infidel** rejects the Bible as the inspired Word of God, as well as the idea of direct revelations from God, and opposes orthodox Christianity.

3. **The agnostic** neither affirms nor denies the exisence of a God, professes a neutral attitude on the tenets of Christian faith, his creed being confined to the three words, "I don't know." In reality, he is an infidel.

4. **The freethinker** assumes the liberty of coming to his own conclusions independent of what the Bible has to say on such things, thus rejecting the authority of the Holy Scriptures.

5. **The rationalist** depends upon human reason rather than divine revelation as the foundation of his beliefs and conclusions.

6. **The modernist** of today seeks to explain Christian doctrine from the viewpoint of agnostics and infidels of former generations.

7. **The evolutionist** seeks to supplant the Genesis account of the creation with the theory of a gradual development, covering unnumbered millions of years, from the lower to the higher forms of life, man being the highest form of such development to date.

All of these and other classes of unbelievers, while differing widely among themselves and presenting a veritable babel of contradictions and confusion of beliefs, are nevertheless a unit when it comes to opposition to the idea that the Bible is a direct revelation from God to man and therefore infallible and absolutely authoritative. As a result of the productions of their minds the Christian Church of today is confronted with such destructive heresies as atheism, polytheism, pantheism, universalism, unitarianism, materialism, rationalism, higher criticism, Christian Science-ism and many other "isms" too numerous to mention. In the midst of this babel of confusion Satan is reaping a rich harvest in carrying away multitudes of deluded souls. This condition of affairs must be kept in mind as we consider the

## CAUSES OF UNBELIEF

in the world today. That so large a proportion of the intelligent people in the world to-day are in the numerous camps of unbelievers is one of the greatest mysteries of the age.

Christ "marvelled" at the unbelief of the people (Mark 6:6) and well He might. Did He not fulfill every scripture foretelling the coming of the Messiah? and did He not manifest His wonderful miracle-working power, His wisdom and love and grace and goodness to such a marvelous degree that no one then living should have doubted His Messiahship? and did not the unbelieving Jews themsalves "marvel" at the demonstrations of His intelligence and power? Yet they preferred to be murderers of the very Messiah for whom they professed to be looking rather than to believe on Him.

But is the unbelief of the Jews in the days when Jesus of Nazareth was among them a greater mystery than the widespread unbelief in the world today? We are surrounded by evidences of Christianity on every hand. We have not only Moses and the prophets, but also the Gospel of Christ, the witness of the Spirit, the testimony of the lives of the children of God, and manifestations of divine power and grace in the daily happenings of the world. Why then is "the whole world" still lying "in wickedness," wrapped in the mantle of unbelief? There are reasons. Here are a few:

1. **The Wiles of the Devil.**—This subject was presented in previous chapters.

2. **Temptation.**—Likewise considered in previous chapters.

3. **Lusting after Sin.**—We often blame people for leading us into sin when, if we would but take a look in-

ward, we should blame no one but ourselves. "Every man is tempted, when he is drawn away of his own lust, and enticed" (Jas. 1:14). What makes the drunkard hang on to his bottle? the tobacco user to his pipe or plug or cigar or cigarette? the sportsman to the gambling table? the libertine to the brothel? the covetous man to his dishonest business methods? the pleasure-seeker to his favorite places of amusement? the contentious man to his quarrels? the irreverent man to his profanity? the thief to his stealing? Lust for forbidden things. Moreover, the stronger our lusts for these forbidden things, the more lightly we esteem God's warning Word, and the more we conclude that these things are not so bad after all, that the Bible does not exactly mean all that it says about them. You see people who were once loyal to God and His Word, but who later drifted into the ways of sin. Perhaps it was some form of worldliness that they coveted, some unpopular commandment of the Lord they were not willing to obey, some kind of business which their church would not tolerate, some forbidden thing that they lusted after, that started them on their drift downward. At first they sinned against their consciences, but by and by their consciences no longer bothered them. Their lusts had led them into an attitude of disobedience, and disobedience brought on a state of unbelief. The things they once believed they now ridicule. They belong to the class of whom Paul wrote, saying, "For this cause God shall send them strong delusion, that they should believe a lie" (II Thess. 2:11).

4. **Self-concentration.**—You have sat in a room, so absorbed in a book that you noticed nothing else; or you were so interested in something that appeared on the printed page that you did not even see the rest of the things that appeared on the same page. Or, you may have seen people so absorbed in questionable business that they could see nothing wrong in it, though they were warned over and over again. Why were the Jews unwill-

ing to believe in Jesus? They were so intensely set on their Judaism that they were blind to the truth. Why is there so much unbelief in the world today? People are so absorbed in the mad rush after this world's pleasures, riches, vanities, and deceptive splendors that they brush aside all of God's Word that condemns their course as of little consequence, refusing to believe it.

5. **False Ideas of Self-interest.**—This explains much of what we tried to present in the preceding paragraph. Why did Eve reach forth her hand to receive the forbidden fruit? Because she had been deluded into the false idea that she was reaching for something that was better than she already had, and covetousness caused her to disbelieve or ignore God's warning. Why do men rob and steal and gamble and cheat? The tempter has made them believe that this is the best and quickest and easiest way to get hold of money. Other illustrations might be given, showing that as the value of things temporal and carnal is magnified the value of things eternal and spiritual is discredited and disbelieved. For this reason men turn against and disbelieve in the religion of Jesus Christ, believing that they have found something better.

6. **Evil Associations.**—Here lies a fruitful source of unbelief. Especially where unbelievers are cultured, intelligent, congenial, and of persuasive manners, they make dangerous companions for young people. It is in this way that many a home, many a social club, many a church, and many an institution of learning has been turned into an infidel factory.

7. **Pernicious Literature.**—A young bishop was visiting in the home of a more aged bishop. He saw on the library table a copy of Thomas Paine's "Age of Reason." He was astonished. "What, you reading such books!" "Yes; why not? I want to keep posted on such things, that I may know how to preach against them." "But what about your boys?" "No danger; they seldom look at this book." But there was danger—both of the boys turned out

to be infidels. Literature is a power, either for good or for evil. With the Bible *out* of the public school systems, and Evolution and other anti-scriptural heresies *in* them, need we wonder at the alarming increase of unbelief? Recognizing the character-moulding power of literature, our duty toward the rising generation is plain.

### WHAT UNBELIEF DOES

We have noticed only a few of the more fruitful causes of unbelief. One of the sad things about it is that so many who are themselves sound in the orthodox Christian faith are not awake as they ought to be to the inroads which this monster evil is making in so many homes, schools, and churches. For their sakes, as well as for the sake of others, let us take a look at the work of this great evil, as made clear in the light of God's Word:

### 1. It weakens the power of Christian workers.

On several occasions the inspired writers cite instances where even the disciples failed to accomplish what they should have done because of a lack of faith. Matt. 17:19, 20. "All things are possible with God," but to man the measure is given, "According to your faith be it unto you" (Matt. 9:29). Since faith is the victory which overcomes the world (I Jno. 5:4, 5), we conclude that it must have been a lack of faith on the part of Christian people that is at least in part responsible for their not more completely conquering the world for God.

### 2. It hinders the work of Christ.

According to Mark 6:5, 6 Christ could do no mighty works in His own country because of the unbelief of the people. Faith on the part of those labored with, as well as on the part of the laborers, is essential to success in the Christian work. The Gospel of Christ grips no heart that does not believe in the truth. God does not compel people to be good in spite of themselves.

### 3. It keeps people out of the Kingdom of God.

The Jews entered not into rest "because of unbelief" (Heb. 4:6). Of those who lived in the days of Christ upon earth a comparatively few were received into the Christian Church because the body of Jews remained in unbelief. It is as true today, as it was when the words were first spoken, that "he that believeth not is condemned already" (Jno. 3:18). Unbelievers may get into the visible Church —often do—but they have no place in the Church of Jesus Christ. When the jailer inquired the way of salvation he got the answer, "Believe on the Lord Jesus Christ" (Acts 16:31). When the eunuch wanted to know whether he might be baptized, Philip told him, "If thou believest with all thine heart, thou mayest" (Acts 8:37). Taking a final view of what becomes of unbelievers (Rev. 21:8), we are informed that they will "have their part in the lake which burneth with fire and brimstone." The Bible holds out no hope of salvation to any one except through faith in the Lord Jesus Christ.

### 4. It has its culmination in the rankest kind of atheism.

When we think of the anathemas that in all ages of the Christian era have been hurled at revealed religion as promulgated in the Gospel of Christ, it gives an added meaning to the words, "gnashing of teeth," as found in Matt. 24:51 and other scriptures. As noted in a previous chapter, such forms of unbelief as evolution and unitarianism are but way stations on the road to the grosser forms of infidelity—the milder forms of unbelief being but the forerunners of atheism. Sow the milder seed, and sooner or later you will reap the crop of rankest atheism. Already the harvest is appearing. A number of years ago a man appeared at Great Bend, Kans., and startled some people by organizing his "church of humanity" and impiously railing down on all forms of religion, expressing his contempt for God, heaven, hell, the Bible, and everything religious which Christian people hold sacred. He was commonly regarded as a crank, harmless even though pestiferous. But within the last few years a more formidable society has arisen, upholding the same system of unbelief, numbering among its members men of recognized ability and attainments, backed by a large endowment, having for its avowed object the destruction of the faith of young Americans, especially high-school and college students. For a statement of the objects of this society, known as "The American Association for the Advancement of Atheism," we will quote from their own literature, as given out in an official circular which we copied from a reprint in the "King's Business." The circular refers to the work of the Junior Atheist League.

"The League will remove boys and girls from the evil influence of the clergy. It will encourage them to protest against Bible reading and religious worship in public schools......The attainment of happiness in this world rather than eternal bliss in a world to come shall be taught the rising generation as the chief end of man. Dispelling the illusions of immortality, the League will free our sons and daughters from the fear of hell and the hope of heaven. SACRIFICE FOR POST-MORTEM CONSIDERATIONS will be SHOWN TO BE CRIMINAL FOLLY!

"Stress will be laid on forming branches in High Schools, as these will prepare students to serve as organizers of DAMNED SOULS SOCIETIES during college years, and for effective work thereafter in combating the church. A comprehensive program has been arranged. PICNICS AND OUTINGS WILL TAKE THE PLACE OF STULTIFYING SUNDAY SCHOOLS.

"Educators in the A.A.A.A. will supervise the instruction. Morality, based on the findings of modern science, will SUPERSEDE BELIEF BASED ON SPECULATIONS OF ANCIENT, ASIATIC THEOLOGY. These lessons will be printed in large quantities for distribution by locals in recruiting members. As soon as 5,000 members are enrolled the first monthly lesson will be mailed. CONTRIBUTIONS ARE COMING IN FROM MEMBERS of the A.A.A.A. for this IMPORTANT PART of ITS WORK!"

Men of faith have protested vigorously against such propaganda, but the protests coming from evolutionists and unitarians have been few and very feeble. Such organizations are but leaves upon the satanic tree of unbelief, which are not "for the healing of the nations" but agencies through which the poison fumes of hell are emit-

ted with blighting and withering effect upon the lives of
those who might otherwise be noble creatures of God,
honoring Him in time, and sharing His glory in eternity!
They are a standing challenge to the Christian Church to
rise in the strength of the Almighty and promulgate the
everlasting truths of God's Word as brought to us in the
Gospel of Christ. T. C. Horton, discussing this matter in
"The King's Business," has this to say:

> "These Bible-denouncers, Home-destroyers, Church-disrupt-
> ers, Nation-demolishers, boast of the funds that are being con-
> tributed to defray the cost of their dastardly deeds, and of their
> literature which is being profusely distributed. In order to
> stem the tide and save our young people, our homes, and our
> country, sound Gospel literature must be quickly provided and
> broadcasted by citizens, churches, and Christian organizations
> everywhere."

In the following chapters, under "God's Plan of Salvation," we shall consider the subject that is just the opposite
of this one, holding out the faith side of life.

# PART V

# God's Plan of Salvation

# GOD'S PLAN OF SALVATION

## Outline of Chapters

6. REDEMPTION FROM WHAT
   a. From Sin
   b. From Bondage
   c. From Dominion of the World
   d. From Satan's Power
   e. From Death
   f. From Destruction

7. RESULTS OF REDEMPTION
   a. Reconciliation to God
   b. Forgiveness of Sins
   c. Justification
   d. Heavenly Peculiarity
   e. Adoption
   f. Sanctification

III. FAITH

1. INTRODUCTORY THOUGHTS

2. KINDS OF FAITH
   a. Belief, Body of Revealed Truth
   b. Confidence, Special Gift
   c. Natural, Christian
   d. "Dead," Living

3. ESSENTIAL TO SALVATION

4. HOW FAITH COMES
   a. By Hearing
   b. By Word of God
   c. By Prayer
   d. By the Spirit
   e. Through the Example of Others

5. WHAT FAITH DOES
   a. Assures Salvation
   b. Assures Place in Family of God
   c. Insures Justification
   d. Brings Joy and Peace
   e. Secures Healing for the Body
   f. Shield for Christian
   g. Puts End to Boasting
   h. Christian's Guide
   i. Sanctification
   j. Binds Us to God
   k. Assures Power
   l. Overcoming Life

6. THE TRIAL OF OUR FAITH
   a. Proves the Genuineness of Our Profession
   b. "Worketh Patience"
   c. The Crown of Life

7. THE CHRISTIAN'S ATTITUDE TOWARD
   FAITH
   a. "Believe on the Lord Jesus Christ"
   b. "Contend Earnestly for the Faith"
   c. "Stand Fast in the Faith"
   d. "Be Thou an Example. . . .in Faith"
   e. "Continue in the Faith"
   f. "Lord, Increase Our Faith"

## IV.  REPENTANCE

### 1. WHAT REPENTANCE IS
a. Conviction
b. Godly Sorrow
c. Confession
d. Forsaking Sin
e. Restitution
f. A Change of Heart

### 2. WHAT REPENTANCE IS NOT
a. Not Mere Change of Mind
b. Not Merely Being Sorry
c. Not Joining Some Church
d. Not Merely Confessing Guilt
e. Not Mere Reform

### 3. WHAT BRINGS REPENTANCE
a. The Goodness of God
b. Hearing the Truth
c. Convicting Power of the Spirit
d. Knowledge of Sin
e. Abhorrence of Sin
f. Faith in God
g. Rewards and Penalties

### 4. FUNDAMENTAL FACTS
a. Repentance Commanded
b. Essential to Salvation
c. Coupled with Remission of Sins
d. Precedes Christian Ordinances
e. Beyond Repentance

## V.  JUSTIFICATION

### 1. HOW WE ARE JUSTIFIED
a. By the Grace of God
b. By Faith
c. By Works
d. By the Blood of Christ
e. "It is God that Justifieth"

### 2. WHAT JUSTIFICATION MEANS FOR US
a. Obedience to God
b. Freedom from Condemnation
c. Peace with God
d. Eternal Salvation
e. Eternal Inheritance
f. Glorification

## VI.  CONVERSION

### 1. THE DOCTRINE STATED

### 2. NO CHANGE, NO CONVERSION

3. EXAMPLES OF CONVERSION
    a. Woman in Simon's House
    b. Saul of Tarsus
    c. Cornelius
    d. The Jailer

4. FACTS CONCERNING CONVERSION
    a. Change of Life Rather than Change in Personal Traits
    b. Accomplished Through the Grace of God
    c. No One Good Enough without Conversion
    d. The More Contrite the Heart, the More Striking the Conversion
    e. Repentance Precedes Conversion
    f. Word of God Essential to Conversion
    g. God Uses Human Instrumentalities
    h. Youth the Time to Turn to God
    i. God Does the Turning

5. RESULTS OF CONVERSION
    a. "A New Creature"
    b. Adoption
    c. Humility
    d. Righteousness
    e. Sanctified Zeal
    f. Spirituality
    g. Christian Fellowship

## VII. REGENERATION

1. HOW CHARACTERIZED IN SCRIPTURE
    a. "Born again"
    b. "A new Creature"
    c. "Begotten"
    d. "Begotten again"
    e. "Washing of Regeneration"
    f. "Newness of Life"
    g. "Created in Christ Jesus"
    h. "The Divine Nature"
    i. "A new Heart"
    j. "The new Man"

2. WHAT REGENERATION IS NOT
    a. Not Mere Reformation
    b. Not Mere Conviction of Sin
    c. Not Joining Some Church
    d. Not Merely Being Moral
    e. Not Mere Social Uplift
    f. Not Merely Correct Doctrine

3. THE WORK OF REGENERATION
    a. The Work of God
    b. Wrought through the Word
    c. Man's Co-operation
    d. Not Needed by Innocent Child
    e. Essential to Salvation

4. EVIDENCES OF REGENERATION
   a. Righteousness
   b. The Sinless Life
   c. Spirit-filled Life
   d. Obedience
   e. Love
   f. Hatred of Evil
   g. Faith
   h. Victorious Life

## VIII. ADOPTION

1. ADOPTION PRESUPPOSES—
   a. People not of the Family of God
   b. God's Willingness to Adopt Them
   c. Their Willingness to be Adopted

2. SCRIPTURAL CONDITIONS FOR ADOPTION
   a. Faith
   b. Regeneration
   c. Scourging
   d. The Grace of God

3. THE BLESSINGS OF ADOPTION

4. EVIDENCES OF SONSHIP
   a. Following after the Spirit
   b. Obedience
   c. Confidence in God
   d. Love of the Brethren
   e. Peaceableness
   f. Godliness
   g. Love of Enemies

## IX. SANCTIFICATION

1. DEFINITIONS
   a. A Preparation
   b. To Hallow
   c. A Setting Apart
   d. Cleansed, Pure, Holy

2. SANCTIFYING AGENTS
   a. Divine Workmanship—Father, Son, Holy Ghost, the Word
   b. The Human Side—Faith, Knowledge, Obedience, Etc.

3. TIME OF SANCTIFICATION
   a. Instantaneous—at Time of Conversion
   b. Progressive—throughout the Christian's Experience

4. **RESULTS OF SANCTIFICATION**
    a. Union with Christ
    b. Christian Perfection
    c. Eternal Inheritance
    d. Preparation for Service
    e. A Continual Growth in Grace

## GOD'S PLAN OF SALVATION

The wisdom of God is evident when we remember that in His plan of redemption for lost souls human merit is entirely eliminated as a basis for salvation. Since it is the goodness and grace of God, rather than the goodness and judgment of man, through which our eternal salvation is wrought, it not only places salvation within the range of possibility for every human being, but it puts us under everlasting obligations to Him for the priceless boon which He gives us upon our fulfilling the necessary conditions.

As to what should be the proper arrangement of the chapters belonging to this group, opinions differ. Were we to study the subject from the standpoint of man we would begin with Faith; but since God accomplished our redemption even from the foundation of the world, we decided to begin with the work of God in the Atonement. But the arrangement of these subjects is more or less arbitrary, as there is no chronological order for their arrangement. They are all so completely interwoven that none of them can be dropped out of God's perfect plan of salvation.

For a description of this PLAN we turn to the language of inspiration:

"We ourselves also were sometimes foolish, disobedient, deceived, serving divers lusts and pleasures, living in malice and envy, hateful, and hating one another. But after that the kindness and love of God our Saviour toward man appeared, not by works of righteousness which we have done, but according to his mercy he saved us, by the washing of regeneration, and renewing of the Holy Ghost; which he shed on us abundantly, through Jesus Christ our Saviour; that being justified by his grace, we should be made heirs according to the hope of eternal life" (Tit. 3:3-7).

In the nine chapters which follow, this doctrine is presented in more extended detail, as taught in the Word of God.

# CHAPTER I

## THE ATONEMENT

Being reconciled, we shall be saved by his life. And not only so, but we also joy in God through our Lord Jesus Christ, by whom we have now received the atonement.—Romans 5:10, 11.

### THE DOCTRINE STATED

We were once far away from God. When man fell he not only became a creature of sin, but he was also without recourse or resource to get back to God. Of fallen man it is written: "All we like sheep have gone astray;" "All have sinned, and come short of the glory of God;" "Death passed upon all men, for that all have sinned." Neither by good works, nor by human goodness, nor by wealth, nor even by the law, could any man redeem himself from his sin-cursed state. Man was LOST—that tells the whole story.

But God, who had created man in His own image, was not willing that man should be without opportunity to shine in His image in eternity. So He made provision for man's redemption, in the person of His own dear Son. Jesus Christ, the only begotten of the Father, as "the Lamb of God that taketh away the sin of he world," died upon the cross as a ransom for our sins. "By his stripes we are healed," and "by one offering he hath perfected for ever them that are sanctified." Through the atoning merits of the shed blood of Jesus Christ we again have access to the Father, and as fellow heirs with Jesus Christ we may again face the future with hope.

### THE DAY OF ATONEMENT

The atonement, like other New Testament doctrines generally, is made clearer to us because of the things written in the Old Testament. Let us notice the day of atonement in both dispensations:

1. **Jewish.**—The Jews had a day of national humilation, kept the tenth day of the seventh month (Lev. 23:26, 27), on which occasion they came confessing their sins and an offering was made for the atonement of their sins. Two goats were prepared, one to be slain and the other to be allowed to escape into the wilderness as the scapegoat, through which sacrifice their sins were remitted and the guilty sinner allowed to go home free. The day was observed as a sabbath, and the atonement made in the holy place, for the high priest, and for the whole congregation. There were severe penalties prescribed for its nonobservance. The importance of the day becomes more apparent when it is remembered that it was on this day that the year of jubilee began. Ex. 30:10; Lev. 25:9; Heb. 9. This sacrifice was typical of the perfect Sacrifice to come. Heb. 9:8, 24; 10:14.

2. **Christian.**—We also have our day of atonement. As already noted, the Jewish sacrifices were but typical of the perfect Sacrifice, Jesus Christ. There was no efficacy in the sacrifices offered up under the law, except as they typified the perfect Sacrifice in which all the sacrifices under the law were fulfilled. "The law having a shadow of good things to come, and not the very image of the things, can never . . . make the comers thereunto perfect" (Heb. 10:1). We today can look upon our day of atonement in two senses: (1) We can look back to the day in which Jesus Christ hung bleeding on the cross, where "by one offering he hath perfected forever them that are sanctified" (Heb. 10:14). (2) The entire Gospel dispensation is a day of atonement, for we have continual access to the altar of the Lord our great High priest, not a moment in which we may not accept this Sacrifice as the atonement for our sins and go on our way rejoicing, forgiven and sinless. Through this wise providence of God

### The Death of Christ

becomes our eternal hope. We therefore look upon Him as:

1. **Our Ransom.**—In other words, He is our Redeemer, having offered Himself and paid the price for our redemption. Read Lev. 25:47-49. As Christ Himself said, He came "to give his life a ransom for many" (Matt. 20: 28). Peter tells us that we are redeemed by "the precious blood of Christ, as of a Lamb without blemish and without spot" (I Pet. 1:19). Paul adds his testimony, saying, "There is . . . one mediator between God and men, the man Christ Jesus, who gave himself a ransom for all" (I Tim. 2:5). By the payment of this ransom we have been freed from the curse of the law, and as "heirs of glory" we are under everlasting obligations to Him who paid the price for our redemption.

2. **Our Propitiation.**—"He is our propitiation" (I Jno. 2:2), the one "whom God hath set for a propitiation through faith in his blood" (Rom. 3:25). In other words, through the atoning merits of the blood of Jesus Christ we have been reconciled to God. Justice and mercy have met, and He is the "reconciliation for the sins of the people" (Heb. 2:17), the anger of a just God has been appeased, and we can now approach God with full confidence that the price has been paid, that the ends of justice have been met.

3. **Our Substitute.**—In the sacrifice of Jesus Christ in our stead, He became our substitute. As the ram caught in the bushes by his horns (Gen. 22:13) became the substitute for Isaac in that he was offered up in Isaac's stead, and as the paschal lamb in Egypt (Ex. 12) became the substitute for the firstborn in all the homes where the sign of the blood was found upon the door, so Christ, having "died for all" (II Cor. 5:15), became our substitute in paying the penalty for our sins. "All we like sheep have gone astray . . . and the Lord hath laid on HIM the iniq-

uity of us all" (Isa. 53:6). "He hath made him to be sin for us, who knew no sin; that we might be made the righteousness of God in him" (II Cor. 5:21).

4. **Our Advocate.**—The death of Jesus Christ on earth released Him to become our advocate in heaven. He was slain, paying the price for our redemption; rose in triumph, and became "the firstfruits of them that slept;" "shewed himself alive after his passion by many infallible proofs;" made provisions for "another Comforter" during the time of His absence from earth, after which He ascended to glory and is now at the right hand of the Father as our representative, our intercessor, our advocate. It is here that Stephen saw Him (Acts 7:55, 56), here that "he ever liveth to make intercession" (Heb. 7:25) for all "who come to God by him." "If any man sin, we have an advocate with the Father, Jesus Christ the righteous" (I Jno. 2:1).

### Some Erroneous Views

When a man says, "I believe in the atonement," he hasn't said very much unless he means to say that he believes that Jesus Christ died in our stead, that His blood was shed to atone for our sins, and that all who accept this redemptive price are thereby reconciled to God. It is customary for liberalists to speak in the language of orthodoxy and thus mislead unsuspecting people who would not be misled in a straight issue between faith and unbelief. There are a number of theories concerning the nature of Christ's death which on the face of them seem plausible, but which in reality are antagonistic to the doctrine of the atonement for sin through the shed blood of Jesus Christ upon the cross. Let us notice a few of them.

### 1. That Christ simply died the death of a martyr.

If His death was simply that of a martyr, why is it that the disciples never refer to it in that sense? So far as His persecutors were concerned, they were guilty of an even blacker crime than if as a mob they would simply have crucified an innocent man; but the death of Christ meant more than simply a martyr's death. This tragedy would never have been committed had martyrdom been the only consideration, for Christ had it within His power to call to His assistance more than twelve legions of angels from heaven. Matt. 26:53; 28:18. If His death was not vicarious and expiatory, then it was not only unnecessary but very foolish for Him to die under such circumstances. But Christ makes it plain that He died not because He was overpowered but because He voluntarily laid down His life for our sakes. Jno. 10:17. Peter says that He was "delivered by the determinate counsel and foreknowledge of God" (Acts 2:23). "Stephen died a martyr's death, but Paul never preached forgiveness through the death of Stephen. Such a view of Christ's death may beget martyrs but it can not save sinners."—Evans.

2. **That the death of Christ is simply a moral example of supreme heroism.**

If that was the purpose of His death, then it was indeed a lamentable failure. How many Jews have been converted through the influence of this heroism? Christ's heroism has been an inspiration to many of His followers, but His death was no more heroic than the rest of His life was. What the sinner needs is not example but salvation. Expiation, not example, is the great achievement of Christ upon the cross. As an example, His whole life furnishes a perfect object lesson on heroism.

3. **That the death of Christ was but an accident.**

Years ago we read a letter which was claimed to have been written by Pontius Pilate. In that letter the statement was made that had he had one more day to make preparations he would never have permitted Jesus to be crucified. Men have contended that the tragic death of Christ was but a mere incident, and that it would not have been necessary had it not been for the unfortunate combination of circumstances which brought His career to an untimely end. If that is the case, then much of the Bible ought to be rewritten. His declaration of His own power

(Matt. 26:53; 28:18) would be mere pretense, and the numerous scriptures showing that His death was necessary to bring about the redemption of man would be as accidental as that of His death. But why all this foolishness? Why not take God at His word, believe it, and thus believe the doctrine of the atonement as it is taught in the Bible?

4. **That Christ died to show people how much He loved them.**

Just as though God had not already shown His love to sinful men over and over again. Wherever the Bible refers to the love of God as connected with the death of His Son it is also in connection with the thought of salvation. "God so loved . . . gave his Son . . . everlasting life" (Jno. 3:16). "Herein is love . . . sent his only begotten Son . . . propitiation for our sins" (I Jno. 4:10). There are many ways in which God manifests His love to men, but there is but one way (through blood atonement) in which He accomplishes the salvation of men.

The one test by which all theories of the atonement may be proved to be either genuine or spurious is the question of what provisions are made for the BLOOD. Do they make room for Christ's vicarious suffering and substitutionary sacrifice, for our cleansing through the efficacy of His blood? The following, from the pen of Joseph Parker, states the Christian view of the atonement very forcibly: "As I speak now, at this very moment, I feel that the Christ on the cross is doing something for me, that His death is my life, His atonement is my pardon, His crucifixion the satisfaction for my sin, that from Calvary, that place of the skull, my flowers of peace and joy blossom forth, and that in the cross of Christ I glory."

### The Nature of Christ's Death

1. **It was by Divine decree.**

He was "delivered by the determinate counsel and foreknowledge of God" (Acts 2:23), this being God's plan for the redemption of sinful men.

## 2. It was voluntary.

There is abundant scriptural evidence that Christ was crucified, not because He was overpowered by superior force but because He willed it so. Read Matt. 26:47-57; Jno. 10:17, 18; 18:4-13. Little did His murderers think that it was through them that God was "causing the wrath of men to praise him," that they were but carrying out the plan of God whereby they themselves and others might have access to the cleansing power of the blood of the Lamb they were slaying.

## 3. It was penal.

The whole world was guilty before God. The penalty for guilt must be paid. On the cruel cross Christ paid the penalty, "A ransom for many" (Matt. 20:28), for "the Lord hath laid on HIM the iniquity of us all" (Isa. 53:6).

## 4. It was expiatory.

"The blood of Jesus Christ his Son cleanseth us from all sin" (I Jno. 1:7). In the crimson flood that flowed from Calvary there is cleansing power to wash away the sins of all who come to Him in faith. Looking toward "the Lamb of God which taketh away the sin of the world," we pray, "Wash me, and I shall be whiter than snow" (Psa. 51:7).

## 5. It was vicarious.

It was God's plan of "the just (dying) for the unjust" (I Pet. 3:18). The death of Jesus Christ upon the Cross means nothing to us if it does not mean that He was offered up in our stead, as our substitute. Upon the spotless Lamb the Lord laid the iniquity of a sinful world (Isa. 53:6), and the price was paid which let the guilty world go free—upon condition of our acceptance of God's terms.

Was this just? Yes; in this sense: The great heart of God went out to poor, lost, weak, fallen, sinful, helpless man; and like a generous-hearted philanthropist who assumes the just debts of one who is hopelessly involved in financial ruin and lets him go free, so this greatest of all benefactors assumed our debts and gave us another chance before God. A just debt has been justly paid, and all who accept this liberation thereby own their Deliverer, are reconciled to God, and are justified in His sight.

### 6. It was mediatorial.

"He is the mediator of the new testament, that by means of death, for the redemption of the transgressions that were under the first testament, they which are called might receive the promise of eternal inheritance" (Heb. 9:15). Read also Eph. 2:12-19.

### 7. It was heart-rending.

If you can imagine a favorite, lovable boy in your own home, whose innocence and purity and goodness have captivated your heart, ruthlessly taken hold of by a vicious mob, shamefully persecuted, nailed to a cross, and compelled to hang there in excruciating pain for six long hours, you have some idea of what Mary the mother of Jesus suffered on that occasion. Then add the thought of this innocent boy's becoming the scapegoat of all criminals in that the sins of the whole world are laid upon Him, and you have some idea of why the sun refused to shine upon Him and the face of the Father, who was too pure to look upon sin, was turned away from Him. The climax is reached when this innocent, spotless Lamb, now burdened with the sins of the world, betrayed by a friend, forsaken by His disciples, treading the wine press alone while even the sun withholds its light and the Father turns aside His face, cries out from the innermost depths of His soul, "My God! my God! why hast thou forsaken me?" The Son of man was dying! He "cried with a loud voice, and gave up the ghost!"

> "What did thine only Son endure,
> Before I drew my breath,
> What pain, what labor, to secure
> My soul from endless death!

> "Well might the sun in darkness hide,
>   And shut his glories in,
> When God's own Son was crucified
>   For man, the creature's sin."

## 8. It was glorious.

See the Son of God upon the cross. In the midst of His sufferings He prays for His enemies, speaks the words of peace and pardon to the wretched thief by His side, makes provisions for His mother, and commits His all to the Father. The marvelous power of God was manifest in the rending of the rocks, the quaking of the earth, and the veil of the temple was rent in twain from top to bottom—so wonderful and awe-inspiring were the last three hours of the crucifixion that even the Roman centurion and they who were with him were impelled to cry out and say, "Truly, this was the Son of God." By His death Christ effected our reconciliation with God (Rom. 5:10; II Cor. 5: 18-20; Heb. 2:17), the remission of our sins (Matt. 20:28; I Tim. 2:6; Heb. 9:12), our justification (Rom. 5:9; II Cor. 5:21), our deliverance (Rom. 8:3; Gal. 6:14; Heb. 2: 14, 15), our sanctification (Eph. 5:26, 27; Tit. 2:14; Heb. 13:12), and unnumbered millions of souls will be glorified together with Him in eternity. "Oh that men would praise the Lord for his goodness, and for his wonderful works to the children of men!"

> "When all Thy mercies, O my God,
>   My rising soul surveys,
> Transported with the view, I'm lost
>   In wonder, love, and praise."

### WHO IS BENEFITED

## 1. The whole world is included in God's terms of salvation.

God's invitation is extended to "all the ends of the earth" (Isa. 45:22), and salvation is free to "whosoever believeth" (Jno. 3:16). It is not God's will that "any should perish" (II Pet. 3:9), and Christ gave Himself "a ransom for all" (I Tim. 2:6). In God's great plan of salvation there is provision made for all men, in every clime and age, as He "is no respecter of persons." Christ's commission to His disciples to "teach all nations . . . to observe all things whatsoever" He commanded them is in keeping with the Divine Plan that provisions should be made for the salvation of all people.

2. **The atonement is available to all penitent believers.**

While the atonement is for all, it is available to such only as are willing to accept the conditions; for salvation is forced upon no one. The Scriptures abound in evidence that only penitent believers who accept Jesus Christ as their Saviour and Lord can be saved. This point is made clear in the chapters on Faith and Repentance.

To use a familiar illustration: A billionaire makes a huge deposit in a bank and invites all people involved in debt to draw on this fund until all their debts are fully paid. While the offer is to "whosoever" and all have an opportunity to become debt-free, only such as will avail themselves of the opportunity will share in the benefits of the generous offer. So with the redemption price paid by our Lord—it is free for all, but only such as avail themselves of the opportunity will become debt-free.

The fact that *only* penitent believers may be saved, emphasizes the other fact that *all* penitent believers *will* be saved, subject to the promises of God and His terms of salvation. To all such the message comes: "Ye are bought with a price: therefore glorify God in your body, and in your spirit, which are God's."

# CHAPTER II

## REDEMPTION

*We have redemption through his blood, the forgiveness of sins, according to the riches of his grace.—Eph. 1:7.*

No sooner had man fallen than God provided a plan for his redemption. This chapter is very closely related to the one that precedes it. It is impossible to speak of the atonement without including redemption, and the only possible redemption for man is through the atoning merits of the blood of Jesus. But while in the former chapter we emphasized the work of Christ in securing redemption for us, in this chapter we mean to place the emphasis upon what this redemptive work means for us.

The meaning of redemption is to buy back, to liberate, to deliver. Lev. 25:25-27; I Cor. 6:20; 7:23. As land that has been confiscated for debt may be redeemed by the payment of a required sum of money or upon other considerations, so the soul of man, hopelessly lost in sin, has by the grace of God, been redeemed by the blood of the Lamb.

### "Sold under Sin"

The condition of man in his fallen state is pathetically stated in the words, "I am carnal, sold under sin" (Rom. 7:14). As Esau, for a mere mess of pottage, sold his birthright, so the poor sinner sells his birthright in the world beyond for a mere "morsel of meat" with which the tempter effects his eternal ruin. Being sold, he is without recourse,—a poor, lost, helpless, miserable mortal, destined to be doomed forever in the eternal flames.

### "Redeemed by the Blood"

It being impossible for man to effect his own redemption (Psa. 49:7); his only chance for redemption is through the shedding of the precious blood of Jesus, and through which the redemptive price is paid. I Cor. 1:30. Peter tells us that we are redeemed, not with corruptible things as silver and gold, "but with the precious blood of Christ" (I Pet. 1:18, 19). Listen to the song of the redeemed in glory: "Thou art worthy . . . for thou wast slain, and hast redeemed us to God by thy blood out of every kindred, and tongue, and people, and nation" (Rev. 5:9). Thank God, we may begin to sing that song here.

### God's Redemptive Plan

**1. He sent His Son into the world.**
Read carefully Eph. 1:1-14.

**2. He sent His Spirit into the world.**
His mission is to "reprove the world of sin, of righteousness, and of judgment" (Jno. 16:8). Through the convicting power of the Spirit sinful man is impelled to cry out, "Who shall deliver me from the body of this death" (Rom. 7:24)?

**3. He has decreed that man must be redeemed through sacrifice.**
"Without shedding of blood is no remission" (Heb. 9:22). Man must continue under the curse of the law until redeemed by the sacrifice of "the Lamb of God, which taketh away the sin of the world" (Jno. 1:29).

**4. Human sacrifice can not avail.**
Of human effort it is written, "Not of yourselves . . . not of works, lest any man should boast" (Eph. 2:8, 9). Man can not be redeemed by corruptible things as silver and gold (I Pet. 1:18, 19), nor "by works of righteousness" (Tit. 3:5), nor by the law (Heb. 10:1); for there is no other avenue left for man but to turn to God for His redeeming grace.

**5. Christ is our only hope.**
"When the fulness of time was come, God sent forth his Son, made of a woman, made under the law, to re-

deem them that were under the law, that we might receive the adoption of sons" (Gal. 4:4, 5). The price for our redemption was paid in "the precious blood of Jesus," and our gratitude goes out to God in that "by one offering he hath perfected for ever them that are sanctified" (Heb. 10:14). Read Lev. 17:11; Acts 20:28; Rom. 5:6-8; II Cor. 5:14; Heb. 9:12, 22.

### REDEMPTION FOR ALL

One of the refreshing thoughts connected with God's plan of redemption is that it is for all people, in all nations, in every clime and age. That not all people will be privileged to sing Redemption's blessed story in eternity is wholly the fault of man, for God made every provision for the eternal redemption of all people. Redemption is—

1. **For the Old Testament Saints.**—"He is the mediator of the new testament, that by means of death, for the redemption of the transgressions that were under the first testament, they which are called might receive the promise of eternal inheritance" (Heb. 9:15).

2. **For the New Testament Saints.**—"Who gave himself for us, that he might redeem us from all iniquity, and purify unto himself a peculiar people, zealous of good works" (Tit. 2:14).

3. **For the Wicked.**—"For Christ hath once suffered for sins, the just for the unjust, that he might bring us to God, being put to death in the flesh, but quickened by the Spirit" (I Pet. 3:18). Read also Rom. 5:8.

4. **For all the World.**—"Thou art worthy to take the book, and to open the seals thereof: for thou wast slain, and hast redeemed us to God by thy blood out of every kindred, and tongue, and people, and nation" (Rev. 5:9).

### REDEMPTION FROM WHAT

1. **From Sin.**—"He shall save his people from their sins" (Matt. 1:21). Read also Rom. 6:18-24; 8:3.

2. **From the Bondage and Curse of the Law.**—"Christ

9

hath redeemed us from the curse of the law . . . to redeem them that were under the law, that we might receive the adoption of sons" (Gal. 3:15; 4:5). Read also Rom. 8:1, 2.

3. **From the Dominion of the World.**—"Who gave himself for our sins, that he might deliver us from this present evil world" (Gal. 1:4). It was this deliverance in which Paul rejoiced, saying "God forbid that I should glory, save in the cross of our Lord Jesus Christ, by whom the world is crucified unto me, and I unto the world" (Gal. 6:14).

4. **From the Power of the Devil.**—"That through death he might destroy him that hath the power of death, that is, the devil; and deliver them that through fear of death were all their lifetime subject to bondage" (Heb. 2: 14, 15).

5. **From Death.**—"The last enemy to be destroyed is death" (I Cor. 15:26). The promise is, "I will ransom them from the power of the grave; I will redeem them from death" (Hos. 13:14). The grave has no terrors for the ransomed of the Lord, for the return of the body to dust means also a return of the spirit to God, and in the end there will be a "redemption of the body" (Rom. 2:23) as well as of the soul.

6. **From Destruction.**—While the wicked will be "punished with everlasting destruction" (II Thess. 1:9), the righteous rest assured in the hope of Him "who redeemeth thy life from destruction" (Psa. 103:4). The redemption through the blood of Jesus is perfect and complete, reaching all people who accept the price paid for their redemption and delivering them from the curse of sin, both in this life and in that which is to come.

### Results of Redemption

We have already seen that the work of redemption is universal in its application, reaching "whosoever will" in every clime and age. Let us notice, in conclusion, that it means not only a deliverance from every form of evil but also an inheritance of every form of blessing. It procures for the redeemed—

1. **Reconciliation to God.**—"And you, that were sometime alienated and enemies in your mind by wicked works, yet now hath he reconciled in the body of his flesh through death, to present you holy and unblameable, and unreprovable in his sight; *if ye continue* in the faith grounded and settled, and be not moved away from the hope of the gospel" (Col. 1:21-23). Two things are especially mentioned: (1) Reconciliation of man to God through the death of His Son; (2) "if ye continue . . . and be not moved from the hope of the gospel." Another thought worthy of note is that God has at all times been willing to be reconciled, sacrificing His only begotten Son to that end. He has done His full part, and made it possible for man to do his. Are *we* willing?

2. **Forgiveness of Sins.**—"In whom we have redemption through his blood, even the forgiveness of sins" (Col. 1:14). In his letter to the Ephesians Paul states this same truth, adding that we get this forgiveness "through the richness of his grace." In other words, when we accept God's proffered terms of redemption we are only "sinners, saved by grace."

3. **Justification.**—"Being justified freely by his grace, through the redemption that is in Christ Jesus" (Rom. 3:24). The redemption wrought through Christ not only saves us from sin but also brings the recognition from God that justifies us in His sight and imputes unto us the righteousness of Jesus Christ.

4. **Heavenly Peculiarity.**—"That he might redeem us from all iniquity, and purify unto himself a peculiar people, zealous of good works" (Tit. 2:14). Peter gives us a similar thought, declaring the people of God to be "a chosen generation, a royal priesthood, an holy nation, a peculiar people" (I Pet. 2:9). We call this a "heavenly peculiarity," for it portrays the people of God as having

been called out from a sinful world, as "a people for God's own possession" (R.V.).

5. **Adoption.**—"The adoption of sons" (Gal. 4:5), Paul calls it. We thank God that through the redemptive work of Christ we belong to a new family, the family of God.

6. **Sanctification.**—"Christ also loved the church, and gave himself for it; that he might sanctify and cleanse it with the washing of water by the word, that he might present it to himself a glorious church" (Eph. 5:25-27). Read also Tit. 2:11-14; Heb. 10:9, 10, 14; 13:12. It is the crowning work of God for His people.

When we remember that the redeemed of the Lord, saved and "sanctified and meet for the Master's use," are His own "purchased possession" (I Cor. 6:20; Heb. 1:14), that they walk safely on the King's highway of holiness (Isa. 35:8, 9) awaiting the time when with the ransomed hosts of God they will return to Zion with joy (v. 10), and they alone will sing together redemption's blessed story in heaven, we have reasons to praise the Lord with overflowing gladness and to serve Him faithfully and willingly the remainder of our days.

# CHAPTER III

## FAITH

Faith is the substance of things hoped for, the evidence of things not seen.—Hebrews 11:1.

The three essential elements of faith are: belief, confidence, trust. It is (1) "the substance of things hoped for," (2) "the evidence of things not seen." In other words, it supplements the things of which we gain our knowledge through the special senses. Some things we know because we have perceived them through the sense of sight, of hearing, of touch, etc.; other things we know only upon the assurance of others in whom we have confidence. For instance, you believe that such men as Caesar, Luther, Washington, and other historic characters existed, not because you have seen or heard them but because you have perfect confidence in the channels through which you get your information. Things that come to us direct through the special senses are not faith but knowledge.

Faith rests upon evidence. We believe in God because we have such substantial assurances, such incontrovertible evidences of His existence that all doubt on this point has vanished and we accept it without question. Another thought about faith is that we can not get through life without it. Men cry out against it, claiming that it is ignorance which prompts people to accept something as a fact without direct and positive first-hand evidence; but their very life belies their claim, for there is scarcely a day but that they take others' word for things without question. For instance, in taking a train for a distant point which they have never seen, they take the word of the railroad men without first investigating for themselves as to whether the things said by the men or found in the railroad guides are true. So on every hand they are surrounded by things or circumstances concerning which they know absolutely nothing except what others have told them. As Christian faith is essential to Christian life, so faith in the abstract is essential to any kind of life. This leads us to a consideration of the first of our subjects; namely, the

### Kinds of Faith

Of these we may make several classifications. The term "faith" may be applied in a general way, as "We walk by faith," or, as in Luke 18:8 and Jude 3, it may be applied to "the body of revealed truth."

Again, faith may be the result of our confidence in men or causes, or it may be a special gift as set forth in I Cor. 12:9.

Again, we may speak of faith as being either a natural or a Christian faith. To recall a former illustration: When you go to a ticket window you take the agent's word for any information he may see fit to give you with reference to route, change of trains, time when you are expected to reach your destination, etc. You hear announcements made in church, read of some frightful accidents, hear of some unexpected death in your community, and you accept all these things as facts, though you have only other people's word for it. This is what we choose to call natural faith, a matter-of-fact confidence which human beings have in each other.

When it comes to Christian faith, we enter a new realm. The persons or beings whom we are called upon to believe are not seen but unseen. The man with natural faith only, stops at the limit of his own personal knowledge or the knowledge of others in whom he has confidence. His faith stops with the creation (or, perhaps, with the dawn of history) on the one hand, and with death on the other. But the man possessed with Christian faith goes beyond this. He believes that the Bible is a divine and miraculous revelation from God to man; that Jesus Christ

is the Son of God, was born of a virgin, gave us an unerring Gospel, died for our sins, rose for our justification.
In short, while man with only a natural faith has a faith
that is earthly, man with a Christian faith has a faith that
is heavenly. This is the kind of faith discussed in this
chapter.

From this viewpoint we also wish to consider two
other kinds of faith; namely, a dead faith and a living faith.

1. "Dead" Faith.—We get this name from what is
often called a "historical faith" from the writings of James
(2:14-26), who makes works a test of real faith. The keynote of his teaching on this point is that "faith without
works is dead." In other words, where works are lacking
it is an evidence that the faith is not genuine. For illustration: you hear of a land where expenses are nominal
and riches are easily acquired; where society is ideal, home
seems like heaven, the climate is healthful, sickness is rare,
and everybody is happy and contented. Are you going?
No? Why not? You may have some good reasons for not
going, but the probable explanation for it is your lack of
faith in the correctness of the report. If you give any
credence to reports, your faith is so weak that it does not
move you to act. You may build air castles, but you stay
where you are.

Now the Bible tells us of a land that is all that, and
much more. We call the land heaven. The most enticing
country known to man is as nothing compared with this
celestial land. Yet there are multitudes of people who profess to have faith in God and His Word who are no more
stirred by the prospects of heaven than if they had never
heard of such a place; their life is as devoid of spiriutality
as is that of the average worldling around them. If they
have any faith at all, it is a "dead" faith, for it produces
little or no works.

2. Living Faith.—It is the "faith which worketh"
(Gal. 5:6) that constitutes the living faith. It is the faith
that grips the soul and moves the individual to act. Why

does the farmer sow his grain? He has faith that there will be a harvest. Why do men deposit money in a bank? They have faith in its stability. What if there were no expectation of a harvest, no faith in the stability of the bank? No seeding, no money deposited. What moved the eunuch to call for baptism (Acts 8:37, 38) and Cornelius to send for Peter (Acts 10)? Faith. Why do some people fall away from God? Because of lack of faith. It is the living faith that grips the heart of man, moves him to seek God's pardoning grace; and having found this grace, to keep it to the end.

### ESSENTIAL TO SALVATION

"Believe on the Lord Jesus Christ, and thou shalt be saved" (Acts 16:31). "He that believeth not is condemned" (Jno. 3:18). God warns us that "without faith it is impossible to please him" (Heb. 11:6). These positive declarations assure us that the only possibly way to the saving grace of God is through the avenue of living faith. According to the plan of God it is: No faith, no salvation.

### HOW FAITH COMES

1. **By Hearing.**—"Faith cometh by hearing, and hearing by the word of God" (Rom. 10:17). It is the plan of God that people are to be brought to a knowledge of the truth through the instrumentality of their fellow men. Of the unsaved millions it is said, "How shall they believe in him of whom they have not heard? and how shall they hear without a preacher" (Rom. 10:14)?

2. **By the Word of God.**—The burden of Rom. 10:14-17 is, "Faith cometh by hearing . . . the word of God."

3. **By Prayer.**—The prayer of the disciples to their Lord, "Increase our faith" (Luke 17:5), should be ours also. It was the prayer of Cornelius (Acts 10:30, 31) that brought the messenger who led him and his household into the living faith. Do you feel a lack of overcoming faith? Pray. Do you feel that others should be blessed with a

stronger faith? Pray. Do you feel the need of a revival that will bring both saved and unsaved into the realms of a victorious faith? Pray.

4. **By the Spirit.**—"To another, faith by the same Spirit" (I Cor. 12:9). It being the mission of the Spirit to lead us into all truth (Jno. 16:13), to testify of Christ (Jno. 15:26), to bring the Gospel of Christ to our remembrance (Jno. 14:26), we can see that through Him the saints of God are led into fuller faith, while through His convicting power sinners are moved to accept the faith brought to sinful men through the preaching of the Word.

5. **Through the Example of Others.**—"Be thou an example of the believers" (I Tim. 4:12). As your faith becomes stronger through the influence of others, so your influence over others will strengthen or weaken their faith, depending upon the kind of example that you are.

## What Faith Does

Faith is the key that unlocks the door to all the blessings of a saved life. Christ sums it all up when He says, "He that believeth and is baptized shall be saved; but he that believeth not shall be damned" (Mark 16:16). That we may know what is the richness of this treasury of faith, let us turn to the Word of God and learn through the language of inspiration what faith means to the believer:

1. **It assures salvation.**

"Believe on the Lord Jesus Christ, and thou shalt be saved" (Acts 16:31). Read also Jno. 3:16; Rom. 3:28; 5:1.

2. **It assures us a place in the family of God.**

"As many as received him, to them gave he power to become the sons of God, even to them that believe on his name" (Jno. 1:12). "For ye are all the children of God by faith in Christ Jesus" (Gal. 3:26).

3. **It insures justification.**

"By him all that believe are justified" (Acts 13:39). "Therefore we conclude that a man is justified by faith, without the deeds of the law" (Rom. 3:28).

#### 4. It brings joy and peace.

"Though now we see him not, yet believing, we rejoice with joy unspeakable and full of glory" (I Pet. 1:8). "Being justified by faith, we have peace with God through our Lord Jesus Christ" (Rom. 5:1).

#### 5. It secures healing for the body.

"The prayer of faith shall save the sick, and the Lord shall raise him up" (Jas. 5:13-15). The day of miracles, even in the healing of the body, is not past.

#### 6. It affords a shield to the Christian.

"Above all, taking the shield of faith, wherewith ye shall be able to quench all the fiery darts of the wicked" (Eph. 6:16).

#### 7. It puts an end to boasting.

"Where is boasting then? It is excluded. By what law? of works? Nay: but by the law of faith" (Rom. 3:27).

#### 8. The Christian is guided through faith.

"We walk by faith, not by sight" (II Cor. 5:7). Walking by sight, we walk "according to this world." Walking by faith, our heavenward steps are directed by our trust in God.

#### 9. Through it we are sanctified.

"To open their eyes, and to turn them from darkness to light, and from the power of Satan unto God, that they may receive forgiveness of sins, and inheritance among them which are sanctified by faith" (Acts 26:18).

#### 10. It binds us to God.

"In whom ye also trusted, after that ye heard the word of truth, the gospel of your salvation: in whom also, after that ye believed, ye were sealed with that Holy Spirit of promise" (Eph. 1:13). Read also Jno. 6:67-69; I Pet. 1:5.

#### 11. It assures power.

"If ye have faith as a grain of mustard seed, ye shall say unto this mountain, Remove hence to yonder place, and it shall remove; and nothing shall be impossible unto you" (Matt. 17:20). "All things are possible to him that believeth" (Mark 9:23). There is an inseparable connection between faith and power. Mountains of difficulty vanish before the power of the prayer of faith.

**12. It assures** OVERCOMING **power.**

"This is the victory that *overcometh the world,* even our faith" (I Jno. 5:4). For a further study of what faith does for the believer, read the eleventh chapter of Hebrews.

### THE TRIAL OF OUR FAITH

James presents the practical side of faith when he reminds us that "faith without works is dead." It is easier to say, "I believe," than it is to demonstrate this belief in actual trial or test. So long as there were only loaves and fishes to hand out everybody seemed to believe in Jesus; but when He preached His Bread of Life Sermon (Jno. 6) which put people to the actual test it is said that "many of his disciples went back and walked no more with him." Their faith had been tried, and found wanting. The trial of faith, therefore,

**1. Proves the genuineness of our profession.**

Christ's searching sermon on the Bread of Life resulted in a culling out of the faithless disciples. The faithful ones remained with Him; the rest "went back." Another example is furnished in the story of Ruth. She stood the test, went all the way with Naomi, while Orpah, much as she would have liked to go along, turned back when she was brought face to face with all that going along would mean. So today there is a sifting out of the unfaithful among church members in every time of great opposition or temptation, in which case the faithful ones remain while the unfaithful ones become backsliders.

**2. "Worketh patience."**

James' testimony, "The trying of your faith worketh patience" (1:3), is often verified in the lives of Christian people. There is a refining power in the trials of life which burn out the dross and brings out the best that is in man. Examples: Abraham, when he was called upon to offer up the child of promise; Joseph, persecuted by his brothers and enslaved and imprisoned in Egypt; Daniel and his three companions in Babylon. "Count it all joy," therefore, "when ye fall into divers temptations" (Jas. 1:2), knowing that God supplies the grace to bear it (I Cor. 10:13) and that every trial when endured adds to the richness of our lives and usefulness in the service of God and men.

### 3. When endured, it insures the crown of life.

They who stand the test can say with Paul in the end, "Henceforth there is laid up for me a crown of righteousness, which the Lord, the righteous judge, shall give me at that day" (II Tim. 4:7, 8).

### The Christian's Attitude Toward Faith

One question remains: What should be the Christian's attitude toward faith? Turning to the Word, we find the following for our admonition:

### 1. "Believe on the Lord Jesus Christ" (Acts 16:31).

This text has been considered before as a condition for salvation. We now submit it for your consideration as a Christian duty. Obey this commandment, and you will naturally comply with all the requirements of the Christian faith. It binds us to Christ in His threefold character: (1) "Lord"—our Master, in authority over us in all things; (2) "Jesus"—the Man from Galilee, who was born of a woman, and came in the flesh; (3) "Christ"—the anointed of God. If your faith includes an acceptance of Christ in this threefold sense, you have met all the requirements of the Christian faith.

If you would be impressed with your Christian duty to believe, take your Bible and see how often we are commanded or exhorted to believe.

### 2. "Contend earnestly for the faith" (Jude 3).

It is not enough that we simply believe; we are exhorted to promulgate this belief. This attitude is admirably exemplified in Luke 1:1-4. We prove the sincerity of our faith in Jesus by faithfully supporting His Gospel and making it known to others.

3. **"Stand fast in the faith"** (I Cor. 16:13).

This suggests several thoughts: (1) Having accepted the faith of Jesus, stick to it—"stand fast." (2) While others fall away, be sure that you "stand fast," be "unmoveable" (I Cor. 15:58). (3) Do not give it passive assent only, but embrace it with your whole heart—"stand fast." (4) Let your steadfastness be in *"the faith," not the doctrines* of man.

Lest any one might get the idea that faith in the abstract—without a thought of obedience—is sufficient, let us remember this warning from God through James: "Faith without works is dead."

4. **"Be thou an example. . . . in faith"** (I Tim. 4:12).

Your obligations do not end with yourself, but extend to others also. Let your example be such as to encourage others to accept the faith, and live it.

5. **"Continue in the faith"** (Col. 1:23; I Tim. 2:15).

The faith of Jesus Christ is not intended for temporary service but for a continuance unto the end. One of the most important words connected with Christian life and service is the word CONTINUE.

6. **"Lord, increase our faith"** (Luke 17:5).

Where this is our daily prayer we will not be disappointed.

# CHAPTER IV

## REPENTANCE

Godly sorrow worketh a repentance not to be repented of.—II Corinthians 7:10.

The first thought to be impressed upon our minds as we study this subject is that repentance is a primary Gospel requirement which none should lightly esteem. It was the opening message in the ministry of John the Baptist (Matt. 3:2), in the ministry of Christ (Matt. 4:17), in the ministry of the Spirit (Acts 2:38), and occupied a prominent place in the teaching of the disciples—all in harmony with this declaration in the ministry to the Gentiles: "God . . . now commandeth all men every where to repent" (Acts 17:30). Our study of the subject will be conducted under four heads: What it is, what it is not, how brought about, other facts.

### WHAT REPENTANCE IS

The essential elements of repentance may be stated in four words: Conviction, contrition, confession, restitution. In other words, it includes a consciousness of guilt, a godly sorrow for sin, a desire to forsake sin, a confession of sin, and a willingness to make restitution for sin. At this point it might be well to note that while the Bible speaks of God as repenting (Gen. 6:6; I Sam. 15:11, in none of these cases did He repent in the sense that man repents, for "God is not a man, that he should lie; neither the son of man that he should repent" (Num. 23:19); and being perfect in every respect He is subject neither to error nor to sin. And while God at times represents Himself as man and speaks as man (as He did to Abraham—Gen. 22:12), and in this sense meets changed conditions in the semblance of repentance, yet we should not forget that with Him "is no variableness, neither shadow of turning" (Jas. 1:17). But to the question: What takes place when one repents?

1. **Conviction.**—This is the first step in repentance. Because of things seen and heard, the conviction grows upon us that we have done wrong—as was the case with the multitudes on the day of Pentecost (Acts 2), the jailer (Acts 16), and Paul after beholding the martyr Stephen (Acts 7:58; 9:5; 22:20). The two powerful factors in bringing about conviction are the Holy Spirit (Jno. 16:8), and the conscience (Rom. 2:15).

2. **Godly Sorrow.**—Let us notice that not all sorrow can be classed as "godly sorrow." People convicted of crime often weep and mourn as though their hearts would break; but it is grief over their dilemma, rather than penitence for sin. Judas Iscariot was sorrowful enough to go and hang himself, yet that did not move him to come back to Christ for restitution and for pardon. Paul in II Cor. 7:10, speaks of a "godly sorrow" and a "sorrow of the world." The first "worketh a repentance not to be repented of;" the second, "worketh death." No man has ever truly repented of any sin without a deep feeling of sorrow because of it. Penitence without sorrow is unheard of in the experience of any penitent sinner; but it is grief for having sinned against God or man, a smitten conscience and consequent contrition, and not grief over being found out.

3. **Confession.**—A sense of shame and humiliation usually accompanies true penitence for sin, but this does not keep back the sinner from confessing his sins. On the other hand, true penitence invariably prompts confession of the things repented of. "Confess your faults one to another," is not only a command, but it is also *the rule* among those who are truly enlightened and truly penitent. Other things being equal, the greater the reluctance in confessing, the less penitence there is in the heart because of sins committed. "With the heart man believeth unto

righteousness; and with the mouth confession is made unto salvation" (Rom. 10:10).

4. **Forsaking Sin.**—Balaam, Saul, Achan, and others confessed, "I have sinned," but they kept right on sinning as though they had never confessed. David, and the prodigal son, and others, also, made the same confession, but they forsook their sins and turned to ways of righteousness. The truly penitent not only confess their sins but they also forsake them. "How shall we, that are dead to sin, live any longer therein" (Rom. 6:2)?

5. **Restitution.**—Were you ever truly penitent for any sin you committed that you did not feel that you wanted to make it right? Restitution belongs to true penitence. This includes making wrongs right with both God and man. Zacchaeus had the right attitude when he said, "If I have taken any thing from any man by false accusation, I restore him fourfold" (Luke 19:8). It was this attitude on his part that enabled Christ to say, "This day is salvation come to this house."

6. **A Change of Heart.**—A man may change his mind and quit his bad habits, but still be an unforgiven sinner. He may be very sorry for what he has done (because he is found out), "but the sorrow of the world worketh death." He may, for policy's sake, even make restitution and live the life of a respectable man, and still his righteousness be as "filthy rags." While all the things so far named are essential elements of repentance, it takes a changed heart to complete the experience. In every case of true repentance there is a change of mind, a change of feelings, a change of attitude toward sin and righteousness, and a change of heart.

## What Repentance Is Not

The closing thought of the last paragraph is the opening thought of the present one. While all the above-named things are essentials, none of them alone (except the last, which includes all the rest) constitutes repentance. Therefore—

## 1. A mere change of mind is not repentance.

A gambler decides that he has about enough money, so he retires from his nefarious business. He is a gambler still—unless a godly sorrow for his sins impels him to forsake his sins, in heart as well as in physical practice, and he makes his wrongs right so far as it lies within his power to do so. The same application may be made to every known sin. Not, Have you changed your mind? but, *Why* have you changed your mind? is the vital question.

## 2. It is not merely being sorry because sins have been committed.

Judas and Peter were both sorry for what they had done, but only Peter returned to the Lord for restitution and pardon. The only sorrow for sin that belongs to repentance is the kind that grips the soul, impels the penitent sinner to come to God for pardon, to forsake his sins, to make his wrongs right.

## 3. It is not joining some church.

Some people actually join some church that it may be easier to keep on sinning without getting into ill repute. Joining the Church is right, provided the applicant is right before God, but it is not a substitute for repentance.

## 4. It is not merely confessing sin.

Thousands, like Balaam, Saul, and Judas Iscariot, have confessed, "I have sinned," and kept right on sinning, the same as before. There is no special virtue in confessing sins—unless it is prompted by godly sorrow for sin.

## 5. It is not mere reform.

True repentance brings genuine reform, in all things where the light of the Gospel makes the penitent sinner conscious of his wrong-doing; but a man may give up all his bad habits, and still cherish them in his heart. A reform, to be recognized in heaven, must be from the heart.

WHAT BRINGS REPENTANCE

### 1. The goodness of God.

In the first place, repentance itself is a gift from God. II Tim. 2:25. While repentance is man's part in God's plan of salvation, no man can claim any credit for it, since it is the goodness of God that leads us to repentance. Rom. 2:4. What was it but the goodness of God that brought Christ our Saviour within the reach of man? that preserved the Bible intact after centuries of desperate effort to destroy or to discredit it? that led such men as Peter, John, Paul, and others of God's servants to repentance and into positions where we, through them, have access to the Gospel? that preserved our own lives until, by the grace of God, we became willing to give our hearts to Him? Yes, it is the GOODNESS OF GOD that leads us to repentance. Let us reverently acknowledge His grace and show by a penitent life that we appreciate this goodness.

### 2. Hearing the truth.

"Faith cometh by hearing, and hearing by the word of God" (Rom. 10:17). How can a man believe himself a sinner without having a knowledge of that fact? The preaching of God's Word in its fullness is a very necessary work in bringing sinners to repentance. It took a Nathan to bring the message of "Thou art the man" (II Sam. 12:7) to David before that erring monarch was brought to dust and ashes. It took the preaching of Jonah to bring the Ninevites to repentance. Because they heard, they repented. The three thousand Pentecostal converts were made such through the preaching of Peter and the other disciples.

### 3. Convicting power of the Spirit.

To "reprove the world of sin" (Jno. 16:8) is one of the principal missions of the Holy Spirit. What we call "conviction" on the part of the penitent sinner is but the result of the operation of the Spirit upon his heart and conscience.

#### 4. A knowledge of sin.

Until the sinner is conscious of his sinful condition there can be no repentance for sin. True, there may be a prodding on the part of the Spirit, so that there is a consciousness that something is wrong, as is the case of the troubled heathen longing after—something; but he must first be shown wherein he is wrong before he can be led to repent of whatever wrong exists.

#### 5. Abhorrence of sin.

People seldom turn away from sin so long as it tastes sweet. The drunkard who loves his liquor, the sportsman who delights in sinful pleasures, the nicotinized man who is charmed with his tobacco, the fashion-monger who loves the glittering sins of this world—all are hopeless victims until they are brought to the point where they abhor the evils which are dragging them downward. The sinner who feels himself "down and out" and like Job abhors himself and repents "in dust and ashes" (Job 42:6), is much more easily reached than is the sinner who is blinded to his condition through love of sin. It is when people "abhor that which is evil" that they are ready to "cleave to that which is good."

#### 6. Faith in God.

You believe that God is your Friend, loving and true. He tells you of your awful condition and of sin's awful results. Knowledge of sin deepens into conviction, and conviction into contrition; your heart is crushed and your soul cries out to God. This takes place only when people believe in God, for people are never moved by any warning which they believe to be untrue.

#### 7. Rewards and penalties.

This should not be our motive in serving God, but there is no denying the fact that it exerts a powerful influence in bringing sinners to their senses. The growing tendency to sneer at the idea of preaching about hell to awaken sinners to their dangers ahead is responsible to a large extent for the rising tide of crime. Why are there so few people destroyed through drinking rank poison, jumping over mighty precipices, or plunging into molten iron? They know the certain results. Why has hell so little terror for the sinner? It is not generally preached; too few people believe that there is such a place. The cause of salvation suffers, and sinners die in their sins, because preachers are faint-hearted in warning sinners to flee from the terrible wrath to come.

### Fundamental Facts

#### 1. Repentance is commanded.

God (Acts 17:30), Christ (Matt. 4:17), John the Baptist (Matt. 3:2), the apostles (Mark 6:12; Acts 2:38; 20:21), all commanded it in unmistakable terms. It is divinely commanded to be taught "among all nations" (Luke 24:47), God commanding "all men every where to repent."

#### 2. It is essential to salvation.

"Except ye repent, ye shall all likewise perish" (Luke 13:3, 5). It is remarkable that the first and last recorded public utterances of Christ (Matt. 4:17; Luke 24:47) on earth were on the subject of repentance. Since "the soul that sinneth, it shall die," it follows that one sin in the soul unrepented of means eternal death. "Repent ye therefore, and be converted, that your sins may be blotted out" (Acts 3:19).

#### 3. It is coupled with remission of sins.

Christ died and rose again, to the end "that repentance and remission of sins should be preached in his name among all nations" (Luke 24:47). God is ready to blot out our sins as fast as we repent of them. There is no promise of remission, except upon condition of repentance.

#### 4. It precedes every act of divine grace and every Christian ordinance.

Notice the quotations: "Repentance and remission of sins." "Repent . . . that your sins may be blotted out." As for ordinances, repentance precedes the first among them, as is evident from the words of Peter: "Repent, and be baptized" (Acts 2:38). We search Scripture in vain for any reference that lends encouragement to the baptizing of impenitent sinners, or to the idea of receiving forgiveness of sins of which we have not repented.

### 5. Beyond repentance.

The most direct reference bearing on this point is found in Heb. 6:4-6: "It is impossible for those who were once enlightened, and have tasted of the heavenly gift, and were made partakers of the Holy Ghost, and have tasted of the good word of God, and the powers of the world to come, if they shall fall away, to renew them again unto repentance: seeing they crucify to themselves the Son of God afresh, and put him to an open shame." While the blasphemy against the Holy Ghost is the only sin that can not be forgiven (Matt. 12:31, 32), there is enough in this warning to impress every child of God with the fact that it is dangerous to trifle with the grace of God. Read I Jno. 5:16.

# CHAPTER V

## JUSTIFICATION

*Being now justified by his blood, we shall be saved from wrath through him.—Romans 5:9.*

Justification is the gracious act of God in which He imputes to all penitent believers the righteousness of Jesus Christ. While the "accuser of our brethren" (Rev. 12:10) is plying his satanic arts in having them condemned before God, the great Judge is virtually saying, "These are mine. They were once guilty, condemned, 'strangers from the covenants of promise,' but things have changed. The price for their redemption has been paid, they have accepted the proffered terms of mercy, have been cleansed by the blood, and are now justified in my sight." Christ having been raised "for our justification" (Rom. 4:25), we praise His name for the privilege of standing before God, uncondemned, justified.

### How We Are Justified

### 1. We are justified by the grace of God.

"Not by works of righteousness which we have done, but according to his *mercy* he saved us" (Tit. 3:5). "By grace are ye saved through faith; and that not of yourselves: it is the gift of God: not of works, lest any man should boast" (Eph. 2:8, 9). "Being justified freely by his grace" (Rom. 3:24), we disclaim all honor or merit for this great distinction, but give all praise and glory to God. Justification, like salvation, is God's free gift to man, unearned, unmerited. The grace of God puts us under everlasting obligations to Him.

### 2. We are justified by faith.

It takes something on our part to put us into touch with God's grace. As "God is no respecter of persons,"

and since some people are justified in His sight while others
are not, it follows that there must be something which
forms the basis of such division. This something we find
to be faith. It is written in so many words that "all that
believe are justified" (Acts 13:39); that "a man is justified
by faith without the deeds of the law" (Rom. 3:28;) that
the just God is "the justifier of him which believeth in
Jesus" (Rom. 3:26). This corresponds with the words of
Jesus: "He that believeth, and is baptized, shall be saved:
but he that believeth not, shall be damned" (Mark 16:16).
Faith, then, marks the dividing line between the saved
and the unsaved, the justified and the unjustified. It is
clear from the above references that God, without waiting
for a single evidence in the form of works, knowing the
thoughts and intents of the heart (Prov. 15:3; Heb. 4:12),
justifies the individual as soon as He recognizes the penitent sinner as a believer in Jesus. It is important that we
keep this fact in mind, as it helps us to keep balanced when
considering the next point.

### 3. We are justified by works.

The most direct scripture in support of this assertion
is that of Jas. 2:14-26. The burden of the argument there
presented is that "faith without works is dead." As illustrations of the doctrine of justification by works James
cites the case of Abraham, who proved his faith in God's
Word by undertaking the seemingly impossible; of Rahab,
who by befriending the spies in preference to her own people proved her faith that the children of Israel were the
people of God. In accord with this teaching is the declaration of our Saviour: "By thy words thou shalt be justified, and by thy words thou shalt be condemned" (Matt.
12:37). Hence the conclusion: "Ye see then how that by
works a man is justified, and not by faith only" (Jas. 2:24).

Some have thought that the teachings of Paul and of
James on the matter of faith and works are antagonistic to
each other, but the Scriptures support no such conclusion.
The burden of Paul's writings is that every believer is jus-

tified; of James, that the absence of works proves that the faith professed is not genuine. There is nothing in the writings of James that is stronger in support of good works than the following in the writings of Paul: Rom. 6:1, 2; Gal. 5:19-21; Eph. 2:10. The faith that justifies in the sight of God is the "faith which worketh;" in other words, produces works that may be seen of men.

### 4. We are justified by the blood of Christ.

All the sacrifices under the law were but types and shadows pointing to Christ. Read Heb. 5—10. It is distinctly stated that "by the deeds of the law there shall no flesh be justified" (Rom. 3:20), and just as distinctly stated that we are "justified by his blood" (Rom. 5:9). Comparing these statements with other references teaching justification by faith, we conclude that all who have faith in the blood of Jesus Christ as the atonement for their sins are justified in the sight of God.

### 5. "It is God that justifieth" (Rom. 8:33).

Self-justification will never make a satisfactory substitute. The lawyer (Luke 10:29), the Pharisee in the temple (Luke 18:10-14), and every other self-conceited man who tried to justify himself made a failure of it. The same is true of all similar efforts today.

## What Justification Means for Us

### 1. It means obedience to God.

This is of necessity true, for only obedient servants of God are justified. Ex. 23:7; Rom. 2:13; 10:5. As to God's attitude toward disobedience, read I Sam. 15:23; Heb. 2:1-3. The Gospel of Christ gives absolutely no assurance of justification to the disobedient.

### 2. It means freedom from condemnation.

"Who shall lay any thing to the charge of God's elect? It is God that justifieth" (Rom. 8:33). Even "the accuser of our brethren" can not prevail against the protective care of God for His own. Read Rom. 8:1, 2.

### 3. It means peace with God.

"Being justified by faith, we have peace with God through our Lord Jesus Christ" (Rom. 5:1). Read also Rom. 8:33, 34; Isa. 32:17; II Cor. 5:18; Eph. 2:14.

### 4. It means eternal salvation.

"Much more then, being justified by his blood, we shall be saved from wrath through him." We may justify ourselves, our friends may justify us; but only they who are justified by the blood, through faith in our Lord Jesus Christ, can rightfully lay claim to the salvation which Jesus Christ alone can bring.

### 5. It means an eternal inheritance.

"Being justified by his grace, we should be made heirs according to the hope of eternal life" (Tit. 3:7). To be fellow heirs with Christ is the Christian's most delightful privilege on earth.

### 6. It means glorification.

"Whom he justified, them he also glorified" (Rom. 8:30). Paul was expounding the doctrine of predestination as based on foreknowledge. The part of the discussion which bears directly upon the subject now under consideration is the statement just quoted. They who would put a "twilight zone" between justification and sanctification have a difficult task in explaining away the meaning of this declaration. Sonship, salvation, inheritance, glorification, all belong to the favored of God who have complied with His conditions for justification. Glory to His hallowed name!

# CHAPTER VI

## CONVERSION

The law of the Lord is perfect, converting the soul.—
Psalm 19:7.

The word "conversion" is used in the Bible but once.
Acts 15:3. Different forms of the word, however, are used
more frequently, and the doctrine of conversion is so prominent in the teaching of Christ and His disciples that if it
were expunged from the Christian faith there would be
nothing left worth saving. The word itself means a turning, a change, a bringing back.

### THE DOCTRINE STATED

We were "by nature the children of wrath" (Eph. 2:2)
—like Ephraim, wedded to our idols. To get back to God
there must be a turning around, a change—a change of
mind, of heart, of affections, of attitude toward God and
toward sin, a change in everything needed to bring us
back to God and in harmony with His Word. While the
exact words, "Things I once loved I now hate, and things
I once hated I now love," are not in the Bible, yet the experience therein expressed is true of every sinner who has
been converted to God. It takes a complete turning around,
a complete about face, a new love in the heart and new
life in the soul, to constitute a real evangelical conversion
to God.

### NO CHANGE, NO CONVERSION

This is the inevitable conclusion that one gets from a
faithful study of the Bible on this subject. To illustrate:
A swampy forest is converted into a fine farming country,
crude iron ore into a mighty ship, silicious sand into the

clearest glass, water into vapor, etc. In each case a fundamental change is essential to the conversion. Now for the application:

A fundamental change must take place before the sinner can become a child of God. There must be a change of mind, of heart, of life. Without such change the sinner may unite with some church but he can not become a child of God, for in Christ Jesus nothing will avail but to become "a new creature" (Gal. 6:15). And no sooner does the "new creature" exist within than the "newness of life" will begin to manifest itself without. "Out of the abundance of the heart the mouth speaketh." "Faith without works is dead." "How shall we that are dead to sin, live any longer therein?" When one is converted to God he will change his ways, forsake all sinful habits, and in his daily walk he will manifest the fruits of a righteous life within. Where such change does not take place—the tongue not being cleansed from filth or profanity, the pride continuing to be manifest in outward appearance, the crooked business ways continuing, the daily habits still indicating more pleasure in the sinful things of this world than in the things pertaining to the world to come—we conclude that since there is no change without, there has been none within, that the individual thus described is not converted to God. Where there is life within there is light without. Matt. 5:14-16.

### EXAMPLES OF CONVERSION

We have an accurate idea of what conversion means as we take note of the changes which take place in the lives of people as they turn to God. Let us notice a few of these examples:

1. **The Woman in Simon's Home** (Luke 7:36-50).— She had been a vile sinner, but having been brought to repentance because of her iniquity, she accepted Christ as her Saviour and Lord, was cleansed, and realizing the wonderful grace of God in saving a wretch like her, her grati-

tude and loyalty knew no bounds. Her sacrificial devotion brought special words of commendation from her Saviour.

2. **Saul of Tarsus** (Acts 9:1-18).—This is perhaps the most conspicuous example of conversion noted in the Bible, hence deserves more than ordinary attention. Upon his conversion he ceased his opposition to Christianity and became the most conspicuous defender of the faith. Penitence, humiliation, submission, complete surrender, obedience to God, willingness to be taught and willingness to suffer for the cause he once so madly opposed, are among the things noted in the change wrought in his conversion.

3. **Cornelius** (Acts 10).—He was a man who had lived up to all the light that he had. God recognized his sincerity, and through the instrumentality of Peter he was converted to Christ, baptized with the Holy Ghost and with water, and continued a devout worshiper of God.

4. **The Jailer** (Acts 16:27-34).—He was apparently a hardened sinner, ready to commit suicide the moment he recognized his danger. Through the grace of God and the instrumentality of Paul and Silas he was led into the light of the Gospel, turned immediately from a persecutor to a friend of the disciples, believed, and was baptized. In the brief account that we have of him we notice his change of attitude, his entrance into the faith of Christ, and his obedience to the commandments of the Lord.

From these and other examples found in the Bible we gather a few

### Facts Concerning Conversion

which will not only help people attain this desirable end but also to appreciate the goodness and love of God in performing this miracle of grace in the hearts of all who grant Him admittance:

1. **Conversion consists of a change of life and service rather than a change in personal traits.**

Take Saul of Tarsus for example. He retained his enthusiasm, energy, courage, and zeal for the cause he loved. The change consisted in transferring his faith from Pharisaism to Christianity, his membership from Judaism to the Church of Christ, and his self-righteousness was exchanged for the righteousness of God. Morally, conversion means a change from the standards of the world to the standards of the Gospel; spiritually, from the standards of Satan to the standards of the Holy Trinity.

2. **The conversion of man is accomplished through the grace of God.**

Behold the grace of God in sending the beam of light upon the archenemy of the Christian faith on the Damascus road; in sending the earthquake to the Philippian jail and bringing about the conversion of the wicked jailer; in opening the eyes of Cornelius and bringing him into touch with the message of salvation. In these and all other cases of genuine evangelical conversion it was and is brought about only by the grace and power of God in the hearts of those willing to receive the transforming power of God into their souls. Jesus says, "No man can come to me, except the Father which hath sent me draw him" (Jno. 6:44). It is when "the hand of the Lord" (Acts 11:21) is with His servants that sinners are brought to the Gospel light and converted.

3. **The best of people fail of salvation except through conversion.**

Nicodemus, Paul, Cornelius, Lydia, and other noble characters needed to be converted to the Lord Jesus Christ before salvation was theirs. Paul's good conscience, Cornelius' devotion to all the light that he had, Lydia's excellent traits of character, all were "filthy rags" until they were brought to the altar and their possessors accepted Christ as their Saviour and their own righteousness was exchanged for that of Jesus Christ. It is remarkable how frail and sinful man appears when put under the light of truth. Paul was a giant in intellect, had a commanding personality, was possessed with a "good conscience," and was zealous of the law; yet when we see all these good qualities absorbed in a murderous fury against the Church of God, we are made to feel that he was far from ideal. Jonah, who by a single message brought a whole city down in sackcloth and ashes, outstripped all our most successful modern evangelists; yet from the Bible description of him we are impressed with the fact that he had some very striking shortcomings. That Pharisee, praying in the temple, who recounted a whole catalogue of good things in his favor, was rated by our Saviour as being less justified in the sight of God than the poor publican by his side. Not good works, not attainments, not worldly renown, not human greatness, but as "a little child" (Matt. 18:3), being nothing of itself but a creature of God, a life "hid with Christ in God" (Col. 3:3), is the Bible standing of goodness and greatness before God. It is in this light only that any one is worthy of the grace of God.

### 4. The more contrite the heart, the more striking the conversion.

The woman in Simon's house, filled with grateful reverence because she had been so wondrously and gloriously saved from sin, was a much brighter example of conversion than was Simon (if, indeed he was converted at all) who seemingly did not feel that he had ever done anything very bad. Saul of Tarsus, after he realized into what depths of iniquity he had fallen, notwithstanding his eminence and apparently good character (I Cor. 15:9, 10; I Tim. 1: 15), stands out to this day as one of the brightest examples of conversion. You have only to look into your own congregation to find at least a few illustrations of the statement at the head of this paragraph.

### 5. Repentance precedes conversion.

The illustrations already cited, as well as the experience of every converted being, are proofs of this fact. "Repent ye therefore, and be converted"—not, be converted and see how sinful you were; but "Repent . . . that your sins may be blotted out" (Acts 3:19); in other words, you will be converted if you truly repent. People who see nothing about their record that moves them to repentance may become willing to unite with a church, but in that frame of mind and heart they will never be converted to God.

**6. The Word of God is an essential element in conversion.**

Peter says, "As I began to speak, the Holy Ghost fell on them" (Acts 11:15). Paul says that the Gospel of Christ is "the power of God unto salvation" (Rom. 1:16); that "in Christ Jesus have I begotten you through the gospel" (I Cor. 4:15). What was it that first directed the mind of the three thousand on the day of Pentecost, of the Ethiopian eunuch, of Saul of Tarsus, of Cornelius, of Lydia, of the jailer, and of others to Christ? The Word of God. "The law of the Lord is perfect, converting the soul."

**7. God uses human beings in bringing about the conversion of others.**

The disciples at Pentecost, filled with the Holy Ghost, were instrumental in bringing about the conversion of three thousand. There is not a conversion mentioned in the epistolary writings but that some servant of God was connected with the event. "He which converteth a sinner from the error of his way shall save a soul from death, and shall hide a multitude of sins" (Jas. 5:29).

**8. Youth is the time to turn to the Lord.**

It means easier turning, less sins to repent of, less wrongs to make right, less influence in leading other souls astray, a longer life of Christian service, and (as a rule) a brighter Christian experience. Many, who in their younger years were under deep conviction but refused to yield, afterwards became so enmeshed in sin that they never gave their hearts to God but died in their sins. "Remember *now* thy Creator in the days of thy youth, while the evil days come not" (Eccl. 12:1).

**9. It is God that does the turning.**

Man has his part, but it is God who performs the miracle of grace in the heart which brings about the wondrous change. "It is God that worketh in you." "No man can come unto me, except the Father. . . . . draw him." Our part is submission and obedience, God does the rest. God draws, man yields, and God finishes the work.

### Results of Conversion

As already stated, conversion means a change, a turning around, an about face, a transformation, a "newness of life." This is what the Bible says takes place when one is really converted:

#### 1. He becomes "a new creature."

"If any man be in Christ, he is a new creature: old things are passed away; behold, all things are become new" (II Cor. 5:17). The life after turning to God is described as a "newness of life."

#### 2. He is adopted into God's happy family.

"If Christ be in you, the body is dead because of sin: but the spirit is life because of righteousness. . . . . For as many as are led by the Spirit of God, they are the sons of God. For ye have not received the Spirit of bondage again to fear; but ye have received the Spirit of adoption, whereby we cry, Abba, Father" (Rom. 8:10-15).

#### 3. He is "clothed with humility."

The true standard of greatness is set forth in Matt. 18:1-3. It is universally true that when people are truly converted to God they become a meek, unassuming, humble people. Christ refers to Himself as being "meek and lowly in heart" (Matt. 11:29). His true disciples are like Him. Read Phil. 2:5-8.

#### 4. He is clothed with righteousness.

"Zion shall be redeemed with judgment, and her converts with righteousness" (Isa. 1:27). When a person is converted he brings his own righteousness to the cross and receives the righteousness of God in its stead. Read Rom. 10:3. This righteousness is no longer the "filthy rags" of

which Isaiah writes, but the real righteousness of Jesus
Christ that becomes the light which causes others to glorify
God.  Matt. 5:14-16.

### 5.  He is zealous in the Master's cause.

"A peculiar people, zealous of good works" (Tit. 2:14;
I Pet. 2:9) is a proper description of God's people of all
ages. The brightest examples of true conversion have invariably been men and women whose zeal for righteousness and truth were known to those about them.

### 6.  He walks, "not after the flesh, but after the Spirit."

Read Rom. 7:9—8:1. No man has ever been converted
to God without becoming like Him, spirituality included.
Before conversion we walked "according to the course of
this world" (Eph. 2:2), "in the flesh to the lusts of men"
(I Pet. 4:2); but all this is changed when the transforming
grace of God turns the individual around and gives him
the heavenly vision.

### 7.  He enjoys Christian fellowship.

"If we walk in the light, as he is in the light, we have
fellowship one with another" (I Jno. 1:7). It is as natural
for people converted to God to have fellowship one with
another while they walk in the footsteps of Christ our
Saviour as it is for the people of this world to keep themselves in the fellowship of those travelling the broad road
to destruction. Our fellowship here is but a foretaste of an
endless and eternal fellowship with God and with saints
in the realms of glory.

10

## CHAPTER VII

## REGENERATION

Marvel not that I said unto thee, Ye must be born again.
—John 3:7.

Literally speaking, regeneration means the act of begetting again. The word is used but twice in Scripture (Matt. 19:28; Tit. 3:5), but, like conversion, the doctrine of regeneration is very much in evidence in all Bible teaching pertaining to salvation. "Regeneration is related to the new birth as cause and effect, the same as atonement and redemption, justification and righteousness, sanctification and holiness. God regenerates, man is born again; God atones, man is redeemed; God justifies, man is reckoned righteous; God sanctifies, man is made holy."—J. B. Smith.

### How Characterized in Scripture

1. **"Born Again."**—"Except a man be born again, he can not see the kingdom of God" (Jno. 3:3). "Being born again, not of corruptible seed, but of incorruptible, by the word of God" (I Pet. 1:23). The first assertion holds out the necessity of the new birth; the second, of its nature, and how brought about.

2. **"A New Creature."**—"If any man be in Christ, he is a new creature" (II Cor. 5:17). The same term is used in Gal. 6:15, showing that it takes a new creation to bring about a right standing before God.

3. **"Begotten."**—"In Christ Jesus have I begotten you through the gospel" (I Cor. 4:15). "Of his own will begat he us with the word of truth" (Jas. 1:18). In both references the idea of a new creation through the Word of God is the prominent thought.

4. **"Begotten Again."**—"Blessed be the God and Father of our Lord Jesus Christ, which according to his abundant mercy hath begotten us again" (I Pet. 1:3). We have here the further thought that this new birth is entirely distinct from our first (natural) birth. As a child born into the world has its first existence on the earth, so a child of God, "born of water and of the Spirit" (Jno. 3:5), thereby gets its first existence in the family of God. And since the first birth is essential to a natural existence in the natural world, so the second birth is essential to a spiritual existence in the kingdom of God. [In this comparison we are not discussing the pre-existence in the kingdom of God of the little child that from its conception to spiritual death at the age of accountability (Rom. 7:9) belonged to the kingdom of God. Matt. 19:14.]

5. **"Washing of Regeneration."**—"Not by works of righteousness which we have done, but according to his mercy he saved us, by the washing of regeneration, and renewing of the Holy Ghost" (Tit. 3:5). The term, "washing of regeneration," is explained by the expression that follows it.

6. **"Newness of Life."**—"As Christ was raised up from the dead by the glory of the Father, even so we also should walk in newness of life" (Rom. 6:4). The matter of Christian duty is here associated with that of Christian life.

7. **"Created in Christ Jesus."**—"We are his workmanship, created in Christ Jesus unto good works" (Eph. 2:10). Notice, this reference ends with the idea of good works—the work of God and the works of men. Both are in evidence in the regenerated life.

8. **"The Divine Nature."**—"That by these ye might be partakers of the divine nature, having escaped the corruption that is in the world through lust" (II Pet. 1:4). Paul gives voice to the same thought when he speaks of "Christ in you, the hope of glory" (Col. 1:27). Every one born of God has "the divine nature" in him; for, "If any

man have not the Spirit of Christ, he is none of his" (Rom. 8:9).

9. **"A New Heart."**—Ezekiel, speaking prophetically, gave voice to the promise of God, saying, "A new heart also will I give you, and a new spirit will I put within you: and I will take away the stony heart out of your flesh" (Exek. 36:26). With this new heart our affections are set "on things above," whereas, while the old stony heart is still in the flesh the affections are set "on things on the earth."

10. **"The New Man."**—"And have put on the new man, which is renewed in knowledge after the image of him that created him" (Col. 3:10). This is a companion thought of the crucifixion of "the old man" (Rom. 6:6), because there can be no "new man" without having "the body of sin" destroyed.

It will be seen by the references quoted that regeneration consists not in merely working over or reforming the old man of sin, but that it is an entirely new creation, the calling into being of "a new creature," "which after God is created in righteousness and true holiness" (Eph. 4:24).

## What Regeneration Is Not

### 1. It is not mere reformation.

This thought is taken care of in a preceding paragraph. Regeneration does indeed bring about reformation, but the change is similar to that which takes place in a nation when a new dynasty of kings begins to reign. The "new heart" within brings about a reformed life without.

### 2. It is not mere conviction of sin.

Conviction is a favorable sign that the Spirit is working, but a man becomes "a new creature" only when he surrenders to God and allows Him to work the miracle of grace in his heart.

### 3. It is not joining some church.

The curse of modern churches is that there are too many members in whom "the old man" still reigns. We do not become children of God because we belong to some church, but we unite with the church that we believe to be most completely in harmony with the Word of God, after we have been "born again."

#### 4. It is not living a mere moral life.

If the good moral man who is so sure that he never did anything very bad would take a good, honest look at himself in the Gospel mirror (II Cor. 3:18) he would find himself to be but a poor, deluded, self-righteous sinner.

#### 5. It is not mere social uplift.

"Social regeneration" has no connection whatever with the "washing of regeneration" that quickens the soul and through that cleans up the outer life. No community is ever saved except as individuals living in it turn to the Lord and become "new creatures" in Christ.

#### 6. It is not merely espousing correct Christian doctrine.

"In Christ Jesus neither circumcision availeth any thing, nor uncircumcision, but a new creature" (Gal. 6: 15). You may hold to a theology that is faultless and still be an unsaved sinner. It is one thing to accept the Gospel in the mind as being correct, and quite another thing to accept it in the heart as "the power of God unto salvation."

All of the things herein mentioned are good in their place, but they have no place as substitutes for salvation.

### The Work of Regeneration

#### 1. It is the work of God.

Father, Son, and Holy Ghost are all recognized in this work. Jno. 1:13; 3:6; Tit. 3:5; I Pet. 1:3; I Jno. 2:29. It is "the washing of regeneration," not "mighty works," that brings about salvation. It is "not by works of righteousness which we have done, but according to his mercy he saved us." We are not born of works, but "born of

God;" "it is God which worketh in you, both to will and to do of his good pleasure."

### 2. It is wrought through the instrumentality of the Word.

The Gospel of Christ, we are told, "is the power of God unto salvation" (Rom. 1:16). "Begotten you through the Gospel," is another way of stating the same truth. "The word of God is quick, and powerful, sharper than any twoedged sword" (Heb. 4:12). The work of regeneration is described by R. A. Torrey as follows:

> "In the new birth the Word of God is the seed: the human heart is the soil: the preacher is the sower, and drops the seed into the soil (Acts 16:14); the Spirit quickens the seed into life in the receptive heart; the new divine nature springs up out of the divine Word; the believer is born again, created anew, made alive, passed out of death into life."

### 3. It is not accomplished without man's co-operation.

While salvation is wholly the work of God, that does not mean that man has no part in it. In the first place, God uses men to bring other men to Him. Besides, God never saves any one contrary to his will. God does indeed smite men mightily through the convicting power of the Spirit, but not until man responds with what virtually means, "Lord, what wilt thou have me to do?" is he created anew in Christ Jesus. Salvation is offered upon conditions which man must meet in order to receive it. Regeneration is the result of faith on man's part. Jno. 1:12; Gal. 3:26.

### 4. It is not needed by the innocent child.

When mothers brought their children to Jesus He blessed them, saying, "Of such is the kingdom of heaven" (Matt. 19:14). Little children are under the blood, fit subjects for heaven, until they come to the time when it is true of them that "sin revived, and I died" (Rom. 7:9)—after which they must be "born again" to enter the Kingdom.

### 5. It is essential to salvation.

As proof of this we cite you to the scriptures already quoted, the most direct among which is Jno. 3:3, 5, 7.

#### EVIDENCES OF REGENERATION

The Bible is not wanting in evidences whereby we may know whether or not we are the children of God. Following are the more prominent among these evidences:

1. **Righteousness.**—"Every one that doeth righteousness is born of him" (I Jno. 2:29). "God is no respecter of persons: But in every nation he that feareth him, and worketh righteousness, is accepted with him" (Acts 10:34, 35). The righteousness of Christ, imputed and imparted to men, is invariably manifested in *doing* righteousness as well as *being* righteous; for, "How shall we that are dead to sin live any longer therein?" There can be no such thing as an "inside religion" without it becoming manifest on the outside. Matt. 5:14-16.

2. **The Sinless Life.**—"Whosoever is born of God doth not commit sin" (I Jno. 3:9). Whatever your interpretation of this scripture may be, be careful that you do not explain it away. It is there for a purpose. The Bible makes plenty of allowance for the infirmities of the flesh, but it offers no excuse for wilful sinning. Read Rom. 8:1; Eph. 2:1-12; Tit. 3:3-7; I Jno. 1:4-7. "They that are Christ's have crucified the flesh with the affections and lusts" (Gal. 5:24). People who are born of God do not *commit* sin, not because they make no mistakes but because they do not wilfully go against better knowledge, and therefore sin is not imputed unto them. Psa. 32:2; Rom. 4:8.

3. **The Spirit-led Life.**—The contrast between carnality and spirituality is forcefully set forth in Gal. 5:19-23. Whether we are walking "after the flesh" or "after the Spirit" (Rom. 8:1) is determined by the other question as to whether in our daily life we manifest "the works of the flesh" or "the fruit of the Spirit." When you see a person whose daily record shows clearly that his whole life

is directed by the Spirit of God you may be sure that such person has been "born again."

4. **Obedience.**—"Hereby we do know that we know him, if we keep his commandments" (I Jno. 2:3). Christ puts a similar test to His disciples when He says, "Ye are my friends, if ye do whatsoever I command you" (Jno. 15:14). James adds a further warning, saying "Be ye doers of the word, and not hearers only, deceiving your own selves" (Jas. 1:22).

5. **Love.**—"We know that we have passed from death unto life, because we love the brethren" (I Jno. 3:14). For the same reason, "He that loveth not his brother abideth in death." "Beloved, let us love one another: for love is of God; and every one that loveth is born of God, and knoweth God. He that loveth not, knoweth not God" (I Jno. 4:7, 8).

6. **Hatred of Evil.**—"He that is begotten of God keepeth himself, and that wicked one toucheth him not" (I Jno. 5:18). "Abhor that which is evil" is to him as sacred as to "cleave to that which is good." The Spirit-filled child of God, like the psalmist, is able to say, "I hate every evil way."

7. **Faith.**—"Whosoever believeth that Jesus is the Christ is born of God" (I Jno. 5:1). This is as plain as language can make it. But faith, like love, may be put to the real test by determining whether we believe all of God's Word, and are as ready to obey those commandments of the Lord which are crucifying to the flesh as we are those which are more popular and not objectionable to the carnal man. "As many as received him, to them gave he power to become the sons of God, even to them that believe on his name" (Jno. 1:12).

8. **The Victorious Life.**—"Whatsoever is born of God overcometh the world" (I Jno. 5:4). The overcoming life is manifest in a number of ways. One rooted and grounded in the faith is not easily moved from the hope of the Gospel. It makes a marked impression on the world. Of

Christ it was said, "He hath done all things well" (Mark 7:37), though He suffered the severest opposition. It is through the power and influence of Spirit-filled lives that men are won for God. "Ask of me, and I shall give thee the heathen for thine inheritance, and the uttermost parts of the earth for thy possession" (Psa. 2:8).

In speaking of love and hatred as evidences of regeneration it is important to bear in mind that the children of God, as far as they have the light, love the things which God loves and hates the things which He hates. The rule is, love everything pertaining to God and godliness, and hate everything that is in opposition to Christ and Christianity. Therefore, "If any man love the world, the love of the Father is not in him" (I Jno. 2:15). Every one that is an ardent lover of that which is good, is also a strong hater of that which is evil. This is one of the fundamental evidences of sonship.

# CHAPTER VIII

## ADOPTION

As many as are led by the Spirit of God, they are the sons of God. For ye have not received the spirit of bondage again to fear; but ye have received the spirit of adoption, whereby we cry, Abba, Father.—Romans 8:14, 15.

This chapter logically follows, rather than precedes, the chapter on Regeneration; for we can not conceive of God receiving unregenerate people into His family. The two subjects have much in common; the distinction being that while in regeneration the emphasis is on spiritual life, in adoption we think of spiritual relationship.

Adoption is the gracious act of God in receiving into His happy family, upon certain conditions, the children of this world. As Moses was adopted as a son of Pharaoh's daughter (Ex. 2:1-10) and Mephibosheth (II Sam. 9:1-10) was sheltered in the family of David as his son, so does God receive into His family, as His sons and daughters, those who have become heirs of glory through becoming new creatures in Christ Jesus.

### Adoption Presupposes—

1. **That there are those who are not of the family of God.**

And of this we have abundant scriptural proof. Christ told the Pharisees that "Ye are of your father the devil" (Jno. 8:44). In the parable of the wheat and the tares Christ explains that "the good seed are the children of the kingdom" while the tares are "the children of the wicked one" (Matt. 13:38). Because Elymas persisted in perverting "the right ways of the Lord" (Acts 13:10) Paul reminded him that he was a "child of the devil." When man fell he lost his place in the family of God, and can be restored only through regeneration and adoption. The theory of "the universal brotherhood of man and fatherhood of God" has been anti-scriptural ever since the fall of man.

**2. That God is ready to adopt as His own, those who are not members of His family.**

Here again we find the supposition true to fact. In Eph. 1:4, 5 we are told that God "hath chosen us in him before the foundation of the world . . . predestinated us unto the adoption of children by Jesus Christ unto himself, according to the good pleasure of his will." In this the wonderful love of God is manifest, in that He made provision for the wayward sons of earth, thousands of years before many of them were born.

**3. That there are those willing to be adopted.**

This also is a fact which God foreknew when He made provisions for man's restoration. One of the well-established principles which God follows in His dealings with man is that He never forces any one to become His child. Ours is a "whosoever" religion, we having the power of choice. Forcible adoption is something unknown in His dealings with men. Even "predestination," over which some people stumble, is based upon the foreknowledge (Rom. 8:29) rather than upon the foredetermination of God. As such it never contradicts the "whosoever will" provision of God for our salvation and adoption. So God, while He made provision for the adoption of every soul, opens the divine family hearth to those only who are willing to come. Read Isa. 55:1; Jno. 1:12; 3:16; Rev. 22:17.

### Scriptural Condition for Adoption

**1. Faith.**—"As many as received him, to them gave he power to become the sons of God, even to them that believe on his name" (Jno. 1:12). "Ye are all the children of God by faith in Christ Jesus" (Gal. 3:26).

**2. Regeneration.**—This thought is sustained in John's testimony that they which "believe on his name" are "born of God." Christ's declaration that no one can get to heaven without being "born again" (Jno. 3:3, 5, 7) makes it positive that regeneration is essential to adoption.

**3. Scourging.**—"Whom the Lord loveth he chasteneth, and *scourgeth every son* whom he receiveth (Heb. 12:6). Perhaps it is the *fact* of scourging, rather than as *a condition,* that Paul desires to emphasize; but it is a fact that no sinner, especially none who has spent years in sin, is ever brought to Christ without a remorse of conscience. "O wretched man that I am!" expresses a common experience among sinners under deep conviction. As a young lady expressed it soon after she felt that the burden of sin had rolled away, "There is nothing so cruel as conviction." This is the way it seemed to her at the time. But on the other hand, conviction is one of God's kindest acts, because it leads us to a closer relationship with Him.

**4. The Grace of God.**—Adoption, like justification, is something that is not based upon human merit. It is not intelligence, not mighty works, not innate goodness, nor attractiveness in any form that moves the loving Father to take any one into His family; but alone His wondrous grace, His infinite goodness, His tender mercies, His loving kindness that prompts Him to claim us as His own. Just as no child can become a member of any family without adoption by the head of the family, so no child of the devil can get into the family of God save through the pardoning grace of God. Our part is acceptance of His conditions; He does the rest.

### THE BLESSINGS OF ADOPTION

are many. In the first place, it admits us into all the privileges of the children of God. The prodigal son was satisfied to be made one of his father's hired servants, but his father graciously restored him to his former position as a favored son. This is typical of the grace of God, who freely forgives the penitent prodigal and adopts him into His happy family. In other words, we are by invitation and action of God made His children. As such we are joint heirs with Christ, having in store the eternal inheritance of the "saints in light." The Spirit's indwelling and guidance, the fellowship of God and of saints, the privilege of shining in the image of our heavenly Father, the opportunity of being in His service, the comfort attending the knowledge that we have made our "calling and election sure," and finally the blessed hope which fills and thrills our souls with glorious anticipations presents to us an array of priceless blessings of sonship that should fill our souls with overflowing gratitude toward God, and our mouths with unstinted praises of Him from whom all blessings flow.

## Evidences of Sonship

1. **Following** After the Spirit.—"As many as are led by the Spirit of God, they are the sons of God" (Rom. 8:14). According to Rom. 8:1, to be led of the Spirit is the very opposite of walking "after the flesh." "It is the Spirit that quickeneth" (Jno. 6:63). The children of this world are under the dominion of the flesh, while the sons of God are under the dominion of the Spirit. "The Spirit himself beareth witness with our spirit, that we are the children of God" (Rom. 8:16, R.V.).

2. **Obedience.**—"Hereby we do know that we know him, if we keep his commandments" (I Jno. 2:3). Read also I Jno. 5:1-3. They who willfully disobey God thereby confess that they do not know Him and can not therefore be His children. I Jno. 2:4; Rom. 6:16-22.

3. **Childlike Confidence in God.**—There is a remarkable similarity between the "little ones" in the family of God and the little ones in our homes. Matt. 18:1-3. They are trustful, unassuming, guileless, incapable of holding a grudge, pure. Look into the face of a little, helpless, trustful, innocent child, and you have a picture of a real child of God. "Because ye are sons, God hath sent forth the

Spirit of his Son into your hearts, crying, Abba, Father" (Gal. 4:6). Childlike faith and childlike simplicity belong to the child of God.

4. **Love of the Brethren.**—"Every one that loveth him that begat loveth him also that is begotten of him" (I Jno. 5:1). It is one of the surest evidences of sonship when our hearts are melted together in fervent charity for one another, knit together in the faith and service of Jesus Christ, showing our love to God by manifesting love one for another, who together belong to the Spirit-led family of God.

5. **Peaceableness.**—"Blessed are the peacemakers: for they shall be called the children of God" (Matt. 5:9). A further study of this is found in the latter part of the same chapter, closing with the words, "that ye may be the children of your Father which is in heaven" (v. 45). Read Rom. 12:17-21; Jas. 3:17, 18.

6. **Godliness.**—"Be ye therefore followers of God, as dear children" (Eph. 5:1). As children resemble their parents, so do the children of God resemble Him in all matters pertaining to life and godliness.

7. **Love of Enemies.**—Read carefully Matt. 5:43-48. It is significant that Christ ends His exhortation to love our enemies with the words, "That ye may be the children of your Father which is in heaven" (v. 45).

# CHAPTER IX

## SANCTIFICATION

> If a man therefore purge himself from these, he shall be a vessel unto honour, sanctified, and meet for the master's use, and prepared unto every good work.—II Timothy 2:21.

### DEFINITIONS

The primary use of the word sanctification is that of a setting apart or consecration to some special work, cause, or purpose. The word, in some form, is used frequently in both Old and New Testaments, and in no case would the meaning of the sentence be changed very materially if the word "separate" or "set apart to" were substituted for the word "sanctify." As applied to the work of God in setting apart His people to a holy purpose, the word takes on the added meaning of purity, holiness, consecration to God, etc. In this sense we speak of sanctification as—

1. **A Preparation.**—"And Joshua said unto the people, Sanctify yourselves: for to morrow the Lord will do wonders among you" (Josh. 3:5). In other words, purify yourselves and get ready for tomorrow. "Sanctified, and meet for the master's use, and prepared unto every good work." Read also Ex. 19:10, 11.

2. **To Hallow.**—"The Lord spake, saying, I will be sanctified in them that come nigh me, and before all the people I will be glorified" (Lev. 10:3). A similar thought is expressed in Num. 10:12 and Ezek. 36:23; also in the admonition, "Sanctify the Lord God in your hearts" (I Pet. 3:15).

3. **A Setting Apart, or Consecration.**—"And God blessed the seventh day, and sanctified it" (Gen. 2:3); that

is, set it apart as a day to be hallowed. "Sanctify unto
me all the first-born" (Ex. 13:2); that is, set them apart
unto me. Read also Lev. 8:10, 11; Jno. 17:17; I Thess.
4:3; Heb. 9:3.

4. **Cleansed, Pure, Holy.**—Read I Thess. 5:23; II Tim.
2:21; Heb. 10:10, 14. We can not conceive of any one
being set apart to the service of God without being cleansed
by the blood, converted to God, holy in His service. Without holiness (sanctification—R. V.) "no man shall see the
Lord" (Heb. 12:14).

### SANCTIFYING AGENTS

This subject needs to be considered from both the
divine and the human side, as both God and man have a
part in it. True, it is distinctly the work of God, as man
could work on his own sanctification a thousand years and
not be any farther along than when he began. On the
other hand, God never sanctifies any man, in the sense
that we are now considering the word, who is not willing
to co-operate with the Lord in bringing it about. In other
words, God sanctifies those who comply with His conditions. Let us notice briefly what each contributes:

### I. Divine Workmanship

1. **God the Father.**—"And the very God of peace
sanctify you wholly" (I Thess. 5:23). "To them that are
sanctified by God the Father" (Jude 1). This work was
foreshadowed in the prophecy of Ezekiel (37:28).

2. **God the Son.**—"Wherefore Jesus also, that he
might sanctify the people with his own blood, suffered
without the gate" (Heb. 13:12). "We are sanctified,
through the offering of the body of Jesus Christ" (Heb.
10:10). Paul further instructs the Ephesians that Christ
sanctifies the Church through "the washing of water by
the word" (5:15-27).

3. **God the Holy Ghost.**—Paul assures the Thessalonians that their salvation was wrought "through the
sanctification of the Spirit and belief of the truth" (II Thess.

2:13). Peter refers to the Church as the "elect according to the foreknowledge of God the Father, through sanctification of the Spirit" (I Pet. 1:2). Read also Rom. 15:16; I Cor. 6:11.

4. **The Word of God.**—"Sanctify them through thy truth: thy word is truth" (Jno. 17:17). The Word of God is an essential factor in the work of sanctification. Christ says, "The words that I speak unto you, they are spirit, and they are life."

## II. The Human Side

1. **Faith.**—Christ our Substitute—"is made unto us . . . sanctification" (I Cor. 1:30). How? As we take hold of Him, grasp His promises by faith He becomes our sanctifier. "Without faith it is impossible to please him." "He that believeth not, is condemned"—neither saved nor sanctified. "He that cometh to God must believe that he is, and that he is a rewarder of them that diligently seek him" (Heb. 11:6).

2. **Knowledge.**—We have already referred to the efficacy of the Word of God in procuring our sanctification. On God's side, He gives us this Word; we accept it; hence we are sanctified through "the washing of water by the word," are made "clean through the word" (Jno. 15:3). Through a knowledge of the Word we are made cognizant of our sins, and being made conscious of God's provisions for our sanctification we act upon them. Read I Pet. 1:2.

3. **Obedience.**—Read Rom. 6:19-23. The Holy Spirit is given "to them that obey him" (Acts 5:32). The disobedient are without promise.

4. **Separation from the World.**—"The Lord hath set apart him that is godly for himself" (Psa. 4:3). Read Rom. 12:1, 2; II Cor. 6:14-18; 7:1. Conclusion: "Be ye separate, saith the Lord, and I will receive you." In other words, If you will hear my voice, separate yourselves from the world, I will receive you unto myself, and "ye shall be my sons and daughters, saith the Lord Almighty."

5. **Following After.**—The promise is, "Seek, and ye shall find." This is true of all spiritual blessings, sanctification included. "Follow peace with all men, and holiness (sanctification, R.V.), without which no man shall see the Lord" (Heb. 12:14).

## TIME OF SANCTIFICATION

One very live question connected with sanctification is, At what stage in the Christian's experience does he become sanctified? In this, as in all other questions pertaining to this great theme, we do well to keep close to the Word. In pursuance of this course, let us turn the Gospel light upon two important facts:

1. **Sanctification is an instantaneous work, at the time of conversion.**

"And such were some of you: but ye are washed, but ye are sanctified, but ye are justified in the name of the Lord Jesus" (I Cor. 6:11). "By the which will we are sanctified, through the offering of the body of Jesus Christ once for all. . . . For by one offering he hath perfected for ever them that are sanctified" (Heb. 10:10, 14).

There are those who would put a "wilderness experience" between the time of conversion and of sanctification. But there are a few scriptures standing in the way of such conclusion. In the first place, Paul's reference to the Corinthians, "Ye are sanctified," was to a class of people who themselves were living a wilderness life. I Cor. 3:3. Again, Paul assures us that "if any man have not the Spirit of Christ, he is none of his" (Rom. 8:9); that without holiness (sanctification) "no man shall see the Lord" (Heb. 12:14); that "they that are Christ's have crucified the flesh with the affections and lusts" (Gal. 5:24). John also adds his testimony, saying, "Whosoever is born of God doth not commit sin" (I Jno. 3:9). These are scriptures that stand in the way of the theory that provides first for justification, then for an indefinite period of sinning religion, then a great awakening, then sanctification. It is unthinkable that

God should set apart a sinning Christian and as such consecrate him to a holy cause. There are several untenable positions closely allied to this "wilderness life" theory, but the only point we desire to raise at this time is that the theory conflicts with a number of clearly enunciated scripture truths.

But does not the record of Christian people reveal shortcomings after their conversion? Yes; plenty of them —even after the Adamic sin is said to have been eradicated and they are wholly sanctified. For example, Paul and Barnabas who were both "filled with the Holy Ghost" (Acts 15:36-39), Peter (Gal. 2:11-13), and others whose standing before God was beyond question. All people, saints as well as sinners, have their shortcomings.

We conclude, therefore, that at conversion one is saved, justified, sanctified, regenerated; and that, so far as salvation is concerned, the work is instantaneous and complete. But there is, however, a subsequent growth, "in grace," that is as natural and as inevitable as is the physical growth of the natural child. And there are subsequent infillings of the Spirit (Acts 4:31), which mean added joys, greater spiritual attainments, and loftier heights in power, zeal, and service.

2. **Sanctification is a progressive work, continuing throughout one's normal Christian experience.**

Once in grace, we naturally "grow in grace, and in the knowledge of our Lord" (II Pet. 3:18). Because of this growth the children of God "increase and abound" (I Thess. 3:12), "abound more and more" (I Thess. 4:1, 19), going "on to perfection" (Heb. 6:1), "perfecting holiness in the fear of God" (II Cor. 7:1). As the natural child would not be normal if it did not continue to develop from its infancy, so the child of God is not normal if he or she does not continue to grow spiritually.

You see a little child a year or two old. You are impressed with its quick perception, its innocent prattle, its promising intellect. "What a bright, promising child," you say. Disease overtakes it, which puts a check to its development, and years afterwards you see it again, and you call it an idiot, even though it may know a little more than it knew the first time you saw it.

So with the babe in Christ, just born into the Kingdom. "Very good," says the Creator, and you yourself are pleased with the start made. But that child of God, because of neglect of means of grace, fails to develop spiritually. You see that individual years after, and can see no evidence that he is any farther along in the work of the Lord than he was years before. "Spiritual idiot," you say. Growth is a natural result of life, and whoever fails to grow, physically or spiritually, is not normal.

You start in your Christian life, a normal Christian. God is satisfied with your condition, and you have reasons to praise the Lord. You have a clear conscience before God and man. You continue to grow. Your fellowship with God and saints, your companionship with the Bible, your daily devotions and active Christian service keep you well nourished and you grow stronger and better—in knowledge, in understanding, in endurance, in spirituality, in Christian graces, in capacity for service. You look back over your past record, and you wonder how it was possible for you to do some of the things that you did in your earlier Christian experience without a remorse of conscience, as you could not do them at all now. What has happened?

You have been growing. As light dawned upon you, one thing after another that you did in former years appealed to you as being wrong, and one inconsistency after another was repented of and dropped from your life and record. This has continued for years; and as you now compare your record with what it was in former years, you are astonished that you did not see those things then. But you have been growing. During all these years your light has been shining brighter and brighter, and by the grace of God, if you will continue as you have been doing, you will continue to shine more brightly, for "the path of the just is as the shining light, that shineth more and more unto the perfect day" (Prov. 4:18). This is progressive sanctification.

Sanctification, perfect and complete, will be the happy lot of every saint at the coming of our Lord, for then no mortal robe will dim the life and light of God within the soul, and our state will be perfect then, as our standing is now.

### RESULTS OF SANCTIFICATION

1. **Union with Christ.**—"Both he that sanctifieth and they that are sanctified, are all of one" (Heb. 2:11). When God sets us apart to His service it means two things: (1) separation from sin (Rom. 6:1, 2; 12:1, 2; II Cor. 6:14-18); (2) union with Himself (Jno. 17:21-23).

2. **Christian Perfection.**—"By one offering he hath perfected for ever them that are sanctified" (Heb. 10:14). Read also Matt. 5:48. How is Christian perfection possible in the life of an imperfect human? Answer: through the cleansing power of the blood, the keeping power of God. Perfect love was the theme of our Saviour when He commanded His disciples to be perfect—perfect through the Blood is the perfection wrought through the "one offering." In this connection read the paragraph on the sinless life, found in the chapter on Regeneration. Christ's perfection is made ours. I Cor. 1:30.

3. **Eternal Inheritance.**—That all the sanctified ones in Christ are joint heirs with Christ is evident, because: (1) God has promised to all the faithful ones "an inheritance among all them which are sanctified" (Acts 20:32). (2) Holiness (sanctification) is mentioned among the conditions required to "see the Lord." (3) The "all things" of Rev. 21:7 are promised to overcomers—and there are no overcomers outside of the saved and sanctified ones.

4. **Preparation for Service.**—"If a man therefore purge himself from these, he shall be a vessel unto honour, sanctified, and meet for the master's use, and prepared unto every good work." Sanctification insures the power of the Spirit,

a prime essential in efficient service. Consecration, a synonym of sanctification, means the surrender of all to God, which means all human powers upon the altar, to be used of Him to full capacity. This accounts for the fact that some possessing very ordinary talents accomplish more for the Lord than many who are blessed with much greater talents but less consecration.

5. **A Continual Growth in Grace.**—Read Eph. 4:11-16; I Thess. 4:1-10; II Pet. 3:17, 18. There is no more favorable condition for rapid, constant growth than a consecrated, holy life. Such a life means the power of the indwelling Spirit in the work of accomplishing great things for God. It puts one into the heavenlies, fills his soul with the richness of God's grace, prompts spiritual activity which is so essential to spiritual development, and furnishes a fertile soil favorable to abundant fruit of the Spirit—and as vegetation grows most rapidly when it is favored with an abundance of warm sunshine, so does the child of God make most satisfactory progress heavenward when enjoying the sunshine of heaven in a sanctified life.

"And the very God of peace sanctify you wholly; and I pray God your whole spirit and soul and body be preserved blameless unto the coming of our Lord Jesus Christ" (I Thess. 5:23).

# PART VI

## The Doctrine of the Church

### CHAPTERS

# THE DOCTRINE OF THE CHURCH

## Outline of Chapters

I. THE CHRISTIAN CHURCH

   1. DEFINITIONS

   2. HISTORICAL AND PROPHETIC
      a. In Old Testament Times
      b. The Church of Christ
      c. The Church in Figure

   3. CHURCH ORGANIZATION
      a. God the Author
      b. Purpose of Organization
      c. Present-day Applications

   4. WHAT THE CHURCH IS NOT
      a. Not a Community Club
      b. Not a Political Organization
      c. Not a Reform Movement
      d. Not a Playhouse

   5. GOSPEL REQUIREMENTS FOR ADMISSION
      a. Faith
      b. Repentance
      c. Conversion
      d. Obedience

   6. CHURCH GOVERNMENT
      a. The Church an Organism
      b. The Church an Organization
      c. The Church an Absolute Monarchy
      d. Christ the Head
      e. The Bible Our Discipline
      f. Scriptural Form of Government

   7. MISSION OF THE CHURCH
      a. To Glorify God
      b. Light of the World
      c. World Evangelism
      d. Growth and Preservation of Saints

   8. SUPPORT OF THE CHURCH
      a. Loyalty
      b. Public Worship
      c. Prayer
      d. Giving
      e. Promulgating Christian Doctrine
      f. Service

II. THE MINISTRY

   1. THE PURPOSE
      a. A Servant
      b. Vested with Authority

2. **THE CHIEF AIM**
   a. Preaching the Word
   b. Propagating the Church

3. **QUALIFICATIONS OF**
   a. Enduement of the Holy Spirit
   b. A Blameless Life
   c. Influential Reputation
   d. Humility
   e. Unselfishness
   f. Patience
   g. Steadfastness
   h. Sweet-tempered
   i. Not Self-willed
   j. Sobriety
   k. Vigilance
   l. Studious
   m. Soundness in Faith
   n. No Novice
   o. Scriptural Marriage Relations
   p. Apt to Teach
   q. Executive Ability
   r. No Worldly Entanglements
   s. Devotion to Calling
   t. A Living Example

4. **OFFICES OF**
   a. Bishop
   b. Minister
   c. Deacon
   d. Pastor
   e. Evangelist
   f. Missionary
   g. Teacher

5. **THE CALL**
   a. Is from the Lord
   b. Is through the Church

6. **HOW THE CALL IS RECOGNIZED**
   a. Individual Conviction
   b. Qualifications
   c. Witness of the Holy Spirit
   d. Unanimous Voice of the Church
   e. The Lot

7. **MINISTER'S PREPARATION**
   a. Study
   b. Reading
   c. Prayer

8. **WORK OF THE MINISTRY**
   a. Preaching
   b. Administering Church Rites
   c. Care of the Flock
   d. Discipline

9. SUPPORT OF
   a. Is Scriptural
   b. Prayer
   c. Obedience
   d. Words of Encouragement
   e. Assistance in Work
   f. Assistance in Physical Labor
   g. Necessities of Life
   h. Money
10. AGAINST A STIPULATED SALARY
   a. The Gospel is Free
   b. The Minister a Servant of the Lord
   c. The Salary a Muzzle
   d. Commercializes Gospel Work
   e. Becomes an Entangling Snare

III. THE CONGREGATION
   1. INTRODUCTORY THOUGHTS
      a. Organization
      b. Qualification of Membership
   2. RELATION OF LOCAL CONGREGATION TO CHURCH AT LARGE
      a. Part of the Church
      b. Obligations and Privileges
   3. CONGREGATIONAL DUTIES
      a. Of Ministry to Laity
      b. Of Laity to Ministry
   4. THE LAYMAN'S OPPORTUNITY
      a. The Sunday School
      b. The Young People's Meeting
      c. The Mission Sunday School
      d. The City Mission
      e. The Benevolent Institution
      f. The Cause of Christian Education
      g. The Foreign Field
   5. BUILDING UP THE CONGREGATION
      a. Hindrances
      b. Helps

IV. CHRISTIAN ORDINANCES
   1. PURPOSE OF ORDINANCES
   2. SUCCESSORS TO O. T. ORDINANCES
   3. SCRIPTURAL ORDINANCES
      a. Baptism
      b. Communion
      c. Feet Washing
      d. Devotional Covering
      e. The Holy Kiss
      f. Anointing with Oil
      g. Marriage

V. BAPTISM
   1. "DIVERS WASHINGS"

2. KINDS OF BAPTISM
   a. Water
   b. Spirit
   c. Fire
   d. Suffering
3. DESIGN OF SPIRIT BAPTISM
   a. The Baptism that Saves
   b. Inducts Believers into Body of Christ
   c. Purification
   d. Power for Service
4. DESIGN OF WATER BAPTISM
   a. Initiatory Rite
   b. Typical of Spirit Baptism
   c. Typifies Remission of Sins
   d. "Answer of Good Conscience"
   e. An Act of Obedience
5. GOSPEL REQUIREMENTS FOR BAPTISM
   a. Faith
   b. Repentance
   c. Conversion
6. WHAT OF INFANT BAPTISM
7. IN WHOSE NAME
8. BIBLE MODE OF BAPTISM
9. WHY WE BELIEVE IN POURING AS THE BIBLE
   MODE
   a. God's Definition for Baptism
   b. No Other Word Used as Synonym for Baptism
   c. In Harmony with O. T. Scriptures
   d. Apostolic Practice as to Place
   e. It Is Practical Everywhere
10. WHY PRACTICE WATER BAPTISM
   a. Christ Commands It
   b. Practiced by the Church since Apostolic Days
   c. Helps Strengthen Believers
   d. Belongs to Scriptural Church Organizations
   e. A Seal of Our Profession of Faith

## VI. THE COMMUNION

1. WHAT IT SIGNIFIES
   a. A Memorial of Broken Body and Shed Blood of Jesus
   b. Typical of Common Union of Communicants
   c. Demands of Communicants a Holy Life
   d. A Testimony with a Twofold Meaning
2. SOME THEORIES EXAMINED
   a. Transubstantiation
   b. Consubstantiation
   c. Open Communion
   d. Close Communion
3. RULES GOVERNING THE COMMUNION
   a. Communicants to Present Solid Body in Christ
   b. Sinners to be Excluded

c. Self-examination to Precede Communion
d. Those Openly Polluted with Sin to be Excluded
e. Only the Bread and the Cup have Divine Sanction

4. FURTHER OBSERVATIONS
   a. Communion Instituted at Regular Time for Jewish Passover
   b. Daytime the Most Appropriate for Observing It
   c. The Communion a Sacred Privilege

## VII.  FEET WASHING

1. OLD TESTAMENT REFERENCES
   a. As a Custom
   b. As a Ceremony

2. JOHN 13:1-17
   a. The Example
   b. Conversation with Peter
   c. The Explanation

3. FEET WASHING IN HISTORY

4. WHY CALL IT AN ORDINANCE
   a. Instituted by Divine Authority
   b. Resembles Ceremonial Feet Washing of O. T.
   c. Not an Old Custom
   d. Not for Cleanliness
   e. A Religious Ceremony
   f. Disciples Commanded to Continue the Practice

5. WHY IT SHOULD BE LITERALLY OBSERVED
   a. A Christian Ordinance
   b. A Blessing Promised for Its Observance
   c. One of the "All Things Whatsoever" of the Great Commission
   d. A Lesson which All Men Need
   e. Typifies Equality of Saints

## VIII.  THE DEVOTIONAL COVERING

1. INTRODUCTORY THOUGHTS

2. I CORINTHIANS 11:2-16
   a. It is an Ordinance
   b. Founded Upon a Fundamental Fact
   c. A Sign of Relationship
   d. Man Should Worship with Head Uncovered
   e. Woman Should Worship with Head Covered
   f. Natural and Spiritual Relationships
   g. A Covering "In Sign"
   h. The Contentious Man Dismissed

3. OBJECTIONS ANSWERED
   a. Not Part of Gospel
   b. Most Churches Have Discarded It
   c. My Church Does Not Observe It
   d. Only a Local Custom
   e. Long Hair a Covering
   f. Hard to Understand
   g. Others go to Heaven without It

h. Some People Make an Idol of It
i. Some Real Christian Women do not Wear It
j. More Pagan than Christian
k. Ashamed to Wear It

## IX. THE CHRISTIAN SALUTATION
1. THE PERSONAL GREETING
2. THE RIGHT HAND OF FELLOWSHIP
3. THE HOLY KISS
   a. A Symbol of Love
   b. A Command
   c. "An Holy Kiss"
   d. For "All the Brethren"
   e. Very Much Needed

## X. ANOINTING WITH OIL
1. AN ANCIENT PRACTICE
2. ANOINTING FOR HEALING PURPOSES
   a. New Testament Authority
   b. A Religious Ceremony
   c. Is It a Command
   d. Purpose of the Anointing
   e. Not Always Appropriate
   f. Not an Unction for the Soul
   g. Not for Infants
   h. Not for the Unconverted
   i. Sickness No Necessary Proof of Committed Sin
   j. Recognize Elders of Your Own Church
   k. Anointing Not for Saving Souls
   l. "Thy Will Be Done"

## XI. MARRIAGE
1. WHY MARRIAGE WAS INSTITUTED
   a. Value of Associations
   b. Propagation
   c. Purity
   d. Bringing up Children
2. WHAT CONSTITUTES MARRIAGE
   a. Beginning New Family
   b. "One Flesh"
   c. Fulfillment of Betrothal
3. MARRIAGE LAWS
   a. Against Marrying Near Relatives
   b. Against Mixed Marriages
   c. Denominational Intermarriages
   d. Against Divorce and Remarriage
   e. Against Plural Marriages
4. GETTING MARRIED
   a. Associations
   b. The Betrothal
   c. The Ceremony
5. HOME LIFE

# THE DOCTRINE OF THE CHURCH

The doctrine of the Church, like all the other great doctrines of the Bible, is set forth in Scripture with a clearness and fullness befitting its importance.

The chapters which follow present to the reader a view of the Church from two angles: (1) the Church as a body of called out ones; its mission, its organization, its work, together with the duties and relationships of its individual members; (2) the ordinances, through which the most vital principles of the Gospel are magnified in the hearts and lives of its members.

The Church has been declared to be both an organism and an organization. As an organism it consists of one body of believers with Jesus Christ as the head and the members of the body functioning as the Head may direct. We have only to think of the relationship of the mind to the rest of the body, and we have a clear concept of the relationship between Christ and the members of His body, the Church. As an organization the Church is a body of people organized for effectual service and the common welfare. Through divine directions it has its officials and rules of order, that members may be of mutual service to one another, may be fortified against the evils of this world, and may unite their powers in the work of winning the lost.

The ordinances serve as a help in keeping the Church in proper working condition, both as individuals and as a collective body. They were conceived in divine wisdom, instituted by divine authority, and we praise the Lord for the privilege of keeping them as He commanded us to do.

All praise and glory to God for instituting the Christian Church. May we cherish it, and spend our lives in promoting its interests and in glorifying its Head.

# CHAPTER I

## THE CHRISTIAN CHURCH

Upon this ROCK I will build my CHURCH and the gates of hell shall not prevail against it.—Matt. 16:18.

In a former chapter we discussed the Church as one of God's means of promoting the welfare of man. In this chapter we continue the discussion, dwelling more particularly upon the work of the Church, especially in this dispensation.

### DEFINITIONS

"The word Church (ekklesia) is derived from two Greek words meaning 'to call out from.' It has been defined as 'a body of believers who have been called out from the world, and who are under the dominion and authority of Jesus Christ.' "—Evans.

*The visible Church* is the Church on earth, as man sees it.

*The Church militant* is the body of Christ maintaining the standard of righteousness, and waging an aggressive warfare against sin and unrighteousness.

*The Church of Christ* is the body of true believers in the present dispensation.

The innumerable body of overcomers whose faith in Jesus Christ enables them to live the overcoming life here and to share in the complete triumphs of righteousness in the end is known as *the Church triumphant.*

In another sense we speak of the Church as an assembly of believers, and in our day the name is frequently applied to houses of worship and to denominations.

"The Church (which is a mystery) and the Kingdom in mystery are now contemporary. The Kingdom will be fully manifested at the coming of Christ. The Church is within the Kingdom."—Evans. "The true Church is the present manifestation of the Kingdom."—A. B. Christophel.

### HISTORICAL AND PROPHETIC

1. **In Old Testament Times.**—While the word church is not known as such in Old Testament times, yet the congregational form of worship is quite prominent in the early history of the children of Israel, and we have a hint of it in Gen. 4:26—"Then began men to call upon the name of the Lord." Stephen referred to the congregation of Israel during the wilderness wanderings as "the church in the wilderness" (Acts 7:38). David testifies, "In the midst of the congregation (church) will I praise thee" (Psa. 22:32). The Tabernacle, the Temple, and later the synagogue, were erected for convenience in sacrificial offerings and congregational worship. Ever since the calling of Abraham God had a distinct and separate people on earth to preach His Word, to promulgate His cause, and to glorify His name.

2. **The Church of Christ** is the body of God's people in this present despensation. It was first heralded forth in prophecy, preparations were made for it in the ministry of John the Baptist, after which it was organized and commissioned by Christ, and quickened and empowered for service at Pentecost. From that day forth it has been dedicated to the one great cause of making Christ and His Gospel known to the world. The Mosaic law has been superseded by the Gospel of Christ, the Levitical priesthood by the priesthood of Christ, who is "an high priest for ever, after the order of Melchisedec" (Heb. 6:20). His Gospel is our discipline, His Word is both law and life. His salvation endures forever. After His ascension His disciples returned to Jerusalem, continued steadfastly in prayer until they were endued with power from on high, since which time the Christian Church, under the leadership of the Holy Ghost, has been at work preaching the Gospel that all the world may know of His salvation. This work will go on until Christ returns for His own and to judge the world.

3. **The Church in Figure.**—There are three very suggestive figures of the Church used in the Bible: (1) the body of Christ, (2) the temple or building, (3) the Bride of Christ.

As the body of Christ, He is represented as the Head (Col. 1:18) and we as members of the body. I Cor. 12.

For an accurate description of the temple in building, read Eph. 2:20-22; 4:11-16.

A most beautiful figure is held out in Scripture representing the Church as the prospective Bride of Christ, awaiting His coming. The Holy Spirit is at work in this dispensation choosing this Bride. As a picture of the Church in the waiting attitude, see Matt. 25:1-11. All things having been completed, the Lord will come for His Bride, an indissoluble union between Christ and the Church (as between a bride and groom) will take place, "and so shall we ever be with the Lord." Read also Eph. 5:22-33 and Rev. 21:9.

### CHURCH ORGANIZATION

1. **God the Author.**—That God is the Author of Church organization is evident. He supplies the overseers and officers of the Church (Eph. 4:11-16), gives directions for its government (Matt. 18:15-17; Acts 20:28), and Christ is frequently referred to as "head," "door," "foundation," etc., of the Church. Church organization is a very prominent feature in the work of both Christ and His disciples.

2. **Purpose of Organization.**—This is forcibly set forth in Paul's instructions to the Ephesians:

> And he gave some, apostles; and some, evangelists; and some, pastors and teachers: for the perfecting of the saints, for the work of the ministry, for the edifying of the body of Christ: till we all come in the unity of the faith, and of the knowledge of the Son of God, unto a perfect man, unto the measure of the stature of the fulness of Christ.—Eph. 4:11, 13 (Read the entire chapter.)

11

Notice the four reasons given: (1) "perfecting of saints," (2) "work of the ministry," (3) "edifying of the body," (4) "unity" of the entire body.

The history of the Christian Church has proved the wisdom of organization. Churches discrediting it are, as a rule, short-lived. Organization is not only a power in holding members but also a means of uniting forces and winning other souls for God. Had the spirit of Luke 9:23, as exemplified in Acts 2:41, 42; 15:6-32 been put into universal practice since the days of Christ, there would today be but one organization in one body of loyal members of the Church of Jesus Christ.

3. **Present-day Applications.**—By authority of Jesus Christ, and the teaching and example of the apostolic Church, there rests upon us the responsibility of keeping the Church well organized and well disciplined. In every congregation there should be provisions made whereby the Gospel is preached, the needy cared for, the flock shepherded, the unsaved reached with the Gospel, and the light of the Gospel sent into the dark places within reach. Leaders need to be in frequent counsel, for "in the multitude of counsellors there is safety." Hence the need of conferences—congregational, district, and Church-wide—which serve as an effective force in promoting the unity of the faith, uniformity in methods of work, and multiplied power for service.

The organization should be simple, as in apostolic times. Organization, like every other good thing, may be overdone. The way some churches are loaded down with committees, departments, boards, movements, etc, and these supplemented with undenominational, interdenominational, and anti-denominational enterprises and movements is simply astonishing. It is safe to say that fully half of present-day church organizations could be profitably dispensed with.

By way of summary we may say that every well organized church has a Church-wide organization which through a General Conference gives voice to all problems affecting the Church as a whole; district conferences, assuming more direct charge over problems, affecting the work in their respective fields; congregations, for convenience in worship and service; mission stations, as centers of Gospel light in dark places; other institutions needed in taking care of the enterprises needed to strengthen and extend the work. As for the congregation, the unit of co-operative service, it is but reasonable that it be kept well supplied with ministers, deacons, and such other officers as are needed for effective service.

## What the Church Is Not

**1. It is not a mere social organization or community club.**

Christian fellowship, not social friendship, is the thing aimed for in Christian associations. Community betterment always results from proper church activities, but that is simply incidental. Not "social regeneration," but the regeneration of the soul; not polish, but salvation; is the proper aim of the Christian Church.

**2. It is not a political organization.**

A church in politics is out of its sphere. The Church is not an adjunct of the state, whose pulpits are turned over to politicians on the eve of great elections; nor is it the master of the state, as some think it should be, and as it consented to be in the days of Constantine. It is simply a spiritual organization in the hands of God, reaching souls by way of the Throne, and getting individuals in touch with God. The Gospel, not the ballot box, is the weapon with which Christian people should seek to clean up this sinful world.

**3. It is not a reform movement.**

The only reforms in which the true Church labors is the cleaning up resulting from the transformation of the soul. The Church proposes to make the world "a better place to live in" by leading benighted souls to Christ and salvation and thus reforming them from the inside out. Incidentally, every community is bettered, morally and intellectually as well as spiritually, by having a wide-awake Christian Church in it.

### 4. It is not a playhouse.

Its purpose is not entertainment but salvation and godly edification. God's house is a house of worship. The pulpit clown, the pool room, the church opera, the banquet hall, and every other fun-making device ever brought into any place called a church—all are abominations in the sight of God, and means of wreck and ruin to human souls. The joy of the Lord, not "the laughter of fools," is the true object sought in the work of the Church.

### Gospel Requirements for Admission

The popular idea of church membership is to receive all who want to unite with the Church; but the Bible holds to a different standard. Following are the Bible conditions for membership.

1. **Faith.**—In response to the question, "What doth hinder me to be baptized?" Philip replied, "If thou believest with all thine heart, thou mayest" (Acts 8:37, 38). When the jailer asked, "What must I do to be saved?" he received the reply, "Believe on the Lord Jesus Christ" (Acts 16:30, 31). Upon evidence of this faith he was baptized. Since faith is essential to salvation (Mark 16:16; Heb. 11:6), it should also be made a test of membership in the visible Church.

2. **Repentance.**—John the Baptist called for "fruits meet for repentance" as a requisite for baptizing the multitudes of people before him. Matt. 3:7, 8. Peter's admonition, "Repent, and be baptized" (Acts 2:38), is in harmony with John's attitude. Receive into Church any one who is willing to come, and the chances are that you have a Simon the sorcerer, an Ananias, or some other unconverted member. Receive him upon evidence of repentance

and you receive one whose sins have been remitted. Luke 24:47.

3. **Conversion.**—True repentance results in conversion. Peter understood this when he said, "Repent ye therefore, and be converted, that your sins may be blotted out" (Acts 3:19). Conversion is essential to salvation, and should be held essential to church membership. To receive unconverted people into the Church is an injustice to the applicant, for the influence of such a procedure is to blind the applicant with false hopes; an injustice to the Church, because it plants more of the leaven of wickedness into it.

4. **Obedience.**—You may ask, "How can a person not yet in the Church manifest obedience?" He can do as they did on the day of Pentecost: "Gladly" receive "his word" (Acts 2:41). The convert who comes dictating terms to the Church is a convert only in name. While the keeping of ordinances is reserved until the convert is taken into fellowship, there are many other commandments which, if the conversion is genuine, will be obeyed from the time the convert is enlightened. The Church has a right to expect a submissive attitude on the part of every convert.

## Church Government

1. **The Church an Organism.**—It is important that we think of the Church as the mystical body of Christ and every member an integral part of it. Read I Cor. 12; Eph. 2:14-22; 4:11-16.

2. **The Church an Organization.**—Not only is the Church an organism, but also an organization, in which the members are (or ought to be) properly related and organized, properly supplied with officers and leaders, all subject to Christ the Head and directed by the Holy Ghost as Leader and Guide.

3. **The Church an Absolute Monarchy.**—A conception of this fact is essential to the highest interests of the body. Equally important is it to remember that the Mon-

arch is not some pope, bishop, presbytery, council, committee, conference, or board, but none less than God Himself. Here are a few facts: (1) No man was consulted when the Law of God was promulgated. (2) There was no referendum submitted to the apostolic Church as to whether they should accept or reject the Gospel of Christ. (3) There is a fearful penalty attached to any effort to modify, add to, or subtract from any part of God's Word. Jno. 13:8; Gal. 1:8, 9; Rev. 22:18, 19. Reverently we stand in His presence, recognizing that our Gospel was conceived in the mind of the Infinite, and therefore in perfect wisdom and love.

4. **Christ the Head.**—Not only the Law but also the leadership of the Church is furnished by the Almighty. We praise the Lord that it is so, for that insures perfection in both law and leadership. We look to Jesus Christ as our Head (Col. 1:18) and to the Holy Ghost as our Leader and Guide (Jno. 14:26; 15:26; 16:13). And as all normal members of the natural body when in good health are subject to the head, so are all normal members of the body of Christ subject to Him as the great Head of the Church.

5. **The Bible Our Discipline.**—Christ our Head instituted the Gospel as our rule of life, and by it we are governed. In it we find rules and regulations for the conduct of members, for the supplying of proper church officials, for the meeting of problems confronting the Church, for the evangelization of the world. In every trial of life, in every question of dispute, in every difficulty that may arise, we go to the Gospel of Christ as the final word on all these points. Not only is the Bible our discipline, but the Church is vested with the responsible duty of seeing that this discipline is made practicable in the life of every member.

6. **Scriptural Form of Government.**—The three most commonly recognized forms of church government are:

(1) the Episcopal, or government by popes or bishops; (2) Presbyterian, or government through presbyteries, synods, conferences, or committees; (3) Congregational, or government by congregations. A careful examination of the Acts and the epistolary writings makes it clear that in the apostolic Church all of the principles and rules of action underlying these three forms of government were made use of, and that in no single instance was there a government of any apostolic church or congregation by one of these methods exclusively. We do well to pattern after this example. Matt. 18:15-18; Acts 1:15-26; 2:46, 47; 6:1-6; 15; Eph. 4:11-16; Tit. 1:5-11; Heb. 13:7, 17; I Pet. 5:1-6.

Two things to be avoided in every church are (1) liberalism, which takes little or no account of the personal life, faith, and conduct of members, and (2) legalism, which insists on emphasizing technicalities to an extent that spirituality is crowded out. The first leads to anarchy, the second to formalism.

### MISSION OF THE CHURCH

#### 1. To glorify God.

This, we may consider, is the foremost duty of every Christian, of every Christian organization. If the admonition, "Do all to the glory of God," is important for individual members, it is most certainly important to the Church as a whole. God is glorified in us, when through our labors and example people are turned to the true and living God.

#### 2. Serve as the light of the world.

"Ye are the light of the world" (Matt. 5:14), is the way Christ impresses this responsibility upon us. Not only does the world need the Gospel but it also needs living examples of how this Gospel should be translated into actual life. Since Christian people are "this world's Bibles," it behooves them to let their lights shine.

### 3. To evangelize the world.

Read Matt. 28:18-20; Mark 16:15; Luke 24:46, 47; Acts 1:8. The outstanding admonitions found in these scriptures are: "Teaching them to observe all things whatsoever I have commanded you;" "Preach the gospel to every creature;" "Repentance and remission of sins should be preached among all nations;" "Ye shall be witnesses unto me . . . unto the uttermost part of the earth." May we faithfully fulfill our mission.

### 4. To promote the spiritual growth and preservation of all saints.

When the Church has brought people to Christ it has performed only half its mission. Converts are to be instructed and, after they are in the fold of Christ, built up in the faith and service of their Master. Man as a social being needs fellowship that will help rather than hinder his spiritual growth. This we get through Christian fellowship, service, and discipline. To foster this fellowship God has wisely instituted a number of Christian ordinances through which the most vital principles of Christian life and faith are symbolized and a higher state of spiritual life is attained. After conversion the soul longs for and enjoys the fellowship of God and of saints. It is a delightful "foretaste" which encourages the believer, strengthens the body of Christ, and enables the people of God to unite their powers in bringing the whole Gospel to the whole world. Acts 2:46, 47; Eph. 4:11-16.

The organization, sphere, government, work, and mission of the Church having been considered, let us notice briefly one more important subject; namely,

### The Support of the Church

Concerning the excellence of this divinely instituted body there can be no doubt, for God conceives everything in infinite wisdom and never makes any mistakes. But man has a part to perform, if this institution of God is to function as God designed that it should. The two human things essential to the proper functioning of the Church are members and proper support. They who accept Christ as Saviour and Lord become members of His body, and once members they will give the body support as they have enlightenment and opportunity. Following are ways in which we may give the Church its proper and needed support:

1. **Loyalty.**—"Ye are bought with a price: therefore glorify God in your body, and in your spirit, which are God's. . . . be not ye the servants of men" (I Cor. 6:20; 7:23). "Hereby perceive we the love of God, because he laid down his life for us: and we ought to lay down our lives for the brethren" (I Jno. 3:16). Here, in a few words, we are reminded of our supreme duty to God and the Church. In loyal, willing, obedient, self-sacrificing, whole-hearted service, without any reservations of a world-compromising nature, our lives should be upon the altar, in which case God can use the whole powers of our being to the glory of His name and the advancement of His cause.

2. **Public Worship.**—"Not forsaking the assembling of ourselves together, as the manner of some is; but exhorting one another" (Heb. 10:25). One of the most substantial ways of supporting the Church is faithful attendance at her public services. Other things being equal, the more loyal we are to God and the Church, the more vitally interested we are in the welfare of the Church and the more faithful we are in attending public services at the house of the Lord. We have reasons to become alarmed when people, without good reasons, become slack in attending church services. By regular attendance we not only get the benefits of these meetings but we also encourage others to become partakers of these benefits.

3. **Prayer.**—We recall numerous instances recorded in the Bible where the cause of Christ and the Church was strengthened through the instrumentality of prayer. Witness, for instance, the apostolic company in that upper

room in Jerusalem previous to the outpouring of the Holy Ghost on the day of Pentecost (Acts 1:13—2:4); the disciples in the home of Mary praying for Peter (Acts 12:5, 12); the praying church at Antioch previous to the sending forth of Paul and Barnabas as missionaries to the Gentiles (Acts 13:1-4), and numerous other occasions where prayer was resorted to with great faith and power. You need not be seriously alarmed about any church whose membership is given to much fervent, sincere, and intelligent praying.

4. **Giving.**—For some reason this subject has gotten to be connected with the giving of money, and for this reason we shall connect it with the same idea. But let us say, first of all, that when the spirit of giving, accompanied by true enlightenment, takes possession of the heart it reaches every part of the being—heart, mind, hands, affections, pocketbook, all. But speaking of the financial support of the Church, it is essential, for the following reasons:

a. *It is needed for the material support of the various enterprises of the Church*—buildings, traveling expenses, living expenses on the part of those who are giving their time to the work of the Church, literature, support of Church institutions, care of the poor and needy, etc.

b. *It is needed for the spiritual welfare of the givers.* It was Christ who said, "It is more blessed to give than to receive" (Acts 20:35). With this agrees the testimony of Paul when he says, "He which soweth sparingly shall reap also sparingly; and he which soweth bountifully shall reap also bountifully" (II Cor. 9:6). This is true of churches as well as individuals. For the sake of the giver, as well as for the sake of the Church, we need to cultivate the spirit of liberality in giving, whatever may be the nature of our gifts.

c. *It is needed for prosperity.* Hear the testimony of the prophet of God: "Will a man rob God? Yet ye have robbed me. But ye say, Wherein have we robbed thee? In tithes and offerings. . . . . Bring ye all the tithes into the storehouse, that there may be meat in mine house, and prove me now herewith, saith the Lord of hosts, if I will not open you the windows of heaven, and pour you out a blessing, that there shall not be room enough to receive it" (Mal. 3:8, 10). Here, then, are the three Biblical reasons for a liberal material support of the Church: (1) because it is needed by the cause of Christ; (2) because it is needed for the proper spiritual development of the giver; (3) because it is needed that God may be glorified in the spiritual and material prosperity of His people. No wonder that we are told that "God loveth a cheerful giver" (II Cor. 9:7).

As to the amount of our spiritual and material support of the Church, that will take care of itself so long as we obey Bible instructions as to motives and methods. Here is the New Testament standard: "Freely" (Matt. 10:8), "to the poor" (Matt. 19:21), "not grudgingly" (II Cor. 9:7), "as he purposeth in his heart" (II Cor. 9:7), cheerfully (II Cor. 9:7), "to the glory of God" (I Cor. 10:31), "as God hath prospered" (I Cor. 16:2). Follow this standard, and neither God nor sensible men will ever find fault with you that you did not give enough.

5. **Promulgating Christian Doctrine.**—The giving of finances is but one among a number of ways in which the cause of Christ and the Church may be advanced. It was our Saviour's instruction to His disciples that they "teach all nations. . . . to observe all things whatsoever" He had commanded them. Personal loyalty is good as far as it goes, but what is good enough for ourselves is good enough for others. We give the Church substantial support when we obey, defend, and promulgate the doctrines known as her tenets of faith; thereby enlarging the borders of the Church and extending the sphere of her influence and labors, thereby strengthening the Church in giving practical testimony in support of the things "most surely believed among us."

6. **Service.**—The cry for laborers has been heard ever since the Christian Church was in the process of forming.

The last message of Christ to His disciples was that they should go "into all the world, and preach the GOSPEL to every creature" (Mark 16:15). Workers are needed in the home, in the schoolroom, in the social circle, in business life, in the home community, in neglected quarters near our doors, in sparsely settled rural districts, in crowded cities, at home and abroad, everywhere, to maintain the standard of the cross, to carry the banner of King Jesus. to make known His "glad tidings of salvation," to "shine as lights in the world," to support the Church in faithful, humble, loyal service. In the language of God through Paul we conclude this chapter by saying, "Therefore, my beloved brethren, be ye stedfast, unmoveable, always abounding in the work of the Lord, forasmuch as ye know that your labour is not in vain in the Lord."

# CHAPTER II

## THE MINISTRY

### By D. H. Bender

Make full proof of thy ministry.—II Tim. 4 :5.

The Christian minister is a servant. The derivation of the word minister makes this its primary meaning. He is a servant in the truest and fullest sense of the word. In this he but follows the example of his Lord and Master, who "came not to be ministered unto, but to minister." Thus the service of the Gospel ministry was exalted to the highest possible degree. It is the most important, the most vital, the most essential, the most responsible, and the most exalted calling within the province of humanity. It is the one calling on earth that is established, fostered, and controlled directly by the Lord Himself. The representatives of the ministry are called, qualified, supported, and finally rewarded by the Lord.

### THE PURPOSE

The place given the ministry of the Gospel in the Scriptures shows that its purpose has a twofold condition of service: (1) Subservient in nature, (2) authoritative in application. Under the first condition the minister serves under the direct leadership of Christ, the Head of the Church; under the second, he is placed in authority, directing the work to some extent through others, and placed under weighty responsibility.

1. **The Minister as a Servant.**—As such the Bible refers to him as—

        a. A servant.—Jas. 1 :1.
        b. A laborer.—I Cor. 3 :9.
        c. A helper.—II Cor. 1 :24.
        d. A steward.—Tit. 1 :7.
        e. A witness.—Acts 1 :8; Rev. 11 :3.

**2. The Minister Vested with Authority.**—As such the Word declares him—

    a. An ambassador.—II Cor. 5:20.
    b. An overseer.—Acts 20:28.
    c. A pastor.—Eph. 4:11.
    d. A ruler.—I Tim. 5.17.
    e. A bishop.—Tit. 1:7.
    f. An elder.—I Tim. 5:17.

### The Chief Aim

The chief aim of the ministry is to bring men to Christ and to build them up in Christ. It is the perpetuation of the ministry of Christ begun by Himself while on earth. This is accomplished—

**1. By the Preaching of the Word.**—"Go ye into all the world, and preach the gospel to every creature," is the commission that confronts every minister as he steps into his sacred office. There is nothing that can take the place of preaching. It is the means ordained of God, foolish though it may seem to some men, by which men shall find salvation. "It pleased God by the foolishness of preaching to save them that believe" (I Cor. 1:21).

**2. By the Propagation of the Church.**—The Church is the one institution on earth established by Jesus Christ. He is still its spiritual Head. It is made up of believers who have been saved through the ministry of the Word. Here they are built up in Christ. They learn obedience to the ordinances, restrictions, and rites laid down in the Word. They unite their efforts in fighting sin and Satan. They foster missions and benevolent institutions, and support the various movements intended to extend the borders of the Kingdom.

### Qualifications for the Ministry

As the office of the ministry is a calling directly under the control of the Lord; since He calls, qualifies, supports, and rewards His ministers, and yet calls the Church to have a part in the choosing, ordaining and sending forth of the ministry, it follows that the Lord would clearly state the character of the men qualified for this important work so that the Church would make no mistake in setting them forth. The Word of God is clear in pointing out these qualifications:

1. **The Enduement of the Holy Spirit** (Luke 4:8; 24: 49; Acts 1:18; 2:1-21).—The work of the ministry is a spiritual work. It deals directly with the spirits of men and can only be accomplished through the leading and power of the Holy Spirit. Were it possible for a man to attain to all the other qualifications laid down in God's Word, yet lacking the baptism of the Holy Ghost, the call of the Spirit and the infilling of the same in a measure especially adapted to his work, he would be utterly disqualified as a minister of the Gospel; and should he attempt to serve without this vital qualification, his work must prove a dismal failure. Even though the other qualifications may not be so strikingly apparent, with the enduement of the Holy Spirit and a diligent application toward the development of the other requisites, he will be a successful minister.

2. **A Blameless Life** (I Tim. 3:2; Tit. 1:5,6).—God demands the highest type of character in His servants. To be successful in the service of the ministry, a man must necessarily be possessed of a blameless character. His life may not be above criticism, but it must be free from worldly spots and above blame.

3. **An Influential Reputation** (I Tim. 3:7).—A minister's work affects largely the unconverted of the community. He needs to have a "good report" among those on the outside as well as among those within the Church. While reputation does not always correspond with character, reputation is, after all, an essential element in character, and, "a good name is rather to be chosen than great riches." You will never win those over whom you have no influence. Influence is begotten of confidence, and confidence of a "good report."

4. **Humility** (Acts 20:19; I Pet. 5:5).—All successful ministers of the past were possessed of a wholesome degree of Gospel humility. Possibly the two greatest ministers before the Christian era were Moses and John the Baptist. The first has been called "the meekest man of the earth" (Num. 12:3). Of the second, after his marks of genuine humility were set forth—in dress, dwelling, manner of life, position—Jesus says, "Among them that are born of women, there hath not risen a greater than John the Baptist." The foundation of all true greatness is true humility. Nothing is so repellent in a public servant as a proud, vain, self-important, arrogant, honor-seeking spirit. God can do nothing for or with a proud spirit. God exalts the humble.

5. **Unselfishness** (I Cor. 9:20:22).—An intimate companion to humility is unselfishness. Pride and selfishness are twin destroyers of power and influence, but humility coupled with an unselfish disposition assures respect and success in any public calling. Let the Christian minister learn from his Master the lesson of unselfishness.

6. **Patience** (II Cor. 6:4; I Tim. 3:3).—"Let patience have her perfect work," is wholesome advice. A man devoid of patience is not qualified for the trying ordeals of the ministry. No other calling demands the employment of Christian patience more than does that of the ministry. The servant of God in this capacity has to deal with all the shades of disposition of a depraved humanity. All manner of Church problems present themselves, and if there is evidence of hot-headedness and impatience on the part of the heads of the Church, the work will be greatly hindered. Patience and cool-headedness go a long way in adjusting difficulties and winning a point for the cause. "Let patience have her perfect work" in the ministry.

7. **Steadfastness** (I Cor. 15:58; Eph. 4:14-16; Jas. 1:8).—Steadfastness, or firmness and loyalty to the right, is a quality that finds frequent use in the work of the ministry. Doublemindedness is condemned in Scripture. Such

a man "is unstable in all his ways." The minister needs to be very cautious and deliberate in taking a position, especially on points that are debatable; but having found the rock foundation, he needs to stand firmly and unflinchingly by his convictions and the teaching of the Word. An unestablished disposition allows the minister to be "driven hither and thither," and no one dares to trust him with personal problems or serious Church matters.

8. **Sweet-tempered** (Tit. 1:7).—"Not soon angry" is the wording used in Holy Writ in describing this quality of the Gospel minister. An irritable disposition repels and destroys. Nothing is ever gained through anger, but very much is lost through this fault of humanity. A leader who cannot control his own temper certainly is unable to control others. Pray for a sweet temper.

9. **Not Self-willed** (Tit. 1:7).—Stubbornness is not akin to steadfastness. The one is a blind determination not to yield to any influence that crosses his path, whatever the nature or source; the other is a faithful adherence to principle. born of unselfish investigation, deep conviction, and scriptural truth. The self-willed minister is responsible for many sad schisms and divisions in the Church. When considering the men for the ministry, beware of the self-willed brother.

10. **Sobriety** (I Tim. 3:2, 8).—The minister of the Gospel is not required to be funereal, ascetic, or painfully serious, but he needs to be composed, thoughtful, "sober," and "grave." Frivolity, lightness, and boisterous levity are not qualities to make the work of a minister effectual.

11. **Vigilant** (I Tim. 3:2; II Tim. 4:5).—The minister is a "watchman on the walls of Zion." It is his duty to have a watchful eye and give the note of warning of approaching danger. He must be wide-awake, always alert. He must be alive to happenings all about him and the flock. He needs this characteristic for self-improvement and to be of real service to the flock. A sleepy, careless, unconcerned ministry allows the enemy to enter the fold

and scatter the flock. "Watch thou in all things," is the Bible advice to a young minister. This is good advice for all ministers, whether young or old.

12. **Studious** (I Tim. 4:13; II Tim. 2:15).—"Give attendance to reading," the young minister Timothy is admonished. A timely modern admonition to serve as an appendix to the above would be, "and be careful what you read." Let that reading be first of all the minister's standard library, the Bible, and all the rest should be in harmony with it. It is well to regard the admonition, "Study to shew thyself approved unto God," in this age when the temptation to cater to the approval of the world and the popular mind is so dominant. The true minister will study the Word, other good books, his life, the signs of the times, the needs of the Church, the mission and other problems of the Church, and everything that pertains to the success of his work as an effectual minister. The minister needs to be habitually studious.

13. **Sound in the Faith** (Tit. 1:9; 2:1).—The soundness of a member's faith should be thoroughly tested and approved before he is considered eligible for the ministry. Ministers who have held points in doctrine not in harmony with the Word or the orthodox faith of the Church have made shipwreck of their own usefulness and carried others down with themselves. Just as an expert architect would reject an unsound piece of timber and not allow its going into the building where heavy strain is required, so the Church should jealously guard against placing men in the ministry, where so much of weal or woe depends on the position taken by the leader of the flock. How can a minister "speak the things that become sound doctrine," when he himself is unsound? How can he "by sound doctrine" used in his arguments and teaching "convince the gainsayer" when he himself does not subscribe to soundness of doctrine? This is a vital and very important qualification, and is becoming more and more so as we approach the "latter days" in which men "will not endure

sound doctrine." If we would save the Church from the general apostasy that is threatening the religious world, let us be more cautious in selecting men for the ministry who are sound in the faith.

14. **"Not a Novice"** (I Tim. 3:6).—A man just converted to the faith has had neither time nor opportunity to prove himself sound in the faith, so what was said on the preceding qualification would forestall the ordaining of a novice. The Bible does not reject young men from the ministry and demand that only the "elders" be ordained, but it does demand that a candidate for the ministry must be old enough in the service to prove himself qualified for this sacred calling. The Church can better afford to wait a while longer than to ordain a bright and apparently useful man, untried and a novice in the faith. Such hasty steps often lead to bitter repentance when much mischief has been wrought to the cause, and it is too late to retrace and undo the harm resultant from the mistake.

15. **Free from Unsuitable Matrimonial Relations** (I Tim. 3:2, 11).—The minister's wife figures largely in his success or failure, and consequently the weal or woe, of the congregation over which he is set. In this age of easy and unscriptural marriage and divorce laws, it is essential that the minister, especially the bishop, take a firm stand as to what constitutes correct scriptural matrimonial relations. Unless he can stand before his people as a model on these points, his influence will be largely destroyed. A wife who could not and would not be a "help meet for him" in the work of the ministry, but would oppose him in his work, would be a positive hindrance to him and the cause he was ordained to promulgate.

16. **The Gift of Teaching** (I Tim. 3:2; 4:11; II Tim. 2:2, 24).—Knowledge and the possession of facts alone do not make a teacher. The power to teach is a gift, an endowment. It is an aptitude that cannot be acquired by storing up knowledge. The Head of the Church "gave

some . . . teachers." The gift to teach comes from above. Much of the work of the ministry is closely related to teaching. Indeed, Jesus commands in the Great Commission that ministers should be qualified for the teaching of "all things" that He had commanded. When the Bible demands that a minister shall be "apt to teach" and "able to teach others," the obligation of the Church is to select such men for the ministry as have the gift to impart knowledge to others and lead others into the development of *truth*.

17. **Executive Ability** (I Tim. 3:4, 5).—Since the ministry is responsible for the execution of God's order in the Church and the discipline of its members, as well as the general leadership of the body of Christ, it is mandatory that a man give evidence of the ability to lead and govern before placing him in the office of the ministry. The Bible demands that a bishop shall have proved himself a wise and effective executive by the successful administration of the affairs of his household, "one that ruleth well his own house," and emphatically declares that if he have failed in this he is unqualified to take the oversight of the Church. This is strikingly plain language: "For if a man know not how to rule his own house, how shall he take care of the church of God?"

18. **Separate from Worldly Entanglements** (I Tim. 3: 3; II Tim. 2:4).—Coveting worldly power, "greedy of filthy lucre," entanglement with "the affairs of this life," are disqualifications carefully noted by the inspired writer. Secular affairs have their place, even in the life and activities of ministers. Paul emphasizes the fact that he made his own living by secular labor, and helped others to do the same. Honest toil, of brain or brawn, is commendable and healthful for the minister. But he must keep himself free from business and social entanglements of a worldly nature. He must set the riches of God's grace above the riches of the world. He must prize the winning of souls more than the winning of dollars or earthly laurels. He looks forward to "the crown of life" given after the "good fight" is accom-

plished rather than to the fading honor and the hollow applause of the world. He is the pattern for the "peculiar people" of God and an example for a "separate-from-the world" body to follow.

19. **Devotion to Calling** (I Cor. 9:16-18; II Cor. 12: 15.)—Paul was willing to "spend and be spent" for the cause he had espoused, even though he saw no appreciation on the part of those whom he served. In fact, he declares "the more abundantly I love you the less I be loved." His keen devotion to his calling made him insensible to the slights and inappreciation of the people. He made great sacrifices so that the Gospel of Christ would be "without charge," and that in no way he would abuse his power in the Gospel. The spirit of true devotion to a work or a cause makes sacrifice a pleasure rather than a burden. Without the spirit of devotion no one is able to render the best service.

20. **A Living Example** (I Tim. 4:12; Tit. 2:7, 8).— Example is stronger than precept. "Actions speak louder than words." These are maxims whose truth is nowhere more vital in any work than in the Christian ministry. Timothy might well assert his authority and allow none to despise his youth, provided he was "an example of the believers." Titus, another young minister, is exhorted to be "a pattern of good works." The minister who leads an exemplary life preaches a telling sermon as long as he lives. An eloquent orator and expert logician may move his audience wondrously for a half hour while he is dispensing to them the truth fired with brilliant eloquence. but unless his life corresponds with his preaching, he is preaching a silent though powerful sermon for the rest of the day that will be the undoing of both him and his work. That "the world reads the preacher more than it does the Bible," is a saying that has been demonstrated time and again. It is the life that counts in the end.

There has been no attempt made to specially apply these qualifications to the various offices of the ministry—

bishop, minister, deacon, evangelist, missionary, teacher—but they have been treated in a general way. All are good for these offices. Some have greater force in one office than in another. The nature of the office determines the class of qualifications that need special emphasis.

After we have done all, have used our best intelligence and wisdom in selecting men for the ministry, let it be remembered that this is the Lord's work; that the Lord qualifies and calls to the ministry; that our part is only to be used as He directs.

### OFFICES OF THE MINISTRY

According to the inspired report of the apostle, the offices ordained of God for the "work of the ministry" are Apostles, prophets, evangelists, pastors and teachers. Eph. 4:11, 12. The modern Church aims to cover the work of these offices by dividing it up variously and assigning more or less specific work to its various offices. In some denominations, as the Roman Catholic and Episcopalian, the work of each office is very definitely outlined and circumscribed; while in others, as the Congregational, the lines of demarcation between the various offices are not so clear, and often the person serving in one office has full authority to serve in any other office. It is our purpose to keep our discussion confined to such offices as are recognized by the Church generally and bestowed upon individuals by regular ordination.

**Bishop.**—The highest office in the Church is that of bishop. The word itself means overseer, director, superintendent. It is a scriptural word used in a definite sense. The word "elder" is used in a number of places in the Bible to represent the bishop, as is also the word "presbyter" in one instance. I Tim. 4:14.

The word "bishop" is a specific term, used in a special manner and with a definite meaning. This cannot be said of the other two terms. The term elder comes from the custom to set at the head of the people the eldest among them, and may include any office of the ministry. In the Bible it is used interchangeably with bishop and other offices of the ministry. It is hardly to be taken that the "elders" which Paul and Barnabas ordained "in every church" on their first missionary journey were all bishops. Other references carry the weight of argument in favor of the claim that elders were bishops. See Acts 20:17; Jas. 5:14; I Pet. 5:1.

The work of the bishop is that of overseer and general director of the affairs of the Church. Jesus Himself is called a bishop in this sense. I Pet. 2:25. The Revised Version uses the word "bishop" instead of "overseer" in Acts 20:28, making the passage read: "Take heed unto yourselves, and to all the flock, over the which the Holy Spirit hath made you bishops, to feed the church of the Lord, which he purchased with his own blood." The apostleship was the highest office in the Church at the time of its founding, and this office is spoken of as a "bishopric" (Acts 1:20). We conclude therefore that the correct term, technical and practical, is that of bishop.

The bishop should be considered the head of the Church, should be in charge of its official functions, and either perform the same himself or have them performed under his supervision. He needs to keep near to the great "Bishop of souls" and be "an ensample to the flock." As such he should receive and enjoy the confidence and hearty support of the congregation. Adam Clarke says: "The office of a bishop is from God; a true pastor only can fulfill this office; it is an office of most awful responsibility; few there are who can fill it."

**Minister.**—This is also a term of accommodation. The technical meaning of the word is servant, or slave. It is widely used in the sense of special servant in both civic and ecclesiastical economy. Every member of the ministry, of course, is a minister. Already in the Jewish Church was the term officially used. Luke 4:20. The Holy Ghost called Paul to be a "minister" (Acts 26:16). Paul speaks of himself and Apollos as "ministers" (I Cor. 3:5). Timothy, who also became a bishop, is called a "minister" (I Thess. 3:2). It is a correct Bible term, and applies well to the office so styled in contradistinction from that of bishop. All bishops are ministers, but not all ministers are bishops, nor are all qualified to become bishops. The minister serves the Church in preaching the Word, assists the bishop, and under his jurisdiction performs many of the functions and rites of the Church, serving the cause in a general manner.

**Deacon.**—The office of deacon seems to have been created in the early days of the Christian Church. There was need that some one especially appointed to take care of the poor and look after the needy of the Church should be ordained to that work, and so the Church ordered the ordination of seven men "of honest report, full of the Holy Ghost and wisdom." These were selected and duly ordained for the work to which they had been chosen. Acts 6:1-6. That the Church continued to use the office of deacon is evidenced by the records given of church work in the epistolary writings. Paul sends greetings to the "bishops and deacons" in the church at Philippi. Phil. 1:1. That the Word carefully records the qualifications of a deacon (I Tim. 3:8-13) shows that theirs is an important office in the Church of Christ.

The work of the deacon generally is to look after the poor, to see to the visitation work, to take care of church funds, to assist in the administration of the ordinances and rites of the Church, and to serve as a helper to the other officers of the church.

**Pastors.**—In many respects every minister is a pastor —one who looks after the flock. In the Mennonite Church the pastoral work of the Church is usually divided among the bishops, ministers, and deacons. In some instances where there are a number of ministers located at one place, one of them is made especially responsible for the oversight of the congregation, and as such is called the pastor or minister in charge. This custom is, however, not universal in the Mennonite Church. Pastoral work is very important. A careful shepherding of the flock goes a long way in the work of a successful ministry.

**Evangelist.**—This is also a general office in the ministry. There is no order or rule of the Church by which certain persons are especially ordained as evangelists. Evangelists are usually chosen from among the ministry and they go forth carrying the Word of the Gospel throughout the Church, laboring in any congregations to which they are called. It is a scriptural office. Acts 21:18; Eph. 4:11.

**Missionary.**—This is a term not found in the Bible. But from the earliest history of the Church she had her missionaries. For some time the work of the missionary was limited to the regularly ordained ministry, but since the field has been enlarged, other workers were needed, and today we have many faithful missionaries who have not been ordained to the ministry. It is not the part of wisdom that such an important work should be done except under the supervision of the regularly recognized ministry.

**Teacher.**—The apostolic Church made provisions for teachers among them. I Cor. 12:28; Eph. 4:11. Christ was a teacher. John 3:2. Barnabas and Paul were teachers. Atcs 13:1. Teaching as used in the Bible sense has reference to a special kind of Scripture interpretation and general instruction of the people. All true preaching has the element of teaching in it. But that not all the teaching from the ministry is wholesome is proved by the warning of the Word. The Church is warned against "teachers" who strive to please those "having itching ears" (II Tim. 4:3). There is a field for special Bible teaching in this age of the Church, in the Sunday school, mission work, special Bible study classes and in our church schools. It is highly important that the greatest care be exercised in the choosing of teachers. That many of the theological schools of the land employ unsound teachers, and are thereby leading many into error regarding the Bible and religious beliefs ought to arouse the Church to the sense of her duty along this line, and she should see to it that such teachers only are given place as are sound in the faith and orthodox in every true sense of the word.

## The Call to the Ministry

The Gospel ministry is a calling. It is not a mere profession or vocation, a trade or business, one that may be chosen, entered into, or laid down at will. Men are divinely called to the ministry. The Lord controls both the call and the work. A few questions naturally present themselves as this subject is approached: How may one enter the ministry? Is there a special call needed, or may one enter the ministry as he would any other profession— by choice or special fitness? Is a divine call essential to the ministry today? A brief consideration of the subject follows.

1. **The Call is from the Lord.**—God has always exercised an exclusive proprietorship over the call of men as leaders of His people. God called Moses in an unmistakable manner. He did not exercise authority to assign the masses their occupations, but He did call Moses as His minister. What is true of the call of Moses, is true of the call of the prophets. It was "the word of the Lord" that came to the prophets and called them from secular occupations to the sacred office of prophet. This is clear, from the call of Samuel to that of Malachi. These were divinely called, and spoke as the Holy Ghost gave them utterance. The first high priest (Aaron) was especially named and called directly of the Lord. The New Testament declares that "no man taketh this honour unto himself, but he that is called of God, as was Aaron" (Heb. 5:4). Jesus Christ, "made a high priest for ever," made the final sacrifice on the altar of sin-offering "once for all," and the Levitical priesthood was abolished. Jesus abolished the priesthood but established the ministry in its stead. He called a num-

ber to be His special followers, inducted them into office, gave them special authority, and sent them forth to minister to the people. He commissioned them and their successors to go "into all the world, and preach the gospel to every creature;" to teach them "all things" that He had commanded. Thus we have the Christian ministry established for the purpose of bringing men to Christ and building them up in Christ. Jesus, moreover, certified His intention to oversee the work and be with His chosen ministers "alway, even unto the end of the world."

We are commanded to pray "the Lord of the harvest" that "HE will send forth labourers into his harvest." This command indicates two things: (1) that it is the duty of the Church to constantly pray for laborers, (2) that the Lord holds the exclusive right to send them forth. Thus the Christian ministry is subject to the call of the Lord.

2. **The Call is Through the Church.**—The Church usually dates her birth from the day of Pentecost. The nucleus of that body was contained in the Twelve. It was to the chosen men that Jesus said, "Upon this rock I will build my church" (Matt. 16:18). See also Matt. 18:18. It was to the spokesman of that body (Peter) that Jesus said, "I will give unto thee the keys of the kingdom of heaven: and whatsoever thou shalt bind on earth shall be bound in heaven; and whatsoever thou shalt loose on earth, shall be loosed in heaven" (Matt. 16:19). Every divinely sanctioned Christian worker is called and commissioned of the Church. A normal church is the mouthpiece and congress of God.

To the pre-pentecostal body of Christ came the word that the place made vacant by Judas should be filled. The body acted. Matthias was chosen to the "ministry and apostleship," and "he was numbered with the eleven apostles" (Acts 1:15-26).

The Church selected the first deacons and ordained them to their office, acting under the guidance of the Holy

Spirit (Acts 6:1-6), as it did also the first missionaries (Acts 13:2, 3).

The apostle to the Gentiles did not act alone upon his divine call from above, and not until the proper officer of the Church had laid his hands upon him and ordained him, giving him his commission, did he enter the work of the ministry (Acts 9:17; 22:12-15). Taking these Scriptures as our testimony, we conclude that all divinely sanctioned ministers are called of God through the Church.

### How the Call Is Recognized

The vital question that often presents itself to the Church and the individual is to determine whether the Lord has or has not called a certain person to the ministry. There should not and need not be occasion for the Church to make so serious a mistake as to ordain an uncalled worker, or set one aside whom the Lord has called. Here are a few tests:

1. **Individual Conviction.**—"From the beginning" God determines His workers. If the individual is true to his nature, there will be an inward conviction, a holy desire, an evidence of responsibility, an assurance that God wants him for His special service. Care must be exercised in locating the origin of this desire and see that it is not the product of selfish soil. Good men, and some not so good, may have a mistaken idea as to the source of this conviction. The test to be made here is to determine whether the work of the ministry—sacrificing for the cause, leading souls into the kingdom, glorifying God—is the real actuating influence. There are features about the ministry that appeal—the public exercise of literary gifts, social standing in the community, advantageous contact with the masses, a place of honor and authority, etc. These are only points incident to the ministry. They are not the ministry, and if for these reasons a man desires to enter the ministry, his convictions may rightly be questioned. "The ministry is the divine business of rescuing souls and

building them up in Christ to the glory of God." On this point Luther says: "Await God's call. Meantime be satisfied. Yet, though thou wast wiser than Solomon and Daniel, yet, unless thou art called (of God) avoid preaching as thou wouldst hell itself." But if the conviction is of God a conviction of a divine obligation, a holy duty, a consecrated, humble desire will rest in the soul, to glorify God in humble, obedient service.

2. **Possession of Requisite Qualifications.**—God never asks a man to perform a task for which is not qualified. He furnishes the means by which the work can be done. He said to the humble fishermen, "Follow me and I will make you fishers of men." There often accompanies the call a keen realization of unfitness and unworthiness. Moses felt it. Paul realized it. Many a modern minister who afterward became a power for God in the service realized a sensitive degree of unfitness. God makes no mistakes. Sometimes He lays hold of a "diamond in the rough," possibly because in His omniscience He sees that it is safer to polish this one within rather than without the ministry. He knows the heart of man.

3. **Witness of the Holy Spirit.**—While Jesus was upon earth, He called His ministers personally. When He ascended to heaven He sent the Holy Spirit as the abiding and controlling person of the Trinity on earth. The direct call to the ministry now is through the Holy Spirit. We are living in the dispensation of the Spirit who speaks to the inner heart and not to the outer ear. Yet the call is just as direct as it was in the days of Christ. The divine voice is heard and recognized by God's people, for it is the natural voice of the Father speaking to His children. It was the Holy Spirit that said to the Church at Antioch: "Separate me Barnabas and Saul for the work whereunto I have called them" (Acts 13:2). That same voice speaks in an unmistakable manner to the Church today. Listen to the voice of the Spirit.

4. **By the Unanimous Voice of the Church.**—If a congregation is in line with God, especially if it is not a large one, the choice for the ministry is frequently determined by the unanimous conviction of its members. This may be just as true of larger congregations. It is in many respects the ideal way. It shows that God is speaking to all in the same voice, which is evidence that all are in position where God can and will fully reveal His will to them. This, of course, presupposes that no other influences were at work that God could not sanction. Electioneering for the ministry is sacrilege. The unanimous voice of a conference may safely be taken as the voice of the Lord in cases where a minister is to be chosen for special work in the district, or from among the congregations comprising the district.

5. **By the Lot.**—The first person chosen to the office of the ministry after Jesus left the earth was by lot. The lot was very frequently used in the early history of God's people in determining the will of the Lord and in calling men to high and sacred offices. There is a disposition among some modern Christians to recognize the scriptural use of the lot for the earlier ages, but object to its use in the ordination of the ministry in this age. This aversion to the use of the lot is sometimes traceable to the misuse of this sacred order. It is not a means to be trifled with, or to be employed with a view of getting out of the task of selecting properly qualified men. It is to be used only when men have done their duty in selecting the proper one for the ministry and the choice is not unanimous. God sees and knows what man cannot see and know.

The call of Matthias is objected to on the ground that the Holy Ghost was not yet given; that the action of the apostles in calling one to fill the place of Judas was premature and therefore without divine sanction; that Paul and not Matthias was the divinely called apostle to take the "bishoprik" of Judas. Space will not permit extended discussion of these controverted points, but we want to give a few proofs that the action of the apostles in the instance cited was divinely sanctioned and sustained, and that the same evidences sustain the use of the lot in the Christian Church today.

a. There is no ground for claiming that the apostles acted without the sanction of the Holy Ghost, as long before that time holy men "speak as they were moved by the Holy Ghost" (II Pet. 1:21). Read also Acts 1:16-22.

b. Matthias is indeed never again mentioned in connection with the activities of the Church; neither are the majority of the rest of the apostles.

c. Paul is nowhere mentioned as the successor of Judas, but is distinctly "the apostle of the Gentiles" (Rom. 11:13). Barnabas and others are also called apostles (Acts 14:14), so the point raised by some that if Matthias was an apostle there were thirteen apostles, has no virtue. There are more than thirteen persons called apostles in the New Testament.

d. That the call of Matthias had the divine sanction is attested to by the fact that the sacred record gives a very full and detailed account of the action, and nowhere in the Bible is there a hint of disapproval. Is it reasonable that an unauthorized action of such magnitude should be thus divinely recorded and made the means of leading the Church in all succeeding ages into error?

e. The Word expressly declares that Matthias "was numbered with the eleven apostles" (Acts 1:26)—and there is no hint that it was a mistake.

f. After the death of Judas and before the call of Matthias the apostles are spoken of as "the eleven" (Matt. 28:16; Mark 16:14; Luke 24:9, 33); after the call of Matthias, and before the conversion of Saul, they were called "the twelve," or spoken of in such a manner as to make it clear that Matthias was included in "the twelve" (Acts 2:14; 6:2).

For the above reasons, and others equally plausible, the use of the lot in the call of the ministry stands approved in the present day and age of the Church. Its use is sacred. It removes no responsibility from the Church in exercising care. The candidates for the ministry must be just as carefully selected when the lot is used as when any other form of call to the ministry is employed. To take men into the lot not scripturally qualified, or attempt to shift responsibility in this important matter, spells punishment.

All whom the Lord calls find their field of labor, if they submit to Him and the call. The Lord opens the way; unless He does, there is no call. Only unfaithful men can hinder the call of the Lord, none can defeat it.

Lord Jesus, send us faithful ministers.

### The Minister's Preparation

Ministerial preparation is a subject of a peculiar nature. Since the Scriptures assert that the matter of the call to the ministry is from God, it follows that the Lord either calls those who have already been prepared, or He takes them through a process of preparation during the call, or He sees to it that adequate preparation is made subsequent to the call.

The Levites went through a process of training for the priesthood. There seem to have been special schools for the training of the prophets: at Ramah (I Sam. 19: 20), Bethel (II Kings 2:3), Jericho (II Kings 2:5), Gilgal (II Kings 4:38), and elsewhere (II Kings 6:1). Just what was the nature of the work done by the prophets at these religious centers is largely a matter of conjecture. There is no record in the New Testament of the existence of schools for the training of men who would enter the ministry. The deplorable fact that many of the theological schools of the day lead young men away from rather than toward the acceptance of a full Gospel teaching, has caused the orthodox body of believers to look with suspicion and disfavor upon such schools. But it is not the intention at this time to discuss the merits or demerits of a theological education.

God makes no mistakes when He calls to the ministry. He has chosen them from the humble fisherman of Galilee, to the educated man of Tarsus. Here are a few facts:

A well-developed and practically trained mind, stored with useful knowledge is a great help in the ministry.

An education achieved amid erroneous influences and false teachings is a great hindrance in the ministry.

It is reasonable and right for any man to obtain a clean education amid ennobling influences, with a view to being of the best service in life, wherever his lot may be cast, whether that be to dig in the ditch or to preach in the pulpit or both.

No one can effectively use a tool with which he is not acquainted. No one can teach grammar who knows nothing about grammar. No one can use the Bible effectively without knowing the Bible. The Spirit will do much in the way of bringing "to remembrance" passages of Scripture once learned, and lead the worker in the proper use of the same, but he must first learn to know the Scripture. To this end a course in Bible study will serve a good end, as well as a knowledge of the field of labor. Three points of preparation are always in order for the Gospel worker:

1. **Study.**—"Search the Scriptures" is the divine injunction. That the minister needs to give much time to study and meditation needs no argument. "Study to shew thyself approved unto God, a workman that needeth not to be ashamed, rightly dividing the word of truth," carries with it more obligation for constant preparation than is usually given it.

2. **Reading.**—"Give attendance to reading" (I Tim. 4:13) is Paul's admonition to a young minister. This word of admonition is inspired, and effective today as much as ever. The minister who would do effective work in the pulpit or among his flock must have a correct view of all that pertains to his work. He needs to be posted on the issues of the day, as well as the teachings of the Word. It is his duty to cope with the issues of the hour, and this

12

he can do intelligently and effectively only as he has knowledge of them. He needs, above all else, to read his Bible carefully and prayerfully and listen to God as He speaks to him through His Word.

3. **Prayer.**—There is no other preparation for a Gospel sermon or pastoral work that can take the place of prayer. It is the medium through which the minister gets to the Throne. He talks to God and God talks to him. He gets instruction direct from the Throne. His heart is warmed as were the hearts of the two walking to Emmaus, because Jesus speaks to him. The night before Jesus delivered His marvelous sermon on the Bread of Life, He spent with the Father in prayer. Mark 6:46; Jno. 6: 22. If Jesus needed to pray, how much more the minister of today! The sermon that lacks the preparation of prayer is lifeless and without spiritual effect.

To attempt to preach without any preparation is a mistake. It is an insult to the Author of preaching to tell the congregation that you have not looked into the Bible for a week, have not thought of a text, nor tried to settle your mind on any subject; that you will now open your mouth and let the Lord do the preaching. It is the preacher's duty to acquaint himself with the Word, to select, under the guiding influence of the Spirit, a text, subject, or line of thought to present to the congregation, to arrange (either in his mind or on paper, if his memory is poor) the points to be presented, store up some fitting illustrations, then turn this preparation and his powers over to the Lord to be used of Him in the pulpit. It may be that he will find it necessary to use another text, to dismiss the outline he had prepared, to go on an entirely different line from that intended. Let the Holy Spirit take care of the delivery, but make diligent preparation.

### The Work of the Ministry

The work of the ministry is of a fourfold nature:—(1) preaching, (2) administering the rites of the Church, (3) caring for the flock, (4) discipline. These different phases of the work we shall endeavor to consider in the light of God's Word.

1. **Preaching.**—This has been called "a divine art." It is the most important activity of the Christian minister. The primary duty, the work of paramount importance that falls to the lot of the ministry, is that of preaching the everlasting Gospel of Jesus Christ to a lost and ruined world. What is preaching? Literally, to preach means to make known by public proclamation. By common consent, preaching is almost exclusively confined to sacred discourse. The extraordinary use of the term helps to preserve the sacredness of preaching.

Preaching is a divine work. God has chosen this means to bring His Word and will to the ears of the people. Tit. 1:3. The word has special use with proclamations that pertain to the salvation of men. The most striking and significant instance where the term is used in the Old Testament is in Jonah 3:2. Here the prophet is charged in this language: "Preach unto it (Nineveh) the preaching that I bid thee." He speaks in a similar manner to every modern preacher. The preaching of Jonah saved Nineveh. True preaching may save many a city today.

It is in the New Testament, however, where preaching takes its true form. The forerunner of the Gospel dispensation preached "the baptism of repentance" (Mark 1:4). The first Gospel preacher (Jesus) had no sooner entered upon His public mission than He "began to preach" (Matt. 4:17). The Twelve were ordained "that he might send them forth to preach" (Mark 3:14). The early Church leaders were preachers and preached the Gospel. Acts 5:42; 8:35; 17:3. Moreover, it has pleased God to employ this means, foolish as it may seem to the world, to save the world. I Cor. 1:21.

2. **Administering the Rites of the Church.**—In the light of what has already been brought out in this chapter, it is clear that the work of baptizing penitent believers, offi-

ciating at the communion, anointing the sick, solemnizing marriages, conducting funeral services, and serving in the administration of all the rites of the Church belongs to the ministry. See Matt. 28:19, 20; Acts 19:1-6; 20:28; Tit. 1: 5; Jas. 5:14.

3. **The Care of the Flock.**—Pastoral work falls to the ministry. The ministers are the shepherds of the flock. They see that the members are supplied with wholesome food and drink, spiritually. They are also under obligations to see that the needy are cared for, the sick visited and the flock shepherded in a general way. In the care of the flock the deacons have a prominent place. See Acts 6:1-6.

4. **Church Discipline.**—The ministers are the executives of the visible body of Christ. Every wise ruler seeks to govern the people over whom he is set by the consent and help of the governed. So will the wise church executive strive to do. The form of church government that has proved the most satisfactory and the most successful is that in which the congregation has a prominent place. The fact that the ministry has the authority to rule and the responsibility to oversee the flock is clearly taught in the Word. "Let the elders that rule well be counted worthy of double honour" (I Tim. 5:17). The ability to rule must be a qualification already proved before a man may be considered for the office of bishop. "For if a man know not how to rule his own house, how shall he take care of the church of God" (I Tim. 3:5)? The ministers and deacons help the bishop, the chief executive, in keeping the Church in Gospel order, ruling not "as lords over God's heritage, but being ensamples to the flock" (I Pet. 5:2, 3).

## Support of the Ministry

In approaching this subject we are aware of the fact that it is one on which the religious world holds divided opinion; one that has suffered abuse on both sides. There are two extremes to be avoided in the consideration of ministerial support: (1) That since the Gospel is free, it would be a breach of the Scriptures to offer a minister any tangible support. (2) That a minister should receive and live upon a stipulated salary as any other professional man would. There is a golden mean between these two extremes that has the full sanction of the Word and the support of sound reason. The space allotted to an article of this nature forbids any exhaustive discussion of the subject. What is said is in the form of brief statements. The reader may develop the subject further in the light of God's Word.

It is clear from such passages as are cited below that the support of a Christian worker is scriptural:

"The workman is worthy of his meat" (Matt. 10:10). "The labourer is worthy of his hire" (Luke 10:7). "Thou shalt not muzzle the ox that treadeth out the corn: and, The labourer is worthy of his reward" (I Tim. 5:18). "Even so hath the Lord ordained, that they which preach the gospel should live of the gospel" (I Cor. 9:14). Other passages might be cited, but these are sufficient to prove that it is scriptural that those who labor in the Gospel receive support when needed. What the nature of that support should be is answered in the points following:

1. **Prayer.**—Paul never asked for a salary by which he might the better dispense the Gospel, but he repeatedly called for the prayers of God's people. Col. 4:2; I Thess. 5:25; II Thess. 3:1; Heb. 13:18. It was the prayers of the Church that helped an early minister out of a serious difficulty. Acts 12:5. The prayers of the laity are a recognized means in helping the ministry to labor successfully. II Cor. 1:11. When a congregation prays in the true spirit for its minister, he will not lack any other good thing from their hands.

2. **Obedience.**—The Word enjoins the congregation to "obey them that have the rule over you, and submit yourselves: for they watch for your souls, as they that must give account, that they may do it with joy, and not

with grief" (Heb. 13:17). Stand by your ministers by yielding a ready and willing obedience to them in all things scriptural, and you will put heart into them and give them courage and strength to rightly perform the arduous duties devolving upon them.

3. **Words of Encouragement.**—Do not flatter, Flattery can do no one any good, and has been the hurt of many. But a word of encouragement by way of approval for faithful service rendered, spoken at the proper time and in the right spirit, goes a long way in helping ministers over hard places.

4. **Assist in the Work.**—There is much that the laity can do in supporting the ministry in the work—visiting the sick, talking to the careless and unconcerned, speaking a word of encouragement to the despondent, urging the unsaved to accept Christ, admonishing the unruly, taking an active part in the general work of the church, being regular in attendance, etc. Do not attempt to take the minister's place, but be helpful to him.

5. **Assist in Physical Labor.**—The minister is trying to make a living for his family while performing the duties of his office. His ministerial duties require time, money, energy, and absence from his home and from his secular work. See to it that he does not suffer along this line. Plow his field, reap his grain, take his place in the shop: divide up the loss of time and energy with him. Here the mutual "burden-bearing" law is in full force.

6. **Provide the Necessities of Life.**—The minister and his family need to eat, just as other people do. He is handicapped in providing a living because much of his time is spent away from his secular work. You are aware of this, and you happen to know that he needs potatoes. Send him over a bushel or so. Or it may be apples, a sack of flour, a basket of berries, or some other article for the table. You will not miss it and it helps the preacher and the cause. You will have several results from your gift. The minister's needs will be supplied; and you will have

won the lasting gratitude of the minister and his family. It will make his preaching better. You will realize the joy of giving, and the blessing of the Lord will rest upon your head. Read I Cor. 9:11.

7. **Money.**—Your minister may have financial obligations to meet. He has had sickness in the family and doctor's bills to pay. There is probably a mortgage on his property and the interest eats up his earnings. Neither his financial standing nor his ability to accumulate wealth may be of the best. Help him pay his debts. At any rate, do not let the work suffer because your minister needs financial help that the congregation is withholding from him.

However, let it be clearly understood, whatever you do for the minister by way of financial help, that you are not paying him for preaching the Gospel. You cannot do that. You would be out of place if you did it, even though you could. That is the Lord's part. He will reward His servants in His own good way, and according to their deserts. You are helping him because he will be in better position to serve the Lord in the ministry and because it is your Christian duty to do so.

## Against a Stipulated Salary

The Word of God is emphatically against the preaching of the Gospel or doing any other Gospel work for money. Gospel work has no money value; it cannot be measured by dollars and cents. The Bible condemns men who serve in the Gospel for "filthy lucre" and disqualifies from the office of the ministry those who would enter it for money. See I Tim. 3:3; Tit. 1:7, 11; I Pet. 5:2. Below are a few points against a salaried ministry:

1. **The Gospel is Free.**—Salvation is a gift from God. Jesus made the Gospel free. What we are in Christ Jesus we have received without merit. "Freely ye have received, freely give." To put a money price on the Gospel, would make it impossible for a great many to hear or receive it.

The Gospel is for all men. The only way that all men may have the benefit of the Gospel is to offer it universally free. The saying of Paul, "I robbed other churches, taking wages of them, to do you service" (II Cor. 11:8), does not mean that he took wages for his service—that is, was paid money for his preaching the Gospel—but that he accepted from other congregations what represented their wages, that he might serve the Corinthians. He accepted help when it was needed. He testified that he labored with his hands not only to support himself, but at times his colaborers as well. Acts 20:34. It is honorable, healthful, and scriptural for a minister to labor with his hands to support himself and his family.

2. **The Minister the Servant of the Lord.**—A servant naturally looks to his employer for his pay. The minister is the servant of the Lord, qualified of the Lord, called of the Lord, responsible to the Lord, and so dependent upon the Lord for his pay. He is not primarily responsible to man, but to God. "Study to show thyself a workman approved unto God," is the gist of the divine admonition. The Lord sets the "fulness of the earth" before the minister, from which he may draw his livelihood. He also lays it upon the faithful ones with whom he labors to help him bear the burden of obtaining that livelihood, if it becomes necessary. But God gives him his wages in a higher form than that of money. The minister of the Gospel who goes into a contract and sells his heaven-ordained calling, his God-given gifts and his powers dedicated to the ministry for a stipulated amount of money, is taking an unscriptural course and must in the end fall short of the divine approval.

3. **The Salary a Muzzle.**—When a man or a set of men employ another and pay him a stipulated amount of money for his time and his accomplishments, they have a legitimate right to dictate the kind of work to be done and the manner of doing it. When this is applied to the ministry it can readily be seen how such an arrangement would destroy freedom of speech and independence of thought

and action. The minister with a salary attachment has a muzzle on his organs of speech. Concerning many of the popular evils of the day he must keep quiet. If he speaks against them, as his obligation would demand, he either loses his job or his living, or both. Such ministers put themselves into the predicament of becoming "dumb dogs, they cannot bark" (Isa. 56:10), or where they dare not bark at sin.

4. **Commercializes Gospel Work.**—If the minister's work is to be placed upon a plane with all other professions, it is but natural that the commercial phase should go with it, and so it should not be surprising to hear that a certain minister with brilliant talents has been called of the Lord (?) from a lower salaried position to a higher one. This commercial spirit among salaried ministers takes such deep root that the minister often arbitrarily demands his salary and collects by any means the law allows him. The spirit of the Gospel is the spirit of sacrifice. The spirit of commercialism is antagonistic to the spirit of sacrifice and when allowed to get into the work of the ministry it kills the very purpose for which the Gospel was first preached. This commercialistic spirit has reached such proportions that preacher's unions are formed, which fix salaries, make demands on congregations and if they want the Gospel preached they must take it after the fashion of the union and pay the price fixed. God, protect us against a commercialized ministry!

5. **Becomes an Entangling Snare.**—The Word declares: "He that is called in the Lord, being a servant, is the Lord's freeman," and admonishes, "be not ye servants of men" (I Cor. 7:22, 23). To go into a contract to preach the Gospel on a money basis robs the "servants of the Lord" of that freedom from men and places his feet in an entangling and dangerous snare. He is expected to live after the highest order of the day. He has a family to support who also must live like the pastor. This requires all the money he gets. He is tempted to stoop down and please

men, for to them he looks for his support, to them he is responsible, from them comes his living. He cannot please God and man, and so having been caught in the fowler's net, he "makes the most of circumstances" and caters to the vanities of men instead of the glory of God. His people have "itching ears" and he must keep them tickled to hold his place with them. What a deplorable predicament for God's "freeman" to drop into!

Then, again, a salaried ministry is a snare to entrap into its employ brilliant young men who have not the first qualifications for the sacred office. They are unconverted. They know nothing of the inner voice of the Spirit. They disregard many of the fundamental doctrines of the Word. They do not know and do not stop to think whether they care what becomes of the souls of men. They only consider that here is a clean, honorable profession open to them. It does not require the wearing of everyday clothes, or soiled hands, or hard work. It offers the opportunity of moving in the best society, to be called "Reverend," and be respected and honored by the masses; to get off flowery sermons and eloquent orations, to feel the pleasant sensations of carrying an attentive audience with you in thought and argument, to see your name heralded in the papers as being a great orator, a popular preacher. So unregenerate men enter the sanctity of the ministry for the bauble of a high salary and personal aggrandizement, rather than for the saving of lost souls and the glory of God. Thus the whole purpose of the ministry is frustrated, the Church is made a social center, and souls of men are lost because men have chosen to enter the ministry for the shining dollar rather than for the shining crown given to all those who keep the faith and fight the good fight of the Lord.

# CHAPTER III

## THE CONGREGATION

### By D. H. Bender

I was glad when they said unto me, Let us go into the house of the Lord.—Psalm 122:1.

### INTRODUCTORY

The words "church" and "congregation" are often used synonymously. In the Word of God the word "church" is used to represent, (1) the general body of believers (Acts 2:47), (2) a local church or congregation (Acts 8:1), and (3) members of the visible body of Christ without reference to locality, organization, or number (Acts 12:2). The Greek word "ekklesia," usually translated "assembly," is used to represent both the Church and a congregation in the Church. The congregation is the Church in organized form, located in any one place, and is composed of both the laity and the ministry.

1. **Organization.**—Every properly organized congregation consists of a body of converted and baptized members of the Church in sufficient number to form a body which meets regularly for worship. This body is presided over by a bishop or ministers, usually assisted by a deacon or deacons. In most churches the regular congregation also supports a Sunday school and other organizations needed to take care of the various activities of the Church. Members moving into a new community should always see that a sufficient number locate near enough together to effect an organization for a congregation and conduct a Sunday school, thus preserving the order of the worship of God's house, maintaining the spiritual life of the members and

leading their children into the faith once delivered to the saints.

2. **Qualifications of Membership.**—The qualifications for admission into a local congregation should be the same as those for admission into the Church in general. Only such persons as (1) have thoroughly repented of their sins, (2) given evidence of genuine conversion, (3) have been duly baptized on their faith, (4) declare themselves in full accord and harmony with the faith and practices of the Church, (5) live lives separate from the world and consecrated to God, and (6) express a willingness to fully submit themselves to the Word of God and the order and discipline of the Church should be considered eligible for membership in full standing and fellowship in any congregation of the brotherhood.

RELATION OF LOCAL CONGREGATION TO CHURCH AT LARGE

It is important that each congregation take its proper place in relation to the general body of the Church. It is well to keep two points well in mind: (1) that the local congregation owes its existence to the fact that it is a component part of the Church at large, and as such has obligations to meet and support to draw from the parent body; (2) that the Church at large owes a general care over and support to the local congregation and has the privilege to draw on the same for recruits in the service.

1. **The Congregation a Part of the Church.**—The entire Church—north, east, south, west, at home and abroad—comprises the "body of Christ" on earth. As the natural body is made up of parts and members, so the Church is made up of local congregations, and the congregations in turn of individual members. While the local congregation is a working unit in itself, yet as a part of the whole it owes something to every other part, and in turn is dependent upon the head and every other part of that body. In working out this interrelationship between the various congregations and the Church as a whole, there have been

organized institutions and conferences where the various congregations are represented: (1) the local Conference, comprising a number of congregations in a district, which considers questions affecting directly the congregations within the district; (2) the General Conference, composed of the various district conferences, whose province it is to consider questions affecting the various district conferences and the work of the Church at large. In the local conference the congregations within the district come into direct contact with one another and in the General Conference representatives of the local conferences come into direct contact. Thus in a direct or indirect manner each member of a local congregation is connected with all the work of the entire Church. The individual member reports to his congregation; the congregation, if need be, carries it to the district conference; and, if the matter has sufficient merit, it is taken by the district conference to the General Conference. In this way the influence, intelligence, sympathy, energy, and spirituality of each member may be felt throughout the entire body of the Church, and the united influence of the whole Church is available for each individual member. This is the order taught in the Gospel. See Acts 15 and I Corinthians 12.

2. **Obligations and Privileges of the Local Congregation.**—Each individual congregation should be made to realize its obligation in supporting the general work and institutions of the Church at large—its missions, its publications, its educational institutions, its benevolent activities and all the objects of support organized and maintained by the Church. The same may be said of its conferences. Each congregation should be represented in each session of the district conference and also in the general conference. Only as the local congregations ardently support the various institutions and activities of the Church can she hope to accomplish the greatest good for the cause and bring glory to the Head of the Church—Jesus Christ.

### Congregational Duties

The duties of laity to ministry and ministry to laity are discussed at some length in the chapter on THE MINISTRY. It will be the aim here to confine the discussion on these duties more especially to the local congregation rather than to the Church at large.

I. **Duties of Ministry to Laity.**—Much depends upon the ministry in making the work of a congregation successful. A congregation cannot prosper when led by an unqualified or disloyal ministry. "Like priest; like people," is an old adage whose truth is not yet spent. The Word of God lays many obligations upon the servants of the congregation.

1. **The minister is the servant of the congregation.** While the minister is at the head of the congregation, he must not for a moment lost sight of the fact that he is the chief servant of the people under him. Should he lose sight of this fact, become officious, magnify his authority or standing as a leader, look upon the laity as underlings and inferiors, begin to "lord it over God's heritage," he is likely to lose his hold upon God, his influence in the congregation, and his usefulness in the service. Jesus sets the standard as Lord and yet chief servant, both in word and in example. He classes all ministers who do not subscribe to this duty as chief servant with the Gentiles, but teaches a nobler way. See Matthew 20:25-28.

2. **It is the duty of the ministry to "feed the flock,"** to see that the congregation is well supplied with wholesome food in the form of sound Gospel teaching, pure literature, helpful advice; paying special attention to the nurturing of the lambs of the fold, a duty of primary importance devolving upon the ministry. Read Acts 20:28 and I Peter 5:2.

3. **It is the duty of the ministry to clearly and fully teach the doctrines of the kingdom.** The minister must be more than an exhorter to good works and faithful living.

It is his duty to teach, explain, and help the laity to recognize, understand and put into practice the doctrines of the Word. II Tim. 2:2. It is his duty to "rightly divide the word of truth" for his congregation. II Tim. 2:15. He is charged with the responsibility of speaking those things "which become sound doctrine" (Titus 2:1). He must constantly "give attendance to reading" and in every way lawful, qualify himself to serve the congregation by teaching intelligently and forcibly the doctrines of the Word and the Church. The responsibility of keeping the congregation sound in the faith is laid at the door of the ministry.

4. **It is the duty of the ministry to expose and reprove sin.** This is an unpleasant task in many ways, but the command is, "Cry aloud, spare not; lift up thy voice like a trumpet, and shew my people their transgression" (Isa. 58:1). Paul commands Timothy (I Tim. 5:20) to rebuke sin openly. This requires boldness, but also tact and a deep feeling of sympathy and love for the cause. The neglect of this duty brings sorrow and defeat, while the faithful performance of the same will in the end yield a rich reward in a pure religion and a congregation free from the corroding blight of sin in its members.

5. **The minister is the watchman of the congregation.** It is a duty of paramount importance that the ministry watch over the flock and guard it against the encroachment of worldliness and harmful doctrines of which the world is so full in these latter days. The minister should be on the lookout and ready to turn aside the agent with questionable literature, especially along the lines of false religion. "Tramp preachers" with no clear recommendations should be kept out of our pulpits. A preacher worthy of his calling always has a place to preach the Word. He has a home congregation to care for, and need not go begging for a place to serve. These mendicant preachers and religious agents usually have some nostrums to peddle out among the uninformed, the gullible, and the morbid that

are not only worthless but often decidedlly harmful; or they are the advance agents of some fallacious cult whose devotees know it cannot be introduced regularly, and so they "climb up some other way" into the homes and lives of the saints. Beware of them! "Take heed therefore unto yourselves, and to all the flock" (Acts 20:28). "Watch thou in all things" (II Tim. 4:5).

6. **The ministry is responsible for the discipline of the congregation.** The Church must be kept in order. Impenitent sinners must be excommunicated. The penitent require instruction; the unruly, correction. It is the duty of the ministry to take these things in hand and perform them in the order of the Gospel and the Church. The Gospel requires that the Church be ruled well, and promises good rulers a special reward. See I Tim. 5:17.

7. **Visitation work.** It is the duty of the ministry, as much as possible, to visit the members of the congregation in their homes, pray for and with them and by personal appeal and help encourage them in the work of the Church and the Gospel. The value of this line of work cannot lightly be overlooked. Read Acts 20:31 and Romans 1:9.

II. **Duties of Laity to Ministry.**—The work of a congregation is a success or a failure in the degree that the laity is faithful in performing its duty to and the supporting of the ministry, or the neglect of the same. Following are a few of the duties the laity owe the ministry:

1. **To pray for them.** The prayers of a faithful congregation are a marvelous help to the ministry. Paul ascribes his success in a large measure to the prayers of faithful saints. II Cor. 1:11. The prayers of the congregation delivered an apostolic minister from prison and from probable death (Acts 12:5). All true ministers realize the worth of and long for the prayers of their congregations. See Col. 4:2, 3; Eph. 6:18, 19; I Thess. 5:25; II Thess. 3:1. Brethren and sisters, pray for your ministers.

2. **To render them willing obedience.** "Obey them that have the rule over you and submit yourselves" (Heb. 13:17)

is the Gospel command. Where there is a lack of obedience to those in authority there can be no successful work done in any congregation. "Rebellion (disobedience) is as the sin of witchcraft" (I Sam. 15:23) and works havoc wherever found—in the home, in the nation, in the Church. Since the ministers are the legitimate and scriptural heads of the Church, it is the duty of the laity to accord them ready and implicit obedience. Should the minister need disciplining, he is subject to the same rules and regulations as is any other member; or, in case the congregation can not control him, it becomes the duty of the conference to deal with him. It is never allowable for a lay member to take an obstinate position toward a minister. There are occasions when a member may consistently raise a question with a minister, but then he should "entreat him as a father" and never take a rebellious attitude toward him. A disobedient, obstinate, insubmissive spirit on the part of the laity proves fertile soil for the seeds of anarchy to grow, which will end sooner or later in open revolt and schism. Just as a home cannot be successfully managed and kept in order without the ready obedience of the children, so it is impossible to keep a congregation in order without the hearty support of the ministry in governmental matters.

3. **To respect and esteem them.** "We beseech you, brethren, to know them which labour among you, and are over you in the Lord, and admonish you; and to esteem them very highly for their work's sake" (I Thess. 5:12, 13). Nothing tends to cripple the work of the minister so completely as a lack of proper regard for him and his sacred calling on the part of the lay members of the congregation. Parents often unwittingly drive their children from the Church by expressions made in the home reflecting upon the ministry. A young person once fully turned against one whom he should esteem, is rarely ever fully won again. Members should guard and enhance the reputation and standing of the minister whenever and wherever possible.

A congregation can rise no higher in standing than that ascribed to the heads of the congregation. Take care of your minister's reputation. Read Phil. 2:29. Honor is due the ministry—not that hollow honor that finds vent in vain expressions of flattery, but that holy honor that Christ and the Word attach to the high calling. He who brings reproach upon the ministry by disrespect and lack of esteem, brings reproach upon Christ, the Head of the Church, whose ambassadors the ministers are. The "elders that rule well" shall "be counted worthy of double honour" (I Tim. 5:17).

4. **To assist them in their labors.** The Word teaches us to bear one another's burdens. This command applies in this case. Lay members can do much in assisting the ministry in building up and keeping in order the Church of Christ. They can offer suggestions without assuming a dictatorial attitude. They can visit the sick and report their condition to the ministry. They can assist the minister in the preaching of the Gospel by prompt and regular attendance and giving wakeful and prayerful attention. If the message appears dull, spend the time you would feel excused to spend in sleep, in praying for the message-bearer. Be cheerful, polite, and helpful to your minister and note the improved condition in both yourself, the minister, and the congregation.

5. **To support them when in need.** There are many ways by which you can be of help to your minister in the support of both himself and family.

6. **To follow their worthy example.** It is the duty of ministers to set proper examples for the flock (I Tim. 4:12; Tit. 2:7; I Pet. 5:3); but an example, a pattern, loses its value unless used in producing counterparts. The good example set by the ministry should be followed by the laity. Phil. 3:17; II Thess. 3:9. Blessed is the state of that congregation whose ministers set the true Gospel standard in all things, from the holy, consecrated life within to the

consistent garb worn without, and whose laity humbly and consistently copy the standard of their leaders.

7. **To share their burdens and responsibilities.** The minister who realizes that the members of the congregation are willing and actually do share with him the burdens that come upon him, the trials that beset him, sympathize with him in his apparent defeats and rejoice with him in his triumphs, becomes the stronger in the added strength of the members. If, when the battle is fierce and his hands become weary, the Aarons and the Hurs come forward and sustain the drooping hands, he sees only victory ahead. no matter how severe the contest or how great the opposition. With the laity standing loyally by him in all things, the consecrated minister takes new courage and triumphantly declares, "I can do all things through Christ which strengtheneth me."

## The Layman's Opportunity

The day is past when the work of a congregation rests solely upon the shoulders of the ministry. So many avenues of direct service are open to the laity, and so many opportunities await its grasp that no one need pine for work or excuse his inaction because there is nothing for him to do.

1. **The Sunday School.**—The Sunday school is practically an indispensable part of every congregation. Superintendents, teachers, and other officers are needed. These as a rule come from the laity. Qualified and faithful Sunday school workers in their place are as essential to the welfare of a congregation as the ministry and other officials of the Church. With movements on foot for the preparation of Sunday school workers in teacher training classes, teachers' meetings, Sunday school conferences, and minor organizations where the best methods are discussed and the talent of the young people finds exercise, few members need go without some definite form of Gospel employment.

2. **The Young People's Meeting.**—There is scarcely now a live congregation that does not support one or more

Bible meetings especially for the younger members. This work is becoming Church-wide and offers a splendid opportunity for the use and exercise of the God-given gifts of the young people, especially in the building up of the cause of Christ.

3. **The Mission Sunday School.**—In many places there are opportunities for the organization of mission Sunday schools in out-of-the-way localities and yet not so far removed from the congregation as to make it impossible for the work to be conducted from the home base. In this way the Gospel can be brought to those who cannot or do not attend the regularly appointed places of worship. Here is an opportunity for consecrated lay members to assist in the evangelization of the world.

4. **The City Mission.**—Besides these rural missions, which are usually cared for by those in the home congregation, the city mission is constantly calling for workers to help in bringing the good news of the Gospel to the lost and fallen in the dark regions of our cities.

5. **The Benevolent Institution.**—Our homes for the aged, for the orphans, our hospitals, and kindred institutions of the Church, established for the sake of the poor and helpless, are avenues through which our lay members may dispense their Christian energies in bringing cheer, courage, and salvation to the unfortunates, thereby obtaining the reward promised in Matt. 25:34-40.

6. **The Cause of Christian Education.**—Nowhere within the bounds of Gospel activity is there a more important position awaiting the thoroughly consecrated, fully indoctrinated, loyal layman than in the educational institutions of the Church. Here will be found those who have a zeal to attain to a place in life where their developed talents may be used to the best possible advantage. He who is able to control these aspirations (not ambitions) to weave into the fiber of the maturing intelligence and knowledge the nobler thread of Christian loyalty and consecration to God and the cause of the Church, has a gift, an opportu-

nity, a work that is excelled by no other. These institutions are calling for laymen qualified for these positions.

**7. The Foreign Field.**—No quarter of the Gospel realm is calling more loudly for true Christian workers than the foreign field. Here is another golden opportunity for you. Prepare to embrace it and make the best use possible of your opportunity.

Besides these special avenues open for the Christian layman to enter, many others of a more general nature could be mentioned. To guide a Christian home where sons and daughters are reared for Christ and the Church is no mean occupation. To diligently manage a legitimate business or follow a worthy profession, and save our money so that we may contribute liberally for the Lord's cause, affords a royal opportunity to labor in His vineyard in a practical way. Last, but not least, to be an exemplary, faithful, loyal Christian without any special attainments but to stand as a living witness for Christ is a godly art of such importance that the Lord has designed that they shall be used as Bibles for many (II Cor. 3:2) to convince them of the reality and power of the Gospel of Christ in the lives of men, for the people of the world read Christians more than they do the Bible. This opportunity is open to all. Seize it and use it to God's glory, and you will be sure of the crown that fadeth not away. The greatest need of the present-day Church is consecrated laymen.

### BUILDING UP THE CONGREGATION

As this subject is approached, two factors present themselves: (1) the hindrances to be overcome, and (2) the helps to be enlisted. These two factors stare every congregation in the face and retard or enhance the work of building up the brotherhood.

I. **Hindrances.**—It has been said that

> "Where God erects a house of prayer,
> The devil builds a chapel there."

In the endeavor to build up a congregation for the Lord, the forces of Satan must be dealt with and counteracted. Let us look at a few:

1. **Self-righteousness.** The severest rebuke the Saviour hurled at the self-righteous Pharisees was: "Ye entered not in yourselves, and them that were entering in ye hindered" (Luke 11:52). The self-righteous still hinder those who would build up His cause. They are found in some form or other in the professed Church today.

2. **Hypocrisy.** A near of kin monster to self-righteousness is hypocrisy. Where one dwells the other makes his abode. Read Christ's scathing rebuke of the hypocrites in Matthew 23, then set your attention to the cultivation of the flower of humility and the grace of sincerity and thus remove a grave barrier to the advancement of the Church of God.

3. **Indifference.** That which prevented the congregation at Laodicea from prospering in the true sense of the word and brought down upon it the rebuke of heaven, stands in the way of many a modern congregation in its efforts to grow in the Lord's vineyard. Let lukewarmness, carelessness, indifference, and lethargy become entrenched in a congregation and its efforts to develop a strong working body are practically futile.

4. **Worldliness.** "The friendship of the world is enmity with God." It makes no difference in what relationship that friendship is cultivated. The Church of Christ has nothing in common with the kingdom of the world. "Ye are not of the world." "Be not conformed to this world." "Love not the world." These and kindred texts show clearly that the Christian has no part with the world. It is his duty always to avoid its friendship and association. When worldliness creeps into a congregation, godliness is crowded out. Jesus compares the worldly Christian to the seed growing among the thorns (Matt. 13:22). It is difficult to utilize it or even to gather it for the garner. One of the chief hindrances to the growth of spirituality

today in our congregation is the presence of worldliness in some form or other, whether in business relations or methods, in the social life, in the marriage relation, in the adornment of the body or the home, or in other ways. It always has the same effect—that of destroying spirituality and preventing the advancement of God's work. Close the door against the greatest enemy of Christ in the Church —corroding worldliness.

II. **Helps.**—Having disposed of a few of the hindrances to congregational growth, we will turn our attention to a few of the helps that make for genuine advancement.

1. **Unity in the Faith.** According to Gospel order every member of a congregation is co-ordinately a part of the same body, and all are "members one of another" (Rom. 12:5). The worship of God and the testimony of faith should come from the entire body as from "one mind and one mouth" (Rom. 15:6). The measure of the perfect men in Christ consists in approaching that condition in the congregation whence it may be said that they are "all come in the unity of the faith" (Eph. 4:13).

2. **Mutual Love.** The true test of the Christian life is the test of brotherly love. I John 3:14. The cultivation of the spirit of brotherly love makes much for the general advancement of the body of Christ. "Let brotherly love continue," is the admonition of the Word to those who would be truly successful in His service. We are also admonished to "love one another with a pure heart fervently." Where love is the rule, there is peace, mutual sympathy, and helpfulness, and the spiritual uplift of the congregation is assured.

3. **Steadfastness.** The congregation at Ephesus is held up as a model. The leading commendation given with regard to that church is its persistence and steadiness in the service. Four times is this quality mentioned. Their service was not spasmodic. They entered into the work with a sanctified determination that won the favor of the

Head of the Church and that triumphed over all obstacles in the way. The Church needs special occasions of revival and uplift, but they are only stimulants. The quality it needs more is the quality that makes its members "not weary in well doing." A great writer once said that he "likes to read about Moses because he carried a hard business well through."

4. **Personal Influence.** After all, the congregation consists but of a number of individuals, each exerting his own peculiar influence. It is the sum total of these personal influences that make or mar the standing and strength of the congregation. Two companions in sin had been converted. They made claims for religious strength. A third doubted the power of salvation. He decided to watch the lives of these two. He left his office and dogged their steps for a week. They did not know it. He was convinced that they had something he did not have and which was of great value. He sought and found Christ. What would have been the result had these two Christians not allowed the light of Christ and the Gospel to shine out in their lives? Each member of the congregation is under watch. In answer to the question recently asked in a meeting as to what is the weightiest argument for or against Chistianity today, the following was given by a wise member of the meeting: "The weightiest argument for Christ, and the weightiest argument against Christ today is the same argument—Christians." What is your personal influence? Read I Pet. 2:15.

5. **Loyalty.** In civic economy the most serious offender and the one most despised man is the traitor. He who is untrue to the cause he has espoused is without respect or esteem among friends and foes alike. On the other hand, he who is true to his profession, be it popular or ever so unpopular, wins and holds the respect of all who are respectable. How this condition is intensified in the Christian economy! Disloyalty on the part of the member of the Church, be it in ever so small a matter, militates against

the best interests of the Church and the cause of Christ in general. Loyalty in all things to God and the Church carrise with it a mighty influence and power to lift up and promulgate the work of the Church. Let the watchword of each member of the congregation be: *Loyal* to the doctrines of the Church, *loyal* to the work of the Church, *loyal* in separation from the world, *loyal* in supporting the public service and all the activities of the congregation, *loyal* to all that is good and high and noble, LOYAL TO CHRIST.

> "Dare to do right, dare to be true;
> You have a work no other can do;
> Do it so kindly, so bravely, so well—
> Angels will hasten the story to tell."

# CHAPTER IV

## CHRISTIAN ORDINANCES

I praise you, brethren, that ye remember me in all things,
and keep the ordinances, as I delivered them to you.
—I Corinthians 11:2.

### The Purpose of Ordinances

Not the least among the blessings of God through the
Church is the institution of Christian ordinances for our
edification. These ceremonies, usually the outgrowth of
or substitution for corresponding ordinances under the
ceremonial law, bring to our remembrance the vital Christian principles needed in Christian life and service. They
are an aid to the Church in maintaining a scriptural organization, also an aid to individual members in maintaining
their Christian experience.

It is not so important that we know the exact reasons
why God instituted certain ordinances as it is for us to
know that He wants us to keep them; that they were instituted by divine authority, taught and practiced by the
disciples, and enjoined upon the people of God in all generations of the Christian era.

Webster defines an ordinance as "an established rite
or ceremony." A Christian ordinance has also been defined as "a religious ceremony with a heavenward meaning." In other words, these ordinances were instituted to
the end that they who keep them may have their minds
drawn heavenward, meditating upon things divine, and
worshiping Him who called them into being.

As for the ordinances under the ceremonial law, they
were fulfilled in Christ, who nailed them to the cross. Col.
2:14. The ordinances instituted under the Gospel of Christ

are distinct and separate from Old Testament ordinances, having a meaning peculiar to our dispensation, the importance of which we recognize as we enter into the spirit of them in a faithful observance of Christ's teachings concerning them. Nevertheless, these New Testament ordinances may be said to be

## SUCCESSORS TO OLD TESTAMENT ORDINANCES

as a few illustrations will show:

1. **Water baptism** is foreshadowed in the "divers washings and cleansings" (Heb. 9:10) of the Old Dispensation, and also in the consecration ceremony by which the Aaronic priests were set apart for their sacred service. Under the Old Dispensation only the sons of Aaron could lawfully become priests, so no consecration ceremony however perfectly administered could avail for any one not eligible to the priesthood. Under the New Dispensation all the family of God constitute a "royal priesthood" (I Pet. 2:9; Rev. 1:6), and "whosoever will" (Rev. 22:17) is eligible to become a member of this priesthood. The outward, visible, initiatory rite into this priesthood—the Church of Christ—is the ordinance of water baptism; but this baptism, though administered by the scriptural mode, is efficacious for those only who have complied with the scriptural (lawful) conditions for baptism. In the Old Dispensation the priests were set apart for their holy service by washing and anointing with oil (Ex. 29; Lev. 8), and an elaborate service in which sacrifice of animals had a prominent part. In the New Dispensation Jesus Christ is the one all-sufficient Sacrifice, the Holy Spirit is prefigured in the anointing oil, and the water used in the priest's cleansing at the door of the tabernacle is typical of the water in baptism. As the outward ceremony connected with the ordaining of priests was typical of a work of God within, so the outward ceremony of water baptism is symbolical of the baptism of the Holy Ghost, the work of God within, bringing us into the eternal priesthood of

Jesus Christ our great High Priest. The Levitical priesthood having been abolished, the consecration ceremony by which the sons of Aaron were ushered into the priesthood is likewise among the Jewish ordinances which Christ "nailed to the cross," while the Christian ceremony, water baptism, serves a similar purpose in the New Dispensation as the initiatory rite into the visible body of Christ.

2. **The communion,** under the new dispensation, has a place similar to that which the Jewish passover had under the old. From the time of its institution when Israel was delivered from the bondage of Egypt, the Jewish passover was observed as an annual feast in commemoration of this miraculous deliverance. When Christ partook of the last legal Jewish passover (Matt. 26:17-25; Mark 14:12-25; Luke 22:7-20) He said, "With desire I have desired to eat this passover with you before I suffer"—and then proceeded to institute the communion ceremony, which has ever since that time been kept in memory of His broken body and shed blood. The memorial of the deliverance of Israel from Egyptian bondage was thus displaced by the memorial of our deliverance from the bondage of sin. Passing by the sacrifices under the Law, we look to Christ of whom it is said, "Even Christ our passover is sacrificed for us" (I Cor. 5:7).

Similar comparisons might be made with reference to the other ordinances, but enough have been given for illustration. And may we say right here that our zeal in keeping these ordinances should not be one whit behind the zeal of the most faithful Jews in keeping the ordinances under the ceremonial Law. "If ye know these things, happy are ye if ye do them."

### Scriptural Ordinances

There is a difference of opinion as to the number of Christian ordinances, intended as such, that ought to be kept by Christian people. Many of the churches recognize but two—baptism and the communion—classifying them as sacraments—others include a few more. Without entering into a discussion, at this time, as to which ones should be recognized as ordinances, we will name seven ordinances which we believe to have been instituted by divine authority, and which we mean to discuss at greater length in succeeding chapters. Following is the list, together with their meaning and use:

### I. Water Baptism.
1. Initiatory rite into the visible Church.—Matt. 28:19; Acts 2:38-47.
2. Symbol of Spirit baptism.—Matt. 3:11; Acts 1:5; 2:14-18; 10:44-48; 11:15, 16; I Cor. 12:13.
3. Typical of remission of sins.—Acts 2:38; 22:16.
4. Answer of a good conscience toward God.—I Pet. 3:21.
5. An act of obedience.—Matt. 3:15.

### II. The Communion.
1. Memorial of the broken body and shed blood of Jesus. —Luke 22:19, 20; I Cor. 11:23-26.
2. Typical of common union of saints.—I Cor. 10:16, 17.
3. A memorial pointing to both the death and the second coming of Christ.—I Cor. 11:26.

### III. Feet Washing.
1. A symbol of humility.—Jno. 13:14-16.
2. A symbol of brotherly equality and of mutual service. —Jno. 13:14 cf. Gal. 5:13.

### IV. Devotional Covering for Christian Women.
1. Symbol of relationship between man and woman in the Lord.—I Cor. 11:2-16.
2. "Sign of authority."—I Cor. 11:10.

### V. The Christian Salutation.
1. "An holy kiss."—Rom. 16:16.
2. "A kiss of charity."—I Pet. 5:14.

### VI. Anointing with Oil.
1. Symbol of God's grace manifest in healing power.— Jas. 5:14, 15.

### VII. Marriage.
1. A union dissoluble by death only.—Matt. 19:3-6.
2. Domestic felicity.—Gen. 2:23, 24; Matt. 19:3-6.
3. Propagation of the human family.—Gen. 1:22; Psa. 128:3.
4. Purity.—I Cor. 7:2; Heb. 13:4.
5. Typical of Christ and the Church.—Eph. 5:25-28.

# CHAPTER V

## BAPTISM

Teach all nations, baptizing them in the name of the Father, and of the Son, and of the Holy Ghost.—Matt. 28:19.

This subject is first mentioned, as such, in connection with the ministry of John the Baptist (Matt. 3:1-5; Luke 3:3, 12), but the idea of ceremonial washings or baptisms is quite prominent in the Levitical law; so that it is the meaning and use of baptism, rather than the ceremony itself, that became a new thing under the new dispensation. Under the general head of

### "DIVERS WASHINGS"

A. D. Wenger has the following to say:

"Paul's 'diaphorois baptismois' is translated 'divers washings' (Heb. 9:10). This shows that the purifying ceremonies of the Mosaic law were so many baptisms ('baptismoi'). These were performed by applications of oil, water, or blood. Pouring oil upon the heads of those chosen to be priests was a rite that signified consecration and sanctification, preparatory to ministering unto the Lord in their priestly offices. 'And he poured the anointing oil upon Aaron's head' (Lev. 8:12). Aaron and his sons were also sprinkled with blood and oil. Ex. 29:21. Also the Levites: 'And the Lord spake unto Moses, saying, Take the Levites from among the children of Israel, and cleanse them. . . . . Sprinkle water of purifying upon them . . . and after that shall the Levites go in to do the service of the tabernacle of the congregation' (Num. 8:5-15). For leprosy: 'The oil that is in the priest's hand he shall pour upon the head of him that is to be cleansed' (Lev. 14:18). For uncleanness: 'The water of separation hath not been sprinkled upon him; he is unclean' (Num. 19:20). There were many other instances of purifying, by pouring and sprinkling ('divers washings'—baptisms) which did not wash the surface of the body but which ceremonially cleansed the entire being. Moses sprinkled a few millions of people with blood and water and they were baptized. Heb. 9:10, 19."—Bible Doctrine, P. 353.

As a matter of fact, most modern translations of the New Testament do not attempt to translate the Greek words "baptizo," "baptisma," and their modifications. The words "baptize" and "baptism" are only transliterations of the Greek terms with endings suited to the English.

In classical Greek before the time of Christ the ordinance of Christian baptism was unknown, and therefore there is no word to express this act or ceremony. When the ordinance came into use the Spirit through writers of the New Testament used the word which most nearly expressed the meaning of the new ordinance. Among the heathen this term needed to be defined. For this reason we get little help in our search for a proper form or mode of baptism from words in use in classic Greek. Baptism was a new ordinance to the heathen and needed to be defined to them as Christians understood it. It is so to this day. No language among the heathen has a word that expresses the meaning of Christian baptism. To the heathen the ceremony is a new one and receives a name which is new to them. In order to find the meaning and mode of baptism we must look into the Scriptures for the meaning of the terms synonymous with our English word "baptism."

### Kinds of Baptism

As a religious ceremony performed by man we have but one kind of baptism; namely, water baptism, but the Bible speaks of three other kinds, making four in all, as follows:

1. **Water Baptism.**—Webster defines this as "The application of water to a person, as a sacrament or ceremony, by which he is initiated into the visible Church of Christ." The Bible first mentions the word in Matt. 3: 5, 6, and records about a dozen instances where this rite was administered to believers.

2. **Spirit Baptism.**—We are introduced to this kind of baptism in the declaration, "I indeed baptize you with water unto repentance; but . . . . he (Christ) shall baptize you with the Holy Ghost and with fire" (Matt. 3:11).

Christ refers to the same event in Acts 1:5. From such references we gather the thought that while man baptizes with water, God baptizes with the Holy Ghost.

We look upon the baptism with the Holy Ghost as the saving baptism, and upon water baptism as being typical of it; for "by one Spirit are we all baptized into one body" (I Cor. 12:13). Its importance is evident: (1) because it is by the Spirit that we are "all baptized into one body;" (2) because of its frequent mention in the activities of the apostolic Church; (3) because of the prominence given it by the disciples in their work.

3. **Baptism with Fire.**—This is mentioned twice by John the Baptist (Matt. 3:11; Luke 3:16) who in each case couples it with the baptism of the Holy Ghost. When the disciples received the enduement of power at Pentecost both fire and the Holy Ghost are mentioned: "And there appeared unto them cloven tongues, like as of *fire* . . . and they were all filled with the *Holy Ghost*" (Acts 2:3, 4). Being coupled together in both the prophecy and its fulfillment, we take it that both were literally fulfilled at Pentecost. Fire is typical of both zeal and purification, both essential to effective Christian life and service.

4. **Baptism of Suffering.**—This kind of baptism is not named in Scripture, yet distinctly taught. Read Matt. 20: 22, 23; 26:39-42; Luke 12:50; Rom. 8:16-18. The baptism of suffering is as a refiner's fire that tests our qualities as Christians and helps us to "stand fast in the faith" in the midst of the storms of life.

### Design of Spirit Baptism

1. **It is the baptism that saves.**

"By one Spirit are we all baptized into one body" (I Cor. 12:13). "Except a man be born of water and of the Spirit, he can not enter into the kingdom of God" (Jno. 3:5). See also Ezek. 36:25-27; Jno. 6:63; Heb. 12:14.

2. **It inducts penitent believers into the body of Christ.** (See references in preceding paragraph.)

### 3. It purifies the Christian convert in the sight of God.

Read Ezek. 36:25-27; Tit. 3:3-7; Heb. 9:14. This thought does not conflict with John's testimony that "the blood of Jesus Christ cleanseth us from all sin." The Bible contains no promise that the blood of Christ shall cleanse any heart or life that is not under the power of the Spirit. There is no such thing as a Spirit-baptized person who is not also blood-cleansed.

### 4. It confers power for service.

For example, note the difference in the disciples before and after Pentecost. Acts 1:8 is true of disciples to-day, as it was in apostolic times. The power of the Spirit cleans up the life, sanctifies the tongue, puts all the human powers upon the altar and in this sense makes them divine, unifies those "of like precious faith," and puts something into the soul which leaves its impress upon the hearts and lives of others. For reference, see Acts 1:8: 2:1-47; 10:47; Heb. 9:14.

### DESIGN OF WATER BAPTISM

### 1. It is the initiatory rite by which people are received into the visible Church.

The two outstanding duties enjoined upon the Christian Church in the Great Commission are (1) "teach," (2) "baptize." The uniform custom of the apostolic Church was to baptize converts upon evidence of faith, repentance, and conversion. Of the Pentecostal converts it is said that "the Lord added (them) to the church."

### 2. It is typical of the baptism with the Holy Ghost.

As Spirit baptism initiates into the invisible Church (I Cor. 12:13), so water baptism initiates into the visible Church (Matt. 28:19; Acts 2:41-47). The two are very closely connected, both in the teaching and practice of the apostolic Church, Matt. 3:11; Acts 1:5; 10:44-48; 11:15, 16.

### 3. It typifies the remission of sins.

Peter's response to the trembling sinners at Pentecost: "Repent, and be baptized every one of you. . . . .for

13

the remission of sins" (Acts 2:38) corresponds with the instruction of Ananias to Saul: "Arise, and be baptized, and wash away thy sins" (Acts 22:16). Do we understand by this that water baptism washes away sins? By no means. The Bible teaches us that baptism is "not the putting away of the filth of the fiesh" (I Pet. 3:19); that the "washing of regeneration" is accomplished through the cleansing power of the Blood and Spirit (I Jno. 1:7; I Cor. 12:13) and not of anything "corruptible" (I Pet. 1:18, 19). Yet baptism by water, a cleasing element, is typical of the very thing that some people erroneously attribute to water itself. We have an apt illustration in the case of the leper (Mark 1:40-44) whom Christ had cleansed and commanded to show himself to the priest and "offer for thy cleansing" the sacrifices customary under the Law. Water baptism, like the offering referred to, is "for" (because of) a previous cleansing.

4. **It is the "answer of a good conscience toward God"** (I Pet. 3:21).

The "good conscience" comes with conversion. Upon evidence of this, the convert should be baptized.

5. **It is an act of obedience.**

We see Jesus coming to the river Jordan to be baptized of John, who forbade Him, saying, "I have need to be baptized of thee." Jesus quickly assures him, saying, "Suffer it to be so now, for thus it becometh us to fulfil all righteousness" (Matt. 3:13-15). Then John baptized Him. We see the Holy Ghost poured out upon the Gentiles in Cornelius' house. Then Peter said, "Who can forbid water?" (Acts 11:44-48), and he commanded water baptism to be administered. Why insist upon water baptism under such circumstances? Were not Christ and Cornelius good enough without water baptism? They certainly were—just in the right frame of mind and soul to receive it, for they were prepared. It is an act of obedience, not of cleansing—save in a typical way. Nobody ever gets too good to be baptized. Nobody is good enough for heaven so long as he withstands a single one of God's commandments, and water baptism is emphatically commanded.

### Gospel Requirements for Baptism

Baptism should be administered only when the applicant has complied with the scriptural requirements for baptism. Not *willingness* but *fitness* is the Gospel test. These Gospel conditions for baptism are:

1. **Faith.**—"What doth hinder me to be baptized?" asked the Ethiopian eunuch. "If thou believest with all thine heart, thou mayest," replied Philip. Acts 8:36, 37. "What must I do to be saved?" asked the jailer. "Believe on the Lord Jesus Christ," was the reply. Acts 16:30, 31. Upon evidence of such faith he was baptized. When Christ said, "He that believeth and is baptized shall be saved," He did not say, "He that is baptized and afterwards believes." Faith of necessity precedes baptism to make it scriptural.

2. **Repentance.**—"What shall we do?" asked the conscience-smitten men at Pentecost. "Repent and be baptized," was Peter's reply. Acts 2:38. Peter did not say, "Be baptized and then repent." Repentance precedes baptism. John's rebuke to the "generation of vipers," calling upon them to "bring forth fruits meet for repentance" (Matt. 3:7, 8) is further proof for this assertion. Only penitent believers are fit for baptism.

3. **Conversion.** — A number of scripture references point to conversion as one of the requirements before water baptism is administered. Peter's admonition to the Pharisees, "Repent ye therefore, and be converted that your sins may be blotted out" (Acts 3:19), makes no direct reference to water baptism, but it does make it clear that conversion is a requirement that comes before the remission of sins. In the conversion of Saul of Tarsus baptism was administered only after Saul had become a praying man and the scales had fallen off his eyes. See Acts 9:1-18.

Let us also notice the case of Cornelius. This was the way of Cornelius and his house into the Kingdom: a stirred conscience, worship, enlightenment, instructions from a Heaven-directed spiritual overseer, baptism with the Holy Ghost, water baptism. The situation in the house of Cornelius is profitable for us to study as we consider the relationship between conversion and water baptism. Before this ordinance is administered we should look for evidences of faith, repentance, and conversion to God. Failing to find these evidences clear should be considered reasons sufficient for further instruction before water baptism is administered. The best interests of the converts, as well as the welfare of the Church, demand that water baptism be administered to converts only who have experienced real conversion.

## What of Infant Baptism

It may seem harsh, to some, for us to say that the Bible is completely silent on infant baptism, but candor compels us to say that very thing. One of the references frequently quoted in support of infant baptism is Matt. 19:13-15; but that very scripture tells what the mothers brought their children there for—"that he should put his hands on them, and pray"—and does not even hint at a baptism. There are those who tell us that there were infants baptized by the apostles, for there were whole families baptized; for instance, in the case of Cornelius, Lydia, the jailer, etc. But the burden of proof still rests on those putting forth this argument, as the Bible says nothing about little children in those homes. In this connection it may be well to remember that of Cornelius it is said that he "feared God with all his house" (Acts 10:2); and also of the jailer, it is said that he was baptized, "believing in God with all his house" (Acts 16:34). If "all his house" of necessity means that there were infants in the family, then it follows that these infants of necessity "feared" and "believed" God. Moreover, it is a common thing to say even of families belonging to churches that reject infant

baptism that the whole family are "Baptists," or "Mennonites," or "Brethren," etc.; meaning, of course, that all who
have reached accountability are members of the churches
named.

Baptism, like all other church ordinances, is intended
for those who have sufficient understanding to receive it
on terms of the Gospel. As for innocent children, they
are under the blood ("Of such is the kingdom of heaven")
until they reach the age of accountability, after which the
Gospel message is for them and they are proper subjects
for baptism as soon as they have met the scriptural requirements for receiving it.

## In Whose Name

Christ teaches us that baptism should be administered
"in the name of the Father, and of the Son, and of the
Holy Ghost" (Matt. 28:19). This is the only place where
these three words are used, the disciples usually baptizing
in the name of Jesus. This presents no serious difficulty,
however, as doing anything in the name of Jesus Christ is
a virtual recognition of the Trinity; for there is no Jesus
Christ save the only begotten of the Father and the sender
of the "other Comforter" which is the Holy Ghost. No
Christian act is valid that does not give full recognition to
Father, Son, and Holy Ghost.

## Bible Mode of Baptism

This phase of our subject has, in times past, received
more than its just share of attention. Of late years, however, the pendulum has swung to the other extreme, and
a freedom is exercised in ignoring Bible teaching as to
mode that is quite as unjustifiable as over-emphasizing it.
Everything taught in the Bible is given by inspiration of
God and merits our prayerful attention and reverential
obedience as far as God gives us light and understanding.

The two modes of baptism in most common practice
are those of affusion and immersion. There are varieties

in practice in each mode, the former being administered by either sprinkling or pouring, the latter by single immersion forwards or backwards, and by trine immersion. The principal argument for affusion rests upon Old Testament ceremonies and prophecies, while immersion rests its arguments on the alleged meaning of the Greek word "baptizo" and the use of the word "buried" as a figure of baptism.

It will help us to keep from becoming radical in our views of baptism if we remember that the exact manner of applying the water is nowhere stated in describing apostolic baptisms. In view of this fact it is in order to remark that where a person has surrendered to God, has been baptized upon confession of faith, and by the grace of God is serving Him as he has light and understanding, God will not bar him out of heaven if there should have been a mistake made in the manner of administering the water in baptism. Carrying this thought a little farther, when one who applies for membership in your church should have been baptized by a different mode from what you are in the habit of administering it, it is more important for you to inquire as to his "good conscience" and as to whether he is now in the unity of the faith with yourselves, than it is to question him as to the mode by which he was baptized.

Yet we should avoid the opposite extreme of indifference to Bible teaching on this subject, for the Bible does give us some teaching which throws light upon the proper mode of baptism. Every Church should make a faithful study of this subject, decide upon which mode comes nearest the requirement of Scripture, and then adopt that as its mode, its only mode of administering baptism.

Why We Believe in Pouring as the Bible Mode

### 1. It is a Bible definition for baptism.

The two words, "baptize" and "pour," are used in Scripture to designate the same thing, as the following comparisons will show:

The same thing that Joel (2:28) and Peter (Acts 2:17) call "pour," John the Baptist (Matt. 3:11) and Christ (Acts 1:5) call "baptize." The same use of the two ideas is brought together in Acts 11:15, 16, showing that the two words are synonymous—"fill" being used here instead of "pour," thus expressing the same idea.

Paul refers to the Red Sea experience of the children of Israel, saying that they "were all *baptized* unto Moses, in the cloud and in the sea" (I Cor. 10:1, 2). The psalmist refers to the same experience, saying, "The clouds *poured* out water" (Psa. 77:17-21). By comparing these two references, we see that the people were baptized through the pouring out of water from the clouds. This again emphasizes the fact that the two ideas are synonymous.

Things equal to the same thing are equal to each other. Since the two words, "baptize" and "pour," are used interchangeably in Scripture, we conclude that they mean one and the same thing, and that the proper way to baptize a person is to pour water upon him or her.

We, of course, recognize that pouring refers only to the mode of baptism, and that not all pourings constitute baptism. In such references as Matt. 28:19, Mark 16:16, and Acts 2:38, where the ordinance rather than the mode is spoken of, the words may not so readily be interchanged. But even here by supplying the needed words to conform to the grammatical construction the same ideas may be interchanged.

2. **There is no other word which the Bible ever uses as a synonym for baptism.**

When it comes to looking around for some other word that can be used interchangeably with the word "baptize," we fail to find one. In this connection it may be well to notice that the word "immerse" is not found in any unbiased translation of the Bible, neither is there a recorded instance in the Bible where one person put another under the water as a religious ceremony. The kind reader will please bear with us in making such assertions, but candor compels us to state the facts, as well as to say that we hold ourselves ready to be corrected when some one has proof of error on our part.

3. **It is in harmony with terms used in Old Testament Scriptures, as well as terms used in connection with Spirit baptism.**

This has already been shown in the paragraphs on "Divers Washings" and on water baptism being a symbol of Holy Ghost baptism. If the baptism with the Holy Ghost, always referred to as an outpouring, was by affusion, why should not the baptism with water be the same?

4. **In a majority of cases where baptism is referred to in apostolic practice, it was evidently in the house, which points to pouring as the most convenient mode.**

We recognize that this point is not conclusive, as it is possible to have baptistries in houses; but it is not very likely that they were thus equipped at the beginning of the apostolic practice of baptism. After Pentecost the only instance where it is clear that baptism was administered in the water was at the baptism of the eunuch (and some think also in the case of Lydia and her household) but in neither of these cases is there a word as to how the water was applied.

5. **It is practical in every clime, and under all circumstances.**

Baptism by pouring may be administered in the sick room, in the frozen regions of the North, in the desert sands wherever "a handful of water" (Menno Simons) is available, and in every other place and under every other condition where any other mode may be practiced.*

*As a sidelight on the mode of baptism as administered by the early Christians of the first few centuries read Wenger's "Six Months in Bible Lands," Chapter IX, referring to the catacombs of Rome.

## WHY PRACTICE WATER BAPTISM

### 1. Christ commands it.

The last thing that He commanded His disciples to do was to teach all nations and to baptize. Matt. 28:19. That this did not mean Spirit baptism is evident, (1) because the work of baptizing with the Spirit is the work of God and not of man, and (2) because the disciples practiced literal water baptism. Acts 2:41; 8:38; 9:18; 10:47, 48; 16:15, 33; 18:4.

### 2. It has been the custom of the Church since apostolic days.

The practice of the apostolic Church (already referred to), the frescoes in the catacombs of Rome hewn out of the rocks by early Christians, and the subsequent history of the Christian Church, all confirm the truth of the statement. Water baptism can not be "spiritualized" away without doing violence to Scripture.

### 3. It helps to strengthen believers.

A scripturally conducted baptismal service is heartening to both converts and congregation. Often, in times of temptation, has the memory of our baptismal promise come to our aid, and thus today, as in apostolic times, "baptism doth also now save us" (I Pet. 3:21).

### 4. It belongs to scriptural church organization.

As the foremost among church ordinances it is a most appropriate and impressive way of receiving converts into the visible Church.

### 5. It is the seal of our profession of faith and acceptance of Christ.

In other words, it is "the answer of a good conscience toward God."

Baptism, like everything else commanded by Christ, has been abused. Some have taken it as a cloak for their sins, others have tried to put salvation into it, others have made an idol out of mode, others have abused it in other ways; but none of these things can by any stretch of the imagination be manufactured into a good reason against its proper observance. It was instituted in divine wisdom and divinely commanded to be obeyed. Let us accept it in grateful reverence, remembering that "he that believeth and is baptized shall be saved."

# CHAPTER VI

## THE COMMUNION

For as often as ye eat this bread, and drink this cup, ye do shew the Lord's death till he come.—I Corinthians 11:26.

As we approach this solemn ordinance our hearts are filled with reverence for Him in whose memory it is kept. It was instituted by our Saviour on the night of His betrayal. After they were seated around the table He said. "With desire I have desired to eat this passover with you before I suffer: for I say unto you, that I will not any more eat thereof, until it be fulfilled in the kingdom of God" (Luke 22:15, 16). It was at this Passover feast that He took the bread, gave thanks, brake it, gave to His disciples, reminding them that it was to be kept in memory of His broken body. After this He took the cup, divided it among His disciples, and reminded them that it was to be kept in memory of His shed blood. A new ordinance, designed for use in the New Testament dispensation, had been instituted.

### What It Signifies

1. **It is a memorial of the broken body and shed blood of Jesus Christ.**

This is clearly set forth in Paul's first letter to the Corinthians:

I have received of the Lord that which I also delivered unto you, that the Lord Jesus the same night in which he was betrayed took bread: and when he had given thanks, he brake it, and said, Take, eat; this is my body, which is broken for you: this do in remembrance of me. After the same manner also he took the cup, when he had supped, saying, This cup is the new testament in my blood: this do ye, as oft as ye drink it, in remembrance of me. For as often as ye eat this bread, and drink this cup, ye do shew the Lord's death till he come. —I Cor. 11:23-26.

It is a very simple ceremony; so simple that a child may know what it is for, yet so profound and far-reaching that the most scholarly men have never been able to fathom it. In the bread we have a symbol of the sacrifice of Jesus for our sakes; in the cup, a symbol of the atonement through the shedding of His blood. No other things are so necessary to be kept in mind; no other symbols so expressive of what they memorialize.

2. **It is typical of a common union of communicants.**
Let us again turn to the writings of Paul for an exposition of this thought:

> The cup of blessing which we bless, is it not the communion of the blood of Christ? The bread which we break, is it not the communion of the body of Christ? For we, being many, are one bread, and one body; for we are all partakers of that one body.—I Cor. 10:16, 17.

As we meditate upon the setting forth of what this communion means, we are impressed (1) with the appropriateness of the symbols, (2) with the idea of a common union of saints, (3) with the thought that in the communion we observe the ordinance as a body, not simply as individuals, (4) with the importance of the body of communicants being as the communion represents them to be—one in the Lord, one in faith and sympathy, one in loyal devotion to the cause of Christ. As the bread is composed of many individual grains of wheat, so inseparably mixed together that it is impossible to tell the flour from the several grains apart, so the communicant body should be one compact body of worshipers in the Lord, dedicated to the furtherance of His cause.

3. **It demands of communicants a holy life, separated from the world.**
Two excerpts from Paul's writings suggest this very forcibly:

> I would not that ye should have fellowship with devils. Ye can not drink the cup of the Lord, and the cup of devils: ye can not be partakers of the Lord's table, and of the table of devils.—I Cor. 10:20, 21.
>
> For as often as ye eat this bread, and drink this cup, ye do shew the Lord's death till he come.—I Cor. 11:26.

These texts state very clearly and definitely the importance of confining the communion to those who are one in Christ, unstained with unforgiven sin. "I would not that ye should fellowship with devils;"—that is, Hold yourselves aloof from them, both in the matter of communion and of (supposed) Christian fellowship. Such a fellowship is possible only in theory—in fact, "Ye can not . . . . ." Keeping this in mind, we understand what Paul meant when he said, that every time you commune you "shew the Lord's death."

As for sinners communing, we have two admonitions on this point: (1) to the Church—not to commune with such persons (I Cor. 10:20, 21); (2) to the sinner: "Whosoever shall eat this bread, and drink this cup of the Lord, unworthily . . . . eateth and drinketh damnation to himself" (I Cor. 11:27-29).

### 4. It is a testimony wtih a twofold meaning.

In the communion, "Ye do shew" (1) "the Lord's death" (2) "till he come." It emphasizes both the cross and the glory side of the Christian life. And it should be borne in mind that only in case we live a consistent Christian life do we really show this in the presence of all witnesses. Both the sacrifice of Jesus Christ for our sakes and the coming glory connected with His second coming are typified in the communion—and are also typified in our lives, if we are true to what our part in the communion signifies.

### Some Theories Examined

1. **Transubstantiation.**—The Catholic view is that the bread and the wine become the actual body and blood of the Lord through their consecration by the priest. This theory is based on the assertion of our Lord, when He instituted the communion, that "This is my body" . . . . "This is my blood." It ought not to be difficult to see the fallacy of this theory. When Christ spoke these words His literal body was in plain sight of the disciples, so they could

not have understood this language in any other way than that it was a figure of speech. A similar illustration is found in Daniel's interpretation of Nebuchadnezzar's vision, saying, "Thou art this head of gold" (Dan. 2:38). This was literally true; but not in the sense that the king of flesh and blood was the head of pure gold seen in the vision. So in the communion, the bread is the body and the cup is the blood of Christ—in a typical sense. The theory of transubstantiation is erroneous, for two reasons: (1) It is contrary to facts, physically. (2) If it were true, then every communicant, no matter how unregenerate and hypocritical, would be eating the flesh and drinking the blood of our Lord, which, according to Christ's own words (Jno. 6:54) would mean everlasting life—a very clever device for getting sinners into the Kingdom of God. There is no virtue in either the bread or the cup, as elements, but as symbols of the broken body and shed blood of Christ they are very appropriate and very important.

2. **Consubstantiation.**—This is a modification of the theory just considered, the difference being that while the first claims the actual presence of the body and blood of the Lord, the second stands for the belief that while the body and blood of the Lord are literally present it is denied that this change took place through the priestly consecration. This theory is subject to practically the same objections as the other. So far as the physical qualities of the bread and the cup are concerned, they are wholly typical; and as for Christ's figuring in the communion, it is wholly spiritual.

3. **Open Communion.**—By this is understood the policy of admitting to the communion all persons who feel themselves worthy to partake of it. Advocates of open communion look upon the restricted communion as being selfish, believing the policy of open communion to be more in accord with the standard of the Gospel, which is declared to be the Gospel of love. But this theory is open to a number of objections:

a. It is hard to harmonize it with the scriptures already quoted.

b. As for close communion being "selfish," it should be understood that the basis of the communion is not friendship but unity in the faith and fellowship in the Lord Jesus Christ.

c. It minimizes the idea of Christian fellowship in the communion. The open communionist says, "We commune with the Lord, not with men." Then why have a public service at all? If it is true that we do not commune with our fellow communicants, why should we not admit gamblers, thieves, murderers, Mormons, Mohammedans, and all other classes of criminals or heretics?

d. It admits to "the table of the Lord" those who are denied admission to the denominational table. We know of churches that admit all classes of Christian professors to the communion but deny admission to their church to all applicants who have not been baptized by a certain mode, except upon rebaptism. Why be more particular with our own denominational table than with the table of the Lord? Only wide-open churches who admit all classes of people regardless of their faith and practice can consistently advocate open communion.

e. It is in strange contrast with the Bible standard of unity. Why should we profess to have a "comm(on)union" service when it is admitted that the common union does not exist? People who are not willing to fellowship with one another in the same church are not near enough one in faith and life to commune together in the same service. Let us keep the service true to name.

4. **Close Communion.**—According to this standard the communicants are confined to those "of like precious faith," acknowledging the jurisdiction and oversight of the church having charge of the communion. We believe it to be scriptural, for the following reasons:

a. It answers the scriptural requirements for unity.

b. It provides for a "common union" of communicants.

c. It enables the Church to keep the Lord's table in order.

d. It makes it possible for a church to comply with the scriptural requirement, "I would not that ye should have fellowship with devils;" for, restricting the communion to those who acknowledge the jurisdiction of the Church, it gives the Church an opportunity to point unworthy ones back from the communion without passing judgment upon members of other churches.

e. It bases the communion upon Christian unity and Christian fellowship, not upon friendship or sociability.

f. It guards against the inconsistency of members pretending to be one in faith and life, as signified in the communion, when they are not willing to fellowship one another in the same church organization.

## Rules Governing the Communion

1. **Communicants are to present a united body in Christ.** I Cor. 10:15-17.

(Discussed in previous paragraphs.)

2. **Persons apparently in the order of the Church but secretly contaminated with sin should not commune in that condition.** I Cor. 11:27-29.

(Discussed in previous paragraphs.)

3. **Self-examination should precede communion.** I Cor. 11:28; II Cor. 13:5.

(Discussed in previous paragraphs.)

4. **Those openly polluted with sin should be excluded from the communion.** I Cor. 10:18-20.

(Discussed in previous paragraphs.)

5. **Only the bread and the cup have divine sanction as part of the communion.** I Cor. 11:17-26.

It is thought by some who want to obey all the commandments of our Lord that since Christ and His disciples ate a full meal at the time the communion was instituted, God's people in this dispensation should observe that as well as the communion. Such seems to have been the custom (at least in part) in the Church at Corinth at the time Paul wrote to them concerning proper rules for observing Christian ordinances. But there are a number of facts in the way of accepting this theory:

a. Matthew, Mark, and Luke tell us plainly that this was the passover; that the paschal lamb was killed the first day of unleavened bread, the regular time for killing the Jewish passover.

b. When Christ and His disciples spoke of this feast as "the passover" it is very evident that they meant the Jewish passover. Matt. 26:17-19; Mark 14:12-16; Luke 22:7-15.

c. There is no record that Christ ever taught, either publicly or privately, that this was anything else but the Jewish passover; nor can we find that the disciples ever taught, or even hinted, that it was not.

d. Paul, after correcting irregularities, reiterated what he had "received of the Lord," mentioned the bread and the cup, but said nothing about the full meal—only to say, "If any man hunger, let him eat at home." This makes it clear that no full meal at the church was authorized; and that it is the soul, not the body, that is to be satisfied in the eating and drinking in communion.

### FURTHER OBSERVATIONS

1. **The communion was instituted at the regular time for the Jewish passover.**

This is clear from the references already quoted. Some have concluded from the language of John ("They themselves went not into the judgment hall, lest they should be defiled; but that they might eat the passover" —18:28) that the supper which Christ ate with His disciples was not the regular Jewish passover, but that it was something else, a new "passover," to be eaten in connection with the communion. Again let us turn to the Scriptures for light. A glimpse into the German version will help us out on this point. King James' version has but one word (passover) for both the paschal lamb (Luke 22: 7) and the seven days feast of unleavened bread (v. 1), but the German version calls the first "Osterlamm" (Easter lamb) and the second "Ostern" (Easter). When we turn to John 18:28 we find that it was the "Ostern," not "Osterlamm," that they still desired to eat. In other words, they wanted to complete the remaining six days of the feast of unleavened bread. So this verse confirms, rather than conflicts with, the testimony of Matthew, Mark, and Luke as to the time when Christ and His disciples ate the Jewish passover.

2. **The most appropriate time of the day to observe the communion is during the time of the day when Jesus hung on the cross.**

Lest we be misunderstood on this point, let us begin this discussion with the statement that there is absolutely no Bible command telling us what time of the day this ordinance should be kept. But the promise is that "as often" as we observe it we "shew the Lord's death," etc.: so that when we observe it in faith and in purity we are both blessed and will be a blessing, whether this be observed morning, noon, afternoon, or night. But there is an added significance in observing it during the time of the day when the Saviour hung on the cross. If the Jewish passover was eaten after night, in memory of a night-time event, why is it not appropriate to partake of the communion during the daytime, since it is kept in memory of the death of Christ, a daytime event?

3. **To partake of the communion is a sacred privilege.**

It is in this sense that we prize it most. It is a command, and as such it should be kept "with reverence and godly fear;" but what greater joy is there for the child of God than to enter into the spirit of the sacrifice which our Saviour made for us, and in fellowship with those "of like precious faith" "shew the Lord's death till he come"?

As we reach forth our hands to partake of His broken body and shed blood our hearts go back in sympathetic sadness to the eventful time when the price for our redemption was paid, our minds go out to our environments surrounding us with opportunities to do our Master's will, and our hopes forge ahead in fond anticipation of that joyous, glorious time when Christ will come again to claim His own. Blessed be God for repeated opportunities of having part in the communion.

# CHAPTER VII

## FEET WASHING

If ye know these things, happy are ye if ye do them.—
John 13:17.

Twice, in the New Testament, is the washing of saints' feet referred to. The first is found in Jno. 13:1-17, telling of the institution of the ordinance; the second in I Tim. 5:10, where Paul, in enumerating a number of things pertaining to the record of a certain widow to be taken into the number which he tells about, uses the words, "If she have washed the saints' feet." But these are not the only places in the Bible where we read about feet washing. Let us notice a few of the

### OLD TESTAMENT REFERENCES

There are two kinds of feet washing referred to in the Old Testament: (1) as a custom, or service; (2) as a command, or ceremony.

1. **Feet washing as a custom** is mentioned in Gen. 18:4; 19:2; 24:32; 43:24; II Sam. 11:8. That this custom was not unknown in the days of Christ is evident from His implied rebuke to Simon: "I entered into thine house, and thou gavest me no water for my feet" (Luke 7:44). It was a custom in those times for hosts to set out water with which guests might wash their feet, very much like the present custom of hosts to set out water for guests to wash their hands and faces. This custom of washing feet is no longer in general use, for the reason that the style of our footwear has changed.

2. **Feet washing as a ceremony** is mentioned in Ex. 30:17-21; 40:30-32. The first reference gives specific directions from God to Aaron and his sons about that part

of the purification ceremonies pertaining to washing hands and feet, while the second tells about the observance of the command.

As we study these two kinds of feet washing we notice a striking contrast. The first was a voluntary custom begun without specific command or divine authority, and dropped as customs changed. The second was instituted by divine authority, a penalty attached for its nonobservance, and discontinued only with the abolition of the ceremonial law.

As we take up the subject as taught in Jno. 13, it will help us to decide whether the New Testament feet washing should be looked upon as a custom or a ceremony by determining which of these two kinds of feet washing it most nearly resembles.

### JOHN 13:1-17

1. **The Example** (1-5).—Jesus rose from supper, laid aside His garments, took a towel and girded Himself, poured water into a basin, and washed His disciples' feet.

2. **The Conversation with Peter** (6-11).—When He came to Peter, that disciple inquired about what He was doing. Upon being informed that this was something which he did not at this time understand he replied, "Thou shalt never wash my feet." Promptly Christ reminded him that upon that condition he could have no part with Him. Then Peter wanted not only his feet washed but also his hands and his head. Again did Christ fail to grant his request, explaining that this was not for cleanliness; that they were all clean but Judas, who was about to betray Him.

3. **The Explanation** (12-17).—Peter's objections being silenced, Christ proceeded to finish His work of washing the disciples' feet. After that He laid aside His towel, put on His garments, sat down, and began to explain what He had done. He commended them for recognizing Him as Master and Lord, and since He, their Master and Lord,

had washed their feet, they also should wash one another's feet; that He had given them this example for that very purpose; that since they knew these things, and that since a servant ought not to esteem himself above his lord, they are happy if they obey Him.

### Feet Washing in History

It is urged by some that the washing of the saints' feet could not have been intended as a religious ceremony to be literally observed by all believers, or history would not be so silent in this matter. To this we reply that the "silence" is largely in the minds of those who would have it so. It is true that we do not hear as much of this in history as we do about some other things, and there is very good reason for it. A ceremony given under the circumstances in which this ordinance was instituted, and which is described with such painstaking care and minute detail as that narrative found in Jno. 13:1-17 is not liable to be called into question very soon—and when not called into question it is not mentioned with the frequency that something is over which there is much controversy. Then we suspect that later historians who were not friendly to the observance of feet washing as a Christian ordinance were not so eager to search for historical references on the subject as they would have been had the subject been more popular in their day. But to wipe the whole subject off the slate because history is "silent" in the matter is to go contrary to the facts of history.

We have already noticed that feet washing, both as a custom and as a ceremony, has a place in both Old and New Testaments. Coming down to the time of the Nicene fathers, we find enough in the writings of such men as Chrysostom, Cyprian, Augustine, etc., to know that it was observed in their day, as well as the other ordinances such as baptism and communion were. One reference from the writings of Cyprian will suffice on this point:

Of this same thing in the Gospel according to John: "If I have washed your feet, being your Master and Lord, ye also

ought to wash the feet of others. For I have given you an
example, that as I have done, ye also should do to others."
(Scribner's "Ante-Nicene Fathers," Vol. V, P. 545.)

The Catholics have preserved the tradition down to
this day, although they have lost the spirit of it, in the
way the ordinance was instituted by our Saviour.

That our Anabaptist forefathers practiced feet washing is evident from a number of confessions of faith adopted
during Reformation times, as well as books written at
that time, Dietrich Philips being especially strong on the
subject. From a confession of faith adopted in Amster-
dam in September, 1627, we copy the following:

> "Feet washing we confess to be an ordinance of Christ,
> which He Himself performed on His disciples, and after His
> example, commended to true believers that they should imi-
> tate it, saying, 'If I then your Lord and Master, have washed
> your feet; ye also ought to wash one another's feet. For I
> have given you an example, that ye should do as I have done
> to you.' Again: 'If ye know these things, happy are ye if ye
> do them.' Jno. 13:14, 15, 17.
>
> "The purpose for which the Lord has instituted this ordi-
> nance is principally this, That we may remember in true hu-
> miliation, that by grace we are washed from sin through the
> blood of Christ and that He our Lord and Master, by His
> lowly example, binds us to true humility towards one another.
> Jno. 13:8, 10, 14. The apostle classes feet washing among the
> good works. I Tim. 5:10." (Martyr's Mirror, P. 30.)

It is admitted that a number of denominations which
now teach against the literal observance of this ordinance
formerly practiced it. Besides the Mennonites, Brethren in
Christ, and several other denominations holding similar
tenets of faith, the Primitive Baptists are still staunch
supporters of this doctrine and faithful in its practice.

### WHY CALL THIS AN ORDINANCE

**1. It was instituted by divine authority.**

There can be no question on this point, as Jesus clearly
proclaimed His Lordship while explaining to His disciples
what He had done.

**2. It resembles the ceremonial feet washing of the
Old Testament.**

Both were instituted by divine command. In connection with the first there was a penalty attached for its non-observance; with the second, a reward for its observance —corresponding with the spirit of the Law and of the Gospel.

### 3. It was not an old custom.

If it had been, Christ would not have needed to say to Peter, "What I do thou knowest not now." It was something entirely new. They had no such custom as one of a company rising from supper to wash the feet of all the rest.

### 4. It was not for cleanliness.

Jesus' reply to Peter: "Ye are clean, but not all," followed by John's explanation: "For he knew who should betray him; therefore said he, Ye are not all clean," settles this point. Ceremonially they had prepared for the feast, and were therefore clean. Had this been for physical cleansing it would have been attended to before they sat down to the table.

But while this was not for physical or ceremonial cleansing, a beautiful application can be made of it as a symbol for cleansing from sin.

### 5. It was a religious ceremony.

Some have tried to make it appear that this event took place at Bethany, not in the upper room where they ate the passover. But it was at this meeting that Christ informed His disciples that Judas should betray Him (vv. 21-27), while Matthew (26:21), Mark (14:18), and Luke (22:21) all say that this took place on the night they ate the passover. It is important that we remember this, even though if this had been instituted at the Bethany supper Jesus would have been none the less the religious rather than the social Head of His disciples. Had it been a mere social affair, some one else would have been the host, for Jesus had "not where to lay his head."

### 6. The disciples were commanded to continue the practice.

The teaching of vv. 14, 15 is that the washing of the saints' feet is a Christian obligation, and that Jesus instituted it to the end that His disciples should follow His example. As the priests under the Old Covenant practiced feet washing until the ceremonial law was abolished, so let the members of the eternal priesthood of Christ keep this that He has commanded to be kept to the end of the age. The "all things whatsoever" of the Great Commission, in force "even unto the end of the world," include the command to "wash one another's feet." Some object to literal feet washing on the ground that it is not a command. But our Saviour's "ye ought" enjoins an obligation as binding as any command. When God says, "Ye ought," that settles it for all who want to do His will.

## Why It Should be Literally Observed by all Believers

### 1. Because it is a Christian ordinance.

As such it should have the same recognition that all other Christian ordinances have. No other ordinance was instituted and impressed upon the minds of the disciples with more painstaking care than this one is.

### 2. There is a blessing promised for its observance.

"If ye know these things, happy are ye if ye do them." The blessing of obedience is something in Christian service which no one can afford to ignore or to miss.

### 3. It is one of the "all things whatsoever" included in the Great Commission.

There is not a live church anywhere that does not make the Great Commission its battle cry. And while our mission spirit runs high, let us not forget that among the things which Christ commanded His disciples to teach all nations is that Christian people should "wash one another's feet."

### 4. It is a lesson which all men need.

The two things most beautifully and forcefully typified in this ordinance are humility, and brotherly equality and mutual service. Both are an antidote to sefishness, one of the great sins of man. It is natural for man to be proud, vain, selfish—and the indications are that not all church members have forgotten their former weaknesses along this line. It is a notable fact that the ordinance of feet washing is one of the things that leaves a church soon after pride becomes entrenched in it. And when there is a struggle on in any church as to whether pride or feet washing shall remain, let it be taken as Heaven's warning that that church needs a renovation—not of unpopular ordinances, but of purifying from soul-destroying influences.

**5. It typifies an equality of saints.**

A brother belonging to a church that believes in feet washing is introduced to a member of another church. "You say you are a ———? What do the ——— believe?" "Among other things, they believe in feet washing." "Ah, I see. Well, I believe in it too; but it would be a killing thing for one of my rich brethren to stoop so low as to wash my feet."

That man touched one of the vital spots in this ordinance. It is God's will that rich and poor, old and young, educated and uneducated, weak and strong, all should consider themselves on a common level, brethren and sisters in the fullest sense of the word, members of the happy family of God, at peace with one another, serving one another in love. There is nothing that more beautifully and forcefully typifies that happy condition in any church than the humble ordinance of washing the saints' feet. No wonder that Paul, enumerating a number of things belonging to a servant of the Church, should see fit to say, "If she have washed the saints' feet."

"If ye know these things, happy are ye if ye do them."

# CHAPTER VIII

## THE DEVOTIONAL COVERING

> Every woman that prayeth or prophesieth with her head uncovered, dishonoureth her head: for that is even all one as if she were shaven. For if the woman be not covered, let her also be shorn: but if it be a shame for her to be shorn or shaven, let her be covered.— I Corinthians 11:5, 6.

I Cor. 11:2-16 is not the first mention we have of the woman's veiling. The Jewish women, as a mark of modesty, veiled themselves when in the presence of men. A very beautiful type of the Christian woman's veil is seen in Gen. 24:65, where Rebekah put on her veil as she approached her betrothed, Isaac. It is but natural that Paul, writing for the instruction of the Bride-to-be of Christ, finding a congregation where this provision was either not properly understood or not properly obeyed, should explain in detail what it means for the Christian woman to be properly veiled as a mark of her relationship to her head—the man, and also Christ. Let us therefore turn at once to these instructions as found in

### I CORINTHIANS 11:2-16

and study them for our learning and admonition.

The church at Corinth seemingly had some trouble on this question, as it had on a number of other questions pertaining to Christian life and order. One appropriate name for the instructions given in these chapters would be, Rules of Order in the Christian Church. In the eleventh chapter we read of two ordinances: the devotional covering and the communion. Here is what Paul teaches on the first of these subjects:

1. **It is an ordinance.**

"Now I praise you, brethren, that ye remember me in all things, and keep the ordinances, as I delivered them to you" (V. 2).

The only thought that we wish to take time to notice in this verse, at this time, is the fact that Paul lists this as among the "ordinances."

## 2. This ordinance is founded upon a fundamental fact —the headship of the man over the woman, the relationship of man to God.

"I would have you know, that the head of every man is Christ; and the head of every woman is the man; and the head of Christ is God. . . . For the man is not of the woman; but the woman of the man." (Vv. 3, 8).

There is a sphere for man, and a sphere for woman, and each can perform the most effective service when working in his or her own sphere. Read Gen. 3:16; I Cor. 14:34; Eph. 5:22-25; Col. 3:18; I Tim. 2:12; I Pet. 3:1, 2. A glance at both man and the animal creation shows that these scriptures are but a reflection of God's order in the creation —the male excelling in strength and executive capacity, the female excelling in tenderness and the finer qualities. It is important that we bear these facts in mind as we study Paul's teaching on this subject.

## 3. There is a sign of relationship between man and woman in the Lord.

In the light of this statement of relationship between the man and the woman, it is but fitting that a proper sign of such relationship should be manifest, especially among worshipers. Hence,

"Every man praying or prophesying, having his head covered, dishonoureth his head. But every woman that prayeth or prophesieth with her head uncovered dishonoureth her head" (Vv. 4, 5).

Why "praying or prophesying?" Why single out these particular things in connection with these discussions? Let it be understood that Paul is writing to worshipers, people who have given themselves to God, who are supposed to be in God's order. Therefore let both appear in order, according to God's direction, for when they attempt to worship when not in God's order, this worship is a dishonor to God and man. Let man worship with head uncovered, thus signifying that while there is a relationship between him and his Head—Christ—this Head is invisible, requiring no visible sign; and let the worshipful woman wear the visible sign of her relationship to her head—man, and through man, to Christ. Paul writes concerning things as they ought to be in the Christian service, in proper Christian relationship, matters pertaining to the interests of the Church as well as of individuals. In other words, he writes about Christian ordinances.

4. **Man should worship with his head uncovered.**

Read again v. 4. To violate this rule means to dishonor his Head—Christ. For this reason Paul urges that "a man indeed ought not to cover his head, forasmuch as he is the image and glory of God" (v. 7).

5. **Woman should worship with her head covered.**

Inasmuch as "woman is the glory of the man" (v. 7), she should not dishonor him by worshiping with her head uncovered ("unveiled," R.V.). In worshiping with uncovered head she is not only dishonoring man but also Christ, who is the Head of the Church (Col. 1:18) and therefore the Head of both man and woman.

6. **Both natural and spiritual relationships, signified by the two coverings** (veiling and long hair) **are set forth in this scripture.**

> "Every woman that prayeth or prophesieth with her head uncovered dishonoureth her head: for that is even all one as if she were shaven. For if the woman be not covered, let her also be shorn: but if it be a shame for a woman to be shorn or shaven, let her be covered. . . . Judge in yourselves: is it comely for a woman to pray unto God uncovered? Doth not even nature itself teach you, that, if a man have long hair, it is a shame unto him? But if a woman have long hair, it is a glory to her: for her hair is given her for a covering" (Vv. 5, 6, 13-15).

Two coverings are here referred to: (1) the natural covering, or long hair, a sign of relationship naturally; (2) an artificial covering ("veil," R.V.), a sign of relationship between man and woman in the Lord. This is made especially clear in the reading of the Revised Version, the word "veil" being used wherever the artificial covering is referred to.

Paul's appeal to nature to confirm the strength of his arguments is especially striking because women universally —married or single, converted or unconverted; regardless of age, nationality, intelligence, color, or creed—are obedient to the lesson which God through nature (long hair for women) teaches—except when some fad comes along and dictates to Fashion-controlled women and girls that they shear their hair. Likewise men usually wear their hair short—with few exceptions, and these are generally regarded as "queer." The burden of Paul's argument is that both men and women should be as obedient to the lesson that God through revelation teaches as they are to the lesson which God through nature teaches—the long hair a *shame* to man, and a *glory* to woman.

Bearing in mind the argument put forth in vv. 13-15, we get the full force of the argument presented in v. 6: "If it be a *shame* for a woman to be shorn or shaven, *let her be covered.*" In other words, If she discards the veil, let her also cut off her hair; but if that is a shame (and it *will* be, as soon as present fashions change) let her be veiled, In both cases, let her be obedient to God, wear her hair long and keep her head veiled.

7. **It is "a covering, in sign"** (v. 10, margin).

"For this cause ought the woman to have power on her head, because of the angels." "Power" here is translated "sign of authority" in the Revised Version. Thus arrayed, she has upon her head the "sign" which gives the angels the occasion to bear the message home to God that she is taking her place side by side with man as his helper and co-worker in the work and worship of the Lord. What this "sign" should be is already partly determined by the word "veil." As to its form, the Bible does not specifically say; but being a church ordinance it is for the Church to say what it should be. What it should cover is indicated

by the other covering (the long hair) which covers the
top of the head. Another thing settled by the word "sign"
is that the ordinary protection covering worn on the head
does not answer the purpose of the veiling, for that is not
a "sign" in the sense that the devotional covering is intended
to be.

Another thought worthy of notice is that it should
be truly a "sign." When we see this covering upon the
head of woman we naturally expect her to exemplify in
her life what the devotional covering is designed to represent—devotion, piety, modesty, purity, subjection to man,
obedience to God. Too often, when this is found not to
exist, the temptation is to do away with what God commands and to retain what He forbids. But if in your heart,
dear sister, you find that there is not the loyalty and devotion and purity and modesty and will to serve and to
obey the Lord that ought to be there to make the wearing
of the devotional covering appropriate, take it as a warning from God that you should conform your life to what
the veiling stands for rather than to discard the covering
and conform your life to the world.

8. **The contentious man who argues against the devotional covering is dismissed with the assertion that he
has no ground for his contentions.**

The discussion of the subject is practically finished in
v. 15. But Paul gives a parting rebuke to the man who
contends that "my wife or daughter shall never wear the
covering." If you do, says Paul in effect, you are battling
against the Lord, as neither Jewish nor Gentile churches
having the custom for which you contend. Some contend
that Paul, in v. 16, throws away the "custom." If he did,
he must have been a very foolish man—in the midst of
arduous duties and a strenuous life to go to the pains to
explain it in minutest detail and support it by unanswer-
able arguments, and then dismiss it by saying, "There is
nothing to it." Had that been his conviction he would

have said so in the first place and thus saved himself much trouble and some churches much confusion.

"Contentions about what? That which he had just been teaching. 'No such custom.' What custom? Of women praying or prophesying with their heads uncovered. 'Neither the churches of God.' An additional argument appealing to surrounding churches, where no custom of putting aside the covering was to be found."—D. D. Miller.

### OBJECTIONS ANSWERED

1. **"It is not a part of the Gospel—just Paul's writing."**

Christ says of Paul: "He is a chosen vessel unto me, to bear my name before the Gentiles, and kings, and the children of Israel" (Acts 9:15). Paul says, "The things that I write unto you are the commandments of the Lord" (I Cor. 14:37).

2. **"Most churches have discarded it."**

So had most people in Noah's time discarded the idea that God meant what He said when He told about the Flood. Not what others think, but what God's Word says, should govern our lives.

3. **"My church does not observe it."**

Without passing judgment upon your church, we would after all remind you that God through James tells us that "to him that knoweth to do good, and doeth it not, to him it is sin." If your church persists in disobeying God, you had better seek affiliation in a church where you can obey God in *all* the ordinances, in fellowship with those "of like precious faith."

4. **"It was only a local custom."**

The burden of Paul's teaching seems to have been that in that locality it was *not* a custom, as fully established as he wanted it to be; hence his emphatic teaching on the subject. Whatever you may say about customs, it is undeniable that Paul emphasized the necessity of Christian women having their heads covered during worship.

5. **"The long hair is the covering."**

Paul first teaches the necessity of the veiling, and then appeals to nature as an illustration to confirm the arguments put forth. As "the hair is given her for *a* covering," the Christian woman understands that she has an illustration impressing upon her the necessity of wearing *the* covering, or *veiling*, taught in I Cor. 11:2-16.

6. **"It is so hard to understand."**

That depends upon how you look at it. Willingness has much to do with the understanding. By accepting without question the things about it that are easily understood you will be prepared to grapple with the harder problems connected with it. Read especially vv. 5 and 6, which even a child can understand.

7. **"If others can go to heaven without wearing it, I can too."**

Who made you judge over others? The question which should most interest you is not where others are going but what does the Lord want *you* to do? One thing is sure: "To him that knoweth to do good, and doeth it not, to him it is sin" (Jas. 4:17).

8. **"Some people make an idol of it."**

Perhaps so. But what has that to do with your obedience or disobedience? Better be a light, and show them how to wear it to God's glory.

9. **"We know of some real Christian women who do not wear it."**

Perhaps so. But whom do you trust most or whose word do you value most highly; these women, or the God who gave us I Cor. 11:2-16?

10. **"The practice was more pagan than Christian."**

Let us quote from a writer who seems to think he knows:

> "The people of Corinth worshiped idols. Their women wore a veil as they went into their idol temples to show their blind deities that they were subject to their husbands. Paul preached to these people. A number were converted. Now they wished to know whether to continue the custom in the wor-

14

ship of the God of heaven. Paul thinks a moment, and, know-ing the power of the law of expediency, advises them, under the circumstances to keep up the custom, lest the heathen say that the new religion, taught by Paul, did not approve of a woman being in subjection to her husband."

One can hardly believe that a man laying claims to intelligence and fairness would put forth such an argu-ment in all seriousness, but it takes such sophistry to argue away this very plain scripture. Honestly, was Paul joking, or was he in earnest? If in earnest (and it would be sac-rilegious to think that he was not) why did he not handle the subject as he did the question of eating meat (Rom. 14; I Cor. 8) in which he clearly taught that while the meat-eating regulations of the Law were abolished, yet for the sake of expediency those thus free from the law should bear in mind the consciences of their brethren who as yet do not see it in that light? Why was he so careful to go into details in explaining the "custom" to a people who in all probability understood it better than he did—if this was but a heathen custom? Why his positive statements with reference to women worshiping with heads covered, men with heads uncovered, appealing to nature as an impressive illustration of obedience, and coupling this "power" with the holy angels? Let us notice:

a. Paul declares that what he taught at Corinth he taught in all the churches. See I Cor. 4:17.

b. The epistle is addressed to all believers every-where. I Cor. 1:2.

c. Paul shows that the covering signifies a recogni-tion of headship and is connected with the original crea-tion before the fall. I Cor. 11:3, 7-12,

d. It is but fitting that the redeemed from sin should recognize creation order that existed before the fall, and that some sign or memorial should be given, as other vital facts and conditions are symbolized in other Christian or-dinances.

e. Paul was writing about ordinances "as I delivered them to you," not as he found heathen customs to be.

**11. "I would be ashamed to wear it."**

You have probably revealed the secret of most of your objections. It is safe to say that most of the objections to the devotional covering would vanish immediately if it were fashionable or popular to wear it.

# CHAPTER IX

## THE CHRISTIAN SALUTATION

Salute one another with an holy kiss.—Romans 16:16.
Greet ye one another with a kiss of charity.—I Peter 5:14.

The Bible speaks of three forms of salutation, as follows:

### I THE PERSONAL GREETING

This is the most common form, the one most frequently spoken of in the Bible. "Salute no man by the way," was Christ's admonition to His disciples as He sent them among "the lost sheep of the house of Israel." By this we not only understand that He did not want them to lose valuable time, but that saluting one another was a very common custom among the people in that day. "Greet the friends by name," is the loving admonition of the disciple whom Jesus loved. This must have been a remarkable gift of John's, and is today a decided help when one is able to recall readily the faces and names of those met before. If you are able to call friends by their given names, you will seem all the nearer to them, especially the young people.

Not only should we greet our friends by name, but our love to God should be strong enough to be friendly towards enemies as well. "If ye salute your brethren only, what do ye more than others? do not even the publicans so" (Matt. 5:47)? A hearty "Good morning" or "How do you do?" may have the effect of driving away that unfriendly feeling and to win for you a friend. When your soul is overflowing with love to God and man, your words and deeds will manifest a friendly spirit toward friend and foe. One of the ways in which you show your friendship is to speak to people as you pass them.

## II THE RIGHT HAND OF FELLOWSHIP

The handshake is not of modern origin. Paul said that when James and Peter and John perceived the grace that had been given to him and Barnabas they extended to them "the right hand of fellowship" (Gal. 2:9). We understand that this was more than a mere social custom. When extended in sincerity it is an expression of friendship and good will. Usually the character of the individual is revealed in the character of the handshake. By it we form ideas of warmth or coldness, of sincerity or insincerity, and strength or weakness of character on the part of those whose hands we grasp. Thus did the apostles recognize Barnabas and Paul to be on the same level with themselves. Thus do people today give evidence of friendship for one another. There is power in a warm handshake, provided it is prompted by godly sincerity and good will.

## III THE HOLY KISS

This form of the Christian salutation was both practiced (Acts 20:37) and commanded by the disciples. It is an expression of a greater degree of warmth and spiritual fervor than the other forms noticed, and the command for its observance is limited to believers. Therefore, you whose hearts are so full of the love of God that you "love one another with a pure heart fervently," use the divinely commanded symbol of such love and "greet ye one another with a kiss of charity."

### 1. It is a symbol of love.

It is both sacred and precious, when observed in the Spirit of love. In this way husband and wife, parents and children, Christian and fellow Christian, salute each other. It is as naturally an expression of fervent love as the handshake is an expression of warm friendship.

### 2. It is a command.

As proof for this assertion let us read what the Scriptures have to say on this point:

> Salute one another with an holy kiss.—Rom. 16:16.
> Greet ye one another with an holy kiss.—I Cor. 16:20.
> Greet one another with an holy kiss.—II Cor. 13:12.
> Greet all the brethren with an holy kiss.—I Thess. 5:26.
> Greet ye one another with a kiss of charity.—I Pet. 5:14.

Here is plain Scripture, easily understood by those who in the spirit of holy regard for the truth of God's Word, and with fervent love for one another, want to know and to do God's will.

We have heard many objections—unsanitary, inconvenient, making a gazing-stock of ourselves, probability of catching disease, the other fellow a hypocrite, out of date, too little to be noticed, handshake has taken its place, etc., etc., etc.—but honestly, in the fact of the scriptures above quoted, are any of these excuses justified? and will not the spirit of fervent brotherly love cause most of these objections to vanish?

### 3. It is "an holy kiss."

And in this respect it is important to remember that the holiness need not be on the part of the one thus saluted. The father of the prodigal son planted the kiss of love upon the face of his wayward child, the fond mother embraces and kisses her erring son, and with the same fervor should the consecrated child of God greet his stumbling brother with even greater warmth of soul than if he had been more worthy. We should greet our brethren, not with the kiss of judgment but with "the kiss of charity." It is "an holy kiss" provided you yourself are pure, holy, filled with overflowing love to God and man. And whatever you may think of your brother, you should not be satisfied with yourself until in heart and mind you have reached this standard.

### 4. It is for "all the brethren."

Some places where the ministry still keeps up this practice the laity have almost if not wholly discarded it.

Why this distinction? We should remember that the Bible does not say, "Greet all the ministers," but "all the *brethren.*" Brethren among brethren, sisters among sisters, this commandment should be consistently obeyed.

Some profess to believe that the ordinance should not be practiced because it is so very much abused. Honestly, though, is this the *real* reason why people oppose, ridicule, and even revile this Bible-commanded but very unpopular ordinance? Where is the Christian ordinance that has not been abused? And would not this objection vanish immediately if it suddenly became popular for men to greet each other with a kiss as it formerly was for women to greet each other in this way?

5. **It is very much needed.**

It is apparent to every impartial observer that the command to "greet one another with an holy kiss," "with a kiss of charity," is not a mere arbitrary command but a Christian admonition to Christian people to keep alive the symbol of a most important Christian principle. Just as the bread and the cup, as symbols in the communion, are valueless where the communicants do not enter into the spirit of the communion, so there can be no "holy kiss," no "kiss of charity" where those going through the form of greeting each other in this way do not walk "in righteousness and true holiness," do not "love one another with a pure heart fervently." It is because these things are so sadly lacking in the hearts and lives of so many Christian professors that this symbol of holy love is so urgently needed to remind people of this part of the full-Gospel standard. You get most out of this subject when you study it in the light of what it typifies or symbolizes, and of how important it is to keep these things alive in our hearts and lives. Though this holy ordinance is often abused, the most frequent abuse of it is the irreverent language used in talking about it and against it.

Where Christian people "love one another with a pure heart fervently" it is but natural for them to "salute one another with an holy kiss."

# CHAPTER X

## ANOINTING WITH OIL

Is any sick among you? let him call for the elders of the Church; and let them pray over him, anointing him with oil in the name of the Lord: and the prayer of faith shall save the sick, and the Lord shall raise him up; and if he have committed sins, they shall be forgiven him.—James 5:14, 15.

### AN ANCIENT PRACTICE

Anointing with oil was an ancient custom among the people of God.

Ruth was commanded to anoint herself in preparation to meet her future husband. Ruth 3:3.

Bodies were anointed for purposes of refreshment and purification. II Chron. 28:15; Esther 2:12.

The psalmist writes: "I shall be anointed with fresh oil" (Psa. 92:10).

Ointments were used in preparing bodies for burial. Matt. 26:12.

One of Christ's instructions to His disciples was, "When thou fastest, anoint thine head, and wash thy face" (Matt. 6:17).

The disciples "anointed many that were sick, and healed them" (Mark 6:13).

Thus it is seen that anointing with oil was practiced at a very early age, and for various purposes.

### ANOINTING FOR HEALING PURPOSES

**New Testament Authority.**—There are two references which we should keep in mind as we study this subject. The first is Mark 6:13, already quoted in part, and the second is the text that stands at the head of this chapter.

**A Religious Ceremony.**—There are some that tell us that James did not refer to literal oil, but that he referred to "oil of grace." To this we offer the same objections that we would to the man who says that Jesus did not refer to water baptism but that the Spirit baptism is alone sufficient. Man can not baptize with the Holy Ghost, neither can he anoint with the oil of grace. When the disciples "anointed with oil many that were sick" did they anoint with literal oil, or with the "oil of grace?"

Another question: Is the oil applied because of its healing properties, or is there a deeper meaning connected with its application to a person? If James had in mind only its healing properties, it seems to us that he would either have given directions as to its use or advised sending for a physician rather than for the elders of the Church. Furthermore, he says, *"The prayer of faith* (not the oil) shall save the sick,"* This makes it clear that he had in mind not merely the curative powers of the oil but more particularly the greater power of God. The healing properties of oil being recognized, we see in it an appropriate symbol of what God can do and does do for both body and soul; and as such it is used in the anointing, just as water is used in baptism, and the bread and the cup in the communion. In choosing types and symbols to be used in religious ceremonies God always chooses the ones that are most striking and appropriate, and the suitableness of oil in the anointing is apparent to all. We look at this, therefore, as a religious ceremony, enjoined upon believers who are sick.

**Is it a Command?**—Not in the sense that baptism and communion are commands. Of baptism it is said, "Be baptized:" of the communion, "This do ye;" of feet washing, "I have given you an example, that ye should do." Concerning the anointing, however, it comes in the form of a divine suggestion rather than as a divine command. Lest some one may read a meaning into this statement that does not belong there, let us remember that an obedient child of God is as submissive to a divine suggestion as to a divine command. Notice how James approaches the subject:

"Is any among you afflicted, let him pray. Is any merry, let him sing psalms. Is any sick among you, let him send for the elders of the church." When you are afflicted, merry, or sick, think of these suggestions from the Lord.

**Purpose of the Anointing.**—This is plainly stated in the instructions: "And the prayer of faith *shall save* the sick, and the Lord *shall raise* him up." The promise is positive. Look it squarely in the face, believe it, accept it, and you are not likely to become misled or fanatical on this subject.

Then why are not all healed who are anointed? There may be a number of reasons. Possibly it was not the Lord's will that the patient should recover; or there may have been a lack of faith on the part of either the sick or the officiating elders, or both; or it may have been administered as an unction for the soul and not with full faith that "the prayer of faith shall save the sick." Whatever may be the cause of the failure, let not the sick call for the anointing, or the elders advise it, without full faith in the promise. The divine admonition, "Let him send for the elders of the church," is clear enough for the sick to act upon the suggestion. When the elders come and talk matters over with the one who called them, it can then be determined what the proper thing is to do. Spiritual overseers ought to be helpful in this as well as in other problems confronting their members. A careful reading of James 5:14, 15 impresses us with the following:

1. **There are times when the anointing is not appropriate.** It is certainly not appropriate where there is not the prayer of faith. There must be an active, living faith —either on the part of the sick, or of the elders, or both— or there can be no "prayer of faith," no petition with power to reach the Throne. And even if a part of those connected with the ceremony have full faith in the promises

of God in this case, the presence of doubt on the part of any in the room is a hindrance to the work. See Matt. 13:58; Mark 5:36-43; Acts 9:39-41. There are times, also, when it is not God's will that the patient should recover, at least not for the time being, in which case we can not pray for immediate recovery and pray "according to his will." When you pray over the matter of anointing, pray with eyes open to the promise. The anointing is in order: (1) when the Lord's will is that the sick recover; (2) when the sick, after prayerful meditation, believes that the Lord wants him to get well; (3) when the elders thus called can unite with the sick in the prayer of faith that "the Lord *shall raise him up*"—either immediately or at a later time, in such a way as God knows is best.

2. **The anointing should not be administered as an unction for the soul.** Some seek the anointing because they "want to keep this one commandment yet" before they die. Now the Bible does not even hint at any such use for anointing. On the other hand, there is a positive promise that "the Lord *shall raise* him up." Whoever is anointed as a preparation for dying lacks faith in this promise. It is to the blood, not to the oil, to which we look for the cleansing of the soul.

3. **The anointing is not for infants.** They do not "call for the elders of the church." Infant anointing has no more standing in the Bible than has infant baptism.

4. **The anointing is not for the unconverted.** If through their sickness they are moved to send for the elders of the Church, let there first be instructions that will lead them to forsake their sins and accept Jesus as their Saviour, after which it will be in order to speak of baptism and the anointing.

5. **Sickness is not necessarily the result of the sins of the sick.** The statement, *"If he have committed sins,"* settles that point. But when sickness is a direct result

of sin, a confession of the sin before the anointing is necessary.

6. **Recognize the elders of your own church,** in the anointing, just as you would in the case of baptism, the communion, or any other church ordinance. This being a religious ceremony, we want to be as regular in this as we are in every other religious ceremony.

7. **The anointing is not for saving souls.** Lest some should get this idea the apostle goes on to say, "And the Lord shall raise him up; and *if* he have committed sins, they shall be forgiven him." As said before, the anointing is for the healing of the body, not the saving of the soul. Whether or not the sick have committed sins, it is the healing of the body that is under consideration. But one thing is sure: the man who meets God's conditions in this matter will be so fully given up to Him, and in case he has been guilty of sin he will have so fully repented of it that when he is raised in body he will also rise with his sins forgiven.

**"Thy Will be Done."**—This is an ordinance which should be taken seriously. When the sick who pray "according to his will" send for the elders of the Church, and the elders, in harmony with the sick, pray in full faith that "the prayer of faith shall save the sick, and the Lord shall raise him up," we have every reason to believe that God will hear the prayers, raise the sick, and glorify His name. Yet we should not forget that as humans we are liable to err, and that however prayerful or careful we might have been there is a possibility in either the sick, or the elders, or some one else having failed to meet the conditions, and the raising up fails to be realized. We should never be so positive, either as to the time of rising or in the rising at all, but that we include the petition of our Saviour: "Nevertheless, let not my will but thine be done."

# CHAPTER XI

## MARRIAGE

> From the beginning of the creation God made them male and female. For this cause shall a man leave his father and mother, and cleave unto his wife; and they twain shall be one flesh: and so shall they be no more twain, but one flesh. What therefore God hath joined together, let not man put asunder.—Mark 10:6-9.

Marriage is an institution ordained of God. Like the day of rest, it was set apart and sanctified in the creation, and in its purity has ever since that time been held sacred by the people of God. The institution of marriage, after Eve was brought into being as "an help meet for" Adam, is described in this manner: "This is now bone of my bone and flesh of my flesh . . . . therefore shall a man leave his father and mother, and shall cleave unto his wife" (Gen. 2:23, 24).

### Why Marriage Was Instituted

#### 1. Not good for man to be alone.

The first Bible reason given is that "it is not good that the man should be alone." For this reason God created "an help meet for him" (Gen. 2:18). We see the truth of this in the constitutional make-up of every normal man and normal woman. They are essentially different—the counterpart of each other, physically, mentally, temperamentally—it takes one to complete the other. What the normal man lacks the normal woman supplies, and vice versa. God created both to move in their respective spheres. Happy the man, happy the woman, who recognizes this wise provision of the Creator, respects it, and works within its bounds.

### 2. Propagation of the human race.

This is set forth in Gen. 1:28—"Be fruitful, and multiply, and replenish the earth."

### 3. Purity of the human family.

"Marriage is honourable in all, and the bed undefiled: but whoremongers and adulterers God will judge" (Heb. 13:4). It is no mere accident that God decreed that children should be brought into the world through marriage.

### 4. Bringing up of children.

The privacy of the home, the sterner qualities of the husband and father combined with the tenderer qualities of the wife and mother, and the strongest of all earthly ties (parental love) are important factors in child training. There is nothing that can take the place of a normal Christian home as a place for bringing up children "in the nurture and admonition of the Lord."

## What Constitutes Marriage

This, to some, may seem an unnecessary question; but as there are people who hold erroneous views as to what marriage really is, we look upon it as a question worthy of our consideration.

### 1. It is leaving parents and starting a new family.

As Gen. 2:24 expresses it, "Therefore shall a man leave his father and his mother, and shall cleave unto his wife." Though they may remain under the parental roof for the time being, and though they should still acknowledge their obligations to parents as sons and daughters, their obligations are now closer to each other than to parents or any other relatives or friends. It is a new family— "one flesh."

### 2. It is becoming "one flesh" with one of the opposite sex.

The parents having given their children away, these two, having by appropriate ceremony been pronounced "husband and wife," have now joined hearts, hands, minds, possessions, and have become one in thought, in interests, and in aims—that is, if it is an ideal marriage.

### 3. It is the fulfillment of the betrothal.

The betrothal, let it be understood, is not marriage. It is a most sacred obligation, yet it is but a promise of marriage and not marriage itself. Many lives have been wrecked because this fact was either not understood or not respected. Not until the words are said, "I now pronounce you man and wife" (or the equivalent of these words) are the two really married. But marriage is the fulfillment of the betrothal. The two having pledged hearts and hands for life, the laws of the state having been complied with, the ceremony is performed, and the promise of undying fidelity to each other is made in the presence of witnesses—the two are MARRIED.

The question is often raised, Are two married if they are not Christians? They most certainly are—provided they have met the essential conditions for marriage. Remember the words, "one flesh," not "one spirit," are used in designating marriage. "Marriage is honorable in *all*" —and whether the ceremony is performed by preacher or magistrate; and whether the contracting parties are converted or unconverted, Christian or pagan, if they have entered into their marriage agreement in accordance with the laws of their country and not contrary to the higher law of God, they are married. Missionaries in heathen countries recognize this fact. If marriage among non-Christians could not be recognized, then the words, "only in the Lord" would be superfluous, for that would be the only kind of marriage possible. Then why insist that Christians marry Christians only, since all marriage bonds are sacred? The answer to this question will become apparent as we continue our discussions.

### MARRIAGE LAWS

Practically all nations, states, and provinces have some kind of marriage laws. As Christian people we need to be submissive not only to these national, state, and provincial laws, but also to the Divine laws as set forth in the Bible. What has the Bible to say on this subject?

### 1. It teaches against marriage among near relatives.

Lev. 18:1-18 is the most direct scripture on this point, unless I Cor. 5:1-6 could be classed among this line of texts. But we are not considering this point from the standpoint of law alone but also from the standpoint of wisdom. In fact, the wisdom of God is seen in all His marriage laws, in both Old and New Testaments. In every family there are peculiarities. Let there be intermarriages between members of the same family for generations, and these peculiarities become multiplied until they often result in idiocy and insanity among the offspring. For this reason God has wisely taught against such marriages.

### 2. It forbids intermarriage between believers and unbelievers.

Moses (Deut. 7:3), Joshua (23:11-13), Ezra (10:10, 12), and Nehemiah (13:23-25) all testify against such mixed marriages in positive, convincing language. Moses states the reason: "They will turn away thy sons from following me, that they may serve other gods" (Duet. 7:4). Coming to the New Testament we find the same counsel in the mind of God, as made evident in such scriptures as "Be ye not unequally yoked together with unbelievers" (II Cor. 6:14), ". . . . marry, only in the Lord" (I Cor. 7: 39), etc. So today Christian people are warned against mixed marriages among believers and unbelievers, for two reasons: (1) They are unscriptural. (2) The results are disastrous. Read Gen. 6:1-6.

### 3. Bible teachings on the subject of mixed marriages throw some light on the question of intermarriages between members of different denominations.

"Can two walk together except they be agreed" (Amos 3:3)? When husband and wife are so far apart religiously that they can not fellowship one another in the same church, they are divided on the most important question that can come up in any home. Parents owe their children a united front on all moral and religious issues, especially in the matter of Church affiliation. It is imperative, therefore, that those seeking life companionship should seek it among members of their own faith.

This raises another question: What about people who are already bound in mixed marriages? Such people find their instructions in I Cor. 7:13-17. The husband can not go to heaven on his wife's religion, neither can the wife go to heaven on the husband's religion. Let both maintain a clear conscience before God, even if that keeps them in separate churches. What we have to say about mixed marriages is to those whose marriage is yet future.

4. **The Bible forbids marriages with divorced persons having former companions still living.**

This is a truth so generally ignored that it demands special emphasis: We will let the Bible talk:

> Moses, because of the hardness of your hearts, suffered you to put away your wives: but from the beginning it was not so. And I say unto you, Whosoever shall put away his wife, except it be for fornication, and shall marry another, committeth adultery; and whoso marrieth her which is put away doth commit adultery.—Matt. 19:8, 9.
>
> Whosoever shall put away his wife, and marry another, committeth adultery against her. And if a woman shall put away her husband, and be married to another, she committeth adultery.—Mark 10:11, 12.
>
> Whosoever putteth away his wife and marrieth another, committeth adultery: and whosoever marrieth her that is put away from her husband, committeth adultery.—Luke 16:18.
>
> The woman which hath an husband is bound by the law to her husband, so long as he liveth; but if the husband be dead, she is loosed from the law of her husband. So then if, while her husband liveth, she is married to another man, she shall be called an adulteress: but if her husband be dead, she is free from that law; so that she is no adulteress, though she be married to another man.—Rom. 7:2, 3.
>
> The wife is bound by the law as long as her husband liveth; but if her husband be dead, she is at liberty to marry whom she will: only in the Lord.—I Cor. 7:39.

These scriptures merit our prayerful consideration, for they are rich in instructive truth. The one point that we desire to notice at this time is that they make it clear and plain and emphatic that no one has a scriptural right to marry while a former companion is living. Neither has any one a scriptural right to marry a divorced person having a former companion living. The fact is that when two are married they are "one flesh" as long as both live, and during this time neither can become "one flesh" with some one else. To assume to do so makes both adulterers, which they continue to be so long as they keep up such relations.

The Bible mentions two cases for separation (Matt. 19:9; I Cor. 7:15), but in neither case is it stated that this is justification for either party to the divorce to remarry while the other one is still living.*

Some people, finding themselves tied up in an unscriptural way with divorced people, claim that a separation would be doing an injustice and therefore committing a wrong against their families by separating. But from the scriptures above quoted it is a clear case that they are living in adultery so long as they continue their unscriptural alliance. Instead of them doing wrong, therefore, in separating, they would be doing a greater wrong by keeping up their sinful relations. However, a separation under such circumstances would not absolve them from their responsibility of caring for and supporting the children brought into the world, through their unscriptural alliance.

5. **Plural marriages have no place in the New Testament Scriptures.**

Throughout the teachings of Christ and the apostles, where this subject is under consideration, it is invariably from the standpoint of union between one man and one

---

*It is held by some that where the cause for separation is scriptural the securing of a divorce is not wrong in itself, for the reason that without a legal separation conveyances of property can not be made where one party is unwilling to join in executing such titles.

The Scriptures clearly teach, however, that the remarriage of either party, even though legally divorced, while the other is living, is a violation of the marriage vow, and denominate both parties to such marriages as adulterers or adulteresses.

woman. Where reference is made to the husband, the "help meet for him" is referred to as "wife." Where the word "wives" is used you always find the corresponding word "husbands;" never "wives" belonging to "husband," or "husbands" belonging to one woman—except in the case of the Samaritan woman, and she is held up before us as a sinful woman. On the other hand, Paul expressly says, "Let every man have his own *wife* (not wives) and let every woman have her own *husband* (not husbands)" (I Cor. 7:2).

The nearest hint that we have of plural marriages existing in apostolic times in found in I Timothy 3 and Titus 1, where Paul says that the bishop must be "the husband of one wife." Some have construed this to mean that plural marriages existed in the Church at that time but that no polygamist should be ordained bishop; but the Word does not say so. Would it not be more in keeping with the rest of the writings of Paul and other inspired men to construe this to mean that as the early Church was made up of men and women taken from polygamous peoples (Jews or Gentiles) they adopted the same rule that our present-day missionaries do in heathen lands where polygamy is practiced? that when a man with more than one wife unites with the church he renounces allegiance to all other wives except the first one married? and that no man having one or more of these former wives living was eligible for the office of bishop? The question has sometimes been raised as to why God permitted plural marriages in the Old Dispensation and not in the New. We may or may not be able to give the reason, but we are confronted with the fact that such is the case. There are other questions—such as swearing oaths, wars, etc.—in which we are confronted with a similar question for explanation. Many of those things "God winked at"—that is, permitted under the then existing circumstances, but which He clearly forbids in the New Testament Scriptures. While in Old Testament times polygamy was permitted, yet you study in vain the marriage laws of the

Bible—Old or New Testament—to find any that make room for polygamy.

## GETTING MARRIED

There are times and circumstances under which it is best for one not to marry, as Paul explains in I Cor. 7:1, 8, 33; but God has made ample provisions for marriage, with ample regulations governing it, so that the right of marriage under scriptural conditions is beyond question. This, next to conversion, is the most important question that can come up in any one's life, hence we shall consider it at some length. First, let us notice a few of the principal problems to be faced previous to marriage:

I. **Associations.**—It is good for people to associate together, both sexes, regardless of whether the marriage question is considered. Such associations are not only normal, but strengthening to character, fitting one for the duties of home life. And from the fact that people usually choose their life companions from those with whom they associate, there are certain things to bear in mind which no one can afford to ignore:

a. As a Christian you have no right to assume any other attitude than that of the Christian man or woman— pure, chaste, upright in character, worthy of the best, the promoter and protector of others' chastity.

b. Courtship with curtains drawn, lights dimmed, in late hours of the night, especially with those of the opposite sex whose morals are questionable, should never be countenanced by Christian people. Such practices have been the means of ruining many people.

c. When it comes to exclusive associations with one of the opposite sex of questionable morals, that is unthinkable for any pure-minded man or woman. "Evil communications corrupt good manners."

d. There are those who from the standpoint of intelligence and virtue are in every way worthy of you: but because your standards of religion are different and your views of life and life plans are not the same as those of the other party, you are putting yourself in the way of temptation when you consider marriage with such persons.

e. It is not treating the other party right if you keep exclusive company with him or her for any considerable length of time, unless you are seriously considering marriage.

f. There is no scriptural "double standard" in morals. What is right for a man is right for a woman, and vice versa. Never treat any other man's sister in a different way from what you would have another man treat your sister, and never excuse or justify in your own life that which you would condemn in the life of one of the opposite sex. In all things, "Keep thyself pure."

2. **The Betrothal.**—When you have arrived at maturity you have come to the time when you may seriously consider marriage. Here also are a few things to be borne in mind:

a. A continual prayer for divine guidance and confidential relationship with your parents are two essentials for safety and best results.

b. Be sure that you know your intended before you put to her the momentous question. Therefore be not hasty in your proposals.

c. Never consider marriage with any one where you would have to violate Scripture to do so. Better remain single all your days than to lightly esteem God's Word and wisdom on a question so vital as this one.

d. Courtship before the betrothal should not be too long. After you have convictions that marriage under the circumstances would be wise or otherwise, either put the question or quit the courtship. It is a matter that is too serious for either yourself or the other party to be wasting time, to say nothing about the serious misunderstandings and heartaches occasioned by breaking off courtships after one of the parties interested expected the courtship to culminate in marriage.

e. When one desires to discontinue the courtship (before definite obligations are assumed) it should be made known to the other party directly interested in such a way as not to humiliate him or her. Affections are something too sacred to be trifled with. At all times be courteous, and use judgment.

f. Remember that the betrothal is not marriage. "Keep thyself pure."

g. Your pledge of hand and heart to one of the opposite sex is the most sacred of your promises. To break an engagement because, for a trivial or selfish reason you "change your mind," or because you see some one else that you like better, is evidence of fickle-mindedness or unworthiness of character that merits the contempt of all right-thinking people. Such a person is not worthy of any standing in either society or Church. Keep your promise sacred. Except in cases of pure deception or fraud, on the part of the other party to the engagement, or where the unwisdom of the engagement becomes so apparent that both parties to the agreement recognize it and freely release each other from further obligation, no one should ever think of discontinuing an engagement, any more than to violate or prove unfaithful to any other sacred promise. Should you find yourself betrothed to another contrary to Scripture, wait with the marriage till conditions are such that you can go on with the marriage without violating Scripture. Show yourself worthy of the best by being as good as your word.

h. Courtship, after the betrothal, should not be delayed unduly. People who allow this matter to drag on for years, without a good reason for so doing, are disqualifying themselves for ideal life-companionship. Marriage is something serious as well as delightful, and for this reason should not be unduly delayed. Be deliberate but not dilatory.

3. **The Ceremony.**—The day comes when courtship culminates in marriage. But remember that this is not the end of the courtship, which ought to continue throughout the married life. Who should preform the ceremony? Some minister in your own church. Marriage in the Lord, remember, is a religious as well as a social affair, and for this reason there should be unity in worship on the part of all who have a part in the ceremony, as well as unity of the two hearts whose oneness is now being publicly solemnized.

The ceremony should be in keeping with Gospel simplicity and piety. The idea that wedding ceremonies are either a mere compliance with the laws of the land or an occasion for festivities unbecoming a child of God was hatched out in the mind of the enemy of souls. If there ever is a time where I Cor. 10:31 has a practical place in the lives of Christian men and women it is on wedding occasions. Certainly wedding ceremonies should be looked upon as happy occasions, even if they do mean the giving up of old associations that new ones may be formed, but **"fun and foolishness"** are not a necessary part of the real enjoyment that should characterize marriages "in the Lord."

Wedding ceremonies in the house of the Lord afford an excellent opportunity for the minister to impress upon his congregation some of the vital problems connected with courtship and home and family life.

## Home Life

We have now brought our subject to the point where home life for the newlyweds begins. As the subject of the Christian Home is considered at length in another chapter, the reader is invited to turn to this chapter and continue the study.

# PART VII

## Christian Life

### CHAPTERS

# CHRISTIAN LIFE

(Duties, Restrictions, Graces)

## Outline by Chapters

I. CHRISTIAN SERVICE
1. INTRODUCTORY THOUGHTS
2. ESSENTIALS TO ACCEPTABLE SERVICE
   a. Obedience
   b. "Doers of the Word"
   c. Consecration
   d. Ministry to the Needy
   e. Work
   f. Prayer
   g. Love
   h. Spiritual Life
3. SPHERES OF SERVICE
   a. In the Home
   b. In the Social Circle
   c. In Business Life
   d. In Church Work
4. PRECEPTS FOR WORKERS

II. PRAYER
1. WHY PRAY
   a. Essential to Spiritual Life
   b. God Commands It
   c. Gateway to Many Blessings
   d. Uplifting Influence
   e. A Protection
   f. Needed for Power
   g. Brings Fullness of Joy
2. CONDITIONS OF ANSWERED PRAYER
   a. Praying According to God's Will
   b. Praying in Faith
   c. Obedience
   d. Perseverance
   e. Coöperation
3. FURTHER OBSERVATIONS
   a. Simplicity and Directness
   b. For All People
   c. A Loving, Forgiving Spirit
   d. Frequent Prayers
   e. Proper Order
   f. Meetings for Prayer
   g. Power of Secret Prayer

## III. OBEDIENCE
### 1. WHOM TO OBEY
 a. God
 b. Parents
 c. Masters
 d. Magistrates
 e. Rulers
### 2. WHAT OBEDIENCE INCLUDES
 a. The Voice of God
 b. The Son of God
 c. The Spirit of God
 d. The Word of God
 e. The Church of God
### 3. OBEDIENCE AND SELF-DENIAL
 a. Self-denial a Necessary Result of Obedience
 b. Common Ground in a Submissive Spirit
 c. The Two Linked Together
### 4. RESULTS OF OBEDIENCE
 a. The Grace of God
 b. An Upright Life
 c. Deliverance in Time and Eternity
### 5. FURTHER OBSERVATIONS
 a. A Heart Condition
 b. Inner and Outer Obedience
 c. Disobedience and Everlasting Punishment
 d. Partial and Total Disobedience
 e. Unqualified Obedience Essential Duty

## IV. WORSHIP
### 1. SOME FUNDAMENTAL FACTS
 a. All Men Worshipers
 b. God Alone to be Worshiped
 c. In Spirit and in Truth
 d. Commanded to Worship
 e. Not Compelled to Worship
 f. Images
 g. Idolatry Degrading
### 2. WHY WORSHIP GOD
 a. Commanded
 b. Freedom from Idolatry
 c. Fellowship with God and Saints
 d. Essential to Divine Favor
 e. Essential to Holy Living
 f. Fruitful of Good Works

## V. SELF-DENIAL
### 1. NOTABLE EXAMPLES
 a. Christ
 b. Abraham
 c. Moses
 d. Fishermen of Galilee
 e. Saul of Tarsus
 f. Examples of Self-indulgence

2. WHY PRACTICE SELF-DENIAL
    a. Essential to Godly Living
    b. Self-indulgence Corrupting
    c. Essential to Victorious Life
    d. Promotes Prosperity
    e. Produces Good Results
    f. Preferable to Self-indulgence
3. WHAT TO DENY
    a. Things Sinful
    b. Things Doubtful
    c. Things Hurtful to Others
    d. Things in the Way of Usefulness
    e. Highest Form of Self-denial
4. THE UNDERLYING PRINCIPLES
5. REWARDS

## VI. NONCONFORMITY TO THE WORLD

1. AN EXTENSIVELY TAUGHT BIBLE DOCTRINE
2. THE REASON WHY
3. MARKS OF WORLDLINESS
    a. Disobedience to God
    b. Wickedness
    c. Pride
    d. Impurity
    e. Covetousness
    f. Ambition
    g. Intemperance
    h. Fashionable Attire
    i. Worldly Amusements
    j. Irreverence
    k. Dishonesty
    l. Carnal Strife
4. THE "UNSPOTTED" LIFE
    a. Obedience to God
    b. Godliness
    c. Humility
    d. Purity
    e. Charity
    f. Self-sacrifice
    g. Temperance
    h. "Modest Apparel"
    i. The Joy of the Lord
    j. Reverence
    k. Integrity
    l. Peace
5. BIBLE TEACHING ON DRESS
    a. Against Worldly Conformity
    b. Dress Distinction
    c. Modest Apparel Commanded
    d. Against Costly Array
    e. Against Immodest Apparel
    f. Uniformity
    g. "Changeable Suits of Apparel"

# CHRISTIAN LIFE

"What is your life?"

This question brings to our attention the most practical phase of Christian experience. What we believe is important; how we act upon such belief is still more important. "In Christ Jesus neither circumcision availeth anything, nor uncircumcision; but a new creature." Three lines of thought are presented in these chapters; namely, duties, restrictions, Christian graces.

Every child of God is constrained by a sense of duty to discharge his full obligations to God and to fellow men. To fear God and keep His commandments is declared to be "the whole duty of man" (Eccl. 12:13). In this series of chapters we have listed five important Christian duties which, if we obey fully, will, we believe, include every obligation resting upon us. Faithful service, unceasing prayer, perfect obedience, hiding self in the cross, and worshiping God "in the spirit and in truth," tell the whole story of Christian obligations.

"The whole world lieth in wickedness." The Christian is directed to travel on another way. To this end a number of important Christian principles are laid down in the Word. The child of God recognizes them as cherished rules of life, while the worldly-minded feel themselves restrained by such teachings and to them they appear as "restrictions." Five of these are included in the chapters before us.

Faithfulness to duty and freedom from sin cause the child of God to shine in the image of his Maker. The grace of God in the heart means Christian graces in the lives of those thus blessed. Love, purity, humility, and hope constitute a heavenly fortune which the treasures of this world can never equal.

# CHAPTER I

## CHRISTIAN SERVICE

Therefore, my beloved brethren, be ye stedfast, unmoveable, always abounding in the work of the Lord, forasmuch as ye know that your labour is not in vain in
the Lord.—I Corinthians 15:58.

The ideal Christian life is a life of active service.

This is contrary to the opinion of most people, who
seem inclined to favor a life of ease and luxury and leisure,
with plenty to satisfy the needs of body, mind and soul,
without necessity of physical exertion unless one feels so
inclined.

Speaking of God's ideal, we have it exemplified in the
primitive man, whom God commanded to dress and to
keep the garden (Gen. 2:15); in the life of Christ, who
was never idle, but "went about doing good" (Acts 10:38);
in the lives of the apostles, who followed in the footsteps
of their Lord and Master until they were called home.
The most beautiful, heaven-blest life is the life that abounds
in good deeds, devoted to faithful Christian service.

There is no special virtue, however, in merely being
busy. Satan is justly credited with being a very busy
creature. It is the nature of our service, the cause in which
we are engaged, and the way we go about it that determines
the merits of our efforts. Energy may be constructive or
destructive, depending upon how it is spent.

It is impossible for us to be other than servants. In
every walk in life we are confronted with two great wills;
the will of God, and the will of Satan. In all that we do,
we conform to the will of one or the other of these two
great masters. Even though we may be considered as
masters over those who have been placed under our lead-

15

ership, we are at best but undershepherds, doing the will of one or the other of the two super-leaders named.

Service does not necessarily mean physical activity. The watchman who does nothing but sit down to look and to warn is as much in the service of his employer as is the laborer who works long hours to the extent of his powers. The real test of service is the test of obedience. On this point Paul says:

> Know ye not, that to whom ye yield yourselves servants to obey, his servants ye are to whom ye obey: whether of sin unto death, or of obedience unto righteousness?—Rom. 6:16.

This gives us an additional thought. Not only are we servants, but the character of our service is determined by the one to whom we yield obedience. Whoever therefore is obedient to Jesus Christ is the servant of Christ, and his service is distinctly a Christian service.

### Essentials to Acceptable Service

The important question concerning our service is, Is it acceptable to God? The command is, "Study to shew thyself approved unto God" (II Tim. 2:15)—not acceptable to man, to the world, to my own personal feelings. Here are some of the scripturally pointed out essentials to such service:

1. **Obedience.**—"Behold, to obey is better than sacrifice" (I Sam. 15:22). The Bible everywhere commends obedience and condemns disobedience to God. They who think themselves to be in favor with God, and yet at the same time disobey His commandments, are deceived. Matt. 7:21-29; Jas. 1:22-25.

2. **"Doers of the Word."**—"Be ye doers of the word, and not hearers only, deceiving your own selves" (Jas. 1:22). While the promise is, "Hear, and your soul shall live," it is the kind of hearing that produces "doing" that brings results. The concluding parable in the Sermon on the Mount (Matt. 7:24-27) reveals the fact that our eternal

destiny depends upon the things which we do or fail to do in this life.

3. **Consecration.**—"I beseech you therefore, brethren, by the mercies of God, that ye present your bodies a living sacrifice, holy, acceptable unto God, which is your reasonable service" (Rom. 12:1). It is but "reasonable" that we consecrate ourselves to Him, because He gave Himself for us, and the most *un*reasonable thing we can do is to withhold such service.

4. **Ministry to the Needy.**—Read Matt. 25:31-46. "Mighty works" are of less importance than caring for the needy. "He that hath pity upon the poor lendeth unto the Lord" (Prov. 19:17).

5. **Work.**—Christ emphasized this fact in the parables of the talents and of the pounds. The unfaithful servant that hid his talent or money and refused to do anything for his lord did not only fail of his reward but was consigned to outer darkness. The devil wants nothing more of Christian professors than that they do nothing for Christ. The Gospel standard is, "A workman that needeth not to be ashamed" (II Tim. 2:15). God's people on earth are described as "a peculiar people, zealous of good works."

6. **Prayer.**—"Why could not we cast him out?" asked the wondering disciples when they saw Christ casting out devils after they had failed in the attempt. Christ's answer to this question should never be forgotten: "This kind can come forth by nothing but by prayer and fasting" (Mark 9:29). And let us not forget that the word "fasting" adds a necessary meaning to the idea of praying with power. A mere formal prayer amounts to nothing, but sincere and fervent prayer from a sincere and fervent heart, stirred by the Spirit to the extent that the supplicant enters into the spirit of fasting, means power with God and man. Many fail because they depend upon human powers rather than the power of the Throne. The prayerless Christian is also the powerless Christian.

7. **Love.**—It was the love of God to men that constrained Him to give His only begotten Son for our sakes; the love of Christ for us that constrained Him to lay down His life for us. "Love seeketh not her own." It is always giving out. "The love of Christ constraineth us," said Paul in recounting his efforts in furthering the cause of Christ and the Church. Other things being equal, the greater our love for God, the more effective our service in His name. It is but natural that Christ should pronounce love to God and man the greatest of all commandments.

8. **Spiritual Life.**—"I never knew you," will be the response of Christ our King to those at the judgment bar of God who will come before Him boasting of their "mighty works." "If any man have not the Spirit of Christ, he is none of his" (Rom. 8:9). "Be filled with the Spirit" (Eph. 5:18), and the spiritual life within will shine out and become the "light of the world." It takes a real experience of salvation, an infilling of the Holy Spirit, a life "hid with Christ in God," to render Christian service that is more than mere form.

These eight essentials to acceptable service might also properly be called *the secret of success in the Christian life*.

### SPHERES OF SERVICE

When we speak of Christian service we speak of something that touches every department of life. It includes more than a mere professional performance of duty in some form of church work. Some people seem to be satisfied when they perform some religious service in a meritorious way, but when you see in their social or business life a record that resembles that of the ordinary worldling, it makes you wonder whether God is satisfied with them. They are what you might call professional Christians, performing religious duties in about the same way that the lawyer works for his client after being employed to do so. But this falls short of the Gospel standard. Rom. 6:13; Luke

18:10-14. The true servant of God is in His service wherever he goes, and keeps on serving God as long as the Lord gives him breath.

Let us briefly consider the several spheres of Christian service within the realms of opportunity.

1. **In the Home.**—Here is the real test of Christian life. Men whose eloquent prayers have caused church walls to fairly vibrate have proved themselves lacking in this first of vital tests. Every home, like every church, should be a house of prayer. Cornelius, praying in his own house (Acts 10:2, 30); a body of members spending a night in prayer in the home of Mary (Acts 12:12); Philip's four daughters that prophesied (Acts 21:9); the church in the house of Philemon (2)—these are a few of the glimpses into the home life of the early Church. May this kind of home life be duplicated in thousands of homes today. Daily family devotions, a daily habit of prayer and meditation, daily conversations about matters pertaining to the spiritual welfare of souls, a faithful and constant effort to bring up *all* the children "in the nurture and admonition of the Lord," Christian hospitality which makes the home a benediction upon all who come within its walls—these are some of the things which should be encouraged in every home.

2. **In the Social Circle.**—Shall we list this among the spheres of Christian service? Most emphatically, yes: even though many seem to think that religion has no place in the social circle. The fact is, wherever Christianity is barred, no Christian has a right to go. "Whether therefore ye eat, or drink, or whatsoever ye do, do all to the glory of God" —in the social circle and wherever you go. We praise the Lord every time we see a group of young people who are at home with the Bible and who can talk Scripture with the same readiness and fluency that others manifest when they throw their life away in uproarious foolishness. Who says that we can not have "a good time" singing, praying, sensible talking, discussing in a sensible way everything suitable for conversation whether it pertains to this world or

the next? Our stalwart young people can render no more effective service that to take the lead in training their fellow youth in pure, intelligent, noble, manly, womanly service. Both inside and outside the home, the social circle is a most effective means of training young people, either for good or evil." "As we have therefore opportunity, let us do good.

3. **In Business Life.**—What! business life a Christian service? Why not? Is there a greater hindrance to the cause of Christ today than inconsistent business methods on the part of professing Christians? If these inconsistencies are such a great power for evil, why not make the business life on the part of Christian people a genuine power for good? Suppose that all Christian people in business would seek "first the kingdom of God and his righteousness," would put the Golden Rule into daily practice, would "provide things honest in the sight of all men," would make it an unalterable rule of "in honor preferring one another," would do "all to the glory of God," would at all times "remember the sabbath day, to keep it holy," would never be unequally yoked together with unbelievers, would consider it their happy privilege, at all times, to be about their Father's business, what do you suppose would be the effect upon their own lives, upon the lives of their families, of their neighbors, of their competitors? Christian men in business too seldom realize the power that falls within their sphere of opportunity.

4. **In Church Work.**—Here is where fathers, mothers, brothers, sisters, sons, daughters; ministers, deacons, lay members, missionaries, superintendents, teachers, farmers, mechanics, merchants, professional men; the weak, the strong, the rich, the poor; men in every condition and walk in life are invited to meet upon a common level, as equals in the Lord and brothers and sisters of our Lord Jesus Christ, and unite in faithful Christian service. Here is where we unite our forces in a common effort to win the lost, to strengthen one another in faith and service, to

receive the needed encouragement and spiritual vision to prepare for the trials and temptations and struggles just ahead, uniting our voices in singing praises to Him from whom all blessings flow, uniting hearts and hands in a common effort to make the Church on earth what it really ought to be—a foretaste of the glorious congregation in the courts above. This subject is discussed at greater length in the other chapters.

### Precepts for Workers

In the light of the precept given us in II Tim. 2:15, every one desiring to render acceptable service to God joins in the prayer, "Lord, what wilt thou have me to do?" Here, in part, is God's answer:

1. Keep thyself pure.—1 Tim. 5:22.
2. Search the scriptures.—Jno. 5:39.
3. Continue instant in prayer.—Rom. 12:12.
4. In all thy ways acknowledge him.—Prov. 3:6.
5. Let every man *prove* his own work.—Gal. 6:4.
6. Keep yourselves in the love of God.—Jude 21.
7. Be thou an example of the believers.—I Tim. 4:12.
8. Study to shew thyself approved unto God.—II Tim. 2:15.
9. Owe no man anything, but to love one another.—Rom. 13:8.
10. He that glorieth, let him glory in the Lord.—II Cor. 10:17.
11. Prove all things; hold fast that which is good.—I Thess. 5:21.
12. Whatsoever ye do, do it heartily as to the Lord.—Col. 3:23.
13. Do all things without murmurings and disputings.—Phil. 2:14.
14. Speak thou the things which become sound doctrine.—Tit. 2:1.

15. Abhor that which is evil; cleave to that which is good.—Rom. 12:9.

16. Let the word of Christ dwell in you richly in all wisdom.—Col. 3:16.

17. Be not overcome of evil, but overcome evil with good.—Rom. 12:21.

18. Be ye not unequally yoked together with unbelievers.—II Cor. 6:14.

19. Bear ye one another's burdens, and so fulfill the law of Christ.—Gal. 6:2.

20. Go ye into all the world, and preach the gospel to every creature.—Mark 16:15.

21. Be ye kind one to another, tenderhearted, forgiving one another.—Eph. 4:32.

22. Take heed unto thyself, and unto the doctrine; continue in them.—I Tim. 4:16.

23. Whether therefore ye eat, or drink, or whatsoever ye do, do all to the glory of God.—I Cor. 10:31.

24. Have no fellowship with the unfruitful works of darkness, but rather reprove them.—Eph. 5:11.

25. Let your light so shine before men, that they may see your good works, and glorify your Father which is in heaven.—Matt. 5:16.

# CHAPTER II

## PRAYER

Pray without ceasing.—I Thessalonians 5:17.
I will therefore that men pray everywhere, lifting up holy
    hands, without wrath and doubting.—I Timothy 2:8.

We know of no more appropriate definition for prayer
than that which the poet used when he called it "the Christian's vital breath." We sometimes hear of "prayerless
Christians." If by that is meant such professors of religion as are negligent in prayers we will let the expression
go by in silence; but if that means no praying at all, then
they are Christians in name only. No one can long remain a Christian without prayer, without fellowship with
God, any more than a fish can long live out of the water.
It is as natural for a Christian to pray as it is for a live
person to breathe. Yes, prayer is "the Christian's vital
breath."

### Why Pray

1. **It is essential to spiritual life.**
(Note in the preceding paragraph.)
2. **God commands it.**
Such admonitions as "Pray without ceasing," "In
everything give thanks," "Give thanks unto the Lord,"
"Watch and pray," "Pray to thy Father," etc., are so numerous in the Bible that we need only to begin to enumerate them till we are impressed that no one can be
obedient to God without living a prayer life.
3. **It is the gateway to many blessings.**
The Holy Spirit, we are assured, is given "to them
that ask him" (Luke 11:13), and a number of other good
things are enumerated in connection with this assurance.
Among the things promised in connection with sincere

and fervent prayer is power with God and man. Mark 9:29. "The prayer of faith shall save the sick" (Jas. 5:15-17), because the "effectual fervent prayer of a righteous man availeth much." In view of the positive assurance that God hears and answers the prayer of faith (Matt. 21:22; Mark 11:24; Jno. 11:22) it follows that all things which may appropriately be included in believing prayer are at the disposal of those who habitually seek the Lord in prayer.

### 4. It lifts the petitioner into the realms of the heavenlies.

Whoever prays, talks with the Lord. Whoever talks with the Lord is admitted into the goodness and grace of God, and the more time he thus spends with Him the more he becomes like Him. Did you ever see any one who spent much time with the Lord in sincere and fervent prayer that was not heavenly-minded, conscientious, consistent in life and service, having power with God and man? On the other hand, did you ever see any one not accustomed to prayer that manifested such qualities to a marked degree? It pays to spend much time with God in prayer; not only because God has promised to answer prayer, but also for what such prayer life does for the soul.

### 5. It protects us against the power of the tempter.

We think of Christ and the apostles just before the Gethsemane experience. We hear the pathetic, loving, warning plea: "Watch and pray, that ye enter not into temptation; the spirit indeed is willing, but the flesh is weak" (Matt. 26:41). As they enter the garden some disciples stay near the border, three accompany Him into the interior, while He goes still farther on and kneels in prayer. Coming back to His disciples, He finds them asleep? "What, could you not watch one hour?" He says. This was repeated three times, and each time the disciples fell asleep. Are we surprised, therefore, that in the trying moment Christ stands every strain while the disciples give way? "But He was Christ, and the disciples were but men," some one says. True, Christ might have stood every strain, without the prayer life; but He could not have been the devoted Son of God had He not been in constant fellowship with the Father, and this very fellowship took Him into the presence of the Father in fervent prayer in every time of temptation and trial. Such habit belongs to divine relationship. And so does close relationship, on man's part, mean a praying habit, and the closer our fellowship the more frequent and fervent our prayers. Christ's perfect relationship with the Father meant a perfect prayer life. May we learn a lesson from Him. The tempter has hard work making inroads into the lives of those who habitually wrestle with God in prayer. If we would live the victorious life daily, let us make sure of our daily prayer life.

> "Satan trembles when he sees
> The weakest saint upon his knees."

### 6. It is needed for power.

Again let us quote our blessed Master in reference to power to accomplish difficult tasks: "This kind can come forth by nothing but by prayer and fasting" (Mark 9:29). Let us also note the power exercised by the disciples on a certain occasion: "And when they had prayed, the place was shaken where they were assembled together; and they were all filled with the Holy Ghost, and they spake the word of God with boldness" (Acts 3:31). The very fact that God has promised to hear and answer the prayers of His people means assurance that the power of Heaven is at the disposal of those who keep in touch with God in a prayer life.

### 7. It brings fullness of joy.

Perhaps this should be considered covered by what has been said in previous paragraphs; but as prayer seems burdensome to so many people, we feel constrained to emphasize this phase of the prayer life. What was it that brought joy to the disciples in Mary's house when Peter was delivered from prison? They had prayed perseveringly, and their prayer was answered. What was it that brought that inexpressible joy on the day of Pentecost? They had been together praying since their Lord went away, and now they were rewarded by receiving the enduement of power and the abiding presence of the Holy Comforter. Let us never forget that prayer is not only a Christian duty, not only a protection against the power of the tempter, but also a source of exceeding great joy to all the saints of God, a joy which they can get in no other way.

### Conditions of Answered Prayer

You have perhaps noticed that so far we have taken it for granted that God answers prayer, and that He answers in a personal way, without attempting to prove it. We count it a dishonor to God and lack of faith in His Word even to entertain the question as to whether He is as good as His Word. The promise is sure, the Bible contains many instances of definitely answered prayer, and many today have within themselves a living witness to answered prayer. The only thing in this connection that needs consideration is the conditions under which prayers will be answered, according to promise. We may confidently expect answers to our prayers—

### 1. **If we pray according to His will.**

"And this is the confidence that we have in him, that if we ask anything according to his will, he heareth us" (I Jno. 5:14). James gives us the same thought, in a negative way, when he says, "Ye ask, and receive not, because ye ask amiss, that ye may consume it upon your lust" (Jas. 4:3). God did not surrender His judgment when He offered to answer prayer. Many a prayer, so-called, being but an expression of selfishness, or perhaps of affected eloquence intended for the ears of man rather than of God, rises no higher than the petitioner's voice because he is not in praying relations with the Father.

### 2.  If we pray in faith.

On this point James advises, "Let him ask in faith, nothing wavering" (1:6). "And all things, whatsoever ye shall ask in prayer, believing, ye shall receive" (Matt. 21:22). Here again the promise is sure—on the condition of "in faith, believing." Many prayers are as so many idle words, for they are offered up without any hope of divine response. A certain writer strikes at the root of the matter when he urges that we should *pray* our prayers, not simply *say* them.

### 3.  If we are obedient to His will.

Hear the prayer of our Perfect Example: "O my Father, if it be possible, remove this cup from me: nevertheless, not as I will, but as thou wilt" (Matt. 26:39). That was the prayer of submission and obedience. Let us quote a text from Proverbs: "He that turneth away his ear from hearing the law, even his prayer shall be abomination" (28:9). What is wrong? Not on praying terms with God. Being disobedient, his prayer is the voice of a hypocrite, whom God will not hear.

The question is often asked, Does God hear the prayers of sinners? That depends upon the nature of the petition. If it is the prayer of penitence, the sinner coming to God for light or for pardoning grace, God most certainly hears that prayer. Otherwise, it is the prayer of the rebel or the hypocrite, a prayer which God can not hear —unless it be to pronounce it "abomination."

### 4.  If we pray perseveringly.

A group of boys are out in the yard playing. Presently one of them, seeing his mother sitting by a window, calls out, "Mamma, I'm hungry; give me a piece of bread" —and keeps on playing as if he had said nothing. The mother, too, acts as if he had said nothing. It may be that this is the last that the boy thinks of it; or, thinking of it, he may have so little hope of his getting the bread that he pays no further attention to it. On the other hand, if he is really hungry and believes that his mother will give him the bread if she sees that he really wants or needs it, he may come to the window and plead his cause until he gets the bread.

This is an illustration of what happens in answer to prayer. The heavenly Father, like parents usually are, is ready to hear all of our petitions and to give us what He knows is good for us and for the good of the cause, but it depends largely upon ourselves as to whether our prayers are answered or in what particular way they are answered. If we throw our life into our petitions and pray "in faith, believing" our prayers will be heard and answered. He may answer immediately, as Christ usually did when people came to Him for favors, or it may be that it will take repeated petitions in persevering prayer, as illustrated in the importunate widow (Luke 18:1-8) and the case of the man pleading for his afflicted child (Mark 9:14-24). It is safe to conclude that deferred answer to prayer is either because of some hindering circumstance connected with the petitioner or the person or cause prayed for, or that because the heavenly Father knows that under existing circumstances the request should not be immediately granted. But whether prayers are answered immediately or otherwise, the *persevering* prayer of faith is also a *prevailing* prayer.

### 5. If we co-operate with the Lord.

We think of Christ instructing His disciples as He sent them on their mission to "the lost sheep of the house of Israel." We hear the charge: "Pray ye therefore the Lord of the harvest that he will send forth labourers into his harvest" (Matt. 9:38-10:18). When what? Did they pray loud and long—and go back to their nets? No; they stayed right there until they knew whether the Lord wanted them to go out and help answer their own prayers. The fervency and effectiveness of their prayers is evident when we remember that every one of them went out as "labourers," and that seventy others followed on a similar mission. Luke 10:1-20.

Another apt illustration is found in Jas. 2:15-18. James tells of a man praying for a needy brother, saying, "Be ye warmed and filled," and sending him away without furnishing the means wherewith he might be warmed and filled. Such prayers are of no avail. Not only does God want us to pray, but He also wants us to hold ourselves ready to do His bidding in the matter of answering these prayers. No one can offer an acceptable prayer to God without throwing his life into his own petitions.

### FURTHER OBSERVATIONS

1. **Prayer should be simple and direct.**

As an example of simplicity and directness, we have a perfect model in the Lord's Prayer (Matt. 6:9-13), and the instructions of Christ preceding and following this prayer should thoroughly enlighten us as to what spirit we should be in when we pray. "Vain repetitions" are not only valueless but also forbidden. Even in public prayer we are to pray to God, not to or "at" the people, God needs no eloquence or high-sounding phrases to convince Him that we are in earnest, and the eloquence of sincerity ought to be enough to satisfy the people. Let all our prayers come from a heart of faith, going direct to the Throne, whether other people hear us or not.

2. **We should pray for all classes of people.**

A possible exception to this rule is found in I Jno. 5:16. Paul advises supplications and prayers "for all men" (I Tim. 2:1). Some have thought that because Christ in Jno. 17 prayed for His disciples and made it clear that He prayed for no one else that therefore He set the pattern for all people to follow. Yes, at that time He was praying only for His disciples, just as at other times He confined Himself to some other cause. But the fact that He prayed for His executioners on the cross (Luke 23:34) showed that He did not confine all His prayers to His disciples. The Word teaches us to pray for saint and sinner, especially for those who are in positions of authority and responsibility. Eph. 6:18; Phil. 1:8; Col. 4:3; I Thess. 5:23-25; II Thess. 1:11; 3:1; I Tim. 2:1, 2, 8.

### 3. We should pray with hearts filled with love, and with a forgiving spirit.

The prayer of Christ on the cross and of Stephen at the time of his martyrdom are examples of the right kind of spirit in praying for enemies. It is worthy of note that the only thing in the Lord's Prayer to which He refers afterwards is this very point. This is what He said: "If ye forgive men their trespasses, your heavenly Father will also forgive you; but if ye forgive not men their trespasses, neither will your Father forgive your trespasses." Divinely approved prayer and malice do not mix.

### 4. Frequent, fervent prayer belongs to the devoted Christian life.

Have you noticed how often such expressions as "Pray without ceasing," "Watch and pray," "Pray for us," etc., are found in the Bible? Prayer is the Christian's daily breath, and the deeper our spiritual life the deeper and oftener we breathe. How can any one of living faith in God who is burdened for the cause of Christ and the welfare of man get along without spending much time in prayer? The members of your own family, the sick in your community, your ministers and others bearing heavy loads, the many trials and temptations to which you and others are subjected, the great obstacles in the way of the cause—these are but a very few of the many things that may be remembered in daily prayers. With the earnest soul it is not a question of what there is to pray for, but how to find time to remember in prayer the many, many things and causes that should be remembered.

### 5. There should be proper order in prayer.

Let there be a stillness, during congregational prayers, that impresses all with the nearness of God—no whispering, no turning of leaves, no unnecessary moving, no babel of voices, all hearts beating in unison as the leader in prayer gives voice to the desires of the congregation—and the congregation is in proper frame to receive the divine response to prayer. And whether the prayer is by congregations, by families, by groups, or by individual petitioners, nothing should be allowed between us and God, everything dismissed from the mind except the persons or causes laid before the Lord in our petitions. It should be borne in mind, also that hands uplifted in prayer should be "holy hands" (I Tim. 2:8), unless it be the hands of penitent sinners coming to God for pardon.

The posture in times of prayer is important enough to merit notice. While there are a few cases recorded in Scripture where people stood during prayer, in most cases the supplicant bowed before the Lord, sometimes falling upon their faces. Psa. 95:6; Num. 16:22; II Chron. 6:13. A mere bowing of the head, and, as is too often the case, a listlessness on the part of the congregation while the minister or some one else recites a prayer, is not in harmony with the reverence and humble expectancy which should characterize all true prayer. Speaking of the kneeling posture, it was in this attitude that we find Solomon at the dedication of the temple (I Kings 8:54), Daniel when under a heavy load (Dan. 6:10), Jesus in Gethsemane (Luke 22:41), Stephen at the time of his martyrdom (Acts 7:60), and Paul and his company just before the departure (Acts 21:5). Every humble supplicant should be able to say, "I bow my knees unto the Father" (Eph. 3:14).

Speaking of proper order in prayer, let us not forget the Gospel order presented in I Cor. 11:4-6.

### 6. Meetings for prayer.

They are edifying, when people come together in the spirit of prayer—not worth the effort where the prayer service is mere form. The Bible mentions a number of prayer meetings that proved a mighty power in advancing the cause. Acts 1:12-14; 4:23-31; 12:5, 12. Naturally when people are in the spirit of prayer, those of like mind and faith delight to be together, talking with the Lord.

### 7. The power of secret prayer.

There should be an altar in every heart, in every home, in every congregation. As for public prayer, it was practiced in apostolic times, it should be practiced today. But the real test is not in the public prayer but in the prayers where there is none but God within hearing distance. Men have prayed eloquently in public without a spark of faith or reverence; but when one prays in secret, where there can be no possible motive but a desire to bring matters before the Lord, there is no question about the sincerity of the prayer or about its being heard in heaven. "When thou prayest, enter into thy closet, and when thou hast shut thy door, pray to thy Father which seeth in secret, and thy Father which seeth in secret shall reward thee openly" (Matt 6:6).

Prayer is said to be "the power that moves the Hand that rules the world." Read Matt. 17:20, 21. Whoever comes before God in sincere, believing, persevering prayer has hold of the arm of Him with whom all things are possible. There are mountains of difficulty on every hand, but through the power of God, moved by the prayer of faith, every one of them may be removed. In the secret chambers of the heart, where none can prevent us from approaching God in prayer, there are mighty fortresses which no enemy of souls can overthrow, for "with God all things are possible."

> "Sweet hour of prayer, sweet hour of prayer,
> That calls me from a world of care,
> And bids me at my Father's throne
> Make all my wants and wishes known.
> In seasons of distress and grief,
> My soul has often found relief,
> And oft escaped the tempter's snare,
> By thy return, sweet hour of prayer.

> "Sweet hour of prayer, sweet hour of prayer,
> May I thy consolation share,
> Till from Mt. Pisgah's lofty height,
> I view my home and take my flight.
> This robe of flesh I'll drop, and rise
> To seize the everlasting prize,
> And shout, while passing through the air,
> Farewell, farewell, sweet hour of prayer."

# CHAPTER III

## OBEDIENCE

Behold, to obey is better than sacrifice.—I Samuel 15:22.
If ye love me, keep my commandments.—John 14:15.

Obedience is twofold: (1) that which is due to God, (2) that which is due to man. The former is due from men and angels, the latter from fellow men and the lower animals. Obedience may also be classified as voluntary or compulsory, complete or partial, indifferent or wholehearted. The first question of interest to those who wish to discharge their full duty toward God and man is that of

### Whom to Obey

To this the Bible answers:

1. **"Obey God"** (Acts 5:29).

This, according to the testimony of the apostles, is our paramount duty. John teaches it as a test of standing before Him (I Jno. 2:3, 4) and Christ places it in the same class. Jno. 14:15, 15:14. John mentions obedience as an evidence of true discipleship. I Jno. 2:3-5. The wise man sums up the question of duty as follows: "Let us hear the conclusion of the whole matter, Fear God, and keep his commandments: for this is the whole duty of man" Eccl. 12:13).

2. **"Children, obey your parents in the Lord"** (Eph. 6:1).

This is "the first commandment with promise." The Bible assigns four reasons for giving the command: (1) "This is right;" (2) "That it may be well with thee;" (3) "This is well pleasing unto the Lord;" (4) "That thou mayest live long on the earth." Obedience to parents is not only the stepping stone to an obedient life in other relationships but also the stepping stone to the highest sphere of usefulness to God and fellow men.

3. **"Obey . . . . your masters according to the flesh"** (Col. 3:22).

That we may get the full force of this commandment, let us notice the explanation that follows: "not with eye-service as menpleasers, but in singleness of heart, fearing God."

4. **"Obey magistrates"** (Tit. 3:1).

In other words, "Let every soul be subject unto the higher powers" (Rom. 13:1).

5. **"Obey them that have the rule over you"** (Heb. 13:17).

Submission to constituted authority, whether in domestic, governmental, or religious affairs, is one of the fundamentals of ideal Christian living. There is a blessedness and a power in the Christian grace of humble submission which none who are proud in heart and rebellious in spirit can ever know.

### What Obedience to God Includes

It will help us to appreciate the importance and far-reaching nature of our obedience to God to take a little time in studying what it includes. They who obey God are submissive to—

1. **The Voice of God.**—"Obey my voice, and I will be your God" (Jer. 7:23). It is this voice that Noah heard when he builded the ark (Gen. 6); that Abraham heard when he left home and kindred and started for the land of promise (Gen. 12:1-5); that Moses heard when he accepted the task of leading his people out of bondage (Ex. 4); that Elijah heard when he was brought back into a state of humble submission to God (I Kings 19:12); that the Church at Antioch heard when Paul and Barnabas were sent out among the Gentiles (Acts 13:1, 2; that we hear at the present time when we give our hearts to Him

OBEDIENCE 469

(Jno. 5:25); that all *must* hear when God will call "all that are in the graves" (Jno. 5:28, 29) to come forth.

2. **The Son of God.**—We hear the call to obedience as the Father commends His Son to the world, saying, "This is my beloved Son, in whom I am well pleased; hear ye him" (Matt. 17:5). It is in this dispensation that God is speaking to us "by his Son" (Heb. 1:2). Therefore, "See that ye refuse not him that speaketh" Heb. 12:25) when He says, "If ye love me, keep my commandments."

3. **The Spirit of God.**—Stephen reminded the Pharisees of the condemnation that was coming to them because they resisted the Holy Ghost, as their fathers had done. Acts 7:51. It is the Spirit of God that guides into all truth. Jno. 16:13. No one can truthfully claim obedience to God without submission to the wooings and leadings of the Holy Spirit.

4. **The Word of God.**—It is impossible to separate God from His Word. The power of God being in His Word, we understand what Paul meant when he declared the Gospel of Christ to be "the power of God unto salvation" (Rom. 1:16). It is idle to think of being right with God without being obedient to His Word. Jno. 14:15; 15:14; Jas. 1:22-25; I Jno. 2:3, 4.

5. **The Church of God.**—As the Word of God is the message of God to man, so the Church of God is the organization through which this message is brought to a lost world, Matt. 28:18-20. This is clearly and emphatically set forth in the teachings of Christ, as for instance, His instructions in cast of disobedience to the Church: "Let him be unto thee as an heathen man and a publican" (Matt. 18:17). See also Matt. 16:19; 18:18; Jno. 20:23.

### Obedience and Self-denial

1. **Self-denial is a necessary result of obedience.**

Drop out this thought, and you have obedience in name only. Jesus said: "If any man will come after me (be obedient), let him deny himself, and take up his cross daily, and follow me" (Luke 9:23). No man knows from experience "the obedience of Christ" but that his will, desires, aims, pleasures, have become subject to the will of God. Self-denial is not merely a Christian duty; it is inseparably connected with an obedient life. "They that are Christ's have crucified the flesh with the affections and lusts" (Gal. 5:24).

2. **Both find common ground in a submissive spirit.**

There can be no submissive spirit without the thought of obedience. To obey means to submit, to submit means to obey. Likewise, there can be no submissive spirit without a willingness to sacrifice any personal interests or desires that conflict with the plans and purposes of the one to whom we are submissive or obedient. Obedience to God means self-denial in all things where there is a conflict between the desires of the flesh and the will of God. Read Rom. 8:1, 2.

3. **Combined obedience and self-denial keeps us in the spirit of both.**

Some people are willing to obey God so long as such obedience does not seriously interfere with their privileges. Others practice (seeming) self-denial so long as they seem to get glory out of it. But you search in vain for some one whose willingness to sacrifice prompts him to obey God and whose obedience to God prompts him to live a self-sacrificing life, who has not entered into the spirit of both self-denial and obedience.

## Results of Obedience

1. **It admits us into the grace of God and the blessings of the Gospel.**

The Holy Ghost is given "to them that obey him" (Acts 5:32). It is essential to our right standing before God. Jno. 15:14; I Jno. 2:3, 4. It is coupled with our justification. Rom. 5:19. It means Christian fellowship and a sinless life. I Jno. 1:7. In short, all the blessings of the Gospel are for the obedient, and there are no promised

blessings for the disobedient to be found in the Bible.
"Through the obedience of faith (Rom. 16:25, 26) we are
delivered from the darkness, thunderings, and tempests of
Sinai with the terrible sense of impending doom, to the
blue sky and bright sunlight of Mt. Zion, where we have
peace with God, union with Christ, ministration of angels,
and fellowship with saints."—Geo. R. Brunk.

2. **It means an upright, wise, sinless life.**

God's counsel is unerring, His Word is perfect, His
power is infinite. Obedience to God means to travel in
the path of righteousness; whole obedience to the world
means to travel in the paths of sin. Truth, justice, righteousness, godliness are all found in the path of obedience
to God.

3. **It assures deliverance in time, and glory in eternity.**

It is the "doers of the word" who stand in line with
God's blessings; who are safe against the coming storms
that will sweep the unsaved into the realms of eternal despair. Matt. 7:21-29; II Thess. 1:7-9. "Blessed are they
that do his commandments, that they may have right to
the tree of life, and may enter in through the gates into
the city" (Rev. 22:14).

### FURTHER OBSERVATIONS

1. **Obedience is a heart condition.**

We now speak of the kind that God takes notice of,
for "The Lord looketh on the heart" (I Sam. 16:7). It
was obedience "from the heart" (Rom. 6:17) that brought
to the Roman brethren the commendation they deserved.
Obedience that does not spring from the heart is worth
nothing as a justifying virtue.

2. **Obedience in the heart produces obedience in outer
life.**

How did Paul know that the Romans were obedient
"from the heart?" He saw it in their works. You never
saw a man with an inward experience that did not manifest

it outwardly, sooner or later. While a man who is right at heart may have his shortcomings, yet his imperfections are such that his acquaintances may be reasonably sure that the errors are due to a mistaken head rather than a rebellious heart.

### 3. Disobedience to God brings everlasting punishment.

When Paul writes to the Thessalonians about the impending judgment upon sinners he says not a word about their grievous sins; but he does say that when the Lord Jesus Christ will be revealed from heaven that "in flaming fire" He will take "vengeance upon them that know not God, and that *obey not* the gospel of our Lord Jesus Christ" (I Thess 1:7-9). Right standing before God is conditioned upon obedience. I Jno. 2:3-5.

### 4. Disobedience in one thing makes a man a rebel in God's sight.

For one act of disobedience the whole human family fell under the curse of sin (Gen. 3:1-6; Rom. 5:12); Moses was denied admittance into the promised land (Deut. 32: 50-52); Uzza was smitten dead before men (II Sam. 6: 6,7). As James says, "Whosoever shall keep the whole law, and yet offend in one point, he is guilty of all" (2:10). Criminals, as a rule, are not punished for having committed the whole catalogue of crimes, but usually because they have been convicted of *one* crime. Whoever willingly disobeys God in any one thing is in rebellion against Him, no matter how many good qualities he may have otherwise. The moralist who prides himself on his goodness will be sentenced to eternal banishment from God for the same reason that the lowest reprobate will be sentenced—because they "obey not the gospel of our Lord Jesus Christ." Neither "mighty works" nor human goodness can be acceptable substitutes for the grace of God when it comes to appearing before the judgment seat of Christ.

5. **We owe God unqualified obedience, no matter who stands with or against us.**

"Every one of us shall give account of *himself* to God" (Rom. 14:12). It would have been foolish for Noah and his family to stay outside the ark because nobody else would go in; or for Daniel and his three companions to have thrown away their convictions because nobody else did as they did and because thereby they might escape the den of lions or the fiery furnace—but not any more so than it is for us at the present time to refuse to obey *all* the commandments of our Lord, because "nobody else does." The moment we begin to inquire what other people ought to do we are confronted with the question by our Master: "What is that to thee? follow *thou* me." Our only justifiable attitude toward God is that of willingness to do just as He wishes that we shall do, even though we may be the only ones under the sun who obey Him thus. Partial obedience is nowhere justified. Like Mary, the mother of Jesus, we want to say (to ourselves and to others) "Whatsoever HE saith unto you, *do* it."

# CHAPTER IV

## WORSHIP

O come, let us worship and bow down: let us kneel before the Lord our Maker.—Psalm 95:6.

Worship is an attitude and feeling of reverence, admiration, awe, adoration, and profound respect. It is a condition of the soul rather than a part of the outer life. Such things as prayer, praise, singing, witnessing for Christ, etc., all belong to worship; but they are the fruits of worship rather than worship itself. When the soul is filled with worship such things are seen as the natural results.

Worship may be true or false, depending upon our sincerity or insincerity, or upon the object of our worship. Worshiping the creature rather than the Creator constitutes idolatry.

### Some Fundamental Facts

### 1. All men are worshipers.

This fact is proved by the record of all people. Paul refers to the Gentiles who have not the law but "do by nature the things contained in the law" (Rom. 2:14), thus giving recognition to the fact that God has implanted something into the hearts of all men that even those who are "dead in trespasses and sins" may be reached by the voice of God and brought back to life. Jno. 5:25. Christians, pagans, people in every clime and age, all are worshipers. Religion is an innate principle in man. In most people it is woefully corrupted, but it is there nevertheless. Even men who themselves look upon all forms of religion as "superstition" are themselves abject slaves to some form of idolatry—making a god of gold, of appetite, of pleasure, of some great hero, of self, of some other idol.

2. **God alone is the proper object of our worship.**

This is decreed in the first Commandment (Ex. 20:3), while in the second Commandment idolatry is forbidden. Christ says, "It is written, Thou shalt worship the Lord thy God, and him only shalt thou serve" (Matt. 4:10).

Idolatry is forbidden. Every mention of it in the Bible is to forbid it or to deprecate the practice of it. Neither gods of wood or stone, nor rivers, nor sun or moon or stars, nor any other creatures or creations of men's minds or imaginations should be worshiped; for they are all idols, when used as objects of worship.

Our own appetites or cravings for that which is not our own are not to be idolized. Phil. 3:19; Col. 3:5.

Hero worship is forbidden. Acts 10:25, 26; 14:10-15.

Not even angels are to be worshiped. Rev. 22:8, 9.

This leaves only God as an object worthy of our worship. He is the only one in His class, the only Creator of heaven and earth, the only Infinite Being perfect in all things, and to Him naturally belong all praise and glory and adoration and reverence. Let us worship Him "in Spirit and in truth," and praise His holy name.

When we speak of God as being the only One whom men should worship, we include the Trinity—Father, Son, and Holy Ghost.

3. **"They that worship him must worship him in Spirit and in truth"** (Jno. 4:24).

In other words, unless we enter into the proper spirit, and worship Him sincerely, we do not worship Him at all. God must be in our hearts as well as on our lips, in our lives as well as in our professions. Of the Pharisees Christ says: "In vain do they worship me, teaching for doctrines the commandments of men" (Matt. 15:9). The very fact that they preferred their own traditions to the commandments of God showed that they were not sincere in their worship. Notice the words: "SPIRIT and TRUTH." We may be correct in doctrine and exact in our forms of worship; but unless we worship in fact, as well as in form, there is no true worship in our souls.

### 4. We are COMMANDED to worship God.

For proof, read again the references already quoted. They who have already entered the true spirit of worship do not need this commandment; but the good works' apostle and the moralist, who imagine that because of their good works and excellent characters they are right with the Lord, are here confronted with a fact that absolutely bars them out. No one who ignores the commandments of the Lord can justly lay claims to being a true worshiper of Jehovah. Matt. 7:21-29; Jno. 14:15; 15:14; I Jno. 2:3, 4.

### 5. We are not COMPELLED to worship God.

While we are *commanded* to worship God we are not *compelled* to do so. The very fact that most people do *not* worship Him sincerely is evidence of the truth of our statement. Man being a free agent, he can do as he pleases about this matter. An illustration of this fact is found in a statement in Joshua's farewell address: "If it seem evil unto you to serve the Lord, choose you this day whom ye will serve . . . but as for me and my house, we will serve the Lord" (Josh. 24:15). We today have the same privilege. We may worship God if we choose to do so; if not, we may be idolaters, as most people are.

But this further thought should not be lost sight of: Since God has given us the freedom of choice, He has also placed upon us the responsibility for our choice. It is this: Worship God, and dwell with Him in eternity; worship idols, and spend eternity with "the god of this world." Heaven or hell will be the result of our choice. Read Gal. 6:7, 8.

### 6. We bear the image of God, or the gods, whom we worship.

Why do the Mohammedans so completely show the characteristics of Mohammed? the Chinese so nearly reflect the qualities attributed to Confucius? the Mormons exemplify the traits of character manifested by Joseph

Smith and Brigham Young? In these leaders were found
the ideals cherished by their followers, who became more
and more like them the longer they followed in their leaders'
footsteps. Today the men who are out to destroy the
Christian faith and to lead the souls of men astray, resemble, in their life and tactics, the "god of this world," as he
is revealed in the garden of Eden. And what is true of
false gods is true also with reference to the God of heaven.
In Him we have our ideal—perfection, righteousness, holiness, purity, heavenly splendor and glory. And the longer
we worship Him the more fully we shine in His image.
Rom. 8:29; II Cor. 3:18; Eph. 4:11-16; Col. 3:10.

7. **Idolatry is degenerating, demoralizing, ruinous, destructive.**

It is not because God is envious of "other gods" that
He declares Himself a "jealous God" (Ex. 20:5) : but He
knows, better than any mortal, what idolatry means for
those who embrace it. God's "jealousy" is of the same
kind which Paul avows when he says, "I am jealous over
you with a godly jealousy" (II Cor. 11:2). God knows,
Paul knew, and so does every thoughtful person know,
that the moment that any one turns aside from the living
God, he turns his face away from the heavenly ideal and
begins to imbibe the qualities attributed to the idols whom
he serves. These idols are either rebellious or unenlightened and sinful men, or they are inanimate objects to
whom have been attributed qualities conceived in ungodly
minds and hearts. Turn to your Bibles and begin reading
at Rom. 1:18. From there on to the end of the chapter
you have a graphic pen picture of what idolatry does for
the soul—it results in a continual course downward into
the depths of iniquity and ruin. The history of the world
in all ages proves that the more dense the idolatry of the
people the more degenerate they are. The whole stream
of idolatrous practices is toward the final and eternal consummation of all wickedness—a gaping, yawning hell,
"prepared for the devil and his angels" and to be eternally

inhabited by them as well as by all human victims who are caught in the snare and corruption of idolatry.

## Why Worship God

### 1. God commands it.

His commandments are founded on perfect wisdom and love, and can not be ignored without disastrous results. Disobedience is the gateway to all the ills and woes of man, both here and hereafter. Rom. 5:12; II Thess. 1:7-9.

### 2. It keeps us free from every form of idolatry.

Instances are on record where idolatrous kings gave recognition to the God of heaven (Gen. 41:38-41; Ezra 1:1-4; Dan. 6:25-27) but there is no instance on record where any man of God ever knowingly gave recognition to any idol as an object of worship. And even these idolatrous kings **dishonored** rather than **honored** God when they gave Him recognition as one among many gods whom they worshiped. The religion of God is of necessity monotheistic, as He has distinctly declared, "I am God, and there is none else" (Isa. 45:22). When Israel departed from this principle and set up a golden calf, the heresy was stamped out immediately (Ex. 32:1-29). Whoever worships God "in spirit and in truth" is kept entirely free from idolatry.

### 3. It brings us into fellowship with God and saints.

Christ taught the Samaritan woman that "We know what we worship: for salvation is of the Jews" (Jno. 4:22). In other words, salvation belongs to those who worship the Father "in spirit and in truth." In the light of this we see the blessed privilege held forth in I Jno. 1:4, 7. Being assembled for worship, as the Scriptures enjoin upon us (Heb. 10:25), and being assured that when we meet in the name of Jesus we have Him in our midst (Matt. 18:20), we not only "have fellowship one with another," but together we can say, "Truly, our fellowship is with the Father, and with his Son Jesus Christ." Such fellowship here is but a foretaste of the fellowship in store for the saints of God in the glory world. Read Rev. 7:9-12.

### 4. It is essential to acceptable standing before God.

Let us hear the warning from Moses: "If thou do at all forget the Lord thy God, and walk after other gods, and serve them, and worship them, I testify against you this day that ye shall surely perish" (Deut. 8:19, 20).

### 5. It is essential to holy living.

Purity, righteousness, holiness, the exercise of all the nobler qualities of heart and soul are inseparably connected with the true worship of the one true and living God.

### 6. It is fruitful of good works.

It puts something into the voice that leaves its impress upon the minds and hearts and lives of others. It produces feelings and convictions which prompt the worshiper to testify for the Master "with reverence and godly fear." It brings about an attitude of loyalty and devotion made manifest in fervent prayers, in inspiring music, in reverential praise, in faithful service. It fits the mind for real companionship with God and saints, and from the depths of the soul there is a hearty response to the sentiment, "I was glad when they said unto me, Let us go into the house of the Lord." There is an inseparable connection between real worship, holy living, and sanctified service. There is an uplifting power in worship which words can not describe.

> "Praise God from whom all blessings flow,
> Praise Him, all creatures here below;
> Praise Him above, ye heavenly host,
> Praise Father, Son, and Holy Ghost."

# CHAPTER V

## SELF-DENIAL

And he said to them all, If any man will come after me, let
him deny himself, and take up his cross daily, and follow
me.—Luke 9:23.

Life is a paradox. The way to retain it is to lose it;
and the way to lose it is to selfishly cling to it. Matt. 10:
39; 16:25; Mark 8:34-38; Luke 9:23, 24; 17:33; Jno. 12:25.
They who are most decidedly alive are the ones of whom
it can truthfully be said, "Ye are dead, and your life is hid
with Christ in God" (Col. 3:3). In other words, the life
everlasting is possible in those only who deny self, allow
the old man to be crucified, who give up the first Adam
that the second Adam may live and rule in his stead. As
selfishness is the most destructive enemy to the highest
interests of self, so may our highest interests be attained
through self-denial.

### Notable Examples

We gain our clearest ideas of any thing by looking at
examples in which that thing is illustrated. Our clearest
idea of self-denial is gained through a study of the lives
of those who practiced it. Let us notice a few of these:

1. **Christ.**—Turn to Philippians 2:5-10. Though He
"thought it not robbery to be equal with God, he made
himself of no reputation." Ease, comfort, popularity,
riches, glory, all were sacrificed upon the altar of self-
denial, His life sacrificed to the one effort to promote the
highest interests of those whom He served and for whom
He gave His all. Looking at results, we find that He not
only accomplished the deliverance of millions of souls
from the captivity of sin and death, but that "God also

hath highly exalted him, and given him a name which is above every name."

**2. Abraham.**—At the call of God he forsook home and kindred and friends, spent his entire life among strangers, and died in comparative obscurity. Looking at results, we look at him today as "the father of the faithful," and in his SEED all the nations of the earth are blessed.

**3. Moses is another man of God who sacrificed a** promising earthly career (Heb. 11:24-26), thereby liberating his people from the bondage of Egypt and exchanging the glory of earth for a greater glory in the world to come.

**4. The Fisherman of Galilee.**—Read Mark 1:18; Luke 5:10, 11. At the call of Christ "they forsook all, and followed him." To them it looked as if they were forsaking their living; to us it seems like a very profitable exchange for something infinitely better than they had before they obeyed the call of their Lord.

**5. Saul of Tarsus.**—When we think of the prominence which this young man had already attained at the time when Stephen made the supreme sacrifice in devotion to his faith (Acts 7:60) we are made to feel what it meant for him to turn aside from his promising earthly career to serve the living God. Keeping this in mind, we have a vivid picture of what self-denial means as we study the life of this great apostle to the Gentiles. His justification in making this denial is evident in the multitudes won for Christ as well as in the rapturous vision presented in II Tim. 4:4-8.

From these and other examples we learn: (1) That self-denial requires a sacrifice of what appears to be self-interest; (2) that this sacrifice must be by consent of the mind reinforced by will power; (3) that though it is a sacrifice, it is an investment which repays the investor abundantly in the form of enriched life and greater service to God and man. To renounce self as being crucified

16

with Christ means to obey the resurrected Christ and constitutes Christian self-denial.

**Examples of Self-indulgence.**—Speaking of examples of self-denial, we are the more impressed with them when we consider them in contrast with other examples on the part of those who made self-interest their first rule in life. Among these we may mention the antediluvians, who subordinated all things to their fleshly desires (Gen. 6) and by their wickedness brought the judgment of Almighty God upon the human race; the Israelites (I Cor. 10:1-12). whose self-indulgence and self-will during their wilderness wanderings brought about the overthrow of the original 600,000 able-bodied men who left Egypt for the promised land (Joshua and Caleb excepted); Belshazzar (Dan. 5), whose debauchery ended in his own death and the overthrow of his kingdom; Dives (Luke 16:19-25), whose gorgeous display and sumptuous feasting preceded his opening his eyes in hell!

These examples, both of self-denial and self-indulgence, might be extended to any length. Whether notable or obscure, they tell the same story, and impress upon the minds of all thoughtful people the same lesson.

## Why Practice Self-denial

### 1. It is essential to godly living.

Read Matt. 10:38; 16:24, 25; Mark 8:34, 35; Luke 9: 23, 24; 14:27. Self-denial stands at the very gateway of Christian life and service. The flesh and the Spirit are at enmity against each other—we can not follow both at the same time. Rom. 8:1, 2; Gal. 5:17-23; 6:7, 8. It is idle to think of living a life pleasing to God without keeping the body under subjection.

### 2. Self-indulgence invariably leads to the corruption of self and of others.

Through following after the lusts of the flesh men have become drunkards, gluttons, whoremongers, liars, thieves, murderers, slaves to every form of sin. The three avenues through which Satan approaches human beings and leads them astray are "the lust of the flesh, the lust of the eyes, and the pride of life" (I Jno. 2:16), and no man can withstand the tempter's snares so long as these avenues of approach are not effectively closed against him. They may be closed only through self-denial. For the sake of ourselves, as well as for the sake of those under our influence, we need to practice self-denial—daily.

3. **It is the only way through which the victorious life becomes possible.**

The desires of the flesh, when kept in their proper place, are God-given, essential to normal life, pure and holy; when allowed to rule, they become the avenues through which Satan enters the soul and accomplishes our ruin. Among these desires we may mention the desire for food, the desire for rest or ease, the desire of sex, the desire for power, and other desires belonging to every normal man or woman. And yet it is these very desires, unrestrained, that are made the basis of the world's vilest sins. Of Christ it is said that He "was in all points tempted like as we are, *yet without sin*" (Heb. 4:15). Why? He practiced self-denial, kept His body under, never yielded to temptation. Two men are confronted with an opportunity to gain money through unrighteous means. Both could make good use of the money if they had it, but neither can get it without resorting to trickery, fraud, or theft. One yields, the other does not. Two men are tempted to help themselves to food that does not belong to them. Both need the food, but neither can get it without theft. One yields, the other does not. Similar instances might be cited with references to temptations along the whole line of temptation and sin. Yield to the promptings of the flesh, and you fall into sin; keep your body under, practice self-denial, and you live the victorious life. The secret of the victorious life is the keeping of every desire of the flesh in its God-given place.

**4. People who practice self-denial are, as a rule, contented, prosperous, and happy.**

Even in the midst of suffering they can say with Paul, "The sufferings of this present time are not worthy to be compared with the glory that shall be revealed." As a rule, who are the healthiest people; they who control their appetites, or they who gratify their desires? who are the most free; they who control their passions, or they who give vent to them? who are the most prosperous financially; they who exercise proper oversight over their purses, or they who purchase whatever the flesh desires? who are the happiest; they who deny themselves of the sinful pleasures of this life, or they who gratify the flesh and follow after pleasure and vanity? Self-denial stands at the gateway to happiness and prosperity, both material and spiritual. Self-indulgence gratifies for the time being, but defeat and disappointment await it in the end.

**5. Self-denial is necessary to accomplish great things for God.**

The cause of Christ today is sustained by men and women who have surrendered themselves to God, are keeping the body under, whose life "is hid with Christ in God," and whose hearts, brains, services, and pocketbooks are upon the altar of the Lord. As the salvation of our souls was made possible by the sacrifice of Jesus Christ, so the cause of salvation is advanced and maintained through the sacrifices of men and women whose lives are upon the altar of the Lord.

**6. Self-denial is not only a Christian duty, but is in every way to be preferred to self-indulgence.**

No doubt Esau enjoyed his mess of pottage; but what is that compared with the birthright which he thereby sacrificed? Dives, no doubt, was delighted with his sumptuous feasting; but the wails in hell are an emphatic reminder that self-indulgence does not pay! The pleasures of sin are but temporary, while the pleasures which come as a reward for denying self from sinful indulgence last forever. If you had no other motive for practicing self-denial than good, sound, business sense, it would pay you, even from this standpoint, to do it. The climax to this line of comparisons is found in the fact that self-indulgence ends in hell, while self-denial marks the path that ends in eternal glory.

## What to Deny

### 1. Things absolutely sinful.

"My son, if sinners entice thee, consent thou not" (Prov. 1:10). "Mortify therefore your members which are upon the earth; fornication, uncleanness, inordinate affection, evil concupiscence, and covetousness, which is idolatry: for which things' sake the wrath of God cometh upon the children of disobedience" (Col. 3:5, 6). Be sure to say NO to the flesh every time you are tempted to commit sin, whether the sin be considered small or great, popular or unpopular. Duty, righteousness, and the highest interests of yourself and others demand that you do so. Gal. 5:24; I Pet. 2:11; 4:3, 4.

### 2. Things that are doubtful.

We often meet with things that we are not quite sure whether they are right or wrong. You are sure to stay on the right side if you deny yourself of all doubtful things, remembering that "He that doubteth is damned if he eat, because he eateth not of faith" (Rom. 14:23). You have probably read the tract, "Others may, you can not." To say nothing of the things which we believe to be wrong but which we are tempted to indulge in because others do, those things which we are not sure whether they are right or wrong should be left severely alone. It certainly can not be wrong to abstain; it *may be* sinful and ruinous to indulge.

### 3. Things that may be right in themselves but become wrong when indulged in to the injury of others.

A clear exposition of this is presented in Romans 14. As for eating meat, Paul had no compunctions of conscience on that point whatever, as the meat-eating regulations under the Law were all abolished in the Gospel of Christ. Yet because the exercise of this privilege was an offense to others, and because "it is good neither to eat flesh, nor to drink wine, nor anything whereby thy brother stumbleth, or is offended, or is made weak," Paul was willing to forego this privilege, saying that "if meat maketh my brother to offend, I will eat no flesh while the world standeth." This same principle can be applied to everything else where Christian liberty is the only principle at stake. Any privilege ceases to be such when the exercise of it becomes an injury to others. Now turn to Rom. 14:15. For the word "meat," substitute the name for any cherished privilege which you insist on exercising in the face of severe criticism or in the face of knowledge that your exercise of the privilege means the going astray of others, and then keep on reading that verse over and over again until the principle therein enunciated is thoroughly imbedded in your system.

4. **Things that stand in the way of our highest usefulness.**

For illustration, it may not be wrong for you to operate a $2000 or a $5000 car; but when you reflect that a car that could have been bought at about half or a third that much money would have served your purpose just as well, and that dying souls around you might have been saved had you chosen to put that wasted money into the treasury of the Lord (to say nothing of your example of extravagance), don't you think it would have been better to practice a little self-denial and buy a cheaper car? It may not be wrong for you to hold that position where you realize an income of five or ten times the amount needed to support your family; but when you meditate that your God-given qualities would make it possible for you to serve in a position in which your returns would be measured in terms of souls rather than in terms of thousands of dollars (to say nothing about the temptations that usually harass the family of a man with a princely income), don't you think it would be better to practice a little self-denial and turn your attention to the greater work of winning souls for the Master? Whether it is money-making or money-spending, popularity or unpopularity, ease or hardships, or anything else that is involved, our highest interests and greatest safety and loftiest motives revolve around that God-honoring counsel: "Whether therefore ye eat, or drink, or whatsoever ye do, do all to the glory of God" (I Cor. 10:31).

5. **Things that are right in themselves, but must be given up to heed the heavenly call to highest duty.**

Why should Abraham be called away from home and kindred to become a sojourner in a foreign land? God had a higher purpose for his life—that of becoming the father of the faithful, the head of a mighty nation, in whose SEED all the nations of the earth should be blessed. Why should the missionary of today be called away from home and kindred, to forego the satisfaction of laying up a competency to maintain himself and family, to forsake native country and dearest friends, and to spend his life in heathen lands? Somebody must do it, if the Great Commission to the Church of Christ is to be obeyed. Paul remained unmarried, not because it was wrong for him "to lead about a sister" (I Cor. 9:5) but because his circumstances were such that even this very helpful privilege under ordinary circumstances would have been a hindrance to his usefulness to the cause of Christ and the Church. Self-denial stops not at saying NO when the flesh is prompted to sin, not at excluding harmful luxuries from the daily life, not at abstaining from cherished privileges when by so doing others might be offended or led astray, but it means the denying of self to the most sacred privileges of life when duty calls us to places and circumstances where the exercise of these privileges stands in the way of the heavenly call of duty and service.

## The Underlying Principles

of self-denial are love and obedience. When the love of God enters the heart of man it not only binds that individual to a life of obedience to God, but also to a life of self-sacrifice that the cause of Christ may flourish, the people of God may prosper, and the world may be brought under the influence and privileges of the Gospel. The highest form of self-denial is the willingness to forego even the bliss and glory of heaven that others may be saved. As examples of this we cite you to the case of Moses, who on a certain occasion and in the interests of the Cause prayed that God might blot him out from the book of God's remembrance (Ex. 32:32); and of Paul, who could wish himself "accursed from God" (Rom. 9:3) for his brethren's sake. In this they simply rose to the sublime heights of self-sacrifice so perfectly exemplified by Jesus Christ when He left the courts of glory, "made himself of no reputation," lived the life of a "man of sorrows," and finally gave up life itself that men might be saved and redeemed from the curse of sin.

## Rewards

But self-denial ends not in suffering and defeat. Rather, it means the dismissal of self and the substitution of God in our stead. The giving up of the joys of the sinful life admits one first into the realms of the foretastes of heaven and finally to the realities of the everlasting joys of heaven itself. Psa. 16:11. The giving up of self-righteousness is simply an exchange for the righteousness of Jesus Christ. The denial of riches here is merely an exchange for the eternal riches above. And so with every sacrifice made for Jesus' sake—it is simply an exchange of things desired by the flesh for something that is infinitely better. The self-denial of Jesus was perfect and complete, extending even to the death on the cross. Phil. 2:5-10. Yet though He was "obedient unto death, even the death of the cross," He did not stop there—"God hath highly exalted him, and given him a name which is above every name." Fear not to follow in His steps. By and by the rewards of self-denial will be apparent in the royal diadem in glory, and self-denial will prove to be but an exchange of earth for heaven.

# CHAPTER VI

## NONCONFORMITY TO THE WORLD

Be not conformed to this world.—Romans 12:2.

With this subject we begin the study of a number of scriptural teachings commonly known as "restrictions." they are *restrictions* to the extent that they serve as a warning and a restraining power, but they may more properly be called **Gospel principles** for those whose lives are governed by the Word of God.

The subject before us is one of the most vital among these Christian principles, and one of the most extensively taught subjects to be found in the Bible. The principle of NONCONFORMITY is commonly recognized and commended by Bible students, though in too many cases the inclination to "make provisions for the flesh" has nullified the practical application of it in their own lives. That it is

### An Extensively Taught Bible Doctrine

is evident from the numerous scriptural references to it, a few of which we herewith submit for your consideration:

> I beseech you therefore, brethren, by the mercies of God, that ye present your bodies a living sacrifice, holy, acceptable unto God, which is your reasonable service. And be not conformed to this world: but be ye transformed by the renewing of your mind, that ye may prove what is that good, and acceptable, and perfect, will of God.—Rom. 12:1, 2.
>
> I have given them (the disciples) thy word; and the world hath hated them, because they are not of the world, even as I am not of the world.—John 17:14.
>
> That which is highly esteemed among men is abomination in the sight of God.—Luke 16:15.
>
> Be ye not unequally yoked together with unbelievers.—II Cor. 6:14.
>
> Who gave himself for us, that he might redeem us from all iniquity, and purify unto himself a peculiar people, zealous of good works.—Tit. 2:14.

Pure religion and undefiled before God and the Father is this. To visit the fatherless and widows in their affliction, and to keep himself unspotted from the world.—Jas. 1:27.

Know ye not that the friendship of the world is enmity with God? whosoever therefore will be a friend of the world is the enemy of God.—Jas. 4:4.

Ye are a chosen generation, a royal priesthood, an holy nation, a peculiar people; that ye should shew forth the praises of him who hath called you out of darkness into his marvellous light.—I Pet. 2:9.

Love not the world, neither the things that are in the world. If any man love the world, the love of the Father is not in him.—I John 2:15.

From these and other scriptural testimonies we conclude:

1. That the people of God and the people of this world are two separate bodies or classes of people.

2. That friendship with the world is enmity against God.

3. That it is wrong and sinful for the people of God to conform to the sinful, fleshly practices of this world.

4. That the people of God have been called to holiness, righteousness, purity, faith, commissioned to win the world to God rather than to confirm the world in its wickedness by partaking of its ungodly practices.

5. That in this separate, holy, God-honoring life, the people of God are letting their lights shine "in the midst of a crooked and perverse nation," thus drawing the minds of people to God.

6. That "pure religion" requires a complete separation from the world, on the part of those who have experienced it.

### The Reason Why

This Bible doctrine is not a mere arbitrary dogma which, as some think, interferes with the liberties of men, but the more we study it the more we see in it the wisdom and love of God for His creatures.

At the head of this world is "the prince of the power of the air," "the god of this world." So completely does he dominate the world that "the whole world lieth in wickedness." Whosoever follows after this leadership is not merely "conformed to this world" but is drifting with the world in the maelstrom of sin and folly into the depths of iniquity. True, some do not go as far in this direction as others do, but the whole trend of worldliness is in that direction and it is folly to lend ourselves to it at all. "Worldliness," "fashion domination," and kindred terms are simply synonyms for Satan leadership.

We may know something of the tyranny of fashion domination by looking at results. People who themselves are slaves to fashion often cry out against its tyranny. "Better be out of the world than out of fashion," is but the cry of desperation, showing that after all, in their blindness, they prefer slavery to "the god of this world" rather than freedom in the Lord.

Why is slavery now so universally condemned, whereas formerly even preachers dedicated, with scripture reading and prayer, the auction block from which slaves were sold? Then it was customary to do so, now it is not. Why did the majority of Masons in America leave the lodge soon after the murder of Morgan, whereas now the lodges are growing by leaps and bounds? Then it was not popular to belong to the lodge, now it is. Why do women claiming respectability insist on exposing their partly nude forms to the lusts of sinful men? Fashion demands it. Why are theaters, moving picture shows, ball rooms, swimming pools, and other forms of irreligion and vice so ardently patronized by Christian professors today? Fashion unites with fleshly lusts in demanding it. Why are there so few textbooks upholding the orthodox faith as against Evolution and other anti-scriptural heresies? Liberalism has become fashionable among school men, preachers included.

This list of questions could be extended indefinitely. Whoever follows in the popular current follows it into the depths of iniquity. Some are not so deeply engulfed in this sin-polluted stream as others are, but they are in the current that flows that way. Many who at first determined to wade in ankle deep have long since forgotten their precaution and are completely engulfed in the stream. The only safe course is to renounce Satan-leadership entirely.

The dividing line between the Christian and the worldling is where the choice is made between walking after the Spirit and walking after the flesh. There are times when Christians and worldlings, acting from motives that are purely human, follow the same customs. In the harvest fields the clothing that they wear is much the same, which may be said of their appearance at the carpenter's bench or any other place where service, not pride or vain display, dictates the kind of clothing worn. In a similar way, you see little difference in agricultural implements, house furnishings, etc., etc.,—so long as necessity and service and not pride and vanity dictate what shall or shall not be used. But the moment that pride, lust, vanity, egotism, etc., enter to influence decisions, you reach a line that separates the worldling who walks after the flesh from the Christian who walks after the Spirit. "Friendship of the world is enmity with God" because the leadership of the world is directly against God and godliness; and for this reason it is out of the question for any child of God to forsake the ways of godliness and conform to the sinful ways of the world.

Christ says, "The children of this world are in their generation wiser than the children of light" (Luke 16:8). While fashion devotees conform to the customs (fashions) of this world, let the people of God follow the established customs of the Church. The only safe course to pursue with reference to any of the vain, inmodest fashions of this world is that of total abstinence.

## Marks of Worldliness

1. **Disobedience to God.**—"The carnal mind is enmity against God: for it is not subject to the law of God, neither indeed can be" (Rom. 8:7). The world was disobedient to

God in the days of Noah, of Abraham, of Moses, of Christ. It is disobedient today, and will be so long as it continues to be Satan-controlled.

2. **Wickedness.**—"The whole world lieth in wickedness" (I Jno. 5:19). Every form of wickedness—blasphemy, murder, lying, robbery, intemperance, profanity, pride, licentiousness, etc.—is evidence of the influence of "the god of this world."

3. **Pride.**—This sin is believed to have been the cause of Satan's downfall. Isa. 14:12, 13; Ezek. 28:17. It is still true that "pride goeth before destruction" (Prov. 16:18). God hates even "a proud look" (Prov. 6:17). The proud who justify themselves with the thought that "we must have a little pride," forget that the Bible nowhere speaks of pride approvingly but on the other hand condemns it in severest terms. That which some people call "pride"—as cleanliness, respectability, etc.—is not pride at all, but simply common decency. The Bible holds out pride as something awful, devilish, soul-destroying, something to be shunned by all people as a deadly foe.

4. **Impurity.**—Read Rom. 1:21-32. It is a true picture of sinful men, and the end of worldliness. Impure thought, impure speech, impure social relations, and every other form of impurity are fruits of ungodliness and belong to this world. For an extended discussion on this subject, read the chapter on "Purity."

5. **Covetousness.**—This is another name for selfishness. Paul calls it "idolatry" (Col. 3:5; Eph. 5:5). All other sins are intensified by this one. I Tim. 6:10. Take away the love of money, and the great sins which are now threatening the existence of nations would be comparatively easy to handle.

6. **Ambition.**—Webster defines ambition as "an eager, or an inordinate, desire for preferment, honor, superiority, power, or the attainment of some thing." This desire is often fanned into a flame of passion for fame and preferment, and thus becomes the undoing of many people. The

fate of Absalom—young, talented, popular and aspiring—
should stand out as a warning to every talented young
person tempted in a similar way. An energetic nature and
a desire for usefulness, which some class as ambition,
should in no way be confused with the desire of preferment
centered in the thought of self-aggrandizement. Let not
the glory of God be displaced by the glory of self as the
impelling motive of our lives. Our mission is to serve, not
to be served, "in honour preferring one another" (Rom.
12:10). No man in whom the love of God is supreme and
whose chief desire is to live for the glory of God and the
good of others will ever be ruined through ambition. Luke
9:23, 24; Gal. 6:14.

7. **Intemperance.**—"Wine is a mocker, strong drink
is raging; and whosoever is deceived thereby is not wise"
(Prov. 20:1). Not only "the drunkards of Ephraim," but
also the drunkards of America, and their abettors (boot-
leggers, moonshiners, politicians, and conscienceless mon-
ey-grabbers) must give account to God for ruined lives.
Fortunes spent in dissipation, billions spent annually for
strong drink, tobacco, opiates, and other destroyers of
manhood, and the wretchedness and poverty found in every
place where intemperance has taken a deep hold, are but
indices of the terrible wreck occasioned by this monster
destroyer.

8. **Fashionable Attire.**—"Strange apparel" (Zeph. 1:8),
the Bible calls it. The clothing that people wear is but
an index of what there is in the heart. Pride, haughtiness,
social impurity, and others of this world's sins are all
indicated by the manner of clothing worn by people. Read
Isa. 3:16-24; Jer. 4:30; I Tim. 2:9, 10; I Pet. 3:3, 4.

9. **Worldly Amusements.**—Read Eccl. 11:9; Prov. 15:
2; Eph. 5:4; I Tim. 5:6. "Rejoice, O young man, in thy
youth; and let thy heart cheer thee in the days of thy
youth, and walk in the ways of thine heart, and in the
sight of thine eyes"—Here we pause in the reading and

meditate upon what it means to take this advice as dictated by the fleshly, sinful heart. We think of ball rooms, theaters, movies, gambling dens, circuses, bowling alleys, etc.; of Sabbath desecration in the form of joy rides, popular games, and dissipation in parks and swimming pools; of the hundreds of thousands of girls disappearing from year to year as victims of seductive pleasure and vice; and of other means of carnal pleasure in this pleasure-loving age—and then we return in our reveries to read the remaining portion of the scripture we started to quote: "but know thou, that *for all these things God will bring thee into judgment.*" "She (he) that liveth in pleasure is dead while she (he) liveth."

10. **Irreverence.**—This is the natural result of the different forms of worldliness thus far noticed. No man can turn aside from the ways of God without cultivating an attitude and feeling of irreverence toward God. Ungodliness, profanity, and other fruits of irreverence are the natural results of walking "according to the course of this world."

11. **Dishonesty.**—"Lie not one to another," is advice that all people need. This includes outlandish falsifying, all forms of deception and hypocrisy, exaggerations, and every other form of sin based upon insincerity and untruth. II Cor. 4:2-4. Every form of untruth and dishonesty comes from "the father of lies" (Jno. 8:44).

12. **Carnal Strife.**—This subject is considered at length in the chapter on "Nonresistance." We list it here because it is distinctly a mark of worldliness from which all Christion people should pray to be delivered.

## The "Unspotted" Life

This is the "pure religion" of which James speaks. Let us hear his testimony:

> Pure religion and undefiled before God and the father is this, To visit the fatherless and widows in their affliction, and to keep himself unspotted from the world.—Jas. 1:27.

From this we conclude: (1) that there are other kinds of religion besides "pure religion;" (2) that this kind can be maintained only by keeping "unspotted from the world" —that is, the worldly spots just enumerated must *all* be forsaken, not only a part of them; (3) that we are not pure in the sight of God until we have forsaken *all sin*. The "marks of worldliness" previously enumerated have their counterpart in the lives of those who are "unspotted from the world," and these we shall now briefly notice:

1. **Obedience to God.**—As disobedience is one of the natural marks of worldlings, so obedience is one of the distinguishing characteristics of the children of God. "Lord, what wilt thou have me to do?" is the voice of the convert seeking after God, and this remains a standing question with him as long as he lives. For an extended discussion of the subject of obedience, read the chapter on that subject.

2. **Godliness.**—"Teaching us that, denying ungodliness and worldly lusts, we should live soberly, righteously, and godly, in this present world" (Tit. 2:12). This is true nonconformity to the wicked and ungodly world. "Follow peace with all men, and holiness, without which no man shall see the Lord" (Heb. 12:14).

3. **Humility.**—This is a Christian grace which adorns the heart and life of every true follower of the meek and lowly Nazarene to whom we look as our Example in every human virtue. The subject is considered in a separate chapter, to which the reader is invited to turn.

4. **Purity.**—This includes purity of thought, of life, of speech, of every Christian virtue, freedom from every form of ungodliness. "Blessed are the pure in heart; for they shall see God" (Matt. 5:8). See chapter on Purity.

5. **Charity.**—Match this Christian grace against the sin of covetousness, and you have the contrast between worldliness and true Christianity. One is for taking in, the other for giving out; one for self, the other for the glory

of God and the good of fellow men. "Charity . . . seeketh not her own." Read I Cor. 13.

6. **Self-sacrifice.**—This is the natural fruit of charity. Ambition prompts us to seek places of honor or preferment; self-sacrifice, to sink self-interest in the supreme desire to advance the cause of Christ and the Church. Perhaps we should have called this word *consecration,* but no one can be truly consecrated to God without having a self-sacrificing spirit. With the life "hid with Christ in God," the selfish nature is gone, and the humble desire to be of real service to God and man has taken its place.

7. **Temperance.**—"Every man that striveth for the mastery is temperate in all things" (I Cor. 9:25). Temperance has been defined as "total abstinence from everything harmful, and sinful, and moderation in things lawful and good." This would include abstinence from all strong drink and other poisonous stimulants and narcotics—and, in things allowable, a moderation that is known to all men.

8. **"Modest Apparel."**—This is the opposite from the "strange apparel" noted in a preceding paragraph. Read I Tim. 2:9, 10; I Pet. 3:3, 4. Of this we shall speak later.

9. **The Joy of the Lord.**—We set this in contrast with the vain and foolish pleasures of this world, because so many people are ignorant of the fact that this world has nothing to offer which can in any way compare with the "joy unspeakable and full of glory" which only the children of God can have. The pleasures of this world are at best but temporary, while the joy of the Lord is for both time and eternity. "Rejoice in the Lord alway: and again I say, Rejoice."

10. **Reverence.**—Companionship with God and with saints begets a growing reverence for God and His Word. The more we see of God the more we are impressed with His goodness, greatness, holiness, majesty, and grace. If we have profound respect for those whom we esteem for their superior qualities, how much greater our reverence

for Him who is infinitely greater, in every way, than any of His creatures! They who "walk in the light, as he is in the light" invariably learn to regard Him "with reverence and godly fear."

11. **Integrity.**—One of the outstanding qualities of the child of God is that "his word is as good as his bond." Truth is imbedded in his character, and honesty and uprightness mark his course—not for advantage, but because these things are a part of his system. This quality belongs to true Christian manhood.

12. **Peace.**—"The servant of the Lord must not strive" (II Tim. 2:24), for "The weapons of our warfare are not carnal" (II Cor. 10:4). "Blessed are the peacemakers: for they shall be called the children of God" (Matt. 5:9). The heavenly refrain heard on the night of our Saviour's birth, "On earth peace, good will toward men," gives voice to a distinguishing mark of the children of God.

### BIBLE TEACHING ON DRESS

"Wherewithal shall we be clothed?" is the most widely discussed question known to man. It was the first question raised after the fall of man (Gen. 3:7), is referred to in some form in most of the books in the Bible, is a very prominent topic in social circles, is a means through which the goddess of Fashion rules the world; and that church, family, or social club does not exist in which the subject of dress has not been a prominent theme for discussion. Naturally, therefore, the people of God are interested in knowing what the Bible has to say on the subject. Here are a few points for consideration:

1. **All Bible teaching against worldly conformity is divine testimony against conforming to the fashions of the world in dress.**

To refresh our memories let us again turn to such scriptures as Luke 16:15; Jno. 17:14, 16; Rom. 12:1, 2; II Cor. 6:14-18; Jas, 1:27; 4:4; I Pet. 2:9; I Jno. 2:15-17. The

Bible has specific instructions as to how people ought to and ought not to be dressed, and every one of these instructions is violated in the vain fashions of this world. To conform to these fashions (rather than to heed the instructions of God's Word and conform to these instructions as exemplified in the clothing worn by consecrated men and women who are completely separated from this world in thought, motives, actions, and appearance) is distinctly a violation of God's Word. In other words, when the style of your headgear, neckwear, and clothing worn on other parts of your body is like that worn by the ordinary worldling, or changes along with or soon after the changes in fashion, it shows a disobedience to God and a subserviency to the world that ought not to exist among the people of God.

Some people tell us that they do not believe in being "conspicuous" or "odd" in the kind of clothing that they wear. This is a very good point—provided we avoid the mistake that such people usually make before they bring up the point. As children of God they do not, ought not to want to appear odd while among those "of like precious faith" but rather show by their appearance that they are one with those who have come out from the world (II Cor. 6:17, 18) and with them are traveling the path of "righteousness and true holiness." But to distort this point into an excuse for being in fashion with the world means a perversion of the truth of which no child of God should be guilty.

There are those who tell us that they "believe in nonconformity" but do not believe in "uniformity." This is another artful way of justifying themselves for following the uniform of the world rather than the uniform of the Church. Nobody who really believes in nonconformity and faithfully obeys the Word of God in the kind of clothing worn will ever be bothered by the "uniformity" bogey.

## 2. The Bible teaches sex distinction in dress.

"The woman shall not wear that which pertaineth unto a man, neither shall a man put on a woman's garment: for all that do so are abomination unto the Lord" (Deut. 22:5). Language can make this no plainer. It needs "obedience rather than explanation."

## 3. Modest apparel is commanded.

I Tim. 2:9, 10 and I Pet. 3:3, 4 cover this point. The Christian model is presented in the former reference cited, as follows: "With . . . . not with . . . . but with. . . ." In other words:

> (1) *"With* shamefacedness and sobriety"—the very opposite of that described in Isa. 3:16-24, where "the daughters of Zion" were condemned for walking about "with stretched forth necks and wanton eyes, walking and mincing as they go."
> (2) *"Not with* broided hair, or gold, or pearls, or costly array"—immodest apparel dictated by pride and desire to be conformed to the world, just as indecent exposure of the body is dictated through lust and submission to Fashion's decrees.
> (3) *"But with"*—as described in the language of Peter, "even the ornament of a meek and quiet spirit, which is in the sight of God of great price."

It is but natural that modest people should wish to be clothed in "modest apparel."

## 4. Wearing jewelry and costly array are forbidden.

Turn again to I Tim. 2:9, 10 and I Pet. 3:3, 4. As a sidelight you might also read Jer. 4:30 and Jas. 2:2-4. It will be well to notice that this style of clothing is especially mentioned as the opposite of "modest apparel," which God through the apostles commanded to be worn. Here is a plain "Thus saith the Lord" which no child of God should think of disobeying.

## 5. Immodest apparel is condemned and forbidden.

Aside from the scriptures already quoted the reader is asked to consult Isa. 3:16-24. "But this is an Old Testament reference," some one says. Yes, but it simply shows that God in all ages held bodily ornamentation under the ban. Clothing, it will be remembered, is for the covering, not the display, of the body. Vain display in dress should be avoided and opposed, (1) because it is testified against in both Old and New Testaments; (2) because it means a waste of the Lord's money; (3) because it is immodest; (4) because it fosters pride; (5) because it fosters lust; (6) because it is a mark of worldly conformity; and (7) because it is the exact opposite of the Bible standard of "the ornament of a meek and quiet spirit."

### 6. We are exhorted to unity.

Such exhortations as "unity of the Spirit" (Eph. 4:3), "unity of the faith" (Eph. 4:13), "of one accord, of one mind" (Phil. 2:2), "walk by the same rule . . . mind the same thing" (Phil. 3:16), etc., should not be lightly esteemed by those who are interested in seeing the whole body of believers knit together in love, united in faith and spirit, separated from the world, consecrated to God, unified in Christian service. In the face of the fact that Bible standards and world standards in dress are so widely different, the idea of abandoning Bible standards for the sake of not appearing "odd" in the sight of the world is unthinkable for obedient children of God, for though all Church members might be united in maintaining un-Biblical standards they would thereby forfeit unity with Biblical standards. Read Matt. 6:24; Luke 16:13. Just as fashion devotees subscribe to the standards of the world and follow its fashions in dress or otherwise, so the people of God should subscribe to the standards of the Bible as held forth and practiced by churches which are faithful to such standards.

### 7. We should avoid "changeable suits of apparel" (Isa. 3:22).

The idea of wearing one kind of clothing while among plain people and another kind while among fashionable people is wholly unscriptural. Disobedience to God's Word is never justified because we are disobedient only part of the time. Read Matt. 5:16; I Thess. 5:22; I Pet. 2:9-11.

## What Nonconformity Means

### 1. It means a life of separation from the world.

In the language of God through Peter, He "hath called you out of darkness into his marvellous light" (I Pet. 2:9). The disciples are "not of the world" (Jno. 17:14), even as Christ is not of the world. The condition upon which God receives us is that we "come out from among them" (II Cor. 6:17, 18).

### 2. It means freedom from the unequal yoke with unbelievers.

Turning to II Cor. 6:14-18, we are confronted with a number of searching questions:

"What fellowship hath righteousness with unrighteousness?"
"What communion hath light with darkness?"
"What concord hath Christ with Belial?"
"What part hath he that believeth with an infidel?"
"What agreement hath the temple of God with idols?"

Or, in the language of God through Amos, "Can two walk together, except they be agreed" (3:3)?

Applying this teaching to the fellowship which sometimes exists between believers and unbelievers—such as, in marriage, in the secret lodge, in business associations, in politics, etc.—it is clear that such alliances are contrary to the scriptural admonitions against the unequal yoke.

### 3. It means a life of witnessing for Jesus.

Separation from the world does not mean being out of reach in helping the world. The disciples, though "not of the world," were commissioned to witness for Jesus "unto the uttermost part of the earth." As the rescuer can do most for the drowning man when not entangled with him, so the child of God can do most for the world when free from all worldly entanglements. "No man that warreth entangleth himself with the affairs of this life" (II Tim. 2:4). It is those who are really free from sin that are most burdened to see this freedom extended to others. Read Rom. 12:2; I Pet. 2:9.

### 4. It means a life of holiness.

It is remarkable that the strongest texts connected with the subject of nonconformity are also connected with the idea of holiness. Being called out of a world of sin means of necessity a call to holiness. God's condition for receiving people is, "Come out from among them, and be ye separate . . . and I will receive you" (II Cor. 6:17). Let us notice a few more texts which connect the idea of nonconformity with that of holiness:

Rom. 12:2—"Be not conformed to this world . . . that ye may *prove* what is that good, and acceptable, and perfect will of God."

Tit. 2:14—Redeemed "from all iniquity, . . . a peculiar people."

I Pet. 2:9—"A chosen generation, a royal priesthood, an holy nation, a peculiar people."

### 5. It means a continuation of this separation and holiness in eternity.

Being called out of darkness here, if we continue to walk in the light, we shall reign with the King "for ever and ever" (Rev. 22:5). The final judgment of the wicked will simply mean this: Since you have chosen to follow "the god of this world" here, you shall continue with him in eternity. For the righteous the verdict is: "Thou hast been faithful over a few things, I will make thee ruler over many things." Since humanity is walking on two roads (Matt. 7:13, 14), and in opposite directions, the only possible result is that the wicked will "go away into everlasting punishment: but the righteous into life eternal" (Matt. 25:46).

# CHAPTER VII

## NONRESISTANCE

Glory to God in the highest, and on earth peace, good will
toward men.—Luke 2:14.

We get the word "nonresistance" from the instruction
of Christ to His disciples that they "resist not evil." We
get the doctrine from the teaching of Christ and the apostles. That we may enter into the spirit as well as the letter
of this teaching, let us notice, first of all, the

### 1. It has a place in the Ten Commandments.

The sixth commandment, "Thou shalt not kill" (Ex.
20:13), had a place in the law of God from the very beginning. God's words to Cain, "The voice of thy brother's
blood crieth unto me from the ground" (Gen. 4:10), make
it clear that murder is not only a transgression against a
fundamental law of God, but that it calls for punishment.
"Thou shalt not kill," was as distinctly the law of God under the Old Dispensation as it is under the New.

### 2. Christ is heralded forth in prophecy as "The Prince of Peace."

Read Isa. 9:6. Notice that the name, "The Prince of
Peace," is the last, the climax, of a list of very prominent
titles bestowed upon Him. He is the Prince of Peace (1)
as our Example, (2) as our Teacher, (3) as the One who
effected reconciliation and peace between God and man.
The message of the heavenly host, on the night of His
birth (Luke 2:14), proclaimed two things: (1) the glory
of God; (2) peace on earth—both connected with the advent
of this mighty Prince of Peace.

### 3. Christ taught nonresistance.

In the Sermon on the Mount He discusses a number of subjects pertaining to the practical side of life and the Christian standards of righteousness, and among other things He says:

> Ye have heard that it hath been said, An eye for an eye, and a tooth for a tooth: but I say unto you, That ye resist not evil: but whosoever shall smite thee on the right cheek, turn to him the other also. And if any man will sue thee at the law, and take away thy coat, let him have thy cloke also . . . . Love your enemies, bless them that curse you, do good to them that hate you, and pray for them which despitefully use you, and persecute you; that ye may be the children of your Father which is in heaven.—Matt. 5:36-45.

Some tell us that this language is figurative. Suppose it is. But by what logic may any scripture be interpreted to mean the exact opposite of what it says? Take this at its face value, and it will be found to harmonize with all the other things which Christ teaches on the same subject. Let us examine a few more of His teachings:

> All they that take the sword shall *perish* with the sword.— Matt. 26:52.
> Unto him that smiteth thee on the one cheek offer also the other; and him that taketh away thy cloke forbid not to take thy coat also.—Luke 6:29.
> Peace I leave with you, my peace I give unto you: not as the world giveth, give I unto you.—John 14:27.
> My kingdom is not of this world: if my kingdom were of this world, then would my servants fight.—John 18:36.

Take these statements at their face value, and you have the mind of the Prince of Peace with reference to carnal strife. These teachings are the more impressive because, in His individual life on earth, Jesus taught us by example how to put His precepts into practice.

Some have tried to make it appear, from the way Christ cleansed the temple, that He was not nonresistant in practice; but facts do not sustain that contention. His cleansing of the temple was in keeping with His general attitude toward sin and unrighteousness. But by no stretch of the imagination can that incident be tortured into an act of physical violence to men on His part. Take your Bibles. Turn to Matt. 21:12; Mark 11:15; Luke 19:

45, and read in both Authorized and Revised versions. Does any one suppose that but for His miracle-working power His enemies would have tolerated His course in a temple where He was not supposed to have any authority? And if He had miracle-working power, what use had He for any carnal weapon with which to inflict physical violence on others?

During all His life Christ was mighty in His conflict with sin, but gentle as a lamb and harmless as a dove in the matter of exerting physical power in overawing His enemies. As an illustration let us cite the fact that though He had power to call more than twelve legions of angels to His relief at the time of His betrayal (Matt. 26:53) He offered absolutely no resistance. Neither did He at any time seek to interfere with the affairs of state or meddle in politics in any way. In the matter of nonresistance, as well as in all other things, His life is an exact interpretation of His teachings.

### 4. The apostles taught nonresistance.

In his letter to the Romans Paul pleads:

> Recompense to no man evil for evil . . . . If it be possible, as much as lieth in you, live peaceably with all men. Dearly beloved, avenge not yourselves, but rather give place unto wrath: for it is written, Vengeance is mine, I will repay, saith the Lord. Therefore if thine enemy hunger, feed him; if he thirst, give him drink: for in so doing thou shalt heap coals of fire on his head. Be not overcome of evil, but overcome evil with good.—Rom. 12:17-21.

Writing to the Corinthians he rebukes them sharply for going to law with one another (I Cor. 6:1-8) and asks: "Why do ye not rather take wrong? why do ye not rather suffer yourselves to be defrauded?" In his second letter to the Corinthians he gives voice to a fundamental fact when he says (10:4), "The weapons of our warfare are not carnal, but mighty through God." Paul, like his blessed Master, while emphatic in his teachings against carnal strife, was equally emphatic against sin, encouraging his people to "fight the good fight of faith." Read Eph. 6:10-18; I Thess. 5:15; I Tim. 6:12; II Tim. 4:7; Heb. 10:30.

Peter offers his testimony for nonresistance, saying:

> If, when ye do well, and suffer for it, ye take it patiently, this is acceptable with God. . . . Christ also suffered for us, leaving us an example, that ye should follow his steps , . . . when he was reviled, reviled not again; when he suffered, he threatened not; but committed himself to him that judgeth righteously.—I Pet. 2:20-23.

The same kind of teaching is given in other parts of his letters.

James likewise testifies in support of evangelical peace, saying:

> Whence come wars and fightings among you? come they not hence, even of your lusts that war in your members? . . . Ye fight and war, yet ye have not, because ye ask not.—Jas. 4:1, 2.

The last statement strikes at the very root of the causes for war. Instead of going to God for wisdom, love, grace, and power to overcome we too often make our appeal to carnal force and attempt to overcome by that means. Results: quarreling, lawsuits, contentions, strife, war.

The apostles, like the Prince of Peace whom they followed, practiced nonresistance as well as taught it. They invariably suffered persecution rather than to inflict violence upon others, suffering imprisonment and martyrdom rather than have a guilty conscience before God.

## 5. The apostolic Church practiced nonresistance.

Historians agree that there were no soldiers among the Christians of the first century in the Christian era. The pagan writer, Celsus, who wrote about the close of the second century, accuses the Christians for refusing to bear arms, even in cases of emergency. Among the early Christians who express themselves on this point and defend the doctrine of nonresistance are Tertullian, Origen, Cyprian, Lactantius, and others. During the first two centuries practically the entire Church adhered to the nonresistant faith. Later, however, there was a drifting away from this faith, on the part of some, until, at the beginning of the fourth century, that part of the Church dominated by Rome had so far departed from the original nonresistant ground that Constantine made Christianity the religion of state in Rome.

## OLD TESTAMENT LIGHT ON NONRESISTANCE

Many people, while offering no very serious opposition to the thought that Christ and His disciples taught and practiced nonresistance, nevertheless justify war on the ground that Moses, Joshua, David, and other men of God in Old Testament times were mighty men of war. "If war was right then," they say, "why is it wrong now?" In response to this contention, let us notice a few facts gleaned from Old Testament scriptures:

1. "Thou shalt not kill," and "Love your enemies," were as indelibly stamped upon Old Testament scripture as upon the New. Read Gen. 4:9-11; Ex. 20:13; Deut. 5:17; II Kings 6:13-23; Prov. 25:21, 22.

2. "One difference between the two dispensations is that while the Old was a dispensation of justice, the New is a dispensation of mercy. We can see therefore how that God in former times used His people in meting out justice to His enemies, while under the New dispensation He uses His people only in dealing out mercy, and that therefore it was as consistent for men like David to be faithful warriors as it is for people under the dispensation of mercy to refuse to have any part in anything but that which deals out mercy to offenders."—Bible Doctrine. (p. 545.)  Read Luke 9:51-56; Jno. 1:17.

3. The law and its workings were for our example and admonition. I Cor. 10:6, 11; Heb. 10:1; 12:24. In God's dealings with His people and with transgressors in that day He gives us vivid object lessons on His severity as well as His goodness in bringing judgment upon sinners. While He deals differently with offenders in this dispensation from what He did in the former dispensation, yet the certainty and severity of punishment for unremitted sin is as great today as it ever was. *"Whatsoever a man soweth, that shall he also reap"* (Gal. 6:7).

4. In those days victory depended not upon carnal force and human cunning, as it does today, but upon whether the warriors on God's side were doing His bidding. The conquest of Jericho, the defeat at Ai, the victories and defeats of Saul, and many other conflicts between the children of Israel and their enemies are illustrations of this fact. We have every reason to believe that had the Israelites been absolutely true to God at all times they would have had one unbroken record of victory without having to shed a single drop of blood or taking the life of a single enemy.

5. The mightiest victories in Old Testament times were won without the shedding of a single drop of blood at the hands of the people of God. Examples: The overthrow of Pharaoh in the Red Sea, the delivery of the Syrian army into Elisha's hands, the destruction of Sennacherib's army, etc. Nonresistance and love were God's desire and wish under the Old Dispensation, as well as under the New.

### The Power of Peace

The wisdom of God in His provisions for peace is evident as we compare the power of peace with that of war. Men usually associate the idea of power with that of physical force, but God has ordained otherwise. It is in peace, not in war, that we find real power. A few examples will suffice:

1. When Christ sent out His disciples He did not arm them with swords and spears and other instruments of destruction, but He sent them forth "as sheep in the midst of wolves" (Matt. 10:16). They went forth, did a mighty work, even the devils being subject to them.

2. After the Christian Church was established the disciples went out preaching "the Gospel of peace" (Rom. 10:15). They had not only the nonresistant faith and therefore could not fight (Jno. 18:36), but they faced the fiercest opposition, first from the Jews and afterwards

from the Romans, and multitudes died a martyr's death. Yet in the face of all this the Church had a marvelous growth, so that before three centuries had rolled away the mighty power of Rome succumbed before the onward march of the Gospel, and a compromise was effected which made nominal Christianity the religion of state in Rome.

3. Now we would expect the Church to grow by leaps and bounds, as the Roman government was turned in defence of rather than in opposition to Christianity. But the reverse was true. No sooner had the sword of the Spirit been replaced by the sword of steel than the Church became corrupt, the power of Rome kept on crumbling, and the era of the "dark ages" was ushered in. The power of the sword is only a seeming power. It is in peace that we find the real power and the most substantial conquests.

4. Nations prosper in times of peace. No nation today enjoys prosperity but that this prosperity is due to peace rather than war. On the other hand, no nation has ever been able to long survive an era of conquest. While "successful" wars have been known to bring prosperity temporarily, they also brought evils which sooner or later made those nations to crumble in the dust. The history of fallen nations is an eloquent commentary on the destructiveness of war.

5. The mightiest triumph of peace will be apparent when the Prince of Peace will have put "all enemies under his feet" and "shall have delivered up the kingdom to God, even the Father" (I Cor. 15:24, 25). See Rev. 22:5.

### Why Advocate and Practice Nonresistance

1. **It is scriptural.**

For proof, read the references already cited in this chapter.

2. **It harmonizes with the Bible doctrine of peace in the soul.**

In other words, nonresistance is but the outward manifestation of the peace of God within the soul. It has well been defined as "love in action," as the peace of God applied to our relations with fellow men. Read Matt. 5:38-45; Rom. 12:17-21; Phil. 4:7.

3. **"All they that take the sword shall perish with the sword."**

Put the emphasis on the word "perish," and you get this testimony of our Saviour in its full force.

4. It is the power that wins.

It is the man or the nation that goes armed that is most likely to get into trouble. History furnishes abundant proof of this. Read Prov. 16:7; Rom. 12:19, 20. The promise of God, "I will never leave thee nor forsake thee," was not given in vain.

5. **War has proved itself a failure.**

The most conspicuous example of this is the recent World War—during which, according to reliable statistics, 10,000,000 lives were lost, $311,000,000,000 were added to national debts, and the total dollar loss is estimated to be $1,600,000,000,000 or "more than twice the total estimated wealth of all the nations of the world."—C. M. Sheldon.

6. **It is God's plan for our lives.**

Were this not so this doctrine would not have such a prominent place in the teaching of the Prince of Peace. Its wisdom has been demonstrated over and over again, man's substitute (war) has proved itself a disastrous failure, and we should not hesitate to take God at His word and to put His precepts into daily practice.

WAR APOLOGISTS' QUESTIONS

1. "If war is wrong for God's people, why was David, 'a man after God's own heart,' such a great warrior?"

As already stated in this chapter, his was a dispensation of justice in which the judgments of God were sometimes meted out to His enemies through the instrumentality of His people; ours is a dispensation of mercy, and therefore God's people are no longer used as they were in

David's time. Because something is right in one dispensation is no proof that the same thing is right under another dispensation. A father may tell his son to go to town today and to stay at home tomorrow. What is the right thing for him to do today, would be wrong tomorrow. For a number of similar illustrations, read the Sermon on the Mount. Matt. 5-7. "The priesthood being changed, there is made of necessity a change also of the law" (Heb. 7:12).

2. "What would become of a nonresistant nation?"

Even admitting that God uses nations as instruments in His hands through which judgment is brought upon other nations, and that through the instrumentality of the sword protection is afforded to the law-abiding against the violence of the lawless, would not change the established fact that the Gospel of Christ forbids that Christian people have any part in carnal strife of any kind.

But taking this question as it stands, the Pharisees expected to make capital out of it, just as people today are doing, when they soliloquized thus: "If we let him (Christ) thus alone, all men will believe on him: and the Romans shall come and take away both our place and nation" (Jno. 11:48). Today people are saying, "If we were all nonresistant they (an enemy nation) would come and take away our place and nation." The fact is, no nation has ever fully obeyed God literally on the war question, so we have no means of answering the question at the head of this paragraph. The nearest approach to a nonresistant nation was the colony of Pennsylvania under the peaceful rule of the Quakers. In those days the colony prospered while the neighboring colonies, relying upon a sword of steel, were harassed by Indian wars.

3. "What if a thief should break into your home?"

We should never think of this question without also thinking of God's many promises to care for His own. There are several things that you might do under such circumstances, but one thing is sure: Should you kill the thief, you would not only be violating the divine law against murder but you would send an unsaved soul to hell, without a chance for repentance; whereas, if the thief would kill you, your soul would be released for glory that much sooner. Such men have repented, made restitution, and afterwards rendered valuable service; but you, by killing him on the spot, would forever bar him from such opportunity. Better obey God, He will take care of results.

4. "Is not military service a good training in discipline?"

Look at the 10,000,000 slain men of the recent World War for your answer. Such lessons in discipline are too costly, even if we would admit their disciplinary value—which we do not. Not one man in a million would give his consent to have his boy exposed to the ravages of war for the disciplinary value there is in it. Even military men have denied that a soldier's life is worth the while for the discipline there is in it.

5. "What would happen if everybody practiced nonresistance?"

Then we would have a paradise on earth, and all the world could join in the song of peace heard by the shepherds of Bethlehem at our Saviour's birth. Luke 2:14.

6. "Should we not be submissive to our government?"

Yes. Read Rom. 13:1; Tit. 3:7. We should be submissive to all constituted authority, remembering that we owe our first allegiance to the highest of all authority, namely God Himself. Acts 5:29. The submissive spirit belongs to the nonresistant heart. Even in case of laws which we can not obey without disobeying the higher law of God, we should be submissive enough not to resist but rather to do as the apostles did—keep our consciences clear, even if that means going to jail or dying a martry's death.

7. "If you consider it wrong to fight, why not take noncombatant service?"

The word "noncombatant," as applied to military service, is a misnomer. It is the business of war to kill and to terrorize until the enemy surrenders. The man who manufactures the munitions of war, the man who hauls them to the battle field, the man who shoots the bullet or shell, and the man who is hired to pray while others shoot, all share in the responsibility of taking human life. If war is right, it should be supported; if wrong, it should not be supported, even in a noncombatant capacity.

8. "Is there not a difference between individual and national nonresistance?"

Yes; one is individual, the other collective. The principle is the same. If it is wrong for you to kill as an individual, what difference does it make whether you do it alone or in company with thousands of others? What would you do if you were a citizen of Turkey and got word to enlist in a war of extermination against all Christians?

### TESTIMONY OF WARLIKE MEN

"The more I study the world, the more I am convinced of the inability of brute force to create anything durable." —Napoleon Bonaparte at St. Helena.

"There never was a time when, in my opinion, some way could not be found to prevent the drawing of the sword."—Ulysses S. Grant.

"I confess without shame that I am tired and sick of war. Its glory is all moonshine. It is only those who have neither heard a shot nor heard the shrieks and groans of the wounded, who cry aloud for more blood, more vengeance, more desolation. . . .War is hell."—W. T. Sherman.

"If you had seen but one day of war, you would pray God never to see another."—Duke of Wellington to Lord Shaftesbury.

"Unless some such move be made we may as well ask ourselves whether we are thus doomed to go headlong down through destructive war into darkness and barbarism."—General Pershing, in an address in New York, Dec. 29, 1920.

"My first wish is to see this plague of mankind (war) banished from the earth."—George Washington in a letter to David Humphreys, July 25, 1785.

"War is the denial of Christianity and of all the most sacred things of life."—John F. O'Ryan in the "New York World" for January 22, 1922.

### Testimony of God through Inspired Men

Thou shalt not kill.—Ex. 20:13.

Resist not evil.—Matt. 5:39.

Love your enemies.—Matt. 5:44.

Do good to them that hate you.—Matt. 5:44.

Avenge not yourselves.—Rom. 12:19.

Whosoever shall smite thee on thy right cheek, turn to him the other also.—Matt. 5:39.

If any man will sue thee at the law, and take away thy coat, let him have thy cloke also.—Matt. 5:40.

As much as lieth in you, live peaceably with all men. —Rom. 12:18.

All they that take the sword shall perish with the sword.—Matt. 26:52.

The weapons of our warfare are not carnal.—II Cor. 10:4.

Be not overcome of evil, but overcome evil with good. —Rom. 12:21.

The servant of the Lord must not strive.—II Tim. 2:24.

# CHAPTER VIII

## SWEARING OF OATHS

Swear not at all.—Matthew 5:34.
Above all things, my brethren, swear not.—James 5:12.

Christian people have their instruction on this subject by the following teaching of Christ our Saviour in the Sermon on the Mount:

> Ye have heard that it hath been said by them of old time, Thou shalt not forswear thyself, but shalt perform unto the Lord thine oaths: but I say unto you, Swear not at all: neither by heaven; for it is God's throne: nor by the earth; for it is his footstool; neither by Jerusalem; for it is the city of the great King. Neither shalt thou swear by thine head, because thou canst not make one hair white or black. But let your communication be, Yea, yea; Nay, nay: for whatsoever is more than these cometh of evil.—Matt. 5:33-37.

Here we observe:

1. That there had been previous teaching on this subject, Christ referring to the Levitical Law. See Ex. 20:7; Lev. 19:12; Num. 30:2; Deut. 5:11.

2. That there are different kinds of oaths, some permissible under the Law, some forbidden.

3. That Christ, in one single statement, makes all kinds of oaths unlawful, giving reasons.

Turning to the teachings of the apostles, we find the same kind of teaching in the book of James. Among other things he says:

> But above all things, my brethren, swear not, neither by heaven, neither by the earth, neither by any other oath: but let your yea be yea; and your nay, nay; lest ye fall into condemnation.—Jas. 5:12.

Comparing these two scriptures, we notice:

1. That there is perfect harmony, both in thought and method of presenting it, between the teaching of Christ and of James. We attribute the positiveness and remark-

able clearness to the fact that the Old Testament teaching on this subject is hereby changed, and all people should know it.

2. That the teachers are of the very highest authority, one of them being the Son of God Himself.

3. That since we accept the New Testament as God's teaching for our times, and Jesus Christ as the authoritative Teacher in the present dispensation (Heb. 1:1, 2; 10: 29), we should unhesitatingly take Him at His Word, not using the oath under any circumstances.

### DEFINITIONS

Webster defines the oath as (1) "a solemn affirmation or declaration, made with an appeal to God for the truth of what is affirmed." (2) "A careless or blasphemous use of the name of the divine Being, or anything divine or sacred, either by way of appeal or as a profane exclamation or ejaculation." Cruden defines the oath as "a solemn action, whereby we call upon God, the searcher of hearts, to witness the truth of what we affirm, for the ending of strifes or controversies."

There are many kinds of oaths, depending upon the application of the obligation; such as the judicial oath, lodge oaths, religious anathemas, etc. In the absence of all seriousness, especially when spoken irreverently or blasphemously, it constitutes a profane oath. Stripped of all appellations to the Deity, for which other names are substituted, it is sometimes called a "wooden oath" or "by-word." But in all these applications the oath is essentially the same, it being an obligation in the name of the Deity (or some idol) with penalty for its violation.

It may be well to note, in passing, that there is an essential difference between an oath and an affirmation, even though some people insist that they are the same. The laws of our land recognize the conscientious scruples of those who can not consistently take the oath and allow them to take the affirmation instead—in which the following essentials of the oath are missing: The declaration ("I do solemnly swear"), the uplifted hand, the appeal to God. In other words, when we take the affirmation we simply state that we mean to tell the truth so far as we understand it, knowing that if we violate this promise we are held under the same penalties as if we had violated an oath. Let us notice also, that while we are positively commanded to "swear not at all," the inspired writer does not hesitate to write, "I will that thou affirm" (Tit. 3:8).

### FURTHER OBSERVATIONS

1. **The oath was frequently used by God's people in Old Testament times.**

Deut. 29:12, 14; Gen. 24:8; 26:3; Psa. 105:9; Judges 21:5; I Sam. 14:26; Neh. 5:12; 10:29. In the light of these scriptures we understand the reason for the carefulness and positiveness of Christ's teaching when He instituted this change in the Law. Matt. 5:33-37.

2. **It was never right to use the profane oath, it being forbidden in the Law.**

"Thou shalt not take the name of the Lord thy God in vain" (Ex. 20:7). It is important that we bear this in mind, as it throws light on the claim of some that Christ, in forbidding the oath, meant only the profane oath. Since that was as distinctly forbidden in the Old as it is in the New Testament, it follows that the only change which Christ taught was to discontinue the oath permitted under the Old Covenant, namely, the judicial oath.

3. **Things which may be right when there is no law against it, become wrong when there is a law against it.**

Example: There was no Old Testament law against the use of the oath other than the profane oath, and it was not wrong for God's people to use it *then*. But there is a New Testament law against it now, hence it is wrong to use it *now*. Some people have been taught to believe that our Saviour did not mean what He said when He commanded Christian people to "swear not at all," on the ground that God never changes. To this objection we reply in the language of George R. Brunk:

> "God is unchangeable in nature and attributes, but changes His law and attitude to meet the changed conditions in man. In Jer. 31:31 the prophet foretells a change, in Heb. 7:12 an apostle declares the necessity of it, and in the Sermon on the Mount the Saviour gives examples of it." (Bible Doctrine, P. 556.)

### 4. The affirmation has taken the place of the oath.

We have already called attention to the difference between the two. In the former dispensation the oath served its purpose, for that was a dispensation of LAW, when people were governed through fear, and it was but fitting that under this system of strict law and drastic penalties there should be something to curb the tendency of degenerate men to bear false witness. Now, however, under the reign of "GRACE and TRUTH," when Christian people are constrained by the love of God to obey the truth from inward principle, the oath is not needed for them. And even, in the light of existing circumstances in this age, it is questionable whether the oath has any practical value for even the non-Christian. As Adam Clarke says, "An oath will not bind a knave or a liar, and an honest man needs none."

### 5. The affirmation serves all the purposes of an oath before a court of justice.

For the honest Christian the declaration of intention to tell the truth should satisfy any court; for the hypocritical church member the clause, "under pains and penalty of perjury," has all the binding qualities of an oath. The free man in Christ Jesus needs no oath to bind him to the truth; the church member in bondage will not be set free by violating the confidence placed in him as a professed follower of the TRUTH.

### 6. A "Thus saith the Lord" should satisfy all Christian people.

There is a what and a why connected with every Bible doctrine. We may not always see the latter, even if we do see the former. Like Peter, who did not understand why the Lord wanted to wash his feet, we sometimes feel like saying, "Thou shalt never . . ." But that was no excuse for Peter, neither is it for us. It is enough for us to know what our Lord wants with us or of us, and we should be ready to obey, whether or not we understand why the command was given. When Christ says, "Swear not at all," and James later emphasizes the same truth, there should be no hesitation on our part to obey, even though there may be some things that do not seem clear. Besides, a willing obedience is the quickest way to an intelligent understanding. "Swear not at all" is one of the "all things whatsoever" (Matt. 28:19) which Christ taught His disciples to observe. Let all Christendom obey.

" 'The Lord do so to me, and more also,' is God's form of Old Testament oaths—a binding of judgment upon the soul. From this shackle the Lord frees us when He asks us to 'Swear not at all.' If free from condemnation, why should we invite the judgment by taking the oath?"— S. F. Coffman.

# CHAPTER IX

## SECRET SOCIETIES

Have no fellowship with the unfruitful works of darkness, but rather reprove them. For it is a shame even to speak of those things which are done of them in secret.—Ephesians 5:11, 12.

What should be the attitude of Christian people toward secret societies?

As we proceed with our discussions it will become more and more apparent that the proper answer to this question is the text that stands at the head of this chapter.

Secret societies may be divided into three classes: (1) the old line secret orders—such as Masons, Odd Fellows, etc.—with organized secretism as a prominent feature; (2) fraternal organizations—such as Modern Woodmen, Elks, Moose, etc.—which are largely social organizations with an insurance policy attached as a drawing feature; (3) labor unions—such as the A.F. of L., I.W.W., carpenters' unions, dairymen's associations, etc.—often organized for protection against corresponding organizations of capital.

As for purpose and character, these organizations range all the way from the higher grade which are almost free from objectionable features from the standpoint of organized secrecy, (as, for instance, some organizations which would come under Class 3 above) to the vilest organizations whose purpose is both murderous and revolutionary. To say that all these organizations belong to the same class and one as bad as the other would be about as nearly correct as to say that all churches belong to the same class and that they are about alike in goodness, faith, etc. Some societies are born of a desire for real uplift, while others are of vilest character. Some are of the class which many well-meaning people endorse; others, of the class which all of the better classes of people oppose.

Yet, as churches have one thing—religion, of some sort—in common, so all secret lodges and organizations have one thing—organized secrecy, aided by grips, passwords, signs, some form of ritual, the oath or kindred obligation—in common; and practically all of them are modeled, to a greater or less extent, after Masonry, the mother of modern secret societies.

But to return to our original question: What should be the attitude of Christian people toward secret societies? We do not hesitate to accept the text which stands at the head of his chapter as our answer.

## WHY OPPOSE SECRET SOCIETIES

### 1. Because of their organized secretism.

We understand that all classes of people in all walks of life have things which they hold confidential, things not for public scrutiny. But there is nothing in any well-regulated church, or family, or business, or social organization that needs to be bound down in a system of grips and signs and pass-words to which one must be sworn to eternal secrecy before being admitted to the organization. Organized secretism is entirely contrary to the spirit and letter of the Gospel, and furnishes too much of a harbor for all sorts of mischief and wickedness. "Let your light shine," is one of the prominent traits of the Christian Church. Its doors stand ajar, and a continual invitation is extended for people to come in, examine its tenets of faith, its rules and regulations, and it makes the acceptance of these the basis for membership. On the other hand, applicants for admission into the lodge are sworn to eternal secrecy before they are admitted. The essential difference between the Christian Church and the secret lodge is the difference between light and darkness. "In secret have I said nothing" (Jno. 18:20), should be the testimony of every child of God.

It has been said that Christ was an eminent Mason. This can hardly be, since Christ was crucified nearly thirteen centuries before Masonry was born. (See Encyclopedia Brittanica, Vol. XI, P. 78, Ed. of 1910.) But waiving aside this technicality, if He was a Mason, then Masonry must have changed in at least two particulars: (1) It could not have been a secret society, or Christ could not have testified, "In secret have I said nothing." (2) It could not have banned Him as the Son of God and only means of our salvation, as Masonry does today.

### 2. Because of the unequal yoke.

One of the clearest and most emphatic of all Bible teachings is that found in II Cor. 6:14-18. Let us quote a few verses:

> "Be ye not unequally yoked together with unbelievers; for what *fellowship* hath righteousness with unrighteousness? and what *communion* hath light with darkness? and what *concord* hath Christ with Belial? and *what part* hath he that believeth with an infidel?"

It is the boast of lodge members that they are more closely bound together in fellowship than are members of the same church. And when church members in the average lodge make such claims they boast of something which the Bible emphatically forbids them to do; namely, to be unequally yoked together with their unbelieving lodge brethren. As a rule all lodge members lose their testimony against throwing out false hopes to unbelieving lodge members, and when one of their unconverted members dies they seldom if ever hesitate to take a part in the ceremony that commits them to "the grand lodge above."

### 3. Because they furnish a harbor for criminals and crime.

Do all lodges harbor such criminals? No: we do not say that. But it is under cover of secrecy that all criminals hide, and all lodges refuse to remove such cover. Every secret organization lends at least indirect encouragement to such organizations as the Clannagaels, the Mollie Maguires, the Black Hand, the Mafia, and other orders whose avowed purpose it is to get rid of "undesirables"—in that while maintaining their principle of organized secrecy they give the more vicious organizations a talking point which leads many people to believe that they are not as bad as they are represented to be.

Neither must we shield the secret orders which have the approval of many of the better classes of people. Take, for example, this excerpt taken from the oath taken by the Royal Arch Mason: "Furthermore do I promise and swear that I will aid and assist a companion Royal Arch Mason, when engaged in any cause. . . .whether he be right or wrong." Commenting on Masonic obligations of like nature, Finney's book on "Freemasonary," P. 267, says: "Let it be distinctly pressed upon their conscience that all Masons above the first two degrees have solemnly sworn to conceal each other's crimes, murder and treason alone excepted, and all above the sixth degree have sworn to conceal each other's crimes without exception." It is notorious that some lodges in which the social feature is prominent are often raided by police because their drinking bouts and attendant excesses have become a community nuisance.

The best way to get rid of pests is to destroy their hiding places. May this not be a good way to rid the secret lodge of its pests? Lift the veil of secrecy, let in the light, and whatever pests are there will either reform or go elsewhere.

### 4. Because of their horrible oaths.

Christian people should stay outside the secret lodge because of the oaths administered there. Should any one have any doubts as to the nature of oaths administered in Masonic and other lodges patterned after Masonry, let him read the revelations found in such works as Bernard's "Lights on Masonry," Finney on "Masonry," Blanchard's "Modern Secret Societies," and other reliable works on such subjects. But to say nothing of the character of the oaths taken in any lodge, great or small, let it be remembered that the taking of any oath is contrary to the teaching of the Gospel. Read Matt. 5:33-37; Jas. 5:12. Turning to Old Testament testimony, let us quote a text which fits the lodge oath to perfection:

> Or if a soul swear, pronouncing with his lips to do evil, or to do good, whatsoever it be that a man shall pronounce with an oath, and it be hid from him; when he knoweth of it, then he shall be guilty in one of these. And it shall be, when he is guilty in one of these things, that he shall confess that he hath sinned in that thing.—Lev. 5:4, 5.

In other words, whoever swears that he will keep secret that which has not yet been revealed to him, is called upon to confess that he has sinned in that very thing. If this scripture were strictly complied with, then the lodges would have to change their rituals before they could take in another member.

Any oath is unscriptural. Many lodge oaths are not only unscriptural but shockingly immodest and profane, and, in some cases, treasonable to the government.

### 5. Because of their origin.

The oldest lodge now in existence in Christian lands is Masonry, said to have been born in a grog shop in London in 1713. But heathen lodges had existence long before that time, and it is a knowledge of their iniquities that doubtless inspired some of the scriptures testifying against their practices. And as Masonry is patterned largely after these heathen lodges, so the other modern lodges are patterned largely after Masonry. This accounts for the fact that many of the magic rites of heathen ceremonies are found in modern lodges; that the spade, the white apron, the ax, the "worshipful master," the death penalty for turning traitor to the lodge, and other relics of foolishness, superstition, idolatry, and wickedness are found in lodges of today. All that is religious in modern lodges (especially in lodges where the Bible is used as "furniture" and Christ has no recognition as the Son of God and the only means of man's salvation) is idolatrous rather than Christian.

### 6. Because of their false assurances of salvation.

The average lodge member denies that his lodge holds out any hope of salvation except through Christ. But the fact remains that such false hopes are fostered in lodges where the name of Jesus Christ as our Saviour is banned, and where the Bible is used as "furniture" in Christian countries, just as the Koran, by the same orders, is used as "furniture" in Mohammedan countries. When Masons or Odd Fellows or others of their imitators surround the grave of an unconverted fellow lodgeman and go through the ceremony of sending him to "the grand lodge above," they simply reflect these false hopes as found in their rituals. The present wave of modernism would have been impossible had not the lodge rituals and propaganda prepared the soil. Read Jno. 14:6; Acts 4:12; Gal. 1:8, 9; II Jno. 10: also Finney on "Freemasonry," Chapter XV.

Contrary to the general impression even of lodge members themselves, the lodge is a system of religious teaching wholly contradictory to Christianity. It teaches that the Bible is only an item of furniture; not the will of God, but a symbol of it: that it is not really binding on lodge members; that the sacred book of any other religion would answer the same purpose as it and not be disqualified by the membership. All men are the children of God whether they believe on Jesus Christ or not; heathen religions are just as good in God's sight as Christianity, for they are simply the worship of the Christian's God under different names. Good lodge men do not need Christ as a Saviour. It is even unlawful to pray in Christ's name in some lodges. The religion of the lodge is a universal religion, higher and better than Christianity, that includes Christianity and other religions as sects. Both secrecy and oath-taking are demanded, regardless of what the New Testament says about it. The one great end is to form a world brotherhood, uniting Christians with non-Christians of every sort, even including infidels, deists, agnostics, and atheists. All the lodges of the present are the direct descendants of the ancient heathen religions, and use the same teachings and symbolic methods as they.

Of all this we have positive and abundant proof in quotations from leading lodge authorities themselves, which we have printed in tract form, giving author, book, and page, and arranged in adjoining columns with quotations from the Bible to show the contradictions, And we challenge all Christendom even to try to disprove them.

Read them for yourself. Ten cents for the three tracts, "How the Lodge Contradicts Christianity," "Where the Lodge Comes From," and "Can an Adhering Lodge Member Be an Acceptable Christian?" —A. S. Macklin in March, 1927, "Christian Cynosure."

### 7. Because of their false claims to charity.

Notwithstanding the boast of secret societies of being better than churches as charitable institutions, the fact remains that they deny charity to those who most need it. Only those who are able to pay their dues are admitted and retained as members. To say nothing of the fact that it costs several times as much to maintain a lodge as is ever paid to needy members, the very people who most need relief because of their inability to pay are not even admitted into the lodge. If it is true that "charity never faileth" (I Cor. 13:8), then it is also true that what the lodges claim as their charity should be known by some other name.

### 8. Because of their influence on Home and Church.

The lodge educates men and women to spend in lodge or club room the time that ought to be spent at home with their families. Thus the home is neglected to the extent that lodge life is kept up. Not only so, but many homes are poorly provided for because the money needed to support the families is spent in keeping up the lodge dues. The decline of the American home is due largely through the influence of the lodge. When the lodge apprentice vows that "I will always hail, and ever conceal, and never reveal" the secrets of his lodge, binding himself under the severest penalties never to reveal any of these things to any one, he thereby promises to make of his fellow lodgemen closer confidantes than even his own wife. By what manner of logic can such a course be defended?

As for the Church, we have a similar vision. As a rule, men who are both lodge men and church men take more interest in their lodges than they do in their churches. There are just about enough exceptions to this to establish the rule. The money that is spent in support of the lodges is sorely needed in support of the Lord's cause. As lodge activities increase, charitable work through the churches diminishes. The unequal yoke with unbelievers in the lodge is a curse. Associations formed in the secret councils may be agreeable to the flesh, but they are very hard on religion. In holding out false hopes of salvation, lodges form a fruitful soil for unbelievers to propagate their skepticism. Any church that tolerates secretism among its members tolerates a curse that will sooner or later eat out its vitals. "Wherefore come out from among them, and be ye separate, saith the Lord, and touch not the unclean thing; and I will receive you" (II Cor. 6:17).

### 9. Because they are not necessary.

All the good found in any lodge may be found in any well-regulated church. God has made full provisions for supplying the needs of men through the home, the Church, and the civil government. Let all church people concentrate all their energies in making home and church life what it ought to be, and the result will be not only more godly homes and more vigorous Church life, but much of the attention that is now drawn to outside organizations and enterprises will be directed to the Church. The world, as well as the Church, would be better off without the lodge.

Concerning the superiority of Church over Lodge the "Christian Cynosure" has this to say:

> "Its fellowship is genuine. Its social atmosphere is wholesome in the extreme. It is bound up and centered in One whom even the lodges admit to be a great moral example. We claim more, as He Himself did. Without Him there is no true morality! Without Him fellowship is a hollow mockery! And in fellowship with Him, there are pleasure and joy in the extreme, which express themselves in a joyful, sweet, and uncompelled love to all men, in a harmonious plan of service, in social intercourse which edifies. What has the lodge to compare with this fellowship? Card parties? Dances?"

### 10. Because of their selfishness.

Self-interest is at the foundation of all these organizations. And whether you speak of old lines secret societies, of fraternal organizations, of labor unions, of capitalistic unions, of farmers' organizations, of school fraternities, of religious secret orders, or of any other organization founded more or less upon the principle of organized secretism, the disposition to work for self and to clash with conflicting interests becomes apparent sooner or later. All this is contrary to the spirit of the Gospel, which holds out the idea of doing good to others, of giving out rather than taking in. "It is more blessed to give than to receive." Strikes, lock-outs, violence, sedition, etc., etc., are but after results of what was earlier fostered in the secret place. Anything that would be disturbed by the light of publicity ought to have this light turned on.

### Why Make Lodges a Test of Membership

1. They are unscriptural, and to tolerate lodge members as church members means to encourage unscriptural organizations.

2. They are detrimental to the best interests of the home and Church, and it is suicidal for any church to tolerate or encourage enemy organizations.

3. History has proved that wherever a church tolerates membership in lodges, on the part of its members, it is only a question of time until that church loses its testimony against organized secretism. Ai can not be conquered so long as members with Babylonish garments are tolerated in God's army.

4. History has proved that when churches tolerate lodge-membership among them it is only a question of time until these churches themselves are lodge-controlled. "A little leaven leaveneth the whole lump."

5. Lodge members are a burden on any church that tolerates them. Even in churches that uphold the lodge it is hard to find an active church worker—and where lodge men are active church workers their activities are of a kind that is not conducive to spiritual life and growth.

6. No man can belong to a secret society without violating scriptures pertaining to oaths, the unequal yoke, hiding lights under a bushel, fellowshiping with unfruitful works of darkness, etc. Any church which carries a consistent testimony against the lodge stultifies itself when it tolerates or harbors members who habitually violate all these scripture teachings. Churches, like individuals, should give heed to the apostolic admonition, "Keep thyself pure."

# CHAPTER X

## LIFE INSURANCE

It is better to trust in the Lord than to put confidence in man.—
Psalm 118:8.

Two men, one a life insurance agent and the other a minister, met at a railway station. "May I ask what is your occupation?" said the agent to the minister. "I am a life insurance agent," was the minister's reply. "Glad to meet you, sir," was the quick rejoinder, "that is my business. What company do you represent?" "I represent the King's Great Insurance Company," was the minister's next response, "a company that has never been known to fail, that has never turned down an application because the applicant was too sickly or too poor to pay his dues, and whoever is insured in this company shall not lack any good thing."

The agent understood. He interpreted this reply as a challenge, and an interesting argument followed. The rest of the discussion centered around the question as to whether any one who has his life insured in the King's Great Company should have his life insured in any other company. It is this same question that we are to consider in this chapter.

### FUNDAMENTAL FACTS

#### 1. The Bible teaches us to put our trust in God.

His promise is, "I will never leave thee, nor forsake thee" (Heb. 13:5). David, a man of wide experience, testified, "I have been young, and now am old; yet have I not seen the righteous forsaken, nor his seed begging bread" (Psa. 37:25). God says, "Leave thy fatherless children, I will preserve them alive; and let thy widows trust in me" (Jer. 49:11). In Matt. 6:24-33 we are warned against anxious care for the things of this life and urged to seek first "the kingdom of God, and his righteousness," being assured that "all these things shall be added unto you." There is nothing that is more abundantly and emphatically taught in Scripture than that we should put our supreme trust and confidence in God, believe all His promises, being assured that He is abundantly able to care for His own.

2. **The Bible warns us against trusting men more than God.**

As the psalmist says, "It is better to trust in the Lord than to put confidence in man." Jeremiah voices the same thought when he says, "Cursed be the man that trusteth in man, and maketh flesh his arm, and whose heart departeth from the Lord" (Jer. 17:5). Is it a desire to get rich quick that causes men to turn aside from Gospel paths and seek wealth through methods that are the inventions of men? "He that hasteth to be rich hath an evil eye" (Prov. 28:22). Read also Matt. 6:24-34; Luke 12:16-20. In this connection it may be well to warn against those who "with feigned words make merchandise of you," claiming to be deeply interested in your welfare, while back of their efforts there is a liberal commission for themselves.

3. **The Bible teaches us to provide for our own.**

And the manner of thus providing for them, as well as our duty along this line, is set forth in such scriptures as Ex. 23:6; Mal. 3:5, 6; Eph. 4:28; I Thess. 4:11, 12; II Thess. 3:10; I Tim. 5:8. Relying upon God for our safe keeping and co-operation with Him by industry, economy, thrift, and a conservation of our resources, we need not hesitate to look to Him with full assurance that He will faithfully provide for His own.

4. **The Bible teaches us to care for dependent relatives.**

Read I Tim. 5:4. So long as needy ones can be taken care of by near relatives there should be no effort made to place them on the charities of the Church or of any other body. The spirit of providing for dependent loved ones was exemplified by Christ when on the cross He committed His mother to the care of the disciple whom He loved. and by John the beloved when he graciously accepted the charge. Jno. 19:25-27. It is the service of love which is not without its reward.

5. **God has a Church through which the needy ones without supporting relatives can be cared for.**

Read Acts 6:1-6; 11:27-30; Gal. 6:10. It should not be forgotten that our obligation to care for the needy does not stop with members in the Church but it extends to "all men" as far as we have "opportunity" to help them. "He that hath pity upon the poor lendeth unto the Lord" (Prov. 19:17).

Summing up these heaven-approved and directed means of helping the needy, we find the following order: (1) by individual toil and effort; (2) by near relatives; (3) by the Church. To this may be added the care given to the needy ones through the instrumentality of the State, which is also a means in the hands of God to provide safety and shelter for all who are under the jurisdiction and protection of the government. Some people would reverse this order—making life insurance the first means of support.

### Why Oppose Life Insurance

1. **It is unnecessary.**

God's provisions for the care of the needy ones— whether through near relatives, or the Church, or civil government—are ample, and no outside organization is needed, when churches and governments do their duty. Churches would be better off, spiritually and materially, if none of them had ever tolerated life insurance among their membership, and even the world would be better off if there were no life insurance companions to help absorb the surplus cash in the pockets of the masses of the people. But of this phase of the subject we shall speak later on.

2. **For the average person insured it is not a good business investment.**

We are not unmindful of the many claims made by life insurance companies, nor of the many plausible arguments put forth in their behalf which convince most people that life insurance is a wise, safe, and sound investment. But what we have to say in this paragraph is based on the official reports of life insurance companies themselves, and they are not supposed to publish official reports unfavorable to themselves. It has been our privilege to examine a number of official reports published by insurance departments in several different states. The first of these reports examined, giving official reports of the companies doing business in the state of Missouri in 1901, showed that out of every five dollars paid in premiums by the insured about two dollars got back to the policy-holders. The last one it was our privilege to examine, giving official reports of companies doing business in the same state in 1925, showed that a little over half of the money paid in premiums got back to the policy-holders. Or, to give exact totals in the latter case, the following were extracted from the mass of figures submitted:

| | |
|---|---|
| Total paid in premiums to insurance companies | $1,790,005,892.98 |
| Total paid to policy holders | 1,158,532,992.17 |
| Balance in favor of companies | $631,472,900.81 |

Or, reckoning from the basis of what life insurance costs the people of a single state for a year, let us note of the insurance department of the state of Pennsylvania one comparison of figures, revealed in the official report of the insurance department of the state of Pennsylvania for the year 1912:

| | |
|---|---|
| Amount paid in premiums to life insurance companies | $65,100,871.73 |
| Amount paid to policy-holders for losses | 23,364,321.53 |
| Loss to the people | $41,736,550.20 |

Since these figures are official, they speak for themselves. It will be noticed that the only comparison made was that of money paid in premiums as compared with the money returned in the form of paid up policies. The other sources of income for the companies are not mentioned. The difference is accounted for by two facts: (1) lapsed policies; (2) the special inducements held out to investors are but *seeming* advantages rather than *real* ones.

### 3.  It enriches the few at the expense of the many.

Possibly the reader may have noticed, in reading the preceding paragraph, that the percentage of money paid back to policy-holders was greater in the 1925 report than in the one for 1912. During the time which elapsed between the publication of the two reports there had been a shaking up in the form of investigations and revelations of questionable methods and extortions, and laws enacted which to a certain extent reformed the insurance business. But that the insurance companies did not suffer materially from these reforms is apparent from another comparison that we wish to make showing the net profits of life insurance companies doing business in Missouri in 1901 and those doing business in the same state in 1925:

> Total net profits in 1901, $293,367,799.52.
> Total net profits in 1925, $753,910,156.82.

This shows an increase of net gains, on the part of the companies during the twenty-four year period, of 253+ per cent. With admitted assets on the part of the companies named in the last report, totaling nearly ten billion dollars, with the annual transfer from the pockets of the masses into the coffers of life insurance companies approaching the billion mark and growing larger every year, and with these figures representing the net profits of only one branch of insurance, it requires no expert to foretell what will be the final result if this stream of wealth continues to flow from the masses to the classes year after year, generation after generation.

**4. It means an unnecessary burden in most homes where the burden of life insurance is borne.**

We make allowance for speculators who manage to carry an enormous policy for a few years and leave a princely fortune to their families or others at their death, for men or women who happen to die early and thus beat the company at the game, and for homes of wealth where the income is great enough to cover both insurance premiums and living expenses. But after you make all these allowances you still find by far the greater number of those carrying life insurance belonging to the struggling masses for whom life means a continual struggle to keep even. For these it means an added burden to load up an annual or semiannual premium to the other demands made upon their income, and in many homes it means a denial of the commonest necessities of life that these premiums may be paid and the family kept from losing all that was put in. For many others it means also that the burden becomes too great, the policies are allowed to or compelled to lapse and the hard-earned payments for years are gone. It is from these lapsed policies that the companies reap a rich harvest, so that both companies and favored policyholders are enriched at the expense of the struggling and poverty-stricken masses, many of whom had been talked into taking out policies against their better judgment. Add to this the fact that often the one insured is the last one of the family to die, so that the family gets absolutely no benefit from its long years of sacrifice, and you have an added reason why people of ordinary means should avoid life insurance. As for those who are able to accumulate wealth while carrying the burden of insurance, it simply shows that they did not need the "protection." Life insurance is an unnecessary burden upon most of those it is supposed to help.

5. **Assuming to give relief to the needy, it debars the very people who most need relief.**

Here is where insurance companies make their strongest pleas; but a little investigation reveals the fact that their claims are faulty.

a. They collect huge profits from the people whom they profess to benefit.

b. Only about half the money paid in gets back to the policy-holders.

c. People who are too poor to pay their dues, or too sickly to give promise of long life, can not get in.

d. People who can not keep up the payment of premiums are dropped and their policies are canceled.

6. **It fosters covetousness by appealing to unworthy motives in acquiring wealth.**

Let it be understood that the chief appeal is to selfishness, notwithstanding the fact that ado is made of the "poor widow and children" in case of an early death on the part of the husband and father. The chief thing looked at is the money, not the question of how it is acquired. The question of acquiring means by rightful methods is overshadowed by the thought of the necessity of having the money when you need it. The idea of "man liveth not by bread alone" is ignored and "provide not for his own" is interpreted wholly from the standpoint of dollars and cents. The professed and confessed gambler produces the same arguments why he is the rightful owner of the money he won at the gaming table as does the man who draws the life policy on the death of a friend. "He that hasteth to be rich hath an evil eye." "Wealth gotten by vanity shall be diminished" (Prov. 13:11). Then too, it fosters the spirit of extravagance and improvidence. As a certain man expressed it: "I carry a heavy life insurance policy, also an accident policy, and belong to several beneficiary associations, so that I have need of nothing. It would be foolish for me not to spend money as fast as I get it." It is the same spirit as that expressed by the man who said:

"Soul, thou hast much goods laid up for many years; take thine ease, eat, drink, and be merry" (Luke 12:19). The higher appeals of the Gospel standard—honest toil, frugality, thrift, trust in the living God, making the care for the soul paramount over the care for the body, personal obligations on the part of relatives and Church—are not the most prominent things urged by the average person boosting life insurance.

### 7. It is unscriptural.

Finally, we object to life insurance because it is unscriptural. It is needless to enter into an extended discussion on this point, for the Scripture testimony thus far submitted sufficiently proves the point. While the many promises of God to care for His own are sure and steadfast, it is the business of life insurance companies to make people dissatisfied and to feel insecure unless they have taken out a policy on their lives. While God has made abundant provisions for the care of the needy through near relatives and Church and State, this order is reversed by placing life insurance at the head of the list, thus proposing an unscriptural way of caring for our own. While the care of our own, by Bible standards, means first of all a care for their spiritual welfare, that proposed by life insurance is confined to material things altogether. Even men who endorse life insurance admit that God's plan is a much better one. As one such man expressed himself: "Neither lodge nor life insurance admits the man who is too sickly to live long or too poor to pay his dues, but the Church has a standing invitation for such men to come in." With this we are reminded of what Paul says: "Charity never faileth." Follow the Bible way of caring for the needy, trust in God to be faithful to His promises to care for His own, and you have reasons to rejoice because you have found something more substantial than anything this world has to offer. Life insurance falls short of the Gospel standard when viewed from the standpoint of laying up treasures, of charity, of sound investment, of trust in the living God, of caring for our own. Let us therefore make sure of our membership in the King's Great Company, where our gain does not mean loss to our fellow men, and where every policy-holder is heir to an everlasting crown.

For a further discussion of the subject of life insurance we submit for your consideration

## A FEW EXCERPTS

from the writings of D. D. Miller, as found in *"Bible Doctrine,"* Part VI, Chap. 9:

**The Main Point Overlooked.**—Life insurance strengthens the sordid tendency to accept the view that a life and its influence is measured by the amount of money it may possess or acquire, which is in opposition to our Saviour's question, "What shall it profit a man, if he shall gain the whole world, and lose his own soul?"

**The Social Side.**—A gifted agent called on a good-hearted, easy-going farmer. After telling of a number of cases where men had died and their widows and children were well cared for, then quoting I Tim. 5:8, then telling about Joseph being at the head of a life insurance company in Egypt, the farmer was almost persuaded to invest. As it happened, however, he still had the presence of mind to remember the good judgment of his wife, and suggested that he would go to the house and get the approval of his good companion who would be so well cared for after his death. After explaining carefully to Mary that after his death she should receive the nice sum of $10,000 she at once said, "Do as you think best, John; the fact is that at that rate you are worth more dead than alive." We need not tell you that John did not insure. Many lives have been shortened because such thoughts have been harbored.

**A Few Problems.**—1. A man had his life insured in several companies, amounting to $50,000. On an average it cost him $18 per thousand annually—$900 a year. If he died, this $900 a year would be saved. Besides, the family would have $50,000 to put on interest, which would readily yield (above taxes) three per cent, or $1500 a year—$900 plus $1500 equals $2400. This made him an expensive article. Every year that he lived the family virtually gave up $2400. He no doubt felt the struggle it would take to keep up his yearly dues. His life ended mysteriously. Find cause of his death.

2. We know a man in the thirties who has paid premiums for some years. It has cost him his earnings and several thousands which he inherited from his father, and, worst of all, his religion. He says, "I dare not quit now, or it will all be lost." They have no home, are paying rent, working hard, family affections none too good, religion gone, wife and children may die before he does—unhappy life—all for the possibility

of some one, at some time, getting a large sum of money. Does it pay?

**The Investment.**—A father said to his son, "Do not allow the agents to deceive you. Better not insure." "But father," replied the son, "why do you keep it up, if it is not a good thing?" "I have paid in too much to lose it," was the father's response.

That is the nature of gambling every time. If a man is caught in a loss, he wants to try it again, and next time he may win.

A widow in our town who was in meager circumstances wanted fuel and had no money. She asked the writer for the wood and when it was delivered to her she said, "I would like to pay you, but I can not now. I am expecting insurance money, but it has not come yet. My husband was a member of the lodge and carried insurance. Before he died he had paid in over $1100. He has been dead more than a year, and I still have no money. They claim there is a flaw somewhere about his keeping up his dues. Oh, if I just had the money we paid in; I could get along quite well!"

About a month later our town paper published in bold type: *"Charity to the Widow! Received from such a source $1000!* giving a glowing write-up of the much good done by those organizations. Now, kind reader, was that charity? or even a good business? —Paid in premiums, $1100; received from insurance company, $1000; interest on investment gone.

These illustrations are all actual occurrences that have come under our own personal observation.

**Some Shortcomings.**—It is true that there are many life insurance companies, and that all have not exactly the same rules. It is also true that not one of them is founded upon strictly Gospel principles.

1. **They hold out great inducements to get fortunes with but little investments,** thus tempting the covetous ones to invest a little with hopes of winning much. The wily agent has on his tongue's end a long list of cases where for the payment of a few premiums large sums were paid over to the widow or other policy holders. Remember, however, that no company pays out more than it gets in. Whenever any one gets more than he paid in, then it is a sure thing that others get less than they paid in. Your gain (if you are the winner) is made up at the expense of your disappointed fellow men, usually poor people who are unable to keep up their premiums. This certainly is a violation of the Golden Rule. It is nothing less than a lottery or game of gambling, with life and death as the main elements in the game.

2. **Life Insurance is even more deceptive than a lottery.** In a lottery it is understood that only a few will be winners, while in life insurance the idea is held out that you can not help but be a winner. The fact is, however, that the majority are losers while only the few are enriched. It is safe to assert that the business would soon come to an end if insurance agents made it a rule to guarantee to refund, dollar for dollar, all the money paid in. It is also safe to assert that if all the money paid on lapsed policies were refunded dollar for dollar, that no life insurance company in existence could long survive at the present

methods of doing business. If then the vast majority have taken out policies with the motive of getting something without paying a just equivalent, or to be enriched by the losses of their disappointed fellow men, then they are guilty whether they gain or lose. Their motives will not bear the test of honesty.

**Encourages Unbelief.**—Life insurance encourages unbelief, the besetting sin of mankind. The all-wise God has made provisions for the caring of His own in all ages, for time and for eternity. "Leave thy fatherless children, I will preserve them alive; and let thy widows trust in me" (Jer. 49:11). "I have been young, and now am old; yet have I not seen the righteous forsaken, nor his seed begging bread" (Psa. 37:25). "Be content with such things as ye have: for he hath said, I will never leave thee, nor forsake thee" (Heb. 13:5). "As we have therefore opportunity, let us do good unto all men, especially unto them who are of the household of faith" (Gal. 6:10). "It is better to trust in the Lord than to put confidence in man" Psa. 118:8).

In the face of all these plain Scripture teachings, it is the business of life insurance companies to make people disbelieve these promises. They say in derision: "We know how God cares for them. Look at the poorhouses and orphanages, and you have an example of how He cares;" thus virtually making God out a liar (I John 1:10) and encouraging others to disbelieve God's Word.

**Concluding Thought.**—Consider all these points in the light of God's Word. It is evident that it is wrong to patronize this popular evil. It is therefore evidently right that it be made a test of Church fellowship.

### A FEW QUESTIONS

1. **Is it not about time that we make a restudy of the question of life insurance and consider it in the light of what it is since it has been reformed by law and other influences?**

Truth will never suffer from a fair and thorough investigation of facts. But practically all the points herein submitted for consideration refer to life insurance as it is today, not as it was a half century ago.

2. **If life insurance is wrong, what about property insurance?**

The two have many points in common, but on one point they differ widely. It is right to deal in property, it is not right to traffic in human life. Property insurance makes merchandise of property; life insurance makes merchandise of human life.

3. **Since there are a number of things which are tolerated by churches opposed to life insurance which can hardly be distinguished from it—such as Workmen's Compensation, automobile insurance, etc.—had we not better drop our opposition to life insurance?**

No; not unless it is proved that life insurance is right. Let each of these be considered upon their individual merits. If life insurance is wrong, and we are inconsistent in tolerating things that are about like it, we had better make a restudy of these other things to determine what should be our attitude toward them. Our attitude toward these things, like our attitude toward life insurance, should be determined by what we find in the light of Scripture.

4. **What about fraternal orders, that conduct their business on the assessment plan?**

Their own history furnishes the answer. They flourish for awhile, then slow up, then waver, then go out of business. How many of these fraternal orders that flourished a generation ago are still in business? Let us quote a few illustrations from a pointed booklet on Life Insurance by A. Sims:

> J. W. Caldwell, Chicago, Ill.; "I am now 56 years old, and in very good health. I have outlived seven companies in which I have been insured, and which have since failed."
> Judge E. B. Buck, Winfield, Kans.: "Fraternal life insurance as an economic proposition has no foundation. As a financial enterprise it is untenable. Without a constant supply of new blood, the only way to get even is to die early."

5. **Is it an assured fact that since insurance companies make such great gains annually, that investment in them is absolutely safe?**

One would think so, especially in view of the fact that the investor is to some extent protected by law. But not to raise the question of possible fraud, where would the companies get their money to pay all the claims in case a number of general calamities like war, pestilence, great earthquakes, and storms, like the ones that visit the Gulf regions occasionally, would come in great numbers at or nearly at the same time?

6. Is not life insurance a blessing in that it enables men to borrow money, with a life policy as collateral, when otherwise they could not borrow?

Call it a blessing if you like, but also bear this in mind: To borrow money under such circumstances would mean a double burden: (1) premiums on your insurance policy, (2) interest on your money. Better take your inability to borrow money without this double tribute as a warning, and begin a policy of retrenchment and economy.

7. What is the difference between investing in life insurance and in a savings bank?

Life insurance is a chance to make or lose, depending upon how long you live and whether you will be able to keep up your premiums or not; in a savings bank you may expect to draw out what you pay in, with reasonable interest, no more, no less. In the first, you must keep up your regular payments or lose what you have already put in; in the second, your money is safe even if stringent times compel you to miss some payments. In the first, the company transacts your business for you; in the second you conduct your own business, thus adding to your business acumen.

# CHAPTER XI

## LOVE

If ye love me, keep my commandments.—John 14:15.

In a subject so vast as the one now before us, it will be impossible to do it justice in the limited space allotted to it; but if, by the grace of God, something will be said that will lead some reader to a deeper, fuller love of Him from whom all blessings flow, we will have reasons to praise the Lord.

We think of love as being *natural* (on the part of both converted and unconverted people), *spiritual* (love between God and His people), *connubial, parental, or filial* (pertaining to family life.) A number of other uses and applications of the affections which God has placed within His creatures could be given. The love which absorbs our attention in this chapter is the love of God for His people, which is reciprocated by all who have entered into covenant relationship with Him. The

### ORIGIN OF LOVE

in the lives of God's creatures is explained in the brief statement, "Love is of God" (I Jno. 4:7). And we get further light on this thought when we remember that "God is love" (I Jno. 4:16). It is but natural for people whose "life is hid with Christ in God" to have their hearts filled to overflowing by the love of God which is shed abroad in their hearts by the Holy Ghost. Rom. 5:5. Hence the testimony, "We love him, because he first loved us."

### MANIFESTATIONS OF GOD'S LOVE

**1. In the giving of His Son.**

"God commendeth his love toward us, in that, while we were yet sinners, Christ died for us" (Rom. 5:8). The

18

same thought is given in Jno. 3:16. The surest evidence of love is the spirit of sacrifice. And when our love is perfect and complete, as God's love is toward us, our life is not withheld from the sacrifice.

### 2. In His "longsuffering to us-ward" (II Pet. 3:9).

Peter reminds us that it is not slackness but longsuffering toward us that prompts the Lord to delay His coming, "not willing that any should perish, but that all should come to repentance." When we think of the longsuffering of God—how much and how long He has borne with our infirmities and our stubborn natures, and how many things He has done for us although we were not worthy of the least of His blessings and did not merit a single one of them—it makes us feel that in Him we have a perfect illustration of what Paul meant when he said, "Charity suffereth long, and is kind" (I Cor. 13:4).

### 3. In what He does for His enemies.

It was not for friends that God made His great sacrifices, for "all we like sheep have gone astray" (Isa. 53:6). It was while we were enemies to God that He reconciled us to Himself by the giving of His Son. Rom. 5:10. Not what one does for his friends, but what he does for his enemies, is the true test of his love. Read Matt. 5:38-48.

### 4. In His bountiful provisions for our happiness and well-being.

God was not satisfied by simply making it possible for us to be saved. Even that was more than we deserved, but He did much more. His attitude is not, "Now I have done my part: if you die and go to hell it is your own fault, not mine." We sometimes hear *men* say something like that, but God never. All that He has ever done for us came from a heart overflowing with love. He redeemed us from sin and death and hell, sacrificing His only begotten Son to accomplish that end. Heaven and earth were created for our happiness and well-being as well as for

His glory. He gave us the Gospel, sealed it with the blood of His Son, and sent us the Holy Comforter to guide us into all truth. He provided for us the Christian Church, and commissioned us to bring the Gospel to all people in all nations, that all men might know of His blessed salvation. On every hand we have evidences of His bountiful love for His creatures.

### How Manifest Our Love to God

#### 1. By an obedient life.

Christ sounded the keynote when He said, "If ye love me, keep my commandments." Again, He puts the same truth in different form when He says, "Ye are my friends, if ye do whatsoever I command you" (Jno. 15:14). Again, in the same discourse: "He that hath my commandments, and keepeth them, he it is that loveth me" (14:21). In v. 23 He says, "If a man love me, he will keep my words." Love and obedience are inseparable. You never saw a man whose love for God was greater than his love for the world but that he made it an invariable practice to "obey God rather than men."

#### 2. By love of the brethren.

"If a man say, I love God, and hateth his brother, he is a liar: for he that loveth not his brother whom he hath seen, how can he love God whom he hath not seen? And this commandment have we from him, That he who loveth God love his brother also" (I Jno. 4:20, 21). With this agrees the teaching of Christ in Matt. 22:33-40, where He declared the greatest commandment to be that of supreme love to God, adding that the second is like unto it; namely, loving our neighbor as ourselves.

#### 3. By love for our enemies.

Our most direct scripture on this point is that of Matt. 5:38-48. It is the rock upon which the Bible doctrine of nonresistance is founded. Our real test of love is not that of returning love for those who love us, but in loving those who evilly entreat us and persecute us.

Herein is one important difference between saint and sinner. After Christ taught us a love which extends to enemies as well as friends, He added, "Be ye therefore perfect, even as your Father which is in heaven is perfect" (Matt. 5:48).

It is not remarkable that at times we find among the enemies of God an attachment to friends as strong as that which exists among the people of God. But how about their love for their enemies? And how about *our* love for our enemies? Do we show our love for them by returning good for evil? Are we free from malice and envy? from a desire for revenge? from a desire for "getting even" with enemies? This is the real test—a test which God stood when He sent His Son to redeem His enemies; a test which Christ stood when He laid down His life for His enemies; a test which God wishes us to stand when we are tempted to seek revenge for any cause. "Be ye therefore perfect (in love) even as your Father which is in heaven is perfect."

### 4. By a faithful Christian service.

This point was really covered in the paragraph on obedience. No one can be obedient to God without rendering loyal, faithful service. Rom. 6:16. But the added thought that we wish to present at this time is that of *willing* service. Children who love their parents render faithful obedience, not because they must but because they are by love constrained to do so. As children of the heavenly Father, we are not slaves but freemen. As such "the love of Christ constraineth us" (II Cor. 5:14) to render faithful, obedient, willing service. Wherever we find willing servants of God we know that we see people that love Him. Law-Christians serve God because they *must;* love-Christians, because they *want to.* The first class serves on the first mile stretch, the second class is invariably found on the second mile.

## LOVE IN ACTION

We turn to the thirteenth chapter of First Corinthians for our text. It is a practical exposition of love in action. As a description of what love actually does, we know of nothing that equals this divinely inspired word picture of "the greatest thing in the world." After pointing out that all human attainments are in vain unless actuated by real charity, Paul goes on to say:

> "Charity suffereth long, and is kind;
> "Charity envieth not;
> "Charity vaunteth not itself, is not puffed up, doth not behave itself unseemly, seeketh not her own, is not easily provoked, thinketh no evil; rejoiceth not in iniquity, but rejoiceth in the truth; beareth all things, believeth all things, hopeth all things, endureth all things.
> "Charity never faileth."

Comment is unnecessary. Apply this to practical, daily life; to home life, to social life, to business life, to religious life; make it your daily prayer that the love of God may fill your soul so completely, may pervade your whole being and prompt your every action, that this kind of a feeling may spring from the innermost depths of the soul rather than from the sentimental side of life, and the love of God will be in you a fact and not a theory.

## THE WONDERS OF LOVE

### 1. Manifested in the grace of God.

This is the first and greatest of all wonders connected with this wonderful subject. As John expresses it, "Behold, what manner of love the Father hath bestowed upon us, that we should be called the sons of God" (I Jno. 3:1). David must have had similar feelings when he exclaimed, "When I consider thy heavens, the work of thy fingers, the moon and the stars, which thou hast ordained; what is man that thou art mindful of him" (Psa. 8:3, 4)? In other words, why should the great and mighty God, who at His will can create unnumbered millions of heavenly beings to bless and to praise His name, whose throne is in the heavens while the earth is His footstool, whose greatness and glory are far beyond the comprehension of the most favored of all His creatures, pay any attention to any creature so weak and vile and unworthy as man—to say nothing of adopting us into His glorious family and making us His sons and daughters? He loves us—that tells the story.

### 2. Manifested in the power of God.

We think of the majesty and power of God as we behold His strength displayed in the earthquake, the tornado, and other manifestations of His power on earth; we remember that by word of His mouth the heavens and the earth sprang into existence, that in the days of Noah the whole earth was covered with a flood and wicked man was wiped into oblivion, that at the giving of the law on Mt. Sinai there were demonstrations of His power in the wind and earthquake and fire and smoke and a terrible noise; but the greatest of all manifestations of His power was at Calvary where, through the wonders of His love, the captive heart was set free and that because of this wonderful sacrifice of love unnumbered millions of souls will bless His holy name in the ceaseless ages of eternity. The ransomed hosts in eternity will not be there through any physical demonstrations of physical power but alone through the wonderful, matchless, marvelous power of His grace. As "lambs in the midst of wolves" the defenseless disciples went out on a mission of love, and overcame. In love there is a power which physical force can never equal. Do we grasp it? Is this power used in our dealings with fellow men? May our daily prayer be, Lord, give us more of Thy love.

### 3. "The greatest thing in the world."

Henry Drummond may have been the first to use this expression, but the thought was in the sacred Word many centuries before Drummond was born. We understand, of course, that it is divine love, not human love, which merits this great distinction. The Bible, in a number of places, compares love with other admirable traits of char-

acter, and invariably places love above them all. **Take,**
for instance, "the love chapter," I Cor. 13. After showing
how utterly valueless all human greatness is without the
love of God in the soul, and after giving a vivid word picture of what love is and does, Paul reaches the climax in
the last verse, saying:

> "And now abideth faith, hope, charity, these three; but the
> greatest of these is charity."

Again, we take the remarkable comparison found in the
third chapter of Colossians. After telling us what to lay
off, Paul enumerates a number of excellent things that we
should "put on." He reaches the climax in verse 14, saying:

> "But above all these things put on charity, which is the
> bond of perfectness."

If in this life we have so many evidences of the wonders and greatness of love, what must be our observations
and experiences along this line in the glorious world of
love beyond!

### 4. Casting out fear.

Another of the wonders of love is that it casts out all
fear. I Jno. 4:18. There are two classes of people who
can face death without a tremor: (1) those who are of
reprobate mind and are therefore "past feeling" (Eph. 4:
19); (2) those who are at peace with God and face the
realities of the world to come in the full assurance of hope
and love. Rom. 8:31-39. They whose affections are set
on things above live in such close fellowship with God that
they have nothing to fear. "There is no fear in love; but
perfect love casteth out fear."

# CHAPTER XII

## PURITY

Keep thyself pure.—I Timothy 5:22.

For an example of perfect purity, look to our Lord Jesus Christ.

But none of us need ever expect to attain the standard of purity held forth in the Bible by striving in our own strength and effort to be like Christ. The law was perfect, pure, holy (Rom. 7:12), yet no one ever attained it in perfection. Christ, tempted in all points like as we are, was "yet without sin" (Heb. 4:15); yet none of us, while wearing our mortal robes, need ever expect to attain the same end, for perfection is never reached through human effort or human goodness. Paul pointed out the weakness of the Pharisees when he said, "They being ignorant of God's righteousness, and going about to establish their own righteousness, have not submitted themselves unto the righteousness of God" (Rom. 10:3). If any of us have thought in our own goodness and by our own effort to attain to the purity, holiness, and perfection of God, we had better cease trying and ask God to try in our stead. This is the way it is accomplished:

> Who gave himself for us, that he might redeem us from all iniquity, and purify unto himself a peculiar people, zealous of good works.—Tit. 2:14.
> The blood of Jesus Christ . . . cleanseth us from all sin.— I John 1:7.

Thus, submitting ourselves to God, allowing Him to perform the miracle of grace in our hearts, walking in the light "as he is in the light," with our lives "hid with Christ in God," it is possible for the weakest of mortals to walk in paths of "righteousness and true holiness." This is heaven-secured purity.

## What It Includes

The admonition of Paul to Timothy, as quoted at the head of this chapter, should be taken seriously by all people. Applying it to our own lives, this Christian grace and attainment means:

### 1. Purity in thought and purpose.

We often think of the old-fashioned hour glass. With the upper chamber filled with sand, it is only a question of time when this sand is found in the lower chamber. So with mind and character. Keep the upper chamber (mind) filled with pure thoughts, and it is only a question of time when this purity is reflected in the character. Keep your mind stored with thoughts that are pure, holy, kind, righteous, chaste, worshipful, and these traits of character will shine out in your daily lives. On the other hand, let your minds harbor evil thoughts, impure motives, and it will not be long until tongues and lives will betray the filth that is harbored in the mind. Therefore, keep thy mind pure.

### 2. Purity in Speech.

"Let your speech be alway with grace, seasoned with salt" (Col. 4:6). "Let the word of Christ dwell in you richly in all wisdom; teaching and admonishing one another in psalms and hymns and spiritual songs, singing with grace in your hearts to the Lord" (Col. 3:16). "Neither filthiness, nor foolish talking, nor jesting, which are not convenient: but rather giving of thanks" (Eph. 5:4). Here is a catalogue of things which do not belong to pure speech: idle words, by-words, slang phrases, vulgar language, profanity, gossiping, rehashing stale yarns, etc. Two things are essential to success in eliminating them from your speech; (1) a pure heart; "for out of the abundance of the heart the mouth speaketh;" (2) a persistent, prayerful, persevering effort to overcome former habits. Keep thy speech pure.

### 3. Purity in heart.

"Set your affection on things above, not on things on the earth" (Col. 3:2). Especially where people before their conversion were given over to vile affections do they need to come before the Throne continually for grace to overcome. To every child of God there comes the admonition, "Be thou an example of the believers . . . in purity" (I Tim. 4:12). Keep your affections centered upon things that are pure and true and righteous and holy, and your mind, tongue, hands, and feet will respond. Read Phil. 4:8. Keep thy affections pure.

### 4. Purity in companionship.

This means two things: (1) that you, personally, live a pure life, worthy of the associations of the best of people; (2) that you choose your companions from among those who are pure in thought and mind, holding aloof from an attitude of social equality with those whose characters are tainted with social impurity. Beware of questionable entanglements. "Evil communications corrupt good manners." You are safe in applying this same rule in your companionship with books and other literature. You can not afford to mix in ungodly associations, for stronger people than yourself have succumbed to such influences.

### 5. Purity in social relations.

The Bible nowhere refers to social impurity except to condemn it. Where chastity gives way to impurity, character is ruined—and this is true of men as well as of women, for there is no "double standard" in morals, in the sight of God.

Speaking of social impurity, it is in order to say that many of the things, in which some people see nothing wrong, are the very things that start people down hill morally. Such things as practicing undue familiarity with the persons of those of the opposite sex, courtship at late hours with curtains drawn and lights dimmed, unchaste

conversation and telling vile "jokes," attendance at movies
and theatres and circuses and other places where vulgar
wit and suggestive thrusts are considered "smart"—these
are things which excite the passions and are responsible
for the ruin of thousands who were once pure-minded
young people. As the young man who never takes the
first drink will never become a drunkard, so the young
man or young woman who never allows himself or herself to be caught in these first traps on the downward road
to the social evil will never become a libertine. As a
Christian, you can not afford to act anything else but the
part of a Christian man or woman, boy or girl, no matter
who is around or what may be the nature of the temptation. Keep thyself pure in the social realm.

### 6. Purity in conscience.

This is the monitor which God has placed within you
to sound a note of warning in every time of danger. Be
sure you keep this conscience pure and tender. Keep it
fed up on the pure Word of God, and never fail to heed
its warnings. So long as your conscience is on the altar
of the Lord, and implicitly obeyed, you are safe. Therefore keep thy conscience pure. Read Acts 24:16; I Tim.
1:5; Heb. 9:9, 14; I Pet. 3:16, 21.

### 7. Purity in righteousness.

Righteousness, like every other trait of Christian character, should be maintained in its purity. This includes
an upright life, honest dealings with fellow men, the righteousness of Jesus Christ shining out in every walk in life.
When tempted to compromise for the sake of gain in
wealth, ease, and popularity, remember the admonition,
"Seek ye *first* the kingdom of God, and *his righteousness*"
(Matt. 6:33). A straightforward course in business, social,
home, and religious life will keep you in line with the Gospel standard of righteousness. Keep thyself pure in righteousness.

### 8. Purity in religion.

We have reserved this for last because it is the foundation, the climax, of all purity. We have a perfect definition for pure religion in Jas. 1:27, discussed at length in another chapter. Never be satisfied with anything short of the pure, unadulterated religion of Jesus Christ, unspotted by any of the sins of this world. Keep thyself pure in religion.

### How Promote the Cause of Purity

### 1. By setting proper examples.

Show by your personal daily life what it means to be pure in thought, in speech, in heart, in associations, in social relations, in righteousness, in integrity, in home life, in religion, and your Bible will mean more to your neighbors than if you lived a careless life. Read Matt. 5:14-16; I Tim. 4:12; I Pet. 2:11, 12.

### 2. By carrying a consistent testimony.

When a pure life flows from a pure heart, the testimony for purity and against impurity will mean all the more to your neighbors. We should not hesitate to rebuke unbecoming speech or conduct; to back up a pure life with appropriate testimony whenever and wherever there are evidences of impurity around. We have missed many an opportunity to advance the cause of Christ because we were not ready enough and decided enough with wholesome testimony. Gal. 6:10.

### 3. By maintaining the Gospel standard of purity in the social circle.

The Christian standard is the only standard which should be maintained in the society of Christian young people. This is a problem which should receive the prayerful attention of parents, of teachers, and of pure-minded leaders among our young people. Let there not only be opportunities for young people to mingle together in a *social* way, but also let proper safeguards be thrown around them whereby they may mingle together in a *Christian* way. Maintain the standard of purity in the social circle, and two-thirds of your problem is solved.

**4. By keeping homes supplied with proper literature.**

Since "reading maketh a full man," it is important that the mind be kept filled with things that are conducive to purity, righteousness, and true holiness. Why should Christian people be any the less interested in keeping the rising generation supplied with literature that helps to build up stable Christian character than other people are to supply the world with other kinds of literature. Where lips, lives, associations, and literature all tell the story of purity, and the rising generation is properly safeguarded against the ravages of immorality, there can be but one result. I Tim. 4:13.

**5. By keeping the community as clear as possible of loafing places.**

As a rule, a community loafing place is a pesthole. It is there that men and boys (sometimes women and girls) of reprobate minds gather together, rehashing impure stories, raking up neighborhood scandals, gloating over unfortunate women's shame, keeping the air filled with a mixture of smut, profanity, and nicotine. It is there that many young people get their first poisonous doses of impurity. The almost universal custom of running to town, or to some community loafing place, on Saturday nights, and the swimming pools and gaming places and other similar places on Sunday afternoons, are fruitful sources of vice and other forms of impurity. The fewer the number of these pestholes in your community the better. See Psalm 1.

**6. By keeping the minds of people occupied in something upbuilding.**

This is a direct means of promoting purity. It is in the idle brain, next to the sin-infected brain, that the devil reaps his richest harvests. Build up a strong character, keep it pure in the best and highest sense of the word, and you have not only a most powerful antidote to impurity but a tower of strength that will exert a powerful influence in promoting purity among others. Children and young people should be taught to work, to read the Bible and other literature that leaves the right kind of impressions on the mind, to turn to the Lord early in life, and to serve Him diligently and faithfully. In connection with their social affairs let their minds be habitually occupied in such activities as Bble study, mission study, teacher training, the singing of "psalms and hymns and spiritual songs," and other things that contribute something useful and noble to mind and character.

"Finally, brethren, whatsoever things are true, whatsoever things are honest, whatsoever things are just, whatsoever things are pure, whatsoever things are lovely, whatsoever things are of good report; if there be any virtue, and if there be any praise, think on these things."

# CHAPTER XIII

## HUMILITY

Before honour is humility.—Proverbs 15:33.

Humility has been described as "a temper of the soul that prepares us for faith." It is generally regarded as a jewel, beautiful as a sentiment but scorned as an actual possession, a jewel which too few people are willing to wear. In this respect it is like Christ, who exemplified it in perfection—people are fond of exalting its virtues, but they prefer to crucify it rather than submit to it. It may be recognized in two ways: (1) by the lives of people who are really humble in mind and spirit; (2) by its being the exact opposite of pride, so common to most people.

### PRIDE AND HUMILITY

are compared in Scripture so frequently that we feel constrained to believe that it will help us appreciate our subject by noticing a few of their contrasts:

1. God resisteth the proud, but
   giveth grace unto the humble.—Jas. 4:6.
2. Whosoever exalteth himself shall be abased; and
   he that humbleth himself shall be exalted.—Luke 14:11.
3. A man's pride shall bring him low: but
   honour shall uphold the humble in spirit.—Prov. 29:23.
4. Better it is to be of an humble spirit with the lowly,
   than to divide the spoil with the strong.—Prov. 16:19.
5. The Lord will destroy the house of the proud.—Prov. 15:25.
   The meek shall inherit the earth; and . . . the abundance of
   peace.—Psa. 37:11.
6. Pride goeth before destruction, and an haughty spirit before
   a fall.—Prov. 16:18.
   Whosoever therefore shall humble himself . . . the same is
   greatest in the kingdom of heaven.—Matt. 18:4.
7. And thou . . . which art exalted unto heaven, shalt be brought
   down to hell.—Matt. 11:23.
   Humble yourselves in the sight of the Lord, and he shall lift
   you up.—Jas. 4:10.

Another striking contrast between pride (self-exaltation) and humility (a feeling of unworthiness) is presented in Luke 18:9-14, where the self-exalted Pharisee was declared to be less favored in the sight of God than the poor publican who confessed himself a sinner and prayed for mercy.

God nowhere speaks of pride except in terms of condemnation and reproach, and He nowhere speaks of humility except in tones of tenderness, approbation, and encouragement.

### Evidences of Humility

1. **A Childlike Spirit.**—Our illustration is found in Matt. 18:1-4. When the disciples wanted to know who was the greatest, Jesus set a little child in their midst, saying, "Whosoever therefore shall humble himself as this little child, the same is greatest." Christ Himself exemplified the spirit of humility in His whole earthly life. A very striking example of this is set forth in Phil. 2:5-11. "Who . . . thought it not robbery to be equal with God: but made himself of no reputation." The thought of greatness had no part in His makeup, though since His humiliation "God also hath highly exalted him, and given him a name which is above every name." They who, like Christ, manifest a meek, submissive, childlike spirit, as is manifested in the child, belong to God's "little ones" who will be exalted "in due time." Childlike simplicity, innocence, and inability to harbor a grudge, are evidences of true humility.

2. **Lowliness.**—Humility may truly be described as being "meek and lowly in heart" (Matt. 11:29). This is the standard enjoined upon Christian people in Eph. 4:2: "With all lowliness and meekness, with longsuffering, forbearing one another in love." It has truly been said that such people never fall very far, as it is only those who highly exalt themselves that get the hard tumbles. In this connection it may be well to note that there is a dif-

ference beween humility and humiliation; as one is low-liness, while the other, as a rule, is but wounded pride.

3. **Meekness.**—This is very closely connected with lowliness. Meekness suggests the further thought of being above taking offence. "Ouly by pride cometh contention" (Prov. 13:10). When man's pride is wounded, he quictly resents it, and the result is contention—usually with the tongue, sometimes with fists, sometimes with still more dangerous weapons. But with the meek it is different. Like their Saviour, when they are reviled, they revile not again; when they are persecuted, they suffer it in meekness. When treated in a way that carries insult to the proud, they bear it meekly, pray for their enemies, thus heaping "coals of fire" upon their heads according to Rom. 12:18-20. This is meekness, one of the surest evidences of humility.

4. **Simplicity.**—This may be evident in the countenance, in manners, in dress. "A proud look" springs not from a humble heart. A haughty bearing and pompous display in clothing are never the result of humility in the heart. Humble people are recognized by their unassuming manners, and simplicity marks both their appearance and their daily habits. Boastfulness is absent from their speech, gay clothing has no part in their attire, and a look of "we are the people" is never found in their countenance.

5. **Modesty.**—Besides the thoughts presented in the preceding paragraph, it may be added that "the big I" is never on parade when the heart is filled with humility. Modesty is a natural fruit of humility, as manifest in speech, in appearance, in the absence of self-conceit.

## WHY CHERISH HUMILITY

### 1. God is pleased with it.

Anything of which God speaks approvingly so often and so emphatically as He does of humility is worth having, for God is never mistaken in His judgment. Childlike humility is held to be the standard of greatness in the kingdom of heaven. Matt. 18:4.

## 2. It is commanded.

Saints are commanded to humble themselves "under the mighty hand of God" (I Pet. 5:6), to "put on ... humbleness of mind" (Col. 3:12), to "be clothed with humility" (I Pet. 5:5), to "walk ... with all lowliness" (Eph. 4:1, 2).

## 3. Through it calamities are often averted.

Let us recall the humiliation of the Ninevites when they heard the message of Jonah (Jon. 3), the prayer of Solomon upon the completion of the temple (II Chron. 7: 12-14), the turning away of God from visiting judgment upon Israel upon evidence that the princes of Israel had humbled themselves before Him (II Chron. 12:7), and similar instances recorded in Scripture. Or speaking from a negative point of view, is there a single instance recorded in Scripture where God visited iniquity upon any people after they had humbled themselves before Him?

## 4. God condemns the want of it.

Read II Chron. 33:23; Jer. 44:10. If God hates even "a proud look" (Prov. 6:17), He can not do otherwise than to condemn pride wherever He finds it. His condemnation of pride is as strong as is His commendation of humility.

## 5. It is a treasure of inestimable value.

Read Prov. 16:19; Matt. 5:3, 5. It is the gateway to the grace of God. Jas. 4:6. They who possess it are "the greatest in the kingdom of heaven." "By humility ... are riches, and honour, and life" (Prov. 22:4).

## 6. It is the forerunner of true exaltation.

Has it ever occurred to you how frequently the Bible connects the idea of humility with that of exaltation? While we should never assume a feigned humility for the hope of the exaltation which humility brings, it is important to know that the path of pride invariably leads to disaster, while there is glory ahead for all who humbly submit themselves to God. Neither is it necessary for us to be anxious about when and how and by what means the exaltation will be brought about; God will attend to all that. What we want is to trust in God, to be true to His Word, to keep humble, to stay at the foot of the cross, remembering that the promises of God to the humble are both sure and steadfast.

### FURTHER OBSERVATIONS

1. **We should avoid an assumed humility.**

This might be designated as "a voluntary humility," or "will worship," as Paul calls it. Col. 2:18, 23. Some people, recognizing the merits of humility, covet it because of its excellence or because of the exaltation (either in the sight of God or of men) that it is supposed to bring. This is the thing that the Bible warns us against. Humility is from the inside out, not from the outside in. People who assume an attitude of being "proud of their humility" will some day awaken to the fact that they were simply proud of their delusion, not of their humility, for they really never had the genuine article; for humility takes wings and flies away the moment that pride enters the heart.

2. **God hears the prayers of the humble.**

"He forgetteth not the cry of the humble" (Psa. 9:12). The Ninevites, in sackcloth and ashes before God; Hezekiah, humbled before God and praying for deliverance from the power of Sennacherib; the conscience-smitten publican in the Temple, pleading with God for mercy, all had access to the Throne and their prayers were heard before God. It is worthy of our constant remembrance that the high and holy God delights in answering the prayers of the meek and lowly supplicants at His Throne.

3. **As an example of humility, let us study the life of Christ.**

In Him we have the only perfect model. In the midst of His lowliness the grandeur of heavenly beauty shone out, and from the depths of His humility He rose to the loftiest heights. In meekness, in modesty, in lowliness, in self-sacrificing efforts to advance the cause of salvation, in everything pertaining to the grace of humility, He shone with a peculiar luster. Only as we pattern our lives after His, can we share in that luster.

**4. It is better to let God exalt us than to try to exalt ourselves.**

It is human to have an ambition to rise—and it is God's will that we do rise. But the two ways of rising are as opposite from each other as day is from night. One is an attempted rising by the power of man, the other a real exaltation by the power of God. You may think that your present position is not commensurate with your ability. Perhaps not; but are you sure that God, who knows all things, has overlooked that fact? And may it not be possible that your vaulting ambition, more than any one thing, stands in the way of your highest usefulness? In other words, if you would recognize in God a Being who is infinitely more capable of selecting a place for you than you are of selecting one for yourself, if you would take your place humbly at the foot of the cross, bring all your talents to the altar and humbly pray, "Lord, what wilt THOU have me to do?" He could place you here, and place you in eternity, to a much better advantage than you possibly can yourself. "Humble yourselves therefore under the mighty hand of God, that he may exalt you in due time" (I Pet. 5:6).

## CHAPTER XIV

## THE CHRISTIAN'S HOPE

Which hope we have as an anchor of the soul, both sure and stedfast.—Hebrews 6:19.

Hope has been defined as "expectation coupled with desire." Like faith, it may be considered from a purely natural standpoint, pertaining to things of this life only; or from the viewpoint of the child of God, pertaining to the things of this world and also of the world to come. It is in this latter sense that we shall consider it in this chapter. As such it thrills the souls of the people of God, who are looking forward in happy anticipation of that glorious time when, after their mortal robes will have been laid aside, they will have a part in the eternal reign of Christ and share in the bliss and glory of heaven forever.

For convenience, we shall consider this subject under three heads: What it is, how obtained, what it does.

### What It Is

There is so much in the Christian's hope which cheers the soul and spurs us on to fuller joys and nobler heights, that the longer we study it the more enthusiastic we become. In this, as well as in all other heavenly blessings, we do not realize how great is the wealth at our door until we begin to investigate. Turning to God's Word, we find these assurances concerning the Christian's hope:

1. It is "sure and steadfast" (Heb. 6:19), being "an anchor of the soul."

2. It is "good" (II Thess. 2:16), giving us "everlasting consolation."

3. It is "lively" (I Pet. 1:3), as distinguished from the false hopes of people who have been deceived into hop-

ing for things which they have no right to expect, for it is coupled with the fact that we have been begotten of God "unto a lively hope by the resurrection of Jesus Christ."

4. It is "the full assurance" (Heb. 6:11) of the child of God, which gives us courage to press on in faith and love and buoyant zeal "unto the end."

5. It is "a better hope" (Heb. 7:19) than that which is founded merely upon the Law, for its foundation is that which the Law typified, namely our Lord Jesus Christ and His Gospel, "by which we draw nigh unto God."

6. It is a source of gladness" (Prov. 10:28) in the soul of the righteous; being "both sure and stedfast" while "the expectation of the wicked shall perish."

7. It is "that blessed hope" (Tit. 2:13) which fills and thrills our souls with joy as we confidently expect and await "the glorious appearing of the great God and our Saviour Jesus Christ."

8. It is faith *in God,* which causes us to take Him at His Word, to believe His blessed promises, and to earnestly expect them to be fulfilled in us. Read Psa. 33:18; 39:7; Acts 26:6, 7; Tit. 1:2; I Pet. 1:21. When the psalmist says, "Lord . . . my hope is in thee," he voices the feelings and experiences of every enlightened child of God.

9. It is faith *in our Lord Jesus Christ,* which inspires confidence in Him as the Author of our salvation, the Head of the Church, the "firstfruits of them that slept," and therefore *our hope.* Read I Cor. 15:19; I Tim. 1:1. Because our hope in Him extends beyond the grave, we have a hope which we cherish as something most precious.

10. It is faith *in the Holy Ghost* (Rom. 15:13) through whom we have power to grasp the promises of God by faith. Gal. 5:5. The Christian's hope, therefore, embraces a steadfast faith in the Holy Trinity—Father, Son, and Holy Ghost.

While the hope of the worldling must of necessity end with this life, that of the Christian goes beyond and includes the things eternal. In fact, this world is but a stepping stone to the higher world above. "If in this life only we have hope in Christ, we are of all men most miserable" (I Cor. 15:19). But with the glorious realms of the world to come within range of the vision of faith, our souls are stirred with the blessed hope and we say with Paul, "We know that if our earthly house of this tabernacle were dissolved, we have a building of God, an house not made with hands, eternal in the heavens" (II Cor. 5:1). With this vision we can sing:

> "Hail! sweetest, dearest tie that binds
>     Our glowing hearts in one;
> Hail! sacred hope, that tunes our minds
>     To harmony divine:
> It is the hope, the blissful hope
>     Which Jesus' grace has given;
> The hope, when days and years have passed,
>     We all shall meet in heaven."

## How Obtained

How do we get possession of a treasure so rich and inspiring? The Bible tells us, among others things, that—

### 1. It is obtained through the grace of God.

Like every other blessing which only the children of God can have, the Christian's hope is based upon the grace of God rather than upon human merit. As Paul writes, "Our Lord Jesus Christ himself, and God, even our Father, which hath loved us, and hath given us everlasting consolation and good hope through grace" (II Thess. 2:16). A similar testimony is found in I Pet. 1:3. Without the grace of God there would be nothing but dark, dismal death ahead, for "all have sinned and come short of the glory of God." But through the abounding grace of God He made full provisions for our eternal redemption, and the future is full of radiant hope for all who have accepted the terms of such redemption.

## 2. Our hope is strengthened through Christian experience.

This thought is emphasized in Rom. 5:1-5. Beginning with a reference to faith and consequent justification in the sight of God, Paul continues to enumerate the unfolding of successive Christian experiences until in v. 4 he comes to the words, "and experience, hope." It is a noteworthy fact that the richer and deeper one's experience in the grace and service of God the brighter his hopes become. His Spirit "beareth witness with our spirit, that we are the children of God" (Rom. 8:16). And having this witness we naturally look forward with confidence to that blessed time when all the promises of God will have been fulfilled. Out of the depths of his experience Job was able to say, "I *know* that my redeemer liveth, and . . . in my flesh *shall* I see God" (Job 19:25, 26).

## 3. It is further perfected through a knowledge of God's Word.

"I hope in thy word," says the psalmist in Psa. 119: 81, 114. A knowledge of the Word, of what it has done for our own individual lives, and the evidences (both inside and outside the Bible) that this book is the BOOK of God, gives us confidence that the whole book is authentic and reliable and that therefore the many promises of God in it are sure and steadfast. "Whatsoever things were written aforetime were written for our learning, that we through patience and comfort in the scriptures might have hope" (Rom. 15:4). At first the trembling child approaches God through the medium of faith. As this faith becomes strengthened through experience and a knowledge of the Word, there is confirmation after confirmation of this faith, the knowledge increases, and through the full assurance of hope the believer finally comes out boldly and confidently says, "We know."

### WHAT IT DOES

Hope is more than mere sentiment or expectation. It is an actual help in practical Christian living.

### 1. It helps in overcoming difficulties.

In the forth chapter of Romans Paul tells about the trials of Abraham, especially in the matter of offering up Isaac, "who against hope believed in hope." In Heb. 11: 17-19 we are told that Abraham had such confidence in God that he had faith in the power of God to raise up Isaac from the dead. His faith and hope were undaunted by the seemingly impossible situation before him, and the results justified his hope.

What was it that prompted Paul to press on in the face of the most trying circumstances and march to the very gates of death in confidence and joy? Hope. In the midst of his trials he was able to say, "I reckon that the sufferings of this present time are not worthy to be compared with the glory which shall be revealed in us" (Rom. 8:18). When at the gates of death he exclaimed, "Henceforth there is laid up for me a crown" (II Tim. 4:8).

These are two among thousands of illustrations of what hope means to the child of God in facing the storms of life. No wonder the apostle calls it "an anchor of the soul."

### 2. It encourages boldness in standing for Christ and His Gospel.

"Seeing then that we have such hope, we use great plainness of speech" (II Cor. 3:12). "I am not ashamed of the gospel of Christ: for it is the power of God unto salvation" (Rom. 1:16). When hope grows strong, the heart grows courageous, the tongue grows bold, and faithful service follows.

### 3. It spurs us on to greater efforts.

What moves the farmer to face the storms and bear the hardships required to get out his crops in time? Hope of harvest. What prompts the merchant, the mechanic, the professional man, the tiller of the soil, to remain at the post of duty while others go pleasure-seeking? Hope of reward. What prompts the soldier of the cross to "endure hardness" in fighting the good "fight of faith?" Hope of greater things ahead. This "blessed hope," which gives the people of God the vision of faith, is one of the mainsprings of life which keeps its happy possessors in the forefront of battles for the Lord.

> "It is the hope, the blessed hope
> Which Jesus' grace has given;
> The hope, when days and years are past,
> We all shall meet in heaven."

### 4. It promotes unity among the faithful.

When out traveling you feel a drawing toward a fellow traveler when you learn that he is going to the same place that you are. In like manner the travelers toward the New Jerusalem are drawn together in closer union because they are animated by a common hope. "There is one body, and one Spirit, even as ye are called in one hope of your calling" (Eph. 4:4).

### 5. It brings joy and gladness.

Hear the testimony of the battle-scarred Paul: "The sufferings of this present time are not worthy to be compared with the glory which shall be revealed." In similar vein was Christ's cheering message to His disciples: "Rejoice, and be exceeding glad: for great is your reward in heaven." Is there anything in this world that can bring to the hearts of the children of men that ecstatic joy which the Christian hope does? It is this that gives the child of God (and none other but the child of God) the experience described by Peter as "joy unspeakable and full of glory." "Rejoice in the Lord alway: and again I say, Rejoice."

### 6. It promotes patience.

"If we hope for that we see not, then do we with patience wait for it" (Rom. 8:25). Did you ever notice that people invariably grow impatient as hope wanes? Hope and patience are inseparably linked together. The more hopeful we are, the more patient we become.

### 7. It is an incentive to purer, nobler life.

The Christian's hope is connected with all that is purest and best in life, with all the beauty and splendor and glory in the life to come. It can not therefore have any other effect than to lead us on to nobler, better things. The thought of hope is associated with salvation (I Thess. 5:8), with righteousness (Gal. 5:5), with the resurrection (Acts 23:6), with the second coming of Christ (I Jno. 3:2, 3), with eternal glory (Col. 1:27). After telling about the blessedness connected with the return of our Lord, John goes on to say, "Every man that hath this hope in him purifieth himself, even as he is pure." Peter also, after telling about the things that will surely come to pass, adds, "Wherefore beloved, seeing that ye look for such things, be diligent that ye may be found of him in peace, without spot, and blameless" (II Pet. 3:14).

The Christian's hope keeps his face turned heavenward, which accounts for the heavenly-mindedness of those possessed with such hope. Let us therefore cherish it for ourselves and encourage it in others. By and by this hope will ripen into experience, and the brightest and happiest anticipations of earth will be translated into the reality of bliss and glory in heaven.

"And the very God of peace sanctify you wholly; and I pray God your whole spirit and soul and body be preserved blameless unto the coming of our Lord Jesus Christ."

# PART VIII

## The Doctrine of the Future

### CHAPTERS

# THE DOCTRINE OF THE FUTURE

## Outline by Chapters

### I. THE SECOND COMING OF CHRIST

1. INTRODUCTORY THOUGHTS

2. THE FACT OF HIS COMING
   Witness: Christ, Two Men in White Apparel, Apostles, Job

3. SIGNS OF HIS COMING
   a. Absorption in Earthly Things
   b. World Evangelization
   c. Great Natural Occurrences
   d. Present Day Apostasy

4. MANNER OF HIS COMING
   a. "With Clouds"
   b. With Saints and Angels
   c. With Power and Glory

5. PURPOSE OF HIS COMING
   a. For His Own
   b. To Judge the World
   c. To Reign

6. FURTHER COMMENTS
   a. Truth of God's Word Not Affected
   b. Failure to Comprehend an Incentive
   c. Importance of Being Ready

7. HOW THE HOPE OF HIS COMING AFFECTS THE BELIEVER
   a. Purity
   b. Watchfulness
   c. Diligence
   d. Rejoicing

### II. THE RESURRECTION

1. THE DOCTRINE STATED

2. AN OLD TESTAMENT DOCTRINE

3. A NEW TESTAMENT DOCTRINE

4. PROOFS OF THE RESURRECTION

5. SOME ERRONEOUS VIEWS
   a. "No Resurrection"
   b. "Past Already"
   c. Body of Christ Not Raised
   d. Only Spiritual Resurrection

6. SUMMARY OF RESURRECTION TEACHINGS
   a. Resurrection of Jesus
   b. Spiritual Resurrection
   c. Bodily Resurrection

7. WHAT THE RESURRECTION WILL MEAN
   a. Resurrection of Life
   b. Resurrection of Damnation
   c. Nature of the Resurrection

## III.  THE JUDGMENT

1. INTRODUCTORY THOUGHTS

2. AN OLD TESTAMENT DOCTRINE

3. A NEW TESTAMENT DOCTRINE

4. REASONABLENESS OF THE JUDGMENT

5. THE JUDGE
   a. Judgment Committed to the Son
   b. Not Committed to Man
   c. A Competent Judge

6. THE JUDGMENT
   a. According to Law and Evidence
   b. Fallen Angels
   c. "All Nations"
   d. "Small and Great"
   e. "The Quick and the Dead"
   f. "The Righteous and the Wicked"

## IV.  HELL

1. DEFINITIONS

2. DESCRIPTION OF THE LAKE OF FIRE

3. HELL A PLACE

4. FOR WHOM PREPARED

5. WHO WILL GO THERE
   a. The Devil and His Angels
   b. The Wicked
   c. All Who Forget God
   d. Impenitent Sinners
   e. The Disobedient
   f. The Hypocrites

6. SOME ERRONEOUS IDEAS
   a. No Hell
   b. Second Chance After Death
   c. Limited Duration
   d. Instant Annihilation

7. EXPERIENCES IN THE LAKE OF FIRE
   a. "Tormented Day and Night Forever"
   b. "Worm Dieth Not—Fire Not Quenched"
   c. "Wailing and Gnashing of Teeth"
   d. "No Rest Day Nor Night"
   e. "Outer Darkness"

8. FURTHER OBSERVATIONS
   a. Make the Truth Known
   b. Man Responsible, if Lost
   c. Eternal Punishment Simple Justice
   d. Opportunity of Escape

## V.  HEAVEN

1. INTRODUCTORY THOUGHTS

2. DEFINITIONS

3. HOW GOD DESCRIBES IT
   a. "A Place"
   b. "The High and Holy Place"
   c. "A Better Country"
   d. "Many Mansions"
   e. "A Garner"
   f. "Pleasures Forevermore"
   g. A Place of Spotless Purity and Fullness of Glory

4. HOW TO GET THERE
   a. By Way of the Cross
   b. By Way of Innocence
   c. By Way of the New Birth
   d. By Way of the "Strait Gate"
   e. By Way of Holiness

5. INHABITANTS OF HEAVEN
   a. God
   b. The Holy Angels
   c. Saints

## 6. CONCLUDING THOUGHTS

- a. God No Respecter of Persons
- b. Limited Knowledge
- c. Trust in the Lord
- d. Eternity in Heaven

# THE DOCTRINE OF THE FUTURE

There are three great divisions of time: the past, the present, and the future.

The past is gone—as we may see, but we can not change our record. The present is our time of opportunity —in the light of past experiences we may know better how to improve our opportunities in building for the future. The future is hidden from our sight by a veil beyond which we can not see, save as God sees fit to brush it aside and give us a vision of the things on the other side. It is this division of time with which these chapters have to do.

In the study of that portion of God's Word which throws light upon the future let us not lose sight of the fact that some things are entirely hidden from us, some things partly revealed, and some things clearly shown. We get most out of our investigations if we do not assume to know too much, but meekly take our place as humble learners and diligent students, in faith receiving what God sees fit to reveal. The wisdom of God is nowhere more clearly manifested than in this that He has given us His Word in such a way that we can not grasp it fully at first and second reading, thereby encouraging a continuous reading and rereading, being rewarded by a greater illumination and brighter visions of the future the longer we search His blessed Word.

No one can thus look into the future, as God has seen fit to reveal it to us, without giving Him praise and glory for the unfathomable riches and glory ahead.

# CHAPTER I

## THE SECOND COMING OF CHRIST

Behold, the bridegroom cometh; go ye out to meet him.—
Matthew 25:6.

We will begin our consideration of this subject with
the message heard at the time of the ascension of our Lord.

The scene is in the region of Bethany, of the Mount
of Olives. Christ has just made His ascent to glory, and
the disciples are looking "stedfastly toward heaven." Presently they hear a voice. There stand beside them two men
in white apparel, cheering them with the message, "This
same Jesus, which is taken up from you into heaven, shall
so come in like manner as ye have seen him go into heaven"
(Acts 1:11).

A new vision is now before them. They remember the
words of Jesus directing them to tarry at Jerusalem until
they should be endued with power from on high, and they
proceed immediately to go back to that city. Here they
continue in prayer and thanksgiving and hopeful expectation until in the fullness of time the enduement of power
is theirs and the promise is fulfilled. No longer do they
center their hopes in an immediate, literal, glorious reign
of Jesus their King on earth, but from that time forward
the personal return of our Lord becomes the hope of the
Church.

### THE FACT OF HIS COMING

Concerning this there can be no reasonable doubt in
the mind of the believer, for here is the evidence:

**1. Christ has promised us that He will come again.**

"If I go and prepare a place for you, I will come again,
and receive you unto myself" (Jno. 14:3). The fact of His

coming was frequently referred to in His conversations with and instructions to His disciples. Matt. 25; Luke 19: 12-27.

### 2. The two men in white apparel said that He will come again.

Read Acts 1:9-11. Doubtless they were heavenly messengers, "ministering spirits" whom God sent for the occasion, as He did to His people on a number of other occasions, to direct them into proper channels.

### 3. The apostles told of His coming.

Paul (I Thess. 4:14-18), Peter (II Pet. 3), John (I Jno. 3:2), and others talked about this event in such a matter-of-fact way as to leave no doubt in any one's mind that they fully expected His coming again. It is said that in the apostolic writings about one verse out of seven is connected in some way with the thought of His return. And in all this there is nothing that is inconsistent with the idea of their looking and hoping for His coming.

Job expresses the confident hope of seeing his Lord, and that in the latter day He would stand upon the earth. Job 19:25.

### SIGNS OF HIS COMING

As to the exact time of His second advent, we know nothing. Christ says that only the Father in heaven knows that time, and we should ask no further questions. Men have set dates for His coming, but as these dates passed by these men were proved false prophets. But the Bible is not lacking in instructions concerning signs of His coming, so that we may know that His coming is not far removed. Matt. 24; Mark 13; Luke 21; I Tim. 4:1-3; II Tim. 3:1-5; II Pet. 2. Let us notice a few of these signs:

### 1. People deeply absorbed in the things of this world.

"But as the days of Noe were, so shall also the coming of the Son of man be. For as in the days that were before the flood they were eating and drinking, marrying and giving in marriage. . . . so shall also the coming of the Son of man be" (Matt. 24:37-39). In other words, people will be so deeply absorbed in the things of this world that they will pay little attention to either prophet or prophecy but plunge on in their mad career for wealth and fame and pleasure and power, until all of a sudden—alas, too late! —the voice of God will be heard and all opportunity for repentance and reconciliation with Him will be gone forever. "In such an hour as ye think not, the Son of man cometh."

### 2. The Gospel preached to all the world.

"And this gospel of the kingdom shall be preached in all the world for a witness unto all nations; and then shall the end come" (Matt. 24:14). This growth is typified in the parable of the mustard seed (Matt. 13:31, 32). Apparently the tree has about completed its growth, as the Gospel message has nearly reached the ends of the earth.

### 3. Great natural occurrences.

Christ speaks of famines, pestilences, wars, etc., as occurring previous to His coming. This sign has been abused in two ways: (1) by those who see in every earthquake, falling star, tornado, war, etc., a sure sign that Christ is coming immediately; (2) by those who see the folly of such predictions and therefore go to the opposite extreme and say there is nothing in this sign of prophecy. To keep balanced on this question, we should remember two things: (1) With the Lord one day is as a thousand years, and a thousand years as a day (II Pet. 3:8) and what may appear to the Lord as very near appears to man as far away. (2) These things have been witnessed for thousands of years; so we must recognize in the great natural occurrences an increase in both destructiveness and frequency before we can look upon them as signs of the King's approach. And when we compare the recent World War with all previous wars, compare the frequency and destructiveness of earthquakes with those of former history, and think of the rapidly growing intensity of the present world-wide unrest, it makes us feel that the day of the Lord is near at hand.

### 4. Present day apostasy.

"That day shall not come, except there come a falling away first" (II Thess. 2:3). Is there any one that doubts that that day is here? Fundamentalists tell of the present day apostasy, and warn the people. Liberalists tell about it, and glory in it. The same things that Paine and Hume and Owen and Ingersoll formerly preached as being against Christianity are now being handed out over the pulpit in the name of religion, and even the rank atheism of Marx finds its echoes in some churches. With many of the great institutions of learning becoming centers of liberalism, many churches captured by this wave of unbelief, and atheism rapidly on the increase, we are approaching conditions referred to in the pathetic, warning voice of Jesus: "When the Son of man cometh, shall he find faith on the earth" (Luke 18:8)? No amount of blind optimism can hide the fact that present conditions are accurately portrayed in the language of the prophetic writers.

What shall we say to these things? Look matters in the face as they are, and meet conditions intelligently. Knowing that the signs of our Lord's return are here, and not knowing the exact time of His coming, we should make sure of our readiness for His coming, and labor diligently to the end that others also may be ready.

### THE MANNER OF HIS COMING

It is interesting to note what the Scriptures have to say about this. In this, as well as in the matter of computing the exact time of His coming, we do well not to be too absolutely sure in our deductions. Yet the Bible tells us enough that we may profitably spend some time in meditating upon this phase of our subject.

### 1. "He cometh with clouds, and every eye shall see him" (Rev. 1:7).

Jesus refers to His coming as "in the clouds of heaven with power and great glory" (Matt. 24:30.) With this thought agrees the testimony of the two men in white apparel (Acs 1:9-11) at the time of the ascension of our Lord. Christ's reference to this event—"then shall appear the sign of the Son of man in heaven"—agrees with the words of the revelator, "Every eye shall see him."

## 2. He will be accompanied by saints and angels.

He Himself says that He will come in His glory, "and all the holy angels with him" (Matt. 25:31). As for the saints, Paul says, "Even so them also which sleep in Jesus will God bring with him" (I Thess. 4:14). Couple this with the thought given in Jno. 5:28, 29, and the conclusion is logical that at Christ's second coming He will bring with Him the disembodied spirits of the saints who had fallen asleep, will call their sleeping bodies from the grave, and, with the soul and body reunited and glorified by the power of God, together with the righteous living at His coming they will "meet the Lord in the air; and so shall we ever be with the Lord" (I Thess. 4:17).

## 3. He will come "with power and great glory" (Matt. 24:30).

In this we notice the remarkable difference between His first and second coming. His first coming was as a helpless infant, without influential friends, dependent upon the nursing of those who were older, and He grew up as other children do. In His second advent He will come as King of kings and Lord of lords, clothed with power and majesty, Judge of all the earth. Of these things we shall speak later on.

### PURPOSE OF HIS COMING

## 1. He is coming for His own.

On the night of Christ's betrayal He comforted His disciples, saying: "I go to prepare a place for you. And if I go and prepare a place for you, I will come again, and receive you unto myself; that where I am, there ye may be also" (Jno. 14:2, 3). During the nineteen hundred years that Jesus has been away the Holy Comforter (Jno. 16: 7-13) has been here as the heavenly Representative on earth, and will continue to be here, as the personal Representative of the Father and the Son, until Christ returns. Paul gives us a detailed description of what will happen on that occasion. I Thess. 4:14-17. The last sentence, "and so shall we ever be with the Lord," emphasizes the fact that when Christ will come it will be to receive His own unto Himself. At this time the righteous will be rewarded for their faithful service to the Master. It is a wonderful incentive to a life of devotion and self-denial to think that we shall be abundantly rewarded for everything that we do in His name. II Cor. 9:6; Jno. 12:24-26; Mark 9:41; Luke 14:14.

### 2. He is coming to judge the world.

Paul says that when Christ will be revealed from heaven it will be to take "vengeance upon them that know not God and that obey not the gospel of our Lord Jesus Christ" (II Thess. 1:7-9). The certainty of a judgment or reckoning following the coming of our Lord is as clearly established in Scripture as is the certainty of His coming. Matt. 25:31-46; Rom. 14:10; II Cor. 5:10.

### 3. He is coming to reign.

Here is something in which we are all interested. And the stronger the faith, the fuller the hope, and the more joyful the expectation, the more intense the interest.

There is a sense in which Jesus is with us now and in which all men of faith recognize His Kingship. As Jeremiah expresses it, "The Lord is . . . an everlasting King" (10:10). When Pilate asked Him, "Art thou a king" (Jno. 18:37)? He quickly replied, "Thou sayest;" meaning, "Yes, I am." To His disciples He said, "Where two or three are gathered together in my name, there am I in the midst of them" (Matt. 18:20). Speaking of His kingdom He says, "The kingdom of God is within you" (Luke 17:21). It is what some call "the kingdom in prospect," yet in it is, in

the fullest sense of the word, His Kingdom—here on earth
NOW.

But there is another sense in which we speak of His
kingdom as being yet future. The parables of the talents
(Matt. 25:14-30) and of the pounds (Luke 19:12-27), in
which Christ represents Himself as a nobleman or heir
traveling into a far country to receive for Himself a kingdom, and other references of a similar nature make it clear
that the literal reign of Christ, in which He personally
takes charge of His people, is yet future. It is this phase
of the Kingdom, doubtless, which John saw when the
angel of God brought before him the inspiring message that
the people of God would reign with Christ "for ever and
ever" (Rev. 22:5).

While there is practical agreement among believers
concerning the fact of the reign of Christ, yet concerning
the nature of His reign, especially with reference to the
order of events immediately following His second advent,
there is a wide difference of opinion. Among believers
this difference is not a question of faith and loyalty but
rather a difference in the interpretation of prophecy.
Some interpret literally what others believe to be figurative language. But even on this point the contention among
believers does not seem so sharp as it once was. It is
a matter of genuine satisfaction that Bible students who
accept without question the verbal inspiration and absolute authority of Scripture are recognizing more and more
the importance of the fact that so long as we accept without question any point of doctrine where a plain "Thus
saith the Lord" makes it clear what the word and will of
the Lord is concerning it we may well afford to bear with
one another on points of doctrine where the proper interpretation of Scripture is not so apparent. What will be
the exact order of events from the time of Christ's second
advent until saint and sinner will have been allotted to
their eternal portion will probably never be fully known
by mortal man until the events come to pass.

### Further Comments

The discussion concerning the reign of Christ, together with a number of other and kindred problems, calls for a few more observations which we trust may be of interest to the reader.

**1. The truth of God's Word is not affected by man's failure to comprehend.**

When in the fullness of time our mortal robes will have been laid aside and God's revelation to man will have been made perfect and complete, it will be found out who was right and who was wrong (or whether all were wrong) on all points of Scripture concerning which there were and are differences of opinion, but the truth of God's Word is the same in all ages. God's Word is the same, eternally true, in all ages, no matter what may be the opinions of man about it.

**2. Failure to fully comprehend should be considered an incentive to a more faithful, prayerful study of God's Word.**

It is no disadvantage, but rather an advantage, that we can not, at first or second or twenty-second reading, grasp in fullness all that is written in God's Word. We hold it to be a mark of God's wisdom that the Bible was given to us in a form that finite man can keep on studying it a lifetime and find it richer and more inspiring the longer he reads it. "All scripture is given by inspiration of God, and is profitable." We may think that we have delved deep, broadened out, and soared high in our study of the Word and grasp of eternal truth, but we will never get so far along in our studies but that there are oceans and worlds of unfathomable truth beyond us. Every time we approach a portion of Scripture that is hard to fathom, it is a challenge to us to pray more fervently for wisdom and to study more diligently, knowing that the Word of God becomes more familiar, His truth clearer and sweeter, the longer we study it and the oftener we read it. There is not a book in the Bible but that has its place and ought to be diligently and prayerfully studied.

**3. It is more important that we be found ready for Christ's coming than it is for us to know the exact time of His coming or the exact program of blessings and judgments after He does come.**

The keynote of our Saviour's instructions, in connection with the signs of His coming, was BE READY. What good will it do, though we have studied a lifetime about the manner and purpose of His coming and the exact order of events after He does come, if we then, after His coming, find ourselves, like the foolish virgins, unprepared? Be ready! *be ready*! BE READY! And having assured ourselves, in the light of God's Word, that we are ready for this great event, let our lives be dedicated to the great cause of helping the greatest possible number of lost souls to find their Saviour, to the end that they, too, may be ready for that eventful time.

How the Hope of His Coming Affects the Believer

1. **"Every man that hath this hope in him purifieth himself"** (I Jno. 3:3).

Let no man say that it makes no difference what we believe concerning the second coming of Christ, or whether we believe in it at all or not. There is a very vital connection between this blessed hope and practical daily life. The hope of His coming is more than a mere sentiment, more than a mere talking point in theology; it is a very practical element in the life of the believer. People who are looking for the coming of Christ, waiting for Him to come at a time when the world is least expecting Him (Matt. 24:32-51), have about them a soberness, a sacred regard for the truth, and an air of "other worldliness" that is not found among those not animated by this hope. And the brighter the hope of His coming, the stronger the impulse and desire to be in proper condition to receive Him when He comes. "Wherefore, beloved, seeing that ye look for such things, be diligent that ye may be found of him in peace, without spot, and blameless" (II Pet. 3:14).

2. **"Take ye heed, watch and pray: for ye know not when the time is"** (Mark 13:33).

"This know, that if the goodman of the house had known what hour the thief would come, he would have watched, and not have suffered his house to be broken through" (Luke 12:39). Expectancy makes us watchful, and the strength of hope holds men to a consistent life while they watch. If there were no other practical results from the hope of our Lord's return than this incentive for those who are expecting it to be watchful and prayerful to the end that they "may be found in peace, without spot, and blameless," this alone would justify the wisdom of God in revealing to man the fact of the Lord's return. Read Luke 21:34-36; Jas. 5:8.

3. **"I must work the works of him that sent me, while it is day"** (Jno. 9:4).

Reason: "The night cometh, when no man can work." This was not spoken in connection with the second coming of Christ, as it was the Lord Himself who was speaking, but it recognized a similar situation in which we find ourselves—great work ahead, limited time, with an urge to improve present opportunities. Since we are even now standing on the brink of eternity, ready to be called over any time, let us make good use of our opportunity for service while it lasts.

4. **"Wherefore comfort one another with these words"** (I Thess. 4:18).

What words? A recital of the "glorious appearing" of our Lord Jesus Christ. Read Matt. 25:1-10; I Thess. 4:14-18; Tit. 2:11-14; II Tim. 4:6-8. Confronted with this thrilling prospect, let us press hopefully, joyfully, faithfully on, praising and glorify God for the riches ahead.

"The Lord is coming by and by,
  Will you be ready when He comes?
He comes from His fair home on high,
  Will you be ready when He comes?
To judgment calls at His command,
Drawn thither by His mighty hand,
Before the Throne we all shall stand,
  Will you be ready when He comes?"

# CHAPTER II

## THE RESURRECTION

> The hour is coming, in the which all that are in the graves shall hear his voice, and shall come forth; they that have done good, unto the resurrection of life; and they that have done evil unto the resurrection of damnation. —John 3:28, 29.

### THE DOCTRINE STATED

The clearest exposition that we know of is that found in the language of the text which heads this chapter. The time of this "hour" is the "last day" of Jno. 11:24. From such references as Jno. 5:28, 29; 11:24; I Cor. 15; and Rev. 20:13, we get the idea clearly that after this age every human being will arise from the dead, when soul and body will be reunited and appear before the Lord.

### AN OLD TESTAMENT DOCTRINE

The doctrine of the resurrection is distinctly a Bible doctrine, as it is taught in no other system of theology or belief. While this doctrine is more clearly set forth in the New Testament than in the Old, we are not left in the dark as to whether this doctrine was believed in by the people of God in olden times. Let us call up a few Old Testament witnesses for testimony:

JOB:"I know that my redeemer liveth, and that he shall stand at the latter day upon the earth: and though after my skin worms destroy this body, yet in my flesh shall I see God" (19:25, 26).

ISAIAH:"Thy dead men shall live, together with my dead body shall they arise. Awake and sing, ye that dwell in the dust: for thy dew is as the dew of herbs, and the earth shall cast out the dead" (26:19).

DANIEL:"And many of them that sleep in the dust of the earth shall awake, some to everlasting life, and some to shame and everlasting contempt" (12:2).

HOSEA:"I will ransom them from the power of the grave; I will redeem them from death: O death, I will be thy plagues; O grave, I will be thy destruction" (13:14).

The reader who is acquainted with New Testament teaching on this subject can not but be impressed with the remarkable unity between Old and New Testament writers. The doctrine of the resurrection is not confined to the teachings of one dispensation but it is one of the eternal verities recognized as truth by the people of God in all ages.

Among the Jews, the Sadducees are the only sect of whom it is stated that they did not believe in the resurrection. Matt. 22:23; Mark 12:18. Martha gave voice to the very common opinion on this subject among the Jews when she expressed the hope of her brother rising again "in the resurrection at the last day" (Jno. 11:24). When Paul declared his belief in the resurrection of the dead (Acts 23:6) he won the support of the Pharisees on that issue, for he gave voice to a Jewish as well as a Christian doctrine. Observing the stand of the liberalists among Christian professors on this and related Bible doctrines today, we are not surprised that the liberalists among the Jews should assume a similar attitude.

## A New Testament Doctrine

Here we find the doctrine both taught and exemplified. Christ not only taught it, but by rising bodily from the grave He became "the firstfruits of them that slept" (I Cor. 15:20). It was a prominent doctrine in the teachings of the apostles (Acts 1:22; 2:31; 17:18; 24:15; I Cor. 15; Phil. 3:10; Heb. 11:35; I Pet. 1:3), the Jews being grieved (not because they taught the resurrection from the dead, but) bcause they "preached through Jesus the resurrection of the dead" (Acts 4:2). It was before the Epicureans and the Stoics (two schools of philosophers) that Paul on Mars' Hill preached the doctrine of the resurrection with such power that none could withstand him in any way but through mockery. Acts 17:16-34. So frequently and forcefully did the apostles preach this doctrine that we can truly point to the New Testament as a text-book on the doctrine of the resurrection.

## Proofs of the Resurrection

This being a prominent Bible doctrine, the proofs of the resurrection are coextensive with the proofs of the inspiration and reliability of the Bible.

We have a proof of the resurrection of Jesus in that He "shewed himself alive after his passion by many infallible proofs" (Acts 1:3). Lazarus also, having been seen by many Jews after that he was raised from the dead (Jno. 12:2, 10), stands out as an "infallible" proof of the power of God to raise the dead from the grave. Again, the fact of the appearance of many, after the resurrection of Jesus, who came forth out of their graves through the miraculous demonstrations of the power of God at the time of the crucifixion (Matt. 27:50-54) is another proof of the resurrection.

But aside from Bible evidences, the doctrine of the resurrection is not incredible. The fact is, of course, that the resurrection is a result of God's marvelous use of power. It will be as easy for Him, at His own appointed time, to call us from the grave as it was for Him to create man in the first place. The doctrine of the resurrection is not harder to believe than is the doctrine of the creation through the creative power of the Almighty. As we write this (in the spring of the year) and look out through the window we have an illustration of the resurrection power in the forthcoming vegetation—an illustration which Paul used (I Cor. 15:35-44) in his forceful exposition of this subject.

Concerning the nature and extent of the resurrection, Wakefield says:

"Redemption is the payment of a price in order to the liberation of the captive, an idea which is clearly involved in the sacrifice of Christ. Our redemption is twofold: virtual and actual. Virtual redemption is redemption by price. Virtual redemption in regard to its extent, includes the whole human family; for Christ 'tasted death for every man.' It includes also the whole of man's nature—the body as well as the soul. This is evident from what the apostle says: 'Ye are not your own, for ye are bought with a price: therefore glorify God in your body, and in your spirit, which are God's.' Hence the bodies of the saints, as well as their souls, have been purchased by Christ. The members, though dissolved by death, are still written in His book, and will in due time be raised in beauty and immortality, 'according to the working whereby he is able even to subdue all things unto himself.' In regard to the soul, every true believer is actually redeemed in the present life; but not so with the body. For, though it is virtually redeemed, its actual redemption lies beyond the present state of being. That can only be fully accomplished when our Redeemer shall break the iron grasp of death, and liberate the captives of the grave. Till then we must wait for the crowning blessing of our adoption, to wit, the redemption of our bodies. Till then the purposes of Christ's mediation will not be fully accomplished; 'for he must reign till he hath put all enemies under his feet. The last enemy that shall be destroyed is death.' This, therefore, clearly and necessarily implies the resurrection of the human race. And 'then shall be brought to pass the saying that is written, Death is swallowed up in victory. O death, where is thy sting? O grave, where is thy victory?' " (Christian Theology, P. 617.)

## SOME ERRONEOUS VIEWS

Like all other great Bible doctrines, the doctrine of the bodily resurrection has by unbelievers been ridiculed, reviled, and opposed in many ways. We are not surprised. Upon this doctrine rests the credibility of the entire Gospel of Christ, as Paul clearly sets forth in I Cor. 15. Concede the fact of the resurrection, and you concede the truth of the entire Gospel, foundation and all. Concede that perhaps after all there is no such thing as the bodily resurrection, and you concede that, after all, the Bible may be only a pious system of fraudulent claims. We expect therefore to see the enemies of Christ attack this doctrine so long as the fact of the miracle has a place in the beliefs of men. Some deny the resurrection entirely while others twist it into something meaningless, so that it might as well be discarded altogether. Let us notice a few of these errors:

1. **"That there is no resurrection"** (Matt. 22:23).

This view was held by the Sadducees, but Christ quickly silenced them. Luke 20:27-38. Paul also proves conclusively (I Cor. 15:12-20) that if this doctrine is abandoned, the whole realm of Christian doctrine falls to the ground.

### 2. "That the resurrection is past already" (II Tim. 2:18).

Paul encountered this heresy, mentioning Philetus and Hymenaeus, and declared that this heresy ate into the vitals of people's faith as cancer does into the vitals of the physical body. It is a deceptive argument, having a show of piety and feigned faith, that the resurrection is merely a rising from sin at the time of our conversion. The fact that Paul, being the chosen of God to proclaim His Word among Jews and Gentiles (Acts 9:15), denounced this heresy, is conclusive proof of its being an error. It is also in direct contradiction to Jno. 5:28, 29: I Cor. 15:51, 52; I Thess. 4:16 and many other scriptures referring directly to the bodily resurrection.

### 3. That the body of Christ was not raised from the grave.

Then why did not Peter and John discover His corpse when they explored the grave? Jno. 20:6-8. And why did Christ call special attention to His wounded body? Jno. 20:26-28. But people today who deny the bodily resurrection of Jesus are not, as a rule in the class of doubters with Thomas but rather with that other class mentioned in Matt. 28:11-15.

### 4. That there will be no bodily resurrection, but that glorified bodies will be supplied in their stead.

This objection is all the more dangerous because it has the semblance of truth in it. The risen saints will indeed be supplied with glorified bodies (I Cor. 15:42-54; I Jno. 3:2) but that fact does in no way nullify the teachings set forth in the scriptures already quoted. Just how the change from a natural to a glorified body will be made we can not explain, for it is miraculous; but we deny the possibility of the transformation from one to the other when we deny the first part of the miracle, namely the bodily resurrection. Two things will be true of the resurrection: (1) It will be a literal bodily resurrection. (2) There will be a transformation whereby these vile bodies will be changed into glorified bodies like unto Christ's. A recognition of both facts is needed to make a perfect Bible doctrine of the resurrection.

### Summary of Resurrection Teachings

**1. There was a bodily resurrection of Jesus Christ from the grave.**

"By many infallible proofs" was this fact demonstrated to the disciples, who by these "proofs" were changed from an attitude of doubting and indifference into that of ardent believers and followers.

**2. There is a spiritual resurrection for all penitent believers.**

That is, there is a rising to "newness of life" on the part of all who are "buried with Christ in baptism" (Rom. 6:3-6; I Cor. 12:13; Col. 3:1-3). Some hesitate to call this a resurrection, for fear that some people will confuse it with the thought of a bodily resurrection. But the surest way to get them confused is to remain silent on the one and thus allow some people to stumble unwittingly upon this rising to newness of life and get it confused with the doctrine of a bodily resurrection. It is a fact that all unsaved souls are "dead in trespasses and sins" (Eph. 2:1); that their souls are "quickened" when they hear "the voice of the Son of God" (Jno. 5:25); and that all such as come to "newness of life" are "risen with Christ" (Col. 3:1). Why not call this a spiritual resurrection, just as rising from the grave is called a bodily resurrection? And let all the world know assuredly that, unless we in this world rise to a "newness of life," when at the trumpet call of God there will be a rising from the grave it will mean to us "the resurrection of damnation" rather than "the resurrection of life."

3. **There WILL BE a bodily resurrection of both the just and the unjust.**

That this resurrection will be universal, there can be no question. Jno. 5:28, 29; Rev. 20:13. From every clime and age, no matter how death was brought about or what disposition had been made of the body, all will be called forth, and all will receive "a just recompence of reward" (Heb. 2:2), whether good or evil. And whether this resurrection will mean to us "the resurrection of life" or "the resurrection of damnation;" whether the souls of the righteous and of the unrighteous will appear at the same time, as some believe, or whether the righteous dead will be called up first and the unrighteous dead a thousand years later, as others believe, the resurrection of the body will be an event in the experience of every individual, good or bad —except such as will be alive at the appearing of our Lord, whose going forth to meet the Lord will be according to I Thess. 4:17.

### What the Resurrection Will Mean

**"The Resurrection of Life."**—To the righteous, the resurrection will mean "the resurrection of life." "They that have done good, unto the resurrection of life." All the inspired writers who have expressed themselves on the subject unite in pronouncing the event a most glorious one. Paul in telling about it says, "Behold, I shew you a mystery; We shall not all sleep, but we shall all be changed, in a moment, in the twinkling of an eye, at the last trump: for the trumpet shall sound, and the dead shall be raised incorruptible, and we shall be changed. For this corruptible must put on incorruption, and this mortal must put on immortality. So when this corruptible shall have put on incorruption, and this mortal shall have put on immortality, then shall be brought to pass the saying that is written, Death is swallowed up in victory" (I Cor. 15: 51-54). To those who are alive at the coming of our Lord the event will appear on this wise: "The Lord himself shall descend from heaven with a shout, with the voice of the archangel, and with the trump of God: and the dead in Christ shall rise first: then we which are alive and remain shall be caught up together with them in the clouds, to meet the Lord in the air: and so shall we ever be with the Lord" (I Thess. 4:16, 17). Rising in the strength and glory of the Most High, the saints of God will be glorified together with Christ (Col. 3:4); and with bodies incorruptible, glorious, powerful, and spiritual (I Cor. 15:42-44), "as the angels of God in heaven" (Matt. 22:30), they will ascend in rapturous joy to meet the Lord in eternal fellowship and glory. Glorious day! May God speed its coming—and may we spare neither pains nor sacrifice in the important work of getting the greatest possible number of people ready to join in this wonderful rapture.

**"The Resurrection of Damnation."** — The saddest thought that ever comes to the children of God is the reflection that not all people will have part in the resurrection of life. Daniel says that when the wicked will awake it will be to "shame and everlasting contempt." Let no unsaved soul now living turn away from this awful scene until he has come to himself, turned a listening ear to the heavenly voice (Jno. 5:25), repented before God, and resolved in his heart to spend the rest of his days in turning the hearts of other unsaved ones from the awful path that leads to destruction and pointing them to the glorious light of the Gospel of Christ.

**Nature of the Resurrection.**—Paul describes this very accurately in I Cor. 15:35-58, from which we quote a few extracts:

"But some will say, How are the dead raised up? and with what body do they come? . . . There are also celestial bodies, and bodies terrestrial; but the glory of the celestial is one, and the glory of the terrestrial is another. . . . So also is the resurrection of the dead. It is sown in corruption; it is raised in incorruption: it is sown in dishonour; it is raised in glory: it is sown in weakness; it is raised in power: it is sown a natural body; it is raised a spiritual body . . . and as we have borne the image of the earthy, we shall also bear the image of the heavenly."

As a grain of corn goes down into the ground and by the power of God a new plant comes forth, so the dead body is lowered, returns to dust, and at the coming resurrection will be called forth at the trumpet call of God. At what particular time, and in what particular way, the change is made from the corruptible clay into the "image of the heavenly," into a glorious body like unto Christ's, God has not seen fit to reveal. We know that it is so, and that is enough to satisfy every believer and to cause us to praise His holy name. As John says (I Jno. 3:2): "We shall be like him; for we shall see him as he is."

# CHAPTER III

## THE JUDGMENT

It is appointed unto men once to die, but after this the
judgment.—Hebrews 9:27.

The word "judgment" has been defined as "the pronouncing of an opinion or decision of a formal or authoritative nature." In the matter of its many applications, Cruden makes the following classification:

1. The sentence, or decision of a judge.—I Kings 3: 28.

2. The spirit of wisdom and prudence, enabling one to know and to discern right from wrong, and good from evil.—Psa. 72:1.

3. Those remarkable punishments, which God inflicts on people for their sins and transgressions.—Prov. 19:29; Ezek. 30:14.

4. The spiritual government of the world, which is committed by God the Father to Christ the Mediator, and which He manages with a perfect rectitude and equity.— Jno. 5:22; 9:39.

5. The afflictions and chastisements which God brings upon His children for their trial and instruction.—I Pet. 4:17.

6. God's merciful moderation in chastising His people.—Jer. 10:24.

7. The solemn action and trial at the great and last day.—Eccl. 12:14; Jude 6.

8. The righteous statutes and commandments of God. —Psa. 119:7, 20.

9. The punishment inflicted on Christ for our sins.— Isa. 53:8.

10. The doctrine of the Gospel, or God's Word.—Matt. 12:18.

11. Justice and equity.—Isa. 1:17; Luke 11:42.

12. The deliverance and vindication of mankind from the power and tyranny of the devil.—Jno. 12:31.

13. God's decrees and purposes concerning nations, or persons.—Rom. 11:33.

14. The sentence of damnation upon the wicked, and of absolution in favor of the godly.—Jude 15.

15. Courts of justice.—Matt. 5:21.

16. Differences and controversies to be decided.—I Cor. 6:4.

17. Sentiment, or opinion.—I Cor. 1:10.

18. Advice.—I Cor. 7:25.

19. The Gospel, or kingdom of grace.—Matt. 12:20.

18. Advice.—I Cor. 7:25.

19. The Gospel, or kingdom of grace.—Matt. 12:20.

The judgment of which we wish especially to speak in this chapter is that pertaining to God's dealing with "the children of the kingdom," and His sentence upon "the children of the wicked one."

## An Old Testament Doctrine

As in the doctrine of the resurrection, we find the doctrine of the judgment well supported in both Old and New Testaments.

David speaks of the time when the Lord "cometh to judge the earth" (I Chron. 16:33), and says that He "hath prepared his throne for judgment" (Psa. 9:7); also that "He cometh to judge the earth: he shall judge the world with righteousness, and the people with his truth" (Psa. 96:13). Solomon says, "God shall judge the righteous and the wicked" (Eccl. 3:17). In warning young men to beware of sinful pleasures he adds, "Know thou, that for all these things God will bring thee into judgment" (Eccl. 11:9). From these references we conclude that the Old Testament writers understood that there is certain reward ahead for the righteous and certain punishment for the wicked. They had only to open their eyes, and they could see the judgments of God visited upon the disobedient, while His blessings flowed freely toward them that kept His precepts. Looking forward toward the time when "they that sleep in the dust shall awake," they could also see the day of rewards and punishments.

## A New Testament Doctrine

We find this same doctrine held forth by the inspired writers in the New Testament. Christ says, "Every idle word that men shall speak, they shall give account thereof in the day of judgment" (Matt. 12:36). Speaking of the Holy Spirit, He said, "He will reprove the world of sin, and of righteousness, and of judgment" (Jno. 16:8). As to what God's judgment will mean for the wicked, He says, "These shall go away into everlasting punishment" (Matt. 25:46), adding, "but the righteous into life eternal."

Paul was equally clear and specific in proclaiming this doctrine. He made Felix tremble as he preached "righteousness, temperance, and judgment to come" (Acts 24:25). To the Romans he wrote, "We shall *all* stand before the *judgment seat of Christ*" (Rom. 14:10). Read also II Cor. 5:10. Writing to the Hebrews, he tells of certain ones with "a certain fearful looking for of judgment" (Heb. 10:27). That this judgment is not merely a smiting of conscience, as some would interpret it, is evident from the fact that he tells these same people that "it is appointed unto men once to die but *after this the judgment.*" ment."

Peter also testifies of the judgment of God being visited upon a sinful world, saying, "The heavens and the earth, which are now, by the same word are kept in store, reserved unto fire against the day of judgment" (II Pet. 3:7). Jude speaks of "the judgment of the great day" (6), and John testifies of his Patmos vision, saying, among other things, "And I saw the dead, small and great, stand before God; and the books were opened: and another book was opened, which is the book of life: and the dead were judged out of those things which were written in the books, according to their works" (Rev. 20:12).

Summarizing these teachings in a single doctrinal statement, we find it tersely put in II Cor. 5:10, as follows: "We must all appear before the judgment seat of Christ; that every one may receive the things done in his body, according to that he hath done, whether it be good or bad."

### REASONABLENESS OF THE JUDGMENT

This being clearly established as a Bible doctrine, let us examine into its reasonableness.

Practically all people believe in some form of judgment. Even the rankest atheist believes that justice should be meted out to criminals, and rejoices greatly when some heartless criminal gets his "just dues." Justice calls for the punishment of crime, and practically all people recognize the reasonableness of it, when administered impartially and sympathetically.

It requires no great intelligence to perceive that in this life people are not always punished or rewarded in a way that is commensurate with their sins or their merits. Quite frequently the most hardened sinners fare comparatively well so far as health, wealth, pleasure, honors, etc., are concerned; while some God-fearing men who want to live right in every respect are afflicted, suffer for years from pain and sickness, and die in penury and want. Examples: Job and wicked men with whom he compared himself, Dives and Lazarus, Christ and His persecutors, Paul and his executioners.

It is evident, therefore, that if the justice of God is to be established there must be future retribution; judgment for the wicked, rewards for the righteous "at the resurrection of the just." Only by future retributions and rewards can the truth of Peter's testimony, "God is no respecter of persons," be sustained.

The stripes and afflictions sent us in this world are not a punishment for sin, primarily, but rather a touch of

God's love (See Heb. 12:1-13) for our own or others' good. We know of no better illustration of this fact than that of the life story of Job. Whatever Job's afflictions may have meant for him and his three friends, the world has in him an object lesson which has been a real blessing to thousands of lives in all generations since that time. There is a vast difference between chastisement and retribution. The first is for corrective purposes, the other is for *punishment."*

The doctrine of judgment for the future is not only reasonable, but, on the other hand, the theory of *no future judgment* is so very unreasonable as to make it unworthy of any support, as it would entirely destroy all idea of the justice of God. Both revelation and nature sustain the doctrine of future retribution and rewards.

### THE JUDGE

1. **"The Father . . . hath committed all judgment unto the Son"** (Jno. 5:22).

A number of thoughts are awakened by this statement. The first is the reason assigned for the provision: "That all men should honour the Son, even as they honour the Father." Indirectly this is a rebuke to "the wise and the prudent," in our day as well as in the day of Christ on earth, who see only the human side of Christ. Another thought is that of the complete triumph of Jesus Christ. "Despised and rejected of men," nailed to the cross and dying in ignominy, He rose triumphant over every foe, took His majestic flight to glory, is at the right hand of the Father as the Advocate and Intercessor for all that believe on Him, and in the fullness of time will return as the Judge of "the quick and the dead." Still another thought worthy of our meditation is the fact that since judgment is in the hands of Jesus Christ who died for us we have a true Friend upon the judgment seat.

2. **It is not within the sphere of man to judge.**

We do not here refer to any use that God may make of man during the eventful times beyond the grave (Matt.

19:28; I Cor. 6:2), but rather to the proper sphere of man while still in the flesh. Matt. 7:1; Rom. 2:1; Jas. 4:12. It is not wrong to pass judgment or express opinion on any subject upon which the Scripture light shines (Jno. 7:24), but to pass the sentence of eternal death upon people is a function that belongs not to man. We may express opinions, may differ from other people in views of religion or duty, but we are very thankful that the matter of deciding upon what shall be their lot in eternity is reserved for Him whose knowledge is infinite and whose judgment is perfect.

3. **Our Judge is in every way competent and worthy.**

He is infinite in wisdom, knowledge, and soundness of judgment. He is unchangeable (Heb. 13:8), and therefore thoroughly reliable. He has proved His friendship for us in that He died for us, therefore we have nothing to fear in the form of severity from an unfriendly Judge. He is perfect in righteousness, so we may expect nothing but simple justice. He is impartial, and therefore "no respecter of persons." This is the character of the great Judge before whom we all shall stand—and if in this life we are wise and judge ourselves according to His standard of everlasting truth and righteousness while this opportunity is still ours, we are assured that our judgment at that great day will be commendation rather than the sentence of eternal death because of our sins. Matt. 25:34; I Cor. 11:31.

It may be well to add that no other being, besides the Divine Judge, is qualified to serve in that capacity. Here, as in all other cases, God has manifested His wisdom and grace in the provisions made for our well-being.

### THE JUDGMENT

1. **It will be according to the law and the evidence.**

Christ makes it clear that He is not an arbitrary Autocrat passing judgment upon whomsoever He will, but that His mission in the world was to save men, not to condemn them (Jno. 3:17; 12:47); and that when He comes the second time it will be with the same heart of love, as the same Friend to humanity, meting out justice according to the Word (Jno. 12:48) and according to our works (II Cor. 5:10). As a man in court is brought before a bar of justice to be justified or sentenced according to the law and the evidence, so will our standing before the great Judge depend upon how our record compares with the eternal Word of God. The law being established forever (Psa. 119:89), the only point to be decided is as to whether our record here has been such as to establish our innocence or guilt before the law. "If we would judge ourselves, we should not be judged" (I Cor. 11:31). If we have accepted God's grace in Jesus Christ, we shall then stand justified in the record; if not, we shall remain condemned. All this will appear in the evidence. Here, not yonder, is where our eternal fate is determined. However merciful a judge may be, justice demands that all who are brought before him be declared innocent or guilty, depending upon the law and the evidence. The law being established forever, and our record established at the time of our death, there remains nothing to do for the great Judge but to assign us to the place where our records, according to the law and the evidence, prove us to belong. Matt. 25:41.

### 2. It will be meted out to fallen angels.

"God spared not the angels that sinned, but cast them down to hell . . . to be reserved unto judgment" (II Pet. 2:4). Jude also testifies that "the angels which kept not their first estate, but left their own habitation, he hath reserved in everlasting chains under darkness unto the judgment of the great day" (6). In the end the fallen angels will share the same fate as fallen men—both will be sent "into everlasting fire, prepared for the devil and his angels" (Matt. 25:41).

3. **It will be meted out to "all nations"** (Matt. 25:32).

God as "Judge of all" (Heb. 12:23) will know no class; neither will there be any favored nations or individuals, for "God is no respecter of persons."

4. **It will be meted out to both "small and great"** (Rev. 20:12).

John on Patmos saw a vision which brought out this fact very forcefully. In this vision is represented a picture of the judgment in which both small and great stand before the throne. Books were opened and comparisons made. The mighty conqueror, the king, the humblest subject, the statesman, the scholar, the illiterate man, the beggar, the billionaire, the old and young—every man and woman whom God has ever given existence, without distinction of race, color, social standing, age, or any other condition—all will be judged by the same standard, all judged in righteousness, our eternal fate being determined by the question as to whether in this life we met or failed to meet the conditions of eternal salvation.

Some of the attainments here mentioned find favor in the sight of men; but before God they are counted as nothing—save that He expects greater things of us in proportion to our blessings, favors, talents, or opportunities.

5. **It will be meted out to "the quick and the dead"** (II Tim. 4:1).

In this connection Paul, in I Thess. 4:14-18, gives us a vivid word picture of what will be the experiences of the righteous dead and the righteous living at the time of Christ's second coming. And a similar application, though with opposite experiences, might be made with reference to the unrighteous living and unrighteous dead. Whether living or dead when Christ comes again, all will be judged according to the deeds done in the body.

6. **It will be meted out to "the righteous and the wicked"** (Eccl. 3:17).

There is no favoritism with God. The difference between the two classes mentioned is that the former have accepted the atonement through the blood of Christ while the latter have not. Malachi speaks of "the great and dreadful day of the Lord" (4:5). Whether we speak of the second coming of Christ, the resurrection, or the judgment to come, it means something indescribably great and glorious for the righteous and something incomparably dreadful and dismal for the unrighteous. The future has no terrors for any class but the unsaved, the unrighteous, the guilty. How striking the contrast between John on the Isle of Patmos praying, "Even so, come, Lord Jesus," and the pitiful wail of those haunted by "a certain fearful looking for of judgment," begging, "Rocks and mountains, fall on us!"

Quite a difference, you say. Yes, the difference is vast. Yet we lose the practical effect of this contrast if we fail to remember two things: (1) The judgment is sure for every one, both small and great, both quick and dead, both saved and unsaved. (2) Upon us as individuals, not upon God's arbitrary power, rests the responsibility of what the judgment will mean for us, as in this life we have the opportunity of making preparation for the great events of the future. These will be to us "great" or "dreadful," depending upon whether in this life we prove ourselves faithful or unfaithful to God.

"Wherefore, beloved, seeing that ye look for such things, be diligent that ye may be found of him in peace, without spot, and blameless.

## CHAPTER IV

## HELL

The wicked shall be turned into hell, and all the nations that forget God.—Psalm 9:17.

### DEFINITIONS

The original word *"Sheol"* has a double application, sometimes used to designate the grave, sometimes referring to the place of departed spirits. In the Authorized Version the words "grave" and "hell" are each used thirty-one times as derived from the word "sheol." (Encyclopedia Britannica.)

In several instances in the Authorized Version the word *"hell"* refers to the grave; as in Psa. 16:10 and Acts 2:27. Generally, however, the word designates the place where lost souls are; as in Deut. 32:22, Psa. 9:17, Luke 16:23, etc.

The word *"hades"* is used frequently in the Revised Version where the word "hell" is used in the Authorized. It is sometimes used to designate the grave, as in Acts 2: 31, I Cor. 15:55, but more frequently refers to the place of torment, as in Matt. 11:23, Luke 16:23, etc.

The word *"gehenna,"* used twelve times in the Greek New Testament, means the place of future punishment.

It matters not by what name the place may be known, the Scriptures teach that there is a place of endless punishment for the wicked, and this is the theme to which the thoughts found in this chapter are directed.

### DESCRIPTION OF THE LAKE OF FIRE

Unless otherwise designated, when the word "hell" is found in this chapter it refers to the lake of fire, the eternal abode of the devil and all his hosts. But the vital question is not, What do we call the place? but, What is it like? Turning to the Word of God for light on this question, we find the following terms used in describing the place:

"Devouring fire" (Isa. 33:14).
"Everlasting burnings" (Isa. 33:14).
"Everlasting contempt" (Dan. 12:2).
"Furnace of fire" (Matt. 13:50).
"Unquenchable fire" (Matt. 3:12).
"Hell fire" (Matt. 5:22).
"Damnation of hell" (Matt. 23:33).
"Outer darkness" (Matt. 25:30).
"Everlasting fire" (Matt. 25:41).
"Everlasting punishment" (Matt. 25:46).
"Where their worm dieth not, and the fire is not quenched" (Mark 9:44).
"Vengeance of eternal fire" (Jude 7).
"Smoke of their torment ascendeth up for ever and ever" (Rev. 14:11).
"Tormented day and night for ever" (Rev. 20:10).
"Lake of fire burning with brimstone" (Rev. 19:20).

To get the full force of this description it will be necessary to study these descriptive terms in connection with their contexts. We shudder as we try to imagine what an awful place this will be—and we become speechless as we try to explain why men pretending to believe the Bible should ever entertain the idea that possibly there is no such a place! Let every one know assuredly that such a place is a terrible reality—or the Bible is not reliable.

## Hell a Place

One of the important things to remember is that hell is a "place" (Luke 16:28), not a mere condition. Some tell us that "we make our own hell." That we are personally responsible for our own state and standing before God here, and personally responsible if we will ever be cast into the lake of fire, is beyond question or dispute; but the scripture teachings as to its being *a place* are so emphatic that no true believer doubts it. Hell is a place, just as earth is a place.

20

## FOR WHOM PREPARED

Christ specifically states that it was "prepared for the devil and his angels" (Matt. 25:41). God prepared a different place for us, as we shall notice in the next chapter; but if any of us will deliberately or carelessly refuse or neglect to conform to God's plan for our eternal welfare, in the great consummation of all things, when heaven and hell will be the only places left, God will have no other recourse than to send us to the place prepared for the devil and his hosts. The devils understand what is to become of them. When Christ met a number of them they cried out, "Art thou come hither to torment us before the time" (Matt. 8:29)? Though they "believe, and tremble" (Jas. 2:19), they know their doom, and dread the place to which they will eventually be sent. In Christ's time they preferred to enter swine rather than to go to their long home. Entering the swine, they caused their destruction. They have the same effect upon men whenever they enter their hearts. The demon-possessed swine rushing down over the bank into the waters are typical of the demon-possessed men rushing into the lake of fire.

## WHO WILL GO THERE

### 1. The devil and his angels.

This thought was presented in the preceding paragraph. Read also Jude 6; Rev. 20:10.

### 2. The wicked.

"The wicked shall be turned into hell." Choosing the path of sin in this world, they will reap the fruits of their unrighteousness in the world to come. Read Matt. 7:13, 14; Rom. 1:18-32; 6:23; Jude 8, 16.

### 3. All who forget God.

It will be noted that in the same breath in which judgment was pronounced upon the wicked there was also included God's judgment upon "all the nations that forget God." In some of the nations where Christianity had once gained a foothold the God of heaven has been all but forgotten and Christ has been entirely repudiated. To say nothing about the wickedness prevailing in such countries, the fact of their apostasy alone is sufficient to merit their eternal damnation.

### 4. Sinners who refuse to repent.

"Except ye repent, ye shall all likewise perish" (Luke 13:3, 5). Remission of sins can take place only upon condition of repentance. Luke 24:47. When therefore sinners die without having repented of their sins, the divine edict applies to them: "The soul that sinneth, it shall die" (Ezek. 18:4).

### 5. All who are disobedient to God.

On this point we find our most direct reference in II Thess. 1:7-9. Here Paul speaks of the vengeance that will be meted out to those who are out of the fold of Christ. Notice, he does not say anything about any of them being notoriously wicked, but he does say emphatically that at His coming Christ will, in flaming fire, take "vengeance on *them that know not God,* and that *obey not the gospel of our Lord Jesus Christ;*" adding that they "shall be punished with everlasting destruction from the presence of the Lord, and from the glory of his power." Let it be indelibly impressed upon every mind and heart that a person need not be a notorious criminal—such as a murderer, a thief or robber, an assassin, a whoremonger, an inveterate drunkard or liar or extortioner—to be on the road to hell, but all that he needs to do is to disobey God, walking disobediently in daily life, and, unless he repents and turns to the path of obedience, he will go into the same place where the vilest of sinners will go.

Here some people stumble. They tell you of the man who is upright in business, provides well for his family, lives a cleaner life than most church members, gives liberally to churches and charitable enterprises, and certainly such a person will not be sent to hell, even if he is only a nominal church member or perhaps no member at all.

They do not realize that in their defence of the man they are simply strengthening the case against him. To say nothing of the fact that by their profession they put more faith in the goodness of that man than they do in the truth of God's Word, a man of that caliber is less excusable for disobeying God than is the man whose mind is enfeebled and judgment warped through ignorance or dissipation. Christ said that in the last day it would be more tolerable for the rank and ignorant heathen, even the men of wicked Tyre and Sidon and Sodom and Gomorrah, than it would for those who knew God's Word and yet disobeyed. Matt. 11:20-24; Luke 10:10-16. It is not that those people were better than the Pharisees, but the Pharisees knew what God wanted of them and still did not obey Him. Before God, the most inexcusable sin is that of going against better knowledge. Luke 12:47, 48. Make no excuses for the moralist or the responsible man who in spite of his superior advantages refuses or neglects to obey God; but say to all such, "Except ye repent, ye shall all likewise perish!"

### 6. The hypocrites.

Some people think that only church members are hypocrites. We admit that there are more hypocrites in the churches than there ought to be; but every man who pretends that the reason he is not in the Church is because there are so many hypocrites there is himself a hypocrite; for no sooner is that excuse taken away than he is ready with some other excuse for not being a Christian. But whether hypocrites on earth are in the churches or outside, in the world to come they will all be together—in the lake of fire. Christ tells of the man who has been negligent in the matter of preparing for the coming of the Lord, saying that He will "appoint him his portion with the hypocrites: there shall be weeping and gnashing of teeth" (Matt. 24:51).

QUESTION: Considering who all are going to the lake of fire, do you suppose that you would enjoy being with them in eternity? If not there, why prefer to be in a class with them here?

## SOME ERRONEOUS IDEAS

It is natural for man, especially disobedient man, to try to escape disagreeable facts. Fortunes have been spent trying to find some magical elixir of life. Vain philosophy has been invoked in the cause of somehow getting around the awful reality of hell, notwithstanding God has made it possible for all to escape it who will. Some seek to argue it away entirely, others to make it easier. Let us notice a few of these errors:

1. **That there is no hell.**

Few people take this position, except those who deny the infallibility of Scripture. But even among those professing to believe the Bible there are some who try to make it appear that hell simply means the grave. For answer to this contention, read again the definitions found at the beginning of this chapter. But aside from these definitions, the Bible would have to be revised to accommodate itself to this view. Why the assertion, "The wicked shall be turned into hell," when all other classes go there too? Why did the rich man say, "I am tormented in this flame," when everybody knows that a dead man could suffer no torment, even if there were flames in the grave? Why the expression, "The smoke of their torment ascendeth up for ever and ever," if only the grave is referred to? There is no possible way of adjusting your views to the idea of no place of eternal torment for the wicked without repudiating all that the Bible has to say about such a place.

2. **That the wicked will have a second chance after death.**

There is nothing in the Bible that lends encouragement to such a delusion. When the rich man begged that Lazarus might be sent to bring him some comfort, Abraham informed him that between them there was a great gulf which no man could cross. While death does not end all, it does end all chance for the sinner finding his way back to God. "It is appointed unto men once to die, but after this the judgment."

### 3. That the wicked will not be in torment forever.

There is absolutely no such teaching in the Bible. On the other hand, the descriptive terms quoted near the beginning of this chapter prove conclusively that the punishment is eternal. The same arguments which men use to prove that the punishment of the wicked will not last forever, would, if honestly applied, prove as conclusively that heaven also will be but of temporary duration.

The idea of a "purgatory," even when stripped of the gruesome stories of priests getting the victims through quickly for a money consideration, is mischievous in that it holds out false hopes and encourages wicked men to take chances, even if they will have to suffer for a while instead of being brought to their senses and truly repenting of their sins while they have opportunity.

Some have gotten the idea of a "purgatory" confused with the scripturally supported idea of an "intermediate state" for both saved and unsaved. A reading of such scriptures as Eccl. 12:7; Matt. 25:30; Luke 16:19-31; I Cor. 15; and I Thess. 3:13; 4:14, gives us the idea that during the intervening time between death and the resurrection the disembodied spirits will be in what has been called "an intermediate place"—the righteous in conscious bliss and the unrighteous in conscious torment, the righteous in the presence of God and the unrighteous in the presence of the tormentors—until the time when Christ returns with His saints, when there will be a reuniting of spirit and body. After the consummation of all things earthly, the righteous, with glorified bodies, will be forever with the Lord, while the unrighteous, doomed and damned in hell, will be with the devil and his angels forever. But there is nothing in the Bible that gives any one the idea that any one will enter the intermediate state an unsaved soul and come out of there saved, neither does any scripture justify the idea that souls once in hell will pass from that place on to glory.

4. **That the wicked will be instantly consumed upon being cast into the lake of fire.**

Again we refer to the descriptive terms used near the beginning of this chapter as proof of the fallacy of such a claim. The theory of instant annihilation does not harmonize with such expressions as "everlasting fire" "everlasting burnings," "unquenchable fire," "worm dieth not, and the fire is not quenched," etc., etc. Some quote Mal. 4:1—"All that do wickedly, shall be stubble: and the day that cometh shall burn them up"—as confirmation of the instant annihilation theory. But this scripture, instead of confirming that theory, rather confirms the many other scriptures which teach destruction but not annihilation of the wicked. True, fire destroys the stubble; but there is not one particle of the stubble annihilated, as all that there ever was of the stubble still exists in the form of vapor, smoke, gas, and ashes. So with the wicked. They will be "punished with everlasting destruction from the presence of the Lord" (II Thess. 1:9), and spend eternity in the lake of fire, where they will be "tormented day and night for ever and ever" (Rev. 20:10).

The saddest part of all these palliatives is not only that they are without scriptural foundation but that they are deceptive, holding out a delusive hope to sin-benighted souls that even if they do live in sinful indulgence and ungodliness here that there will be some means of escape from the awful punishment which the Bible emphatically teaches is in store for the wicked who die in their sins. Dear Christian friends, be diligent in sounding the alarm.

### Experiences in the Lake of Fire

Perhaps we ought not to burden the reader with a recital of what is already apparent. But what we have yet to say is a part of God's Word and ought to be proclaimed to all the world. Let the world be awakened to what it means to be lost in an endless hell, and millions will also be awakened to their awful condition and seek the pardoning grace of God while there is opportunity. The "fire alarm" needs to be sounded. Let all the sinful world look the stern realities of the future squarely in the face and know that the following conditions are just a-head:

1. They will be "tormented day and night for ever" (Rev. 20:10).

We have chosen this wording of what constitute: endless punishment, not because the doctrine depends upon this scripture alone but because it is an impressive way of stating what is repeatedly and emphatically taught in other scriptures. Here we suffer, hoping for relief sooner or later; there the suffering will continue forever, without hope of ever getting through. The severest and most prolonged case of suffering on earth is but a mere foretaste of what is in store for doomed souls in hell!

2. There "their worm dieth not, and the fire is not quenched" (Mark 9:44).

As literal fire is to the body, so the fire of hell will be to the soul. And the fire will be like the burning bush which Moses saw—will continue, but the body will not be consumed. Our physical bodies may be burned or destroyed in some other way, but the soul having eternal existence can never be annihilated, though it suffers "the vengeance of eternal fire" forever.

3. "There shall be wailing and gnashing of teeth" (Matt. 13:42).

Notice the two words, "wailing" and "gnashing"—sorrow and rage, weeping and cursing, lamentations and defiance, remorse and desperation, pitiful moaning and fierce and blasphemous raving—but we draw the curtain, the scene can not be described. Only those whose doom it is to spend eternity in hell will know the depth of the agony of this awful suffering.

4. **They will have "no rest day nor night"** (Rev. 14: 11).

People suffering here are usually relieved in resting spells; or, failing to get relief the Lord graciously relieves their suffering here by removing them from time to eternity. No such relief is ever in store for the doomed in hell.

5. **They will be in "outer darkness"** (Matt. 22:13).

What! outer darkness where there is so much fire? Yes, if God could create light without first creating the sun, He can also create fire without light. But this is not the kind of light and darkness we are talking about. We think of light as truth, righteousness, holiness, a knowledge of God, the presence of the Lamb (Rev. 21:23; 22:5) who furnished light without the aid of any sun. Out of this light the sinner is forever banished—away from God, away from the truth, away from holiness, away from glory —banished, forever banished from the presence of the Lord —in the darkness of sin, of gloom, of wretchedness, of woe, without a ray of light from heaven—here the doomed souls must spend eternity, "punished with everlasting destruction from the presence of the Lord and the glory of his power"—this is "outer darkness!"

## FURTHER OBSERVATIONS

1. **Withhold not the facts from a sinful and deluded world.**

A noted infidel was lecturing before a large audience, drawing upon the powers of language to make the Bible doctrine of an endless hell as repulsive as it was possible for the human tongue and imagination to make it. "Suppose," said he, "that this world would be composed of sand, and a little bird would come at the end of each thousand years and carry away a grain. Even by this inconceivably slow process the world would be finally removed, but still there would be an eternity ahead for the doomed souls in hell to suffer the pangs and torments of indescribable misery and woe!" A thoughtful young man was in the audience, greatly stirred by the recital, but it had an opposite effect from what the lecturer intended. "If this is true—and it is," he said, "I will spend my whole life in warning sinners to flee from the wrath to come." That young man was William Booth, afterwards organizer and commander-in-chief of the Salvation Army. And why should we not be moved with a similar resolution? Tell the world the truth. It has been lulled to sleep in a sense of false security, and it will take many thunderings from Sinai to awaken the sleeping millions to a realization of their actual condition and danger.

2. **Whoever is lost, is lost in spite of God's will and mercy.**

It is not God's will "that any should perish" (II Pet. 3:9), for He has "not appointed us to wrath" (I Thes. 5: 9). With a greater sacrifice (Jno. 3:16, 17; Rom. 5:8) than any human being has ever been willing to make to rescue his fellow man, God has done everything that can be done to make it possible for all men to be saved. Notwithstanding the fact that men have cried out against God as cruel and unmerciful, His is one continuous record of love and sacrifice and benevolence, while sinful men have deliberately defied His Word and made it impossible for Him to do anything but to send them where they belong.

3. **Eternal punishment is simple justice.**

The present wave of lawlessness and crime is due to the fact that men have turned a deaf ear heavenward and a listening ear to sin and iniquity. People are reaping what they have sown; and the only thing that will keep them from reaping the full crop in eternity is the grace of God in giving every penitent believer an opportunity for "repentance and remission of sins." What jails and penitentiaries are in this world, the lake of fire will be to the world to come—with this exception: Here mistakes are often made in that guilty ones are allowed to go on in their crimes unpunished while innocent ones are unjustly imprisoned, while over yonder there will be perfect justice, and no one will be cast into the lake unjustly.

### 4. Tell the people of their opportunity.

Thank God, there is a way of escape. Let all the world know that through the grace of God there is opportunity given for "repentance and remission of sins," for "the blood of Jesus Christ his Son cleanseth us from all sin." "Let the wicked forsake his way, and the unrighteous man his thoughts: and let him return unto the Lord, and he will have mercy upon him; and to our God, for he will abundantly pardon."

# CHAPTER V

## HEAVEN

Rejoice, and be exceeding glad: for great is your reward in heaven.—Matthew 5:12.

It is significant that the word "God" (the Creator, the Infinite One) is mentioned in the first verse in the Bible, while the word "Lord" (the One in supreme authority) is found in the last. Between these two verses is written the career of man in time; beyond it is the lot of man in eternity.

"The best last" is not only a sentimental saying of man, but also one of the happy provisions of the Creator for His people. Here we are blessed with many unmerited favors, but the best of human life is mixed with disappointments and sorrows. Over yonder is a world unmixed with the sins and sorrows of earth, abounding in endless bliss and glory of which the most blissful things of earth are but temporary foretastes. It is fitting, therefore, that in harmony with this gracious provision of a loving heavenly Father, we should reserve for the last a subject which, next to God, is the sublimest of all subjects—HEAVEN. The reader is invited to join us in our meditation upon what heaven is, upon the way to get there, upon who will go there, and what will be their experiences after they get there.

### DEFINITIONS

In considering this subject we think of—

1. The aerial heavens—where the birds fly, the clouds float, the rain and snow are formed.

2. The broad expanse—the region of the stars.

3. The "heaven of heavens"—the place where God dwells, the eternal "paradise of God," where God and saints and angels will spend eternity.

## How God Describes It

1. **It is "a place"** (Jno. 14:1-3).

Christ comforted His disciples, saying, "I go to prepare *a place* for you. And if I go and prepare *a place* for you, I will come again, and receive you unto myself." From this and similar scriptures we understand that heaven is not merely *a condition* but *a place,* the eternal dwelling place of God, where God the Saviour dwells, and where saints and angels will spend eternity with Him.

2. **It is "the high and holy place"** (Isa. 57:15).

This gives us the added thought that of all places heaven is "the high and holy" place—high, because it is above all other places; holy, because it is inhabited by holy beings only, and sin will never enter there. The seraphim sang, "Holy, holy, holy, is the Lord of hosts," (Isa. 6:3), and worshipers in glory will continue to take up this sweet refrain. The holy of holies in the tabernacle in the wilderness, and later in the temple, typified heaven. Heb. 9:1-12.

To those who expect to spend eternity in heaven the commandment is, "Be ye holy; for I am holy" (I Pet. 1:16). The angels of God are spoken of as "holy angels" (Matt. 25:31). Nothing unholy will ever be permitted there, for "there shall in no wise enter into it anything that defileth, neither whatsoever worketh abomination, or maketh a lie: but they which are written in the Lamb's book of life" (Rev. 21:27). Without peace and holiness, "no man shall see the Lord" (Heb. 12:14). Holy, thrice holy, forever holy is the eternal dwelling place of God.

3. **It is "a better country"** (Heb. 11:16).

This world seems good enough to many people, considering how they cling to it in the face of all that the Bible has to say of "the high and holy place," the "better country" above; but they who have, with an eye of faith, beheld visions of the glory world, are of one mind in calling that "a better country" than any place ever found here, for the following reasons:

All that is in this world—"the lust of the flesh, and the lust of the eyes, and the pride of life"—will pass away, but the things of the "better country" will last forever. I Jno. 2:15-17.

Here riches are endangered by moth, rust and thieves; there they are safe, will endure, are eternally preserved. Matt. 6:19, 20; II Tim. 1:12.

Here the wicked trouble, we grow weary and worn; there "the wicked cease from troubling;" and the weary are "at rest" (Job 3:17).

Here all flesh, like grass, withers; there we shall live forever. I Pet. 1:24; I Cor. 15:54; Rev. 21:4.

Here we have sickness, heartaches, pain, disappointments, many tears; in the world to come there will be no sickness or pain, and all tears will be forever wiped away. Rev. 21:4.

Here the poor are oppressed, some well-meaning people are led astray, and murder, wars, licentiousness, pride, intemperance, and corruption are in evidence in every land; there such things are unknown. Rev. 7:16, 17; 21; 22.

### 4. It is a place of "many mansions" (Jno. 14:2).

As God makes bountiful provisions for the well-being of His people here, so will He do for His people in the world to come. The question is not, Has God prepared a mansion for us there? but, Have we made the necessary preparations, that we may be so happy as to occupy it when the Lord makes His final call?

### 5. It is a "garner" (Matt. 3:12).

"He will . . . gather his wheat into the garner," is another way of saying that in the final great harvest God will send forth His "reapers" (Matt. 13:39) to bring in the golden sheaves, cast the tares into the fire, and gather the wheat into the garner. It is figurative language, but the meaning is so clear that no one needs an interpreter to understand it. The idea of a garner suggests convenience, protection, safety, and preservation.

6. **It is a place where there are "pleasures for ever-more"** (Psa. 16:11).

This world is pleasure-mad—and in their madness after pleasure people seek it from the wrong source. Following the leadership of the enemy of their souls, their pleasures are but for a season, when the bitter dregs found in every cup of sinful pleasure reveal the folly of it all. Eccl. 11:9; Prov. 23:32; I Tim. 5:6. But if a simple faith in Jesus is an occasion for "joy unspeakable and full of glory" (I Pet. 1:8), what must be the real experience of the saints of God when, in the fullness of joy and glory they shall stand in the presence of the King in His glory and at His right hand share in His pleasures forevermore. "Rejoice, and be exceeding glad: for great is your reward in heaven."

And then to think that this will go on FOREVER. Can you grasp it? Centuries before the Flood, Enoch was translated and has been walking with God ever since; but this is but a mere speck upon the canvas of time as compared with what eternity means. Joy, riches, glory—FOREVER—How long did the pleasure-mad people of that day who despised God's marriage laws (Gen. 6:1, 2) enjoy their pleasures! "FOREVERMORE"—are the pleasures at the right hand of God. Well has the poet said:

> "When we've been there ten thousand years,
>   Bright, shining as the sun,
> We've no less days to sing God's praise
>   Than when we first begun."

7. **It is a place of spotless purity and fullness of glory.**

No vile bodies will be there, for "flesh and blood cannot inherit the kingdom of God" (I Cor. 15:50). No sin will be admitted there, for the "dogs, and sorcerers, and whoremongers, and murderers, and idolaters, and whosoever loveth and maketh a lie" (Rev. 22:15) will all be on the outside. What is more, "the fearful, and unbelieving, and the abominable, and murderers, and whoremongers, and sorcerers, and idolaters, and all liars shall have their part in the lake which burneth with fire and brimstone" (Rev. 21:8). What a place even earth would be if all these things were excluded! And who can fathom the depths of the blessedness and purity and holiness of heaven, where the ransomed hosts of God will be out of sight and out of reach of all danger, forever removed from the corruption and debauchery of the devil and his hosts? As for the glory there, it is beyond the power of the human tongue or pen to describe. Nearly two thousand years ago the heavenly host proclaimed the glory of God, saying, "Glory to God in the highest, and on earth peace, good will toward men." Saints and angels are still proclaiming His glory. Today we look beyond this vale of tears and with an eye of faith behold the King upon His throne surrounded by an innumerable throng of saints and angels. We think of the glory which envelops the throne of God in heaven; of the majesty and power and goodness and purity and wisdom and dominion of the mighty King of kings and Lord of lords; of the saints of God and holy angels in unnumbered millions praising and glorifying His high and holy name; of the ransomed hosts of God singing the song of everlasting deliverance; of the immeasurable space, the indescribable beauty, the matchless purity, and the perfect bliss of those whose happy lot it will be to share in this wondrous glory; of the heavenly light that far outshines the brightness of the noonday sun, the Lamb of God being the light thereof. Glorious and wonderful, both the Throne and He that sitteth thereon—happy the lot of those whose blissful privilege it will be to have a part in His never ending reign. "Praise ye the Lord."

## How to Get There

It is easy, if we take God's way for it; impossible, if we take our own. We reach it—

### 1. By way of the cross.

In other words, it is through Jesus Christ "the door" (Jno. 10:1, 9) that any one may enter, and no one can find entrance by any other means. Acts 4:12. When Thomas asked, "How can we know the way?" Jesus replied promptly, "I am the way, the truth, and the life: no man cometh unto the Father, but by me" (Jno. 14:6). Christ Jesus "is made unto us wisdom, and righteousness, and sanctification" (I Cor. 1:30).

### 2. By way of innocence.

Jesus referred to the child as being typical of and among those who are fit to enter the kingdom of heaven (Matt. 18:1-3, 10; 19:14), saying, "Of such is the kingdom of heaven." God's "little ones" are the innocent ones, those under the Blood whether by reason of childhood innocence or by being "born again"), a prime essential for getting into the Kingdom—otherwise their entrance into heaven would bring defilement into it. But being under (washed, cleansed by) the Blood, they are fit subjects for the eternal Kingdom.

### 3. By way of the new birth.

"Except a man be born again, he can not see the kingdom of God" (Jno. 3:3, 5, 7). This was spoken to Nicodemus, a man of good repute and excellent worth; yet a man of that kind, like the vilest of sinners, can get to heaven only by becoming a child of God. We "must be born again." "In Christ Jesus neither circumcision availeth any thing, nor uncircumcision, but a new creature" (Gal. 6:15).

### 4. By way of the "strait gate" (Matt. 7:13, 14).

"Enter ye in at the strait gate;" says Christ, "for wide is the gate, and broad is the way, that leadeth to destruction. . . . Strait is the gate, and narrow is the way, which leadeth unto life." Turning to Luke 13:24 we read, "Strive to enter in at the strait gate: for many, I say unto you, will seek to enter in, and shall not be able." Christ warns His followers against the teaching of false prophets, who deceive many into traveling the broad road—where they may take their pride, lust, covetousness, sinful amusements, deceitfulness, selfishness, and every other mark of worldliness along. The narrow way is too narrow to admit any of these things, yet broad enough for every human being to travel on, provided they leave their worldliness behind. This way is just as broad as the TRUTH—no broader, no narrower. How eager we should be to know the truth and to obey it in fullness: for who has the power to remove even "one jot or tittle" from the WORD?

### 5. By the way of holiness.

"And an highway shall be there, and a way, and it shall be called The way of holiness; the unclean shall not pass over it" (Isa. 35:8). People are not made holy at the judgment bar; there they will simply get their sentence of reward or punishment, according to the record they make here. Whatever may be the point at which we get on to this "highway" or "way of holiness;" we must be on it at the time death overtakes us, or eternity will find us outside of heaven. "To day; lest any of you be hardened through the deceitfulness of sin . . . harden not your hearts" (Heb. 3:13, 15). The way of the world is condemned. Eph. 2:2. Only holy people can walk the way of holiness. "But if we walk in the light, as he is in the light, we have fellowship one with another, and the blood of Jesus Christ his Son cleanseth us from all sin." They who travel this road will "see the Lord" (Heb. 12:14).

### INHABITANTS OF HEAVEN

We have reached the portals. The way that leads to the pearly gates has been traveled. We hear the blessed invitation, "Come, ye blessed of my Father, inherit the KINGDOM." That glorious land, so vividly described in Scripture and so ardently longed for by every child of God, is in plain sight. The thing that now interests us is, Who is there? Whom shall we meet? Who will be our companions in glory?

1. **God** is there, will be there in power and glory. Psa. 11:4; I Kings 8:27, 30; Dan. 5:23; Matt. 11:25. We have already spoken of heaven as the eternal dwelling place of God—Father, Son, and Holy Ghost. Christ our Mediator entered heaven (Acts 3:20, 21; Heb. 6:20) where He is all powerful. Matt. 28:18. Heaven is God's throne, and He fills heaven and earth. Jer. 23:24. It is the presence and power of the Holy Trinity that makes heaven a land of infinite bliss and riches and glory.

2. **The holy angels** will be there. Matt. 18:10; 24:36. When Christ was under trial He had only to speak the word, and more than twelve legions of angels from heaven were ready to come to His rescue. Matt. 26:53. In the great hallelujah songs of glory the angels will have a prominent part. Rev. 7:9-12. Heaven will mean more for saints because of the presence of those celestial creatures who in this life served as "ministering spirits" to all the "heirs of salvation." Heb. 1:14.

3. **Saints** will be there. These, we understand, will include both those who went in childhood innocence and those who, by the grace of God and through faith in our Lord Jesus Christ, were "born again" and became "heirs of glory." The spirits of those who have gone on before are even now in the realms of glory, in the presence of God, and when Christ will bring them with Him when He comes for His bride they will, with the righteous living, be clothed in glorified bodies and together they will meet the Lord in the air (I Thess. 4:14-18) and be forever with Him. "They that be wise shall shine as the brightness of the firmament . . . as the stars for ever and ever" (Dan. 12:3). To all the saints on earth this cheering message is enough to encourage them to put forth redoubled efforts to win as many other souls for God as it is possible for

them to do. "Rejoice, and be exceeding glad: for great is your reward in heaven."

## Concluding Thoughts

### 1. "God is no respecter of persons" Acts 10:34, 35).

The most scholarly man in the most enlightened country on the face of the globe and the most ignorant person in the jungles of densest heathen lands have like chances before God, so far as salvation is concerned; that is, both must receive salvation through our Lord Jesus Christ, must come to God by way of Calvary, or they will never be saved, will never reach the realms of glory. As Peter says, "In every nation he that feareth him, and worketh righteousness, is accepted with him." People are saved or lost, as they accept or reject the Gospel. That God is impartial is evident from the fact that salvation comes not by wealth or social standing or human goodness or by any other human device, but alone, "by grace, through faith." The "whosoever" provision of God's plan of salvation puts all human beings on a level—there is but one road to heaven; and rich and poor, intelligent and ignorant, great and small, old and young, without distinction of nationality or color, all have God's permission and God's invitation to travel on this road.

### 2. We have only a limited knowledge of heaven.

Notwithstanding the graphic pen pictures of heaven found in the inspired Word, there are many things which have arisen in the human mind in the form of questions which God has seen wise to withhold from us. Shall we recognize our friends there, as we knew them here? Will we know one another there as infants, centenarians, and in-betweens? Will we continue to grow there? Many more questions of similar nature have been raised, and to which, as a rule, the most enlightened human beings must answer, "I don't know." Is it wrong to ask such questions? No—but it is well that in all these things which are not clearly revealed we are not too positive in our views. Some things are plainly taught; others are not so clearly set forth, but we may have a fair estimate of them by the inferences borne in Scripture; while on other things the Bible is completely silent. We do well to remember that the Infinite God saw fit to reveal and to withhold from view, just as much as He knew and knows to be for our good. And in our differing opinions we should be very slow to take away other people's hopes of anything which they expect to see in heaven, unless we have a clear "thus saith the Lord" that they are deluded by false hopes. Another thing to remember is that, on this as well as many other subjects, the more earnestly and prayerfully and perseveringly we study God's Word the more the things which at first seem hazy are transferred into the class of things which are clearly revealed. And whatever is left unrevealed when we reach the portals of death, will be revealed in clearness when we open our eyes on the other shore. "Now we see through a glass, darkly; but then face to face: now I know in part; but then shall I know even as also I am known" (I Cor. 13:12).

### 3. We can afford to trust the Lord.

We spoke of a number of questions which people have raised with reference to how it will be in heaven after we get there. But there are questions which, to us in this world, are still more vital—one of them being: If Christ should come at this time, would we be prepared to meet Him, and to get to heaven at all? In all such questions we can well afford to open our eyes, trust the Lord, and conform to His holy will—not, close our eyes and risk it; but open our eyes, study God's Word, and obey it fully.

### 4. Eternity in heaven.

Here are two unfathomable words in glorious combination which send a thrill of rapturous joy through the hearts and souls of all men who have ever taken time to meditate upon this absorbing theme and who know by personal experience what it is to be saved from sin and adopted into God's happy family. The first thought that comes to us is that of the grace of God in making us heirs of glory. Then we think of the endless ages in which we shall be in His hallowed presence, in the fellowship of saints and angels, in the fullness of bliss and glory in the land where farewell tears are never shed and sorrows never come. Meditating upon these things, may we breathe a prayer to God that He may grant us long lives and healthy bodies here, thus extending the time of our opportunities to give this vision of a blessed eternity to as many people as are willing to receive the message of salvation. Yes, we want to go home, and long for the time to come when we may—but not until we have done all that lies within our power to do to the end that others also may set their faces heavenward, and set their affections upon this eternal home and make that the goal of their lives.

Eternity, *Eternity,* ETERNITY—time is but its advance agent, challenging us to get ready to spend it in the realms of the blest, "where the wicked cease from troubling, and the weary are at rest" (Job 3:17).

> "Oh the clanging bells of time,
>   Soon their notes will all be dumb,
> And in joy and peace sublime,
>   We will feel the silence come;
> And our souls their thirst will slake,
>   And our eyes the King will see,
> When thy glorious morn shall break,
>   Eternity! eternity!"

Need we wonder why the ancient patriarchs, looking steadfastly towards heaven, and looking for "a city which hath foundations, whose builder and maker is God," confessed themselves "strangers and pilgrims on the earth" (Heb. 11:10, 13), and that the disciples so earnestly and hopefully and joyfully glorified God and exhorted others to be steadfast and faithful as they looked forward and thought of the wondrously glorious things which God has prepared for them that love Him? Well may the poet sing:

"I'm but a stranger here,
  Heav'n is my home;
Earth is a desert drear,
  Heav'n is my home;
Danger and sorrow stand
'Round me on ev'ry hand,
Heav'n is my father land,
  Heav'n is my home.

"There at my Saviour's side,
  Heav'n is my home;
I shall be glorified,
  Heav'n is my home;
There are the good and blest,
Those I love most and best,
There, too, I soon shall rest,
  Heav'n is my home."

As we lay down our pen it is with the sincere prayer that the blessed hope of the "glorious appearing of the great God and our Saviour Jesus Christ," who will come to take His own to be with Him forevermore, will appeal with compelling force to all our readers, and that we may all dedicate ourselves anew to the great cause of carrying this Gospel of eternal salvation to the ends of the earth. With heaven as our goal, and earth as our stepping-stone of opportunity to reach it, let us join with the poet in singing,

"'Mid scenes of confusion and creature complaints,
How dear to my soul is communion with saints!
To find at the banquet of mercy there's room,
And feel in the presence of Jesus at home.

"Sweet bonds that unite all the children of peace,
And thrice blessed Jesus, whose love can not cease,
Though oft from Thy presence in sadness we roam,
We long to behold Thee in glory at home.

"We long, dearest Lord, in Thy beauty to shine,
No more as an exile in sorrow to pine,
And in Thy dear image arise from the tomb,
With glorified millions to praise Thee at home."

# SUBJECT INDEX